Gendering International Legal Responses to Environmental Chronic Emergencies

Gendering International Legal Responses to Environmental Chronic Emergencies

Edited by

Sara De Vido

Professor of International Law, Ca' Foscari University of Venice, Italy

Deborah Russo

Professor of International Law, University of Florence, Italy

Enzamaria Tramontana

Professor of International Law, University of Palermo, Italy

Edward Elgar PUBLISHING

Cheltenham, UK • Northampton, MA, USA

Cover image: Sara De Vido

Published by

Edward Elgar Publishing Limited
The Lypiatts
15 Lansdown Road
Cheltenham
Glos GL50 2JA
UK

Edward Elgar Publishing, Inc.
William Pratt House
9 Dewey Court
Northampton
Massachusetts 01060
USA

Authorised representative in the EU for GPSR queries only: Easy Access System Europe – Mustamäe tee 50, 10621 Tallinn, Estonia, gpsr.requests@easproject.com

A catalogue record for this book is available from the British Library

Library of Congress Control Number: 2025949674

This book is available electronically in the Elgaronline
Law subject collection
https://doi.org/10.4337/9781035367795

MIX
Paper | Supporting responsible forestry
FSC® C013604

ISBN 978 1 0353 6778 8 (cased)
ISBN 978 1 0353 6779 5 (eBook)
ISBN 978 1 0353 8979 7 (ePub)

Printed and bound by CPI Group (UK) Ltd, Croydon, CR0 4YY

Contents

List of contributors vii
Foreword ix
Dorothy Estrada-Tanck
Gendering International Legal Responses to Environmental Chronic Emergencies: *Introduction* xi
Sara De Vido, Deborah Russo and Enzamaria Tramontana

PART I CONCEPTUALIZING ENVIRONMENTAL CHRONIC EMERGENCIES

1 Feminist legal methods and environmental chronic emergencies: challenging the anthropocentric and androcentric international legal system 2
Sara De Vido

2 Moving beyond an approach based on crisis and disasters to address environmental chronic emergencies 23
Deborah Russo

3 Environmental chronic emergencies, women's inequality and international law 42
Enzamaria Tramontana

4 Taking the long view: what environmental chronic emergencies require of states 65
Karen Morrow

PART II ENVIRONMENTAL CHRONIC EMERGENCIES ACROSS TIME

5 A fear of falling? The mineshaft as an 'environmental chronic emergency' in modern Cornwall 88
Timothy Cooper

6 Minamata disease as an environmental chronic emergency: institutional failures and global lessons 108
Shuichi Furuya

7 Environmental chronic emergencies and the challenge of temporality 128
David M. Scott

8 Environmental chronic emergencies and future generations 147
Laura Magi

PART III ENVIRONMENTAL CHRONIC EMERGENCIES IN CONTEXT

9 Environmental chronic emergencies, slow-onset events and other anthropocentric dilemmas in times of climate crisis: the need for a reconception 167
Monica Feria-Tinta

10 States and corporations in the context of environmental chronic emergencies: Responsibility and liability at the crossroads 184
Patricio Barbirotto

11 Due diligence obligations and environmental chronic emergencies 206
Björnstjern Baade

12 The duty to cooperate in addressing the adverse impact of environmental chronic emergencies: ensuring gender-sensitive responses 227
Martina Sardo

13 Transforming slow violence into social justice: the quest for reparation for environmental chronic emergencies 250
Francesca Tammone

PART IV CONCLUDING REMARKS

14 Conclusion 274
Meghan Campbell

Index 280

List of contributors

Björnstjern Baade, Privatdozent at Freie Universität Berlin and Visiting Professor at Heinrich Heine University Düsseldorf, Germany

Patricio Barbirotto, Postdoctoral Researcher of International Law, Ca' Foscari University of Venice, Italy

Meghan Campbell, Reader in International Human Rights Law at **the** University of Birmingham, United Kingdom

Timothy Cooper, Honorary Senior Lecturer in History at the University of Exeter, United Kingdom

Sara De Vido, Full Professor of International Law at Ca' Foscari University of Venice, Italy

Dorothy Estrada-Tanck, Tenured Professor of Public International Law at the University of Murcia, Spain; Member of the United Nations Working Group on Discrimination against Women and Girls

Monica Feria-Tinta, LLM (with merit) LSE, Dipl. Hague Academy of International Law; Barrister at Twenty Essex, Bar of England & Wales; Visiting Fellow, Jesus College, University of Cambridge (2021); Partner Fellow, Lauterpacht Centre for International Law (2019–2021)

Laura Magi, Associate Professor of International Law at the University of Florence, Italy

Karen Morrow, Professor of Environmental Law at Hillary Rodham Clinton School of Law at Swansea University, United Kingdom

Deborah Russo, Associate Professor of International Law at the University of Florence, Italy

Martina Sardo, Postdoctoral Researcher of International Law at the University of Palermo, Italy

David M. Scott, British Academy Postdoctoral Fellow at Queen Mary University of London, United Kingdom

Shuichi Furuya, Full Professor of Law at Waseda University, Tokyo, Japan

Francesca Tammone, Assistant Professor of International Law at the University of Catanzaro, Italy

Enzamaria Tramontana, Associate Professor of International Law at the University of Palermo, Italy

Foreword

Dorothy Estrada-Tanck

This book, edited by renowned scholars Sara De Vido, Deborah Russo and Enzamaria Tramontana, and containing contributions from a broad and plural range of prominent authors, is a welcome addition to a corpus of work in crucial need of expansion. It presents an insightful analysis of the gendered dimensions of environmental crises and adopts an ecofeminist lens to critically examine the legal and political framework and practices in place to confront them.

As such, the editors perceptively identify that to fully capture the phenomenon of environmental degradation, we must address its root causes and not merely react to its symptoms. As the editors emphasize, building on the concept of slow violence, such one-time localized responses to any given specific crisis or disaster fail to grasp "the complexity of the whole system of violence that anticipates the disruptive force." Rather, as their proposed understanding of environmental chronic emergencies (ECEs) suggests, the underlying causes of environmental devastation can be found in the social hierarchies and asymmetries of power, resources, and opportunities between women and men, as well as in the disparities of (real or perceived) control between humans and nature, and the interlocking inequalities and precarities that these relationships generate.

While spelling out the damaging gendered consequences of applying dominant models to ECEs, the editors also question commonly held knowledge and challenge, as various authors explicitly hold, the anthropocentric and androcentric international legal system. The vision advanced in the book, framed by the editors and applied by the different authors, intends to move away from approaches based on a reductionist notion of crisis to push for a more holistic, structural and integral understanding of the emergencies themselves and the avenues to prevent, mitigate, address and provide reparations for the violations and harms they provoke. To do so, the authors provide us with a rich tapestry of doctrinal, normative and jurisprudential evaluations, as well as national, regional and international examples and case studies that illustrate the gaps and inconsistencies—and also the opportunities—that the current international legal system holds and that can be best revealed and interpreted through a gendered and intersectional optic.

Indeed, this view recognizes that multiple social identities in combination with gender—such as race, class, disability, religion, sexual orientation, migratory status and age—interact and converge to shape women's and girls' lived experiences of inequality as related to environmental harms. Examples provided by different feminist authors and human rights bodies include the recognition that women's care work and needs increase during health and environmental crises, or how when water and wood become depleted, or when water becomes polluted, women and girls who are typically responsible for collecting these resources must travel farther distances, expending considerable time and energy, which often affects their physical and mental well-being.

Throughout the book, the diverse authors explore the role of the law in confronting emergencies derived from the triple environmental crisis of climate change, pollution and biodiversity loss, and the duties of different actors under international law, including due diligence and international cooperation obligations, tackling state responsibility but also that of non-state actors, such as corporations, with a particular focus on transnational enterprises. The study by contributing scholars of concepts such as the rights of nature, the protection of future generations and the ethics of care interconnecting the care for humans and care for the planet also constitutes a breath of fresh air. At the same time, these perspectives contrast with more conventional approaches within the international legal scenario, adding deeper innovative value to the examination.

This is a must-read book for academics, lawyers, policymakers, civil society organizations and practitioners interested in comprehensively understanding and addressing ECEs with a gendered, structural and sustainable approach. Meaningful activation of such a framework is needed if impact is to be achieved, as illustrated in the concrete proposals and strategies masterfully articulated by the authors. One can only hope this transformative vision permeates our treatment of the planet and the lived reality of billions of women and girls and their communities worldwide. As famous ecofeminist Vandana Shiva affirmed, "We are either going to have a future where women lead the way to make peace with the Earth or we are not going to have a human future at all."[1]

1 See Preface by Vandana Shiva in Maria Mies and Vandana Shiva, with a Foreword by Ariel Salleh, *Ecofeminism (Critique Influence Change)*, (2nd edn, Zed Books 2014); and the position of the Earth Centric, Women Centric and Farmer-led movement for the protection of biological and cultural diversity, Navdanya: https://navdanyainternational.org/ecofeminism.

Gendering International Legal Responses to Environmental Chronic Emergencies: Introduction

Sara De Vido, Deborah Russo and Enzamaria Tramontana

The book is the development of research originally started by one of the editors on the "legalization" of the concept of *slow violence* (elaborated by the US scholar Rob Nixon) and its reflection on the debate on intergenerational equity, using an ecofeminist method of analysis that is rarely endorsed in legal scholarship. This idea has been expanded and developed into a research project, *GenREm – Gendering international legal response to chronic emergencies,* thanks to the close connection among us, the three co-editors of this book, who are also the heads of the three units of the project. We come from the North (Venice), the Centre (Florence), and the South (Palermo) of Italy, and, talking together, we realized that more could be done in Italian international legal scholarship to endorse a feminist method in international law, especially international environmental law.

This research project received funding from the European Union Next-Generation EU – National Recovery and Resilience Plan (NRRP) – MISSION 4 COMPONENT 2, INVESTMENT 1.1 – CUP N. H53D23002940006. This manuscript reflects only the authors' views and opinions; neither the European Union nor the European Commission can be considered responsible for them.

WHY A NEW CONCEPT?

At the origin of the project, we felt that there was a need for a reflection on emergencies that are not mere disasters but deeper and more complex ongoing phenomena that call into question the traditional categories of time, space and legal obligations in international law. The concept of environmental chronic emergencies (ECEs) derives from the innovative idea of slow violence and elaborates further the concept of slow-onset events, developed at the UN level, to appreciate situational vulnerabilities and the disproportionate impact of these emergencies on women and girls. The adjective 'chronic' conveys the idea of something that is rooted, often silent, surely unseen, but that has an impact on present and future generations, on the environment and on women at the intersection of different grounds of discrimination. There is no other concept, legally conceived, that can capture phenomena like the mercury pollution in Minamata that then led to the adoption of a specific Convention, or the slow, gradual degradation of the environment, which is not immediately perceived as a crisis, or a crisis that has an impact on humans, but that surely represents an emergency exacerbated by structural inequalities. We could have used the concepts of disasters or slow-onset events, but these concepts completely fail to understand the underlying causes of discrimination and inequality that exacerbate environmental emergencies. In our opinion, the idea of conceptualizing ECEs is stimulating and challenging at the same time because it calls into question both the rigid categories of law that are based on links of causality, time and space, and the political approach underlying the legal response to their tragic effects. We decided it was important to take up the challenge and to endorse an ecofeminist method of international legal analysis that precisely grasps the dynamics of power and oppression.

THE STRUCTURE OF THE BOOK

The book is divided into three parts. In the first one, *Conceptualizing Environmental Chronic Emergencies,* we provide the legal and conceptual frameworks of the book. In the first chapter, *Feminist Legal Methods and Environmental Chronic Emergencies: Challenging the Anthropocentric and Androcentric International Legal System,* Sara De Vido provides the foundations of the project as an ecofeminist international lawyer. In the second chapter, *Moving Beyond an Approach Based on Crisis and Disasters to Address Environmental Chronic Emergencies,* Deborah Russo focuses on the concept of ECE to discuss what responding to such emergencies entails and why this concept is useful for shaping the international law of tomorrow. Enzamaria Tramontana, in *Environmental Chronic Emergencies, Women's Inequality, and International Law,* examines the intersection of women's inequality and ECEs through an ecofeminist lens. In *Taking the Long View: What Environmental Chronic Emergencies Require of States,* Karen Morrow examines ECEs as key elements of the rapidly shifting planetary context, and applies an ecofeminist conception of the ethics of care to reframe the treatment of the environment in international law.

The second part of the book – *Environmental Chronic Emergencies Across Time* – endorses a temporal perspective in international law. A historical perspective is provided by Timothy Cooper in the chapter *A Fear of Falling? The Mineshaft as 'Environmental Chronic Emergency' in Modern Cornwall,* which offers an overview of the historical applicability of the concept of *ECE* through the enduring legacy of Cornwall's disused mineshafts. In the chapter *Environmental Chronic Emergencies and the Challenge of Temporality*, David Scott focuses on the challenge of time for a global legal response to ECEs. Every international lawyer knows of the existence of the Minamata Convention on Mercury, but few know the story that led to it. From the legal perspective of this case, there is not much literature in English; hence, the focus provided by Shuichi Furuya is of particular interest. In *Minamata Disease as an Environmental Chronic Emergency: Institutional Failures and Global Lessons*, the scholar, a former member of the Human Rights Committee, frames 'Minamata disease' as an ECE. Laura Magi, in the chapter *Environmental Chronic Emergencies and Future Generations*, explores the concept of ECEs and their impact on future generations, emphasizing the importance of intergenerational equity as a principle of international law.

The third part of the book looks at *ECEs in Context*, focusing on legal obligations, actors and reparations. With regard to actors, the chapter *Toward a Paradigm Shift in Case-Law concerning Environmental Chronic Emergencies?*, written by Monica Feria Tinta, reconstructs different approaches to environmental harm, explaining how both international and domestic judges have started to call into question the traditional anthropocentric paradigm to apply more innovative models. In *States and Corporations in the Context of Environmental Chronic Emergencies: Responsibility and Liability at the Crossroad,* Patricio Barbirotto examines the role of transnational corporations in contributing to ECEs and their impact on human rights, particularly women's rights. Björnstjern Baade, in the chapter *Due Diligence Obligations and Environmental Chronic Emergencies,* analyzes the content and scope of due diligence obligations with regard to preventing and countering ECEs, including any gendered effect deriving from them. Martina Sardo's chapter on *Obligation to Cooperate to Cope with the Adverse Impact of Environmental Chronic Emergencies* examines the content and scope of States' duty to cooperate in responding to the gendered effects of ECEs. In *Transforming Slow Violence into Social Justice: The Quest for Reparation for Environmental Chronic Emergencies*, Francesca Tammone endorses a 'transformative' understanding of reparation, which has the potential to address the root causes of these phenomena and reshape the unjust power relationships on which they are grounded.

Meghan Campbell wrote the concluding remarks.

ACKNOWLEDGMENTS

This book is the outcome of great teamwork. We are very grateful to our postdocs: Patricio Barbirotto, Giorgia Berrino, Martina Sardo, and Francesca

Tammone for contributing to the project with their ideas and editing. We would also like to thank Maria-Calina Bordos for helping us with proofreading.

A special thanks to Dorothy Estrada-Tanck, member of the *UN Working Group on discrimination against women and girls,* for taking the time to write the foreword to this book. Her experience with countering discrimination against women and girls is an example for all of us. Our utmost gratitude also goes to David R. Boyd, former UN Special Rapporteur on the human right to a clean, healthy and sustainable environment, for writing the endorsement. His book *Rights of Nature* has been a great inspiration. We would like to express our gratitude to those who participated in our workshops and seminars: Dalia Leinarte, former member of the CEDAW Committee, current member of the Human Rights Committee; Meghan Campbell (University of Birmingham); and Karen Morrow (Swansea University) for contributing to the workshop in Florence on 28 March; Micaela Frulli (University of Florence), who is a guide and a source of support for the three of us; and Eliana Cusato (University of Amsterdam) for her participation in the workshop held in Palermo on 4 October 2024.

We are enormously grateful to our families for the support and the love they give us every day. We dedicate this book to our children, Amanda, Anna, Carlo and Federico. We hope that they will live in a future where ECEs are recognized as drivers and multipliers of inequalities and where environment- and gender-sensitive responses are not the exception, but rather the rule.

PART I

Conceptualizing Environmental Chronic Emergencies

1. Feminist legal methods and environmental chronic emergencies: challenging the anthropocentric and androcentric international legal system

Sara De Vido

1. INTRODUCTION

Environmental chronic emergencies (ECEs), as this concept has been developed in this project,[1] are and have been around us, hidden in plain sight, one could say. Some of the phenomena that fall under this notion are related to climate change, which, as this chapter will explain further, is an example of ECE: desertification, loss of biodiversity, sea level rise, acidification of the ocean and salinization of water can be named. However, other environmental phenomena – caused by (a part of) humanity[2] – could be brought within the terms of this new concept, such as the environmental effects of extractive industries or the end of extractivism, the presence of microorganisms affecting the quality of water and pollutants that are considered relatively innocuous at a certain moment in history, the impact of exploitative animal agriculture.[3] Back

[1] On the definition of the concept, see in more detail Deborah Russo, 'Moving Beyond an Approach Based on Crisis and Disasters to Address Environmental Chronic Emergencies' in this Volume.

[2] Emily Jones, Dianne Otto, 'Thinking through anthropocentrism in international law: queer theory, feminist new materialism and the postcolonial' (*LSE Centre for Women, Peace and Security blog* 2020) <https://www.lse.ac.uk/women-peace-security/assets/documents/2020/Final-Jones-and-Otto-Anthropocentrism-Posthuman-Feminism-Postcol-and-IL-LSE-WPS-Blog-2019-002.pdf> accessed 8 April 2025.

[3] On exploitative animal agriculture, see Maneesha Deckha, 'The One Health Initiative and a Deeper Engagement with Animal Health and Wellbeing: Moving Away from Animal Agriculture' in Irus Braverman (ed.) *More-than-One Health. Humans, Animals, and the Environment post-Covid* (Routledge 2023) 157. On

in 1962, American biologist Rachel Carson denounced in *Silent Spring* the toxic connections between pesticides, environmental degradation and interspecies health.[4] Looking at the situation of Indigenous women, the economist and activist Winona LaDuke wrote:

> The rapid increase in dioxins, organochlorides and PCBs (polychlorinated biphenyls) in the world as a result of industrialization also has a devastating impact on Indigenous peoples, Indigenous women and other women. Each year, according to Environmental Protection Agency statistics, the world's paper industry discharges from 600 to 3,200 grams of dioxin equivalents in water, sludge and paper products. This quantity is equal to the amount that would cause 58,000 to 292,000 cases of cancer every year. According to a number of recent studies, this has significantly increased the risk of breast cancer in women.[5]

The adjective 'environmental' that this project uses as connected to chronic emergencies must be read as considering the environment as 'us', where all the elements are intertwined.[6] This is also the view of the *One Health Initiative*, which recognizes that 'human health (including mental health via the human-animal bond phenomenon), animal health and ecosystem health are inextricably linked'.[7] Some of the research attached to the *One Health Initiative* is relevant for this project as well, whose purpose, however, is not to 'promote, improve, and defend the health and well-being of all species', but to legally analyze what the effects of ECEs are, how they disproportionately affect women and girls, what kind of obligations States have and which forms of reparation are available. Analyzing from a legal perspective, ECE is a matter of time, actors, places and obligations States must abide by.

The scope of this chapter is to provide the theoretical and methodological foundation of the project and to explain why we felt it was necessary to distinguish the concept of ECEs from the well-known one of 'slow violence', coined by the American scholar Rob Nixon, to better grasp the complexity of patterns

---

the effects of extractive industries, see Sara Seck, Penelope Simons, 'Sustainable Mining, Environmental Justice, and the Human Rights of Women and Girls: Canada as Home and Host State' in Sumudu A. Atapattu, Carmen Gonzalez and Sara Seck (eds) *The Cambridge Handbook on Environmental Justice and Sustainable Development* (Cambridge University Press 2021) 314.

[4] Rachel Carson, *Silent Spring* (Houghton Mifflin Company, 1962).

[5] Winona LaDuke, 'Mothers of our Nations: Indigenous women address the world (1995)' in *The Winona LaDuke Reader: A collection of Essential Writings* (Voyageur Press 2002), 211, 216.

[6] Christopher Stone, *Should Trees Have Standing?: Law, Morality, and the Environment* (3rd edn, Oxford University Press, 2010).

[7] Mission statement available here: <https://onehealthinitiative.com/mission-statement/> accessed 9 April 2025.

of discrimination present in our societies and between and across species. The concept of chronic emergencies derives from the innovative idea of slow violence and elaborates further the concept of slow-onset events elaborated at the UN level[8] to appreciate situational vulnerabilities and the disproportionate impact of these emergencies on women and girls.[9] The adjective *chronic* gives the idea of something that is rooted, often silent and surely unseen, but has an impact on women, the environment and present and future generations of both humans and non-humans. It avoids the dichotomy of slow/fast violence, which misses the continuum of violence and strengthens the idea of something that is entrenched in society. The word 'emergency' derives from the Latin *e-mergere*, which is composed of *e* (outside) and *mergere* (sink), showing that the emergency is something that comes to light, that reveals itself if we have eyes open to see it.

ECEs can result in an environmental disaster – and probably all the examples cited will, sooner or later, in the short, medium, long, or very long term, result in a disaster of major proportions – but the peculiarity of this kind of phenomena is that they occur gradually and, for this very reason, are poorly considered, even in legal terms, as stuck in the 'trap' of the present or at least the imminent.

The project adopts a feminist method of analysis to challenge international law as it stands, to highlight patterns of discrimination and address inequalities and to look at the reality of women, especially those at the intersection of different grounds of discrimination, facing those emergencies. GenREm uses international law categories and analyses them from a critical perspective, embracing post-colonial concerns. This chapter also contributes, in line with the view of scholars such as Greta Gaard, to revitalizing ecofeminism, seeing in it its disruptive effect on monolithic categories of international law.

2. THE STARTING POINT: THE CONCEPT OF SLOW VIOLENCE AND ITS FEMINIST (CRITICAL) ANALYSIS

In his book *Slow Violence and the Environmentalism of the Poor,* Rob Nixon was a pioneer in coining the brand-new concept of 'slow violence' and addressing what seems to be an invisible violence 'that occurs gradually and out of sight, a violence of delayed destruction that is dispersed across time and space,

---

8 OCHA *Occasional Policy Briefing Series – Brief No. 6: 'OCHA and slow-onset emergencies'* (April 2011) <https://www.unocha.org> accessed 9 April 2025.

9 See in more detail Enzamaria Tramontana, 'Environmental Chronic Emergencies, Women's Inequality, and International Law' in this Volume.

an attritional violence that is typically not viewed as violence at all'.[10] He was convinced that the very idea of violence needed to be reconceptualized, to take into account other forms of violence, which are 'neither spectacular nor instantaneous, but rather incremental and accretive, its calamitous repercussions playing out across a range of temporal scales'.[11] He mentioned, as forms of slow violence: climate change, the thawing cryosphere, toxic drift, biomagnification, deforestation, the radioactive aftermaths of wars, acidifying oceans and 'a host of other slowly unfolding environmental catastrophes present formidable representational obstacles that can hinder our efforts to mobilize and act decisively'.[12] The author was also aware of not being 'the first one' to realize the impact of substances that at first sight were considered to be devoid of any particular effect: Rachel Carson is one of the authors he mentions.

The concept of slow violence is challenging for lawyers. Many questions indeed arise: Who is responsible for slow violence? Who is affected by slow violence? How can its effects be measured? What kind of legal obligations do States have to prevent and respond to slow violence? What kind of reparations can be envisaged? Personally, as the principal investigator of this project, the idea of 'legalizing' slow violence emerged during the COVID-19 pandemic, while reading multiple sources – during the confinement we were all obliged to undertake – and preparing a chapter on 'Health' for the book *Tipping Points in International Law*.[13] This chapter was the starting point for a legal analysis that could embrace the complexity of slow violence from an international legal perspective. The two words combine an idea of apparent innocuity (slowness) with the idea of disruption and fear (violence). The concept of slow violence has already been intuitively discussed by a few scholars who used it to reinvigorate an argument or to push the boundaries of the interpretation of legal instruments in force. For example, Eliana Cusato, in her book *The Ecology of War*, reflected on conflicts and other security threats, starting from the compelling argument by Nixon, according to whom 'smart wars' and 'precision' warfare, intended to shorten the conflict, produce 'slow violence, inflicting "off camera" casualties'.[14] She encouraged a political ecology of international

10 Rob Nixon, *Slow Violence and the Environmentalism of the Poor* (Harvard University Press, 2011) 2.

11 *Ibid.*

12 *Ibid.*

13 John Haskell, Jean d'Aspremont (eds) *Tipping Points in International Law: Commitment and Critique* (Cambridge University Press 2021).

14 Eliana Cusato, *The Ecology of War and Peace* (Cambridge University Press 2021) 20. See also, on climate change, Julia Dehm, 'Climate change, "slow violence" and the indefinite deferral of responsibility for "loss and damage"' (2020) 29 (2) *Griffith Law Review* 220.

law.[15] She also reflected on the opportunity to use the language of peace and security with regard to the violence of climate change, which she found of limited scope 'without interrogating whose security we are actually concerned about', and she contended, in line with the argument of these pages, that 'current discussion obfuscates the differentiated impacts of climate change according to privilege and vulnerability'.[16] More recently, Nicole Rogers developed the idea of 'climate slow violence', to which both states (mainly through inaction) and transnational corporations (actively through their business) contribute.[17] The Author stressed the pivotal legal issue these pages also look into, namely the 'general failure on the part of governing bodies to recognize and respond to "slow" emergencies', and the incapacity of the criminal justice system to 'address the prolonged timeframe of the slow lethal violence of climate change'.[18]

The concept of 'slow violence' was not devoid of criticism from a feminist perspective, though. Rob Nixon dedicated an entire chapter to slow violence and gender, focusing on the Kenya Green Belt Movement.[19] Looking at the role of both Wangari Maathai and Rachel Carson, he stated that both of them sought 'in their different cultural milieus, to shift the parameters of what is commonly perceived as violence'.[20] He was also attentive to intersectional environmentalism, giving prominence to the special position of rural women. The 'interweaving of environmental and feminist thought' has indeed its roots in African feminist activism, most specifically in the experience of Wangari Maathai, who connected the 'erosion of resources' with the 'erosion of women'.[21] However, despite this important chapter in his book, some scholars argued in an interesting special issue in *Environment and Planning C: Politics and Space* that Nixon did not say much about space. Space, which is explored in critical legal geography,[22] represents a crucial factor in the analysis

---

15 Cusato, *The Ecology of War and Peace* (n 14) 240 ff.

16 Eliana Cusato, 'Of Violence and (In)Visibility: The Securitisation of Climate Change in International Law' (2022) 10 (2) *London Review of International Law* 203.

17 Nicole Rogers, 'Climate change and the word' (2023) 14 (2) *Journal of Human Rights and the Environment* 144, 150.

18 *Ibid.*, 150.

19 Nixon, (n 10) 128.

20 *Ibid.*, 144.

21 Cinnamon P. Carlarne, 'Environmental Law and Feminism' in Deborah L. Brake, Martha Chamallas and Verna L. Williams (eds) *The Oxford Handbook of Feminism and Law in the United States* (Oxford University Press 2021) 573.

22 Critical legal geographers use 'concepts of space as socially produced, and as fluid, malleable and multidimensional to examine the relationships between

because 'slow violence is always situated in historical and geographical contexts that affect and enable it'.[23] Also, it should be stressed that slow violence is not only about environmental issues, but that is what Nixon's book predominantly focused on.

As it will be explained in the next chapter, GenREm also decided to incorporate the adjective 'environmental' in chronic emergencies in order to narrow down the analysis to some of the possible forms of slow violence, being aware nonetheless of other forms, such as 'protracted and subvisible processes of 'slow dissent', but also violence in intimate and domestic domains intersecting with other political violence.[24] Nixon was also criticized for neglecting Black, antiracist, decolonial and feminist theoretical work, but also insights from Indigenous geographies.[25] The vantage point he offered, scholars contend, is 'white, patriarchal, heterosexual, classed'.[26] As an alternative, the authors of the articles included in the special issue delved into feminist standpoint theories and theories of intersectionality, privileging the standpoint of 'those who are most affected by slow violence.[27] They challenged Eurocentric approaches and whiteness and engaged in qualitative methods and historical methods, using biographical interviews or historical accounts. Keeping this powerful feminist critique in mind, how can international law deal with its own limits, including its male and 'Western' DNA?

3. A FEMINIST PERSPECTIVE: INTERNATIONAL LAW IS THE (ANDROCENTRIC) LAW OF CRISIS

International law, Hilary Charlesworth (critically) tells us, is the law of crisis. She argued, more than twenty years ago, using arguments that are still valid today, that 'crises structure our thinking about international law' and that they

---

space and the law, and to understand the consequences of legal spaces on society, and vice versa'; Zoe Pearson 'Feminist Project(s): The Spaces of International Law' in Sari Kouvo, Zoe Pearson (eds) *Feminist Perspectives on Contemporary International Law: Between Resistance and Compliance?* (Hart Publishing, 2014) 47, 56.

23 Rachel Pain, Caitlin Cahill, 'Critical political geographies of slow violence and resistance' (2022) 40 (2) *Environment and Planning C: Politics and Space* 359.

24 *Ibid.*, 361.

25 *Ibid.*, 362.

26 Naya Jones, 'Dying to eat? Black Food Geographies of Slow Violence and Resilience' (2019) 18 (5) *ACME: An International Journal for Critical Geographies* 1076, 1081.

27 Pain, Cahill (n 23) 363.

'dominate the imagination of international lawyers'.[28] She identified a few 'obsessions' international lawyers have with crises: one, particularly relevant for our analysis, being to be 'preoccupied with great crises, rather than the politics of everyday life;' in this way, 'international law steers clear of analysis of longer-term trends and structural problems'.[29] She also identified the silences, including the position of women in the representation of crises: 'the players in international law crises are almost exclusively male. Men are the protagonists, men are at the negotiating table, men are making threats, retaliating and intervening. The lives of women are considered part of a crisis only when they are harmed in a way that is seen to demean the whole of their social group'.[30] The gendered nature of international 'building blocks' is also an issue, because the legal discourses on crises rely on dichotomies – objective/subjective, legal/political, logic/emotion, order/anarchy, mind/body, culture/nature, action/passivity, public/private, protector/protected, independence/dependence – 'with the first term (objective, legal, logical, order etc.) signifying "male" characteristics and the second (subjective, political, emotional, nature etc.) signifying "female"'.[31] Charlesworth encouraged a refocus of international law on issues of structural justice that underpin everyday life.[32] This means, for example, identifying the interconnections of environmental degradation, gender, geographical position and social situation as causes of chronic emergencies, even when those emergencies do not amount to major disasters. It is important to enlarge our vision, not only to include emergencies that do not seem to be as such because they are generally coded as feminine issues (like situations having effects on women's reproductive health), not only to avoid definitions of women as vulnerable subjects, but also to listen to voices that allow for a better understanding of the phenomenon. Ratna Kapur has warned against the risk of using a 'victimization' rhetoric, especially when dealing with the situation of Third World women, and has encouraged a more complex understanding of women's lives along different axes, including race, wealth, class and religion.[33]

The language of the crisis in international law has commonly been a language of securitization that overlooks the importance of prevention and of

---

[28] Hilary Charlesworth, 'International law: a discipline of crisis' (2002) 65 (3) *Modern Law Review* 377, 382.

[29] *Ibid*, 389.

[30] *Ibid.*

[31] *Ibid.*, 390.

[32] *Ibid.*, 391.

[33] Ratna Kapur, 'The Tragedy of Victimization Rhetoric: Resurrecting the Native Subject in International/Postcolonial Feminist Legal Politics' (2002) 15 (1) *Harvard Human Rights Law Journal* 1.

addressing underlying structural inequalities.[34] Migration is a crisis, despite being a structural phenomenon. Climate change has been defined as a crisis, as has poverty, health and the scarcity of food and water. This book stresses the importance of considering environmental phenomena (where the environment is meant as interconnectedness between nature, humans and other-than-human beings) like climate change, not as a crisis – which gives the idea of exceptionalism as opposed to normality – but rather as an emergency that is chronic because it is entrenched in societal mechanisms that reproduce inequalities. The surface of the response to crises has always been a language that mainstreams gender, but does little else, if not nothing, to endorse a policy that questions the underlying axes of power and oppression.

Dianne Otto reflected on the fact that the development of international law has often occurred as a response to a crisis.[35] The example provided in this book, Minamata, explains this point. Minamata, a severe case of mercury pollution, has been neglected for years, despite causing an impact on the environment and on the reproductive health of women. When the emergency exploded into a crisis, that was the moment in which it 'became' relevant to international law with the negotiation and the adoption of a specific Convention.[36] This project argues that an ECE must be taken care of before and even if it does not lead to a major crisis; in a feminist reconceptualization of legal obligations, States must abide by. Dianne Otto reflected, from a queer feminist perspective, on the proliferation of 'sexual and gender panics', meaning actions undertaken to respond to a crisis that, in the end, divert attention from larger injustices perpetrated in the name of the phenomenon.[37] Feminist issues have been deployed, for example, to justify or even legitimize military interventions, such as the US military response to the 'humanitarian crisis' of women

---

[34] See, for example, Shirley V. Scott's 'Securitizing Climate Change: International Legal Implications and Obstacles' (2008) 21 (4) *Cambridge Review of International Affairs* 603. Stressing that environmental degradation is a cause of gendered insecurity, 'particularly in the developing – or 'majority' – world, Laura J. Sheperd, 'Security' in Laura J. Sheperd (ed.) *Handbook on Gender and Violence* (Edward Elgar Publishing 2019) 146, 153.

[35] Dianne Otto, 'Decoding Crisis in International Law: A Queer Feminist Perspective' in Barbara Stark (ed.) *International Law and Its Discontents* (Cambridge University Press 2015) 115.

[36] The Minamata Convention on Mercury was adopted on 10 October 2013 at Kumamoto (Japan) on the occasion of the Conference of Plenipotentiaries on the Minamata Convention on Mercury held from 7 to 11 October 2013, and it entered into force on 16 August 2017. See in that respect Shuichi Furuya in this Volume.

[37] Otto, 'Decoding Crisis in International Law: A Queer Feminist Perspective' (n 35) 117.

in Afghanistan:[38] the same Western country that later concluded an agreement with the Taliban without women's participation and without taking women's issues into account. In environmental issues, the 'sexual and gender panics' are attached to major disasters (the increase of sexual violence as a consequence of natural disasters, for example), neglecting rooted inequalities exacerbated by disasters and the legal forgetfulness of emergencies that disproportionately affect women and girls. This neglect often turns into narratives that trivialize women's experiences: the 'hysterical' and 'overemotional' wives and mothers at Love Canal being one among multiple examples.[39] This approach to crises has consequences in terms of legal response, which is commonly dictated by matters of urgency – 'techno-scientific' solutions, where the priority is 'security'[40] – and linked to repression rather than to prevention.[41]

4. A FEMINIST PERSPECTIVE: INTERNATIONAL LAW IS NOT (YET) THE LAW OF CHRONIC EMERGENCIES

Our international law of the everyday – to use the words by Hilary Charlesworth – is the law of ECEs, which is still underdeveloped and underrecognized. The response to a crisis can be delayed when another crisis takes precedence – the example of the COVID-19 pandemic that slowed down all measures in response to climate change – but a response to an emergency that takes into consideration the interconnectedness between elements must be capable of engaging in critical gender work. That is what climate change and disaster laws have not

38 Dianne Otto, 'Remapping crisis through a Feminist Lens' in Kouvo, Pearson (eds) (n 22) 75, 84.

39 From 1942 to 1953, an area close to Niagara Falls known as Love Canal was filled by Hooker Chemical Company with tons of toxic waste, covered with layers of terrain and later sold to the city, which built a school and a new neighbourhood. A few years later, the effects of pollution started to manifest. Lois Gibbs, one of the women and mothers living there, initiated a case against both Hooker and the city administration. Lois Marie Gibbs, *Love Canal: My Story: Lois Marie Gibbs as told to Murray Levine* (State University of New York Press 1982); Id., *Love Canal: and the Birth of the Environmental Health Movement* (3rd edn, Island Press, 2011); Richard S. Newman, *Love Canal: A Toxic History from Colonial Times to the Present* (Oxford University Press 2016). See also Karen Jan Stults, 'Hysterical Housewives (And Other Courageous Women)' (1989) 13 *On The Issues Magazine* <https://ontheissuesmagazine.com/feminism/hysterical-housewives-and-other-courageous-women/> accessed 8 April 2025.

40 Sherilyn MacGregor, 'A Stranger Silence Still: The Need for Feminist Social Research on Climate Change' (2010) 57 (2) *The Sociological Review* 124, 127.

41 *Ibid*., 128. It has been called 'masculinization of environmentalism'.

accomplished, except for an important but insufficient increase in women's participation in the processes.[42] As Gina Heathcote argued, fragmented feminist reforms have tended to be directed at improving women's issues rather than improving the discipline of international law.[43] Feminist methodologies suggest that the prescription of women's equality must listen to the women 'we think we are helping', incorporating, for example, Indigenous women's rights in the debate and reflecting on their systematic discrimination.[44] International law has been unable to listen to women's instances. Even though feminist legal theories have sometimes struggled with paradoxes, with the tension between, on the one hand, becoming institutionalized, with the risk of reproducing the same dynamics of oppression and, on the other hand, remaining the critical but often neglected and even trivialized voice, they surely shed light on persistent silences in law and explained how law in itself might represent a cause of violence.[45]

In climate change law, the language of crisis is predominant, with climate change being described as an 'apocalypse':[46] however, it is not a monolithic phenomenon, but rather composed of different situations, from acidification of oceans to desertification, which cannot be understood properly without recognizing its social dimension. Climate change is a gendered phenomenon and a matter of social justice, mediated by axes of power, including colonial power

---

42 International disaster management law focuses on legal issues arising from the prevention of, response to and recovery from various natural catastrophic events, but also from human-made disasters, such as large-scale industrial accidents. See Andrea de Guttry, Marco Gestri and Gabriella Venturini (eds), *International Disaster Response Law* (Springer 2012); Flavia Zorzi Giustiniani, *International Law in Disaster Scenarios: Applicable Rules and Principles* (Springer 2021). Hopefully, the forthcoming treaty on the protection of persons in disasters will strengthen a gender approach that only timidly appears in the draft of 2016 elaborated by the International Law Commission. Giulio Bartolini, 'Toward a universal treaty on "Protection of Persons in the Event of Disasters"' (*EJIL:Talk!* 17 December 2024) <https://www.ejiltalk.org/toward-a-universal-treaty-on-protection-of-persons-in-the-event-of-disasters/> accessed 9 April 2025.

43 Gina Heathcote, *Feminist Dialogues on International Law* (Oxford University Press, 2019) 33.

44 Hilary Charlesworth, 'Talking to Ourselves? Feminist Scholarship in International Law' in Kouvo, Pearson (eds) (n 22) 17, 32.

45 On law as a cause of gender-based violence against women, see Sara De Vido, *Violence against Women's Health in International Law* (Manchester University Press, 2020).

46 Sherilyn MacGregor, 'Only Resist: Feminist Ecological Citizenship and the Post-politics of Climate Change' (2014) 29 (3) *Hypatia* 617, 630.

and inequalities. It is a matter of 'women's inequality and climate injustice'.[47] In a perspective that departs from the predominant Eurocentrism, it is important to stress that ecological catastrophes caused by a part of humanity are part of history and not a recent manifestation: Native Americans' ecosystems were destroyed due to colonialism, for example. The risk is that, by insisting on the new threat caused by climate change, which matters only because it also affects 'our' European world, 'the existence of a form of ecological catastrophe that has been going on for at least five centuries, threatening all forms of life, but with the Indigenous people paying the first and highest price' is erased.[48] An apparently neutral phenomenon, climate change exacerbates situations of discrimination, including gender discrimination and ecological domination as a legacy of colonialism, which are already present in societies. Nicole Rogers explained that 'climate crisis' is an 'assemblage of synergistic violences, encompassing violence to human, nonhuman and more-than-human beings, violence to Earth systems, and violence to all forms of property, including but not limited to, the annihilation of the entire territory of individual nation-states. These violences are both direct and structural in nature'.[49] Hence, for example, it has been shown that sea level rise produces negative effects on women's reproductive health.[50] Two authors argued, without however incorporating a gender dimension, that 'climate change has been brought about through the colonial processes implicated in the production and reproduction of those very inequalities: the colonial and racialized dispossessions that severed peoples' access to land and resources to sustain their livelihoods and set them to work in the plantations and factories that went on to drive extraction through industrial development'.[51] It is possible

---

47 Cathi Albertyn, Helena Alviar Garcia, Meghan Campbell *et al.*, 'Introduction' in Cathi Albertyn, Meghan Campbell, Helena Alviar Garcia *et al.* (eds) *Feminist Frontiers in Climate Justice: Gender Equality, Climate Change and Rights* (Edward Elgar Publishing 2023) 1, 10.

48 Chiara Bottici, 'Ecofeminism as Decolonial and Transindividual Ecology' (2021) 2 (2) *(Des)Troços: Revista de Pensamento Radical* 141, 146.

49 Rogers (n 17) 144. On structural inequality, with a focus not only on women's rights, Virginia Mantouvalou and Jonathan Wolff (eds), *Structural Injustice and the Law* (UCL Press, 2024).

50 Mahadi Al Hasnat, Zoya Teirstein, 'The Bizarre Link Between Rising Sea Levels and Complications in Pregnancy' (*Vox* 30 May 2024) *Vox* <https://www.vox.com/climate/351534/salt-water-pregnancy-rising-sea-levels> accessed 8 April 2025. See also Cathi Albertyn, 'Radical connectedness: Reproductive Rights, Climate Justice, and Gender Equality' in Albertyn, Campbell, Alviar Garcia et al. (eds) (n 47) 138, 146.

51 Gurminder K. Bhambra, Peter Newell, 'More than a Metaphor: 'Climate Colonialism' in Perspective' (2023) 2 (3) *Global Social Challenges Journal* 179, 182.

to add a layer of analysis: gender-based discrimination against women as one of the inequalities that have shaped colonial development. Fahrana Sultana captured this aspect, advocating for a feminist climate justice scholarship that 'engages with intersectionality to demonstrate how patriarchy compounds social-ecological crisis', looking at 'the specificities of interlocking systems of oppression and exploitation'.[52] An approach that incorporates systems of oppression and exploitation unveils the inherent masculinities in the law and policies of climate change, which are aimed at addressing the disasters offering 'techno-scientific solutions' devoted to security, missing the point of how climate change exacerbates existing inequalities and forms of oppression that are also interspecies.[53] Indeed, working on these solutions shifts the responsibility from a part of humanity to nature, stressing the inevitability of natural disasters, which are, however, the result of human behaviour: 'absent or hidden is an ethical stance against the exploitation of the planet by humans and for its protection as indivisible from human life'.[54]

5. WHY WE NEED MORE ECOFEMINISM IN INTERNATIONAL LAW

Ecofeminism has rarely been explored in law and has never been included among 'the' methods of international legal analysis. Despite the fact that this chapter cannot do justice to the richness of the debate on ecofeminism and its manifestations,[55] a few words are needed to explain why ecofeminism can play a role in international legal scholarship.[56] For our purposes, combining environmental and feminist legal theory can better grasp the complexity of ECEs because it highlights the intertwining between societal schemes and the environment. The term was coined by Françoise d'Eaubonne in her 1974 work,

---

52 Farhana Sultana, 'Critical Climate Justice' (2022) 188 (1) *Geography Journal* 118, 120.

53 MacGregor, 'Only Resist: Feminist Ecological Citizenship and the Post-politics of Climate Change' (n 46) 626.

54 *Ibid.*, 628.

55 An excellent summary of the development of ecofeminist thought, although limited to North America, in Greta Gaard, 'Ecofeminism Revisited: Rejecting Essentialism and Re-Placing Species in a Material Feminist Environmentalism' (2011) 23 (2) *Feminist Formations* 26; Carlarne, 'Environmental Law and Feminism' (n 21).

56 An example of the application of an ecofeminist method to water governance is found in Kate Darling, 'A Weight for Water: an Ecological Feminist Critique of Emerging Norms and Trends in Global Water Governance' (2012) 13 (1) *Melbourne Journal of International Law* 1.

Le féminisme ou la mort, in which she highlighted the environmental costs of development and argued that the overpopulation of the planet was caused by the patriarchal rejection of women's right to self-determination with regard to their bodies.[57] Puleo explained that it is 'an attempt to hypothesize a new utopian horizon, one that addresses environmental problems arising from the categories of patriarchy, androcentrism, care, sex and gender'.[58] The dialogue between feminism and environmentalism is decisive in emphasizing the impact of environmental degradation on gender and the contributions women can make. Ecofeminism has been a discipline of 'practice'[59] also because of women's environmental activism 'within the context of, and as a result of, their particular socially assigned roles – roles that in many key ways do transcend boundaries of race, ethnicity and class'.[60]

Vandana Shiva, Carolyn Merchant and Maria Mies were among the key authors at the origin of the thought. References to what we call in this book ECEs were present already in the 1960s, without the law, including the human rights system, being capable of seeing them. For example, in 1996, Merchant argued that:

> Environmental equity is an ecofeminist issue. The body, home, and community are sites of women's local experience and local contestation. Women experience the results of toxic dumping on their own bodies (sites of reproduction of the species), in their own homes (sites of reproduction of daily life), and in their communities and schools (sites of social reproduction). Women's leadership and organizing skills gained in grassroots struggles empower them to change society and themselves.[61]

---

[57] François d'Eaubonne, *Le féminisme ou la mort* (P. Horay 1974). On ecofeminism, see, among others, Karen Warren, 'The Power and the Promise of Ecological Feminism' (1990) 12 (2) *Environmental Ethics* 121; Maria Mies and Vandana Shiva, *Ecofeminism* (Zed Books 1993); Karen Warren (ed.) *Ecofeminism. Women, Culture, Nature* (Indiana University Press 1997); Mary Mellor, *Feminism and Ecology* (New York University Press 1997); Chaone Mallory, 'Val Plumwood and Ecofeminist Solidarity: Standing with the Natural Other' (2009) 14 (2) *Ethics and the Environment* 3; Bruna Bianchi, 'Ecofeminism: Thought, Debates, Perspectives' (2012) 20 (8) *DEP Deported, Exiles and Refugees* I.

[58] Alicia H. Puleo, 'What is Ecofeminism?' (2017) 25 *Quaderns de la Mediterrània* 27.

[59] Freya Mathews, 'The Dilemma of Dualism' in Sherilyn MacGregor (ed.) *Routledge Handbook of Gender and the Environment* (Routledge, 2017) 54, 68.

[60] Joni Seager, *Earth Follies: Coming to Feminist Terms with the Global Environmental Crisis* (Routledge, 1994) 269.

[61] Carolyn Merchant, *Earthcare: Women and the Environment* (Routledge, 1996) 191.

Merchant referred in her pioneering book to women's 'intimate knowledge of nature', deriving from their role as caregivers, and called for a 'partnership ethic of earth care'.[62] Maria Mies and Vandana Shiva, who also supported a movement to address ecological challenges through decolonization, talked about a 'feminine principle'.[63] These arguments paved the way for a critique of ecofeminism as being 'essentialist', either by arguing that women were inevitably and inherently connected to nature or socially intertwined with it.[64] As it was pointed out, 'if women are essentialized as an eternal feminine principle, then they are relegated once again to the natural realm, as they have been for such a long time, and to their own detriment, as such nature has, in its turn, itself been situated in the horizon of death'.[65] In other words, the inherent connection between women and nature contradicts the need to disrupt the dichotomy of human/nature. The consequence was a complete silence on ecofeminism: by 2010, 'it was nearly impossible to find a single essay, much less a section, devoted to issues of feminism and ecology (and certainly not ecofeminism), species, or nature in most introductory anthologies used in women's studies, gender studies, or queer studies'.[66] Legal scholarship entirely ignored the debate, except for a few exceptions.[67]

Despite some clear references by authors to this strong connection between women and nature,[68] the critique referring to essentialism casts a shadow on the richness of a debate that has not simply equated women with nature.[69] Ecofeminism has had multiple nuances, only some of which are rooted in

---

62 *Ibid.*, 12.

63 Mies, Shiva (n 57).

64 Mary Mellor, 'Feminism and Environmental Ethics: A Materialist Perspective' (2000) 5 (1) *Ethics and the Environment* 107, 114.

65 Bottici (n 48) 148.

66 Gaard, 'Ecofeminism Revisited: Rejecting Essentialism and Re-Placing Species in a Material Feminist Environmentalism' (n 55). The Italian journal *DEP-Deportate esuli e profughe* dedicated an issue to ecofeminism at a time (2012) when the debate was nonexistent in Italy. See: <https://www.unive.it/pag/31491/> accessed 8 April 2025.

67 For a reflection on the scarce legal scholarship on ecofeminism, see Linda A. Malone, 'Environmental Justice Reimagined Through Human Security and Post-Modern Ecological Feminism: A Neglected Perspective on Climate Change' (2015) 38 (5) *Fordham International Law Journal* 1445.

68 One can read the powerful pages by Mary Huntin Austin, for example, in *The Ford* (Houghton Mifflin, 1917) 233–4, on the androcentric culture in the economic activities in the desert. Mary Hunter Austin, *La terra delle piogge rare* (Nova Delphi 2023).

69 Gaard, 'Ecofeminism Revisited: Rejecting Essentialism and Re-Placing Species in a Material Feminist Environmentalism' (n 55).

'essentialist (cultural) feminisms', while others 'grew out of liberal, social, Marxist, anarchist and socialist feminisms', and 'in the 1990s, ecofeminist theories continued to refine and ground their analyses, developing economic, material, international and intersectional perspectives'.[70] Ecofeminism expresses great potential for application as a legal method of international law because it questions monolithic legal categories and reconsiders them in light of the interdependence between all species (human and non-human) and with nature, prioritizing the needs of communities whose voices have never been effectively heard and that are most affected by climate change and, as this book argues, by ECEs. Feminist theories call into question dichotomies such as male/female, reason/emotion, white/colored, transcendent/material, culture/nature, mind/body, human/animal, which are gendered in the sense that the first word is associated with maleness and masculinity and the second, subordinate one, with women and femininity. One of ecofeminism's points of strength is 'subjected to the subordinating process of dualism, that nature is perhaps the ultimate "Other" upon which the human self gets constructed'.[71] Ecofeminism, in other words, rejects 'false binaries and dualisms such as the human/nature dualism (...), as well as a refusal to privilege "ecological" concerns over so-called "humanist"'.[72]

There are other fascinating theories that have been developed, starting from ecofeminism. For example, MacGregor argued for a project of *feminist ecological citizenship* to develop ecofeminist positions that are non-essentialist, democratic and oppositional. In her book, *Beyond Mothering Earth*, she contended that an ecofeminist approach to citizenship 'recognizes care as a form of work and a moral orientation that has been feminized and privatized in Western societies and that must be distributed fairly within and between societies if gender equality and sustainability are to be realized'.[73] In response and/or opposition to ecofeminism, feminist political ecology developed to provide an intersectional analysis of socio-environmental reactions and to take into

---

70 *Ibid*, 32. There have been several phases of ecofeminism, including vegan ecofeminism. See also Elizabeth Carlassare, 'Socialist and Cultural Ecofeminism: Allies in Resistance' (2000) 5 (1) *Ethics and the Environment* 89.

71 Chaone Mallory, 'Environmental Justice, Ecofeminism, and Power', in Ricardo Rozzi, F. Stuart Chapin III, J. Baird Callicott *et al.* (eds), *Earth Stewardship: Linking ecology and Ethics for a Changing World* (Springer 2013) 251, 254.

72 *Ibid.*

73 Sherilyn Mac Gregor, *Beyond Mothering Earth: Ecological citizenship and the Politics of Care* (UBC Press 2006). See also in that respect Karen Morrow in this Volume.

account complex dimensions of gender and social experiences.[74] Looking at 'political' concepts such as 'citizenship' and challenging political and economic structures and institutions within which oppression and domination have been reproduced are relevant trajectories to lawyers as well. Going back to the 'personal is political', these theories allow an understanding of the role of care, including ecological care, across genders, publicly recognized as a political ideal.[75] However, 'the history of ecofeminism merits recuperation, both for the intellectual lineage it provides and for the feminist force it gives to contemporary theory'.[76] In our case, ecofeminism can and should become a method of international law.

To reply to an obvious objection commonly addressed to feminist lawyers – why they are using ecofeminism and not exploring other methods and theories, such as deep ecology or Marxism[77] – because hardly classic methods of law would be questioned as relevant for the debate, it should be acknowledged that there are indeed several theories that endorse non-anthropocentric perspectives on law. Nonetheless, revitalizing ecofeminism and using it as a method of international law opens new interesting paths of research that can better examine schemes of oppression within and across species. It is not necessarily the best method – each method has points of strength and weakness and mirrors the given author's background and sensitivity – or one that necessarily has to replace the others, but it is a method that combines an understanding of persistent discrimination in our societies with the knowledge that humans belong to the environment and not *vice versa*. It is a method that unravels the dynamics of power and oppression within and between different species, expanding the view of these dynamics beyond humans. In our project on ECEs, we searched for a method that, combined with the classic ways in which rules are adopted and 'performed', challenges patriarchal structures inherent in international law and helps us reconceptualize them. We see in ecofeminism the origin of the debates that followed, including the aforementioned feminist political ecology and feminist ecological citizenship and in its clear message, despite the nuances of the thought – the intersections existing among environmental

---

[74] Dianne Rocheleau, Barbara Thomas Slayter and Esther Wangari (eds), *Feminist Political Ecology: Global Issues and Local Experience* (Routledge, 1996).

[75] MacGregor, 'Only Resist: Feminist Ecological Citizenship and the Post-politics of Climate Change' (n 46) 677.

[76] Gaard, 'Ecofeminism Revisited: Rejecting Essentialism and Re-Placing Species in a Material Feminist Environmentalism' (n 55) 42–3.

[77] One could use Marxism, for example, which examines the relationship between the base and the 'superstructure', and concepts of ideology and hegemony, but not the exploitation of nature by (a part of) humanity.

injuries, destruction of ecosystems and social and economic injustices – the potential to be used as a legal method.[78]

Karen Morrow argued that 'when ecofeminism is pursued in an international context, its goal is to import this paradigm-shifting approach to accommodating alternative/additional procedural and substantive expertise and experience, from the periphery to the mainstream[79] Since international law 'embraces and even embeds dualism at its very core, with entrenched power holders enjoying the advantages of othering non-privileged humans and the environment', an ecofeminist approach 'could offer a corrective [...] entailing at base a radical, relational process of (re)connection – as humans with one another and as humans with the non-human environment'.[80] Ecofeminism, focusing on the processes through which gender, racial and ecological oppression are connected, is 'not merely conceptual': it shows 'how these ideological connections are dialectically entangled with the material condition of women and other oppressed groups'.[81]

Intersectional Legal Ecofeminism

Women, especially those at the intersection of different grounds of discrimination – women of colour, displaced women, Indigenous women, women belonging to minorities, low-income women, women with disabilities, girls etc. – are particularly affected by contamination and ecological degradation. In Colombia, for example, the cultivation of flowers, a largely female

---

78 See Sara De Vido, '*In dubio pro futuris generationibus*: Una risposta giuridica eco-centrica alla slow *violence*' in Micaela Frulli (ed.), *L'interesse delle generazioni future nel diritto internazionale e dell'unione europea* (Editoriale Scientifica, 2023) 419. As it was argued, 'Specifically, ecofeminism stems from the philosophical dissection of the shared subjugation of women and nature as social categories nested within the hegemonic arrangement of global heterosexual patriarchal racialized capitalism; ideas that initially coalesced outside of the academy. Whereas FPE emerged from political ecological thought with strong theoretical affinities to the largely Western urban-centric scholarship of feminist geography': Laura A. McKinney, Devin Wright, 'Gender and Environmental Inequality' in Michael A. Long, Michael J. Lynch and Paul B. Stretesky (eds), *Handbook on Inequality and the Environment* (Edward Elgar Publishing, 2023) 228, 235.

79 Karen Morrow, 'Towards an Ecofeminist Critique of International Law?' in Vincent Chapaux, Frédéric Mégret, Usha Natarajan (eds) *The Routledge Handbook of International Law and Anthropocentrism* (Routledge 2023) 183, 194.

80 *Ibid.* See the discussion of ecofeminism in private international law in Sara De Vido, 'The Privatisation of Climate Change Litigation: Current Developments in Conflict of Laws' (2024) 6 (1) *Jus Cogens* 65.

81 Mallory, 'Environmental Justice, Ecofeminism, and Power' (n 70) 255.

labour drawn from low-income areas, determines a disproportionate impact on women who are exposed to pesticides and very difficult working conditions.[82] Flower production, celebrated as an opportunity for the employment of women, has changed the land and women's bodies: their bodies are poisoned, injured and silent.[83] The position is maintained for many hours, and the chemicals have a negative impact on the body cycles of menstruation and pregnancy.[84] As it was argued:

> The production of poisoned, sick and silent bodies configures an alienated female corporality, an *experience of bodies apparently without pain* and a labor experience in which the pain is unavoidable. From the Indigenous perspective, it could be said that the pain that female workers of the flower agroindustry feel is an expression of the pain of the land; and the alienated corporality is an expression of the alienation of the territory (of their biodiversity and water sources) by the flower sector.[85]

In Ecuador, the interconnection between the exploitation of nature and the exploitation of women is related to the shrimp fishery. *Concheras* women, of African descent, are subject to discrimination because they are women, because of their ethnicity, but also because of the depletion of the ecological resources that are at the basis of their livelihoods. As it was pointed out, 'an ecofeminist lens brings into focus how the power of white supremacist Anglo-European capitalist patriarchy operates to marginalize women and nature simultaneously'.[86] Several studies report that women face additional climate-related health vulnerabilities and that racially minoritized women are doubly disadvantaged.[87] There is also little research, and we are aware that this book is not addressing this aspect in detail, on the femininities of women who were not born female, and on the gender identity and sexual orientation of women vis-à-vis what we call ECEs. For lesbians, for example, ECEs can exacerbate discrimination against them because of the social impact of these phenomena.

---

82 Helena Alviar Garcîa, Maria Carolina Olarte-Olarte, 'Climate change and gender in Colombia: exploring female-led struggle in the flower industry' in Albertyn, Campbell, Alviar Garcia et al. (eds) (n 47) 190.

83 Juliana Flórez Flórez, Guisella Andrea Lara Veloza, Patricia Veloza Torres et al., 'Politics of Place at the Women's School of Madrid: Experiences Around Bodies and Territory' in Wendy Harcourt (ed.) *Bodies in Resistance: Gender and Sexual Politics in the Age of Neoliberalism* (Palgrave Macmillan 2017) 31.

84 *Ibid.*

85 *Ibid.*, 34–35.

86 Mallory, 'Environmental Justice, Ecofeminism, and Power' (n 71) 256.

87 Thilagawathi Abi Deivanayagam, Sonora English, Jason Hickel et al., 'Envisioning Environmental Equity: Climate Change, Health, and Racial Justice' (2023) 402 *Lancet* 74.

It has also been reported that 'homophobia infiltrates climate change discourse, distorting our analysis of climate change causes and climate justice solutions, and placing a wedge between international activists'.[88]

An intersectional legal approach 'listens' to multiple experiences, not to produce a 'single' and irrefutable truth but to interpret States' legal obligations present in the (limited) legal framework that is available. An intersectional ecofeminist method to law guarantees environmental justice that understands the ways in which 'systems of oppression (such as racism, gender discrimination and environmental degradation) are interconnected and mutually reinforcing'.[89] It means, for example, that in deciding cases of ECEs from the perspective of human rights law, international bodies and regional courts should use intersectionality to shape positive obligations of due diligence and to 'measure' reparations. To go back to the example of Colombia, occupational healthcare has been ignored by the flower industry, also because in many cases the effects of pesticides manifest once people retire – and that is precisely what we mean by ECEs, because they manifest (or not) after many years both on women's bodies and on the land.[90] From an international human rights perspective, if the case was brought to the attention of the Human Rights Committee, having Colombia ratified the Optional Protocol to the International Covenant on Civil and Political Rights, the disproportionate impact on women and on nature could shape the way in which legal obligations for States are conceptualized – for example, obligation to classify the level of toxicity of pesticides with studies that include the effects on women – and which reparations should be envisaged (including long-term and gender-sensitive care). There is a lot to be done in legal scholarship to connect race, class, disability and coloniality with gender on issues of environment, especially when it is not related to major disasters. In this project, we try to take on some of these challenges.

6. WHAT AN ECOFEMINIST LEGAL METHOD PRACTICALLY MEANS WHEN DEALING WITH CHRONIC EMERGENCIES

International law has dealt in recent decades with issues of gender equality and non-discrimination. As Dianne Otto pointed out, 'feminist tenacity, now spanning decades, has led to international law's repeated formal commitment to realizing the equality of women'.[91] However, a formal commitment

---

88 Greta Gaard, 'Ecofeminism and climate change' (2015) 49 *Women's Studies International Forum* 20, 24.

89 Mallory, 'Environmental Justice, Ecofeminism, and Power' (n 71) 253.

90 Flórez, Veloza, Torres et al. (n 83).

91 Otto, 'Remapping crisis through a Feminist Lens' (n 38) 93.

is insufficient because international law itself can be a source of violence, contributing to the reproduction of patterns of discrimination and inequality. The representation and participation of women are important but not decisive unless we challenge monolithic categories of analysis, including that of 'crisis'. International law can be the law of ECEs, and we can find some examples of this practice in treaty law, where negotiations were able to (though often partially) respond to an ECE using a feminist lens, and in the interpretation – often encouraged by feminist scholars – of existing legal instruments in a more ecofeminist way. In the Minamata Convention on Mercury, for example, there is a recognition of the disproportionate impact of mercury on women, especially pregnant women, children and on future generations. This is an important step forward, but the reference to women is scarce and not in the operative part of the Convention, especially regarding States' obligations. Women are considered as a vulnerable subject. Their vulnerability is not only related to their reproductive role but also to the societal context in which they operate. This aspect can be taken into account in the adoption of national action plans, interpreting one of the provisions of Annex C to the Minamata Convention on 'artisanal and small-scale gold mining', stating 'strategies to prevent the exposure of vulnerable populations, particularly children and women of child-bearing age, especially pregnant women, to mercury used in artisanal and small-scale gold mining'.[92] This provision does not take into account the interconnection between the exploitation of women and the exploitation of nature, and that women can be placed in a subordinate position in societies where artisanal and small-scale gold mining is performed. Law is surely 'part of the problem' because of its traditional 'anthropocentric' and 'androcentric' structure, and it is not necessarily the only response. This is why 'feminists need to be considerably more sceptical about the embrace of feminist ideas by crisis, searching for ways in which those ideas can be reclaimed for feminist purposes, while at the same time emphasising the continuing complicity of law in women's inequality' (and of the exploitation of nature).[93] An ecofeminist method to ECEs will shift the focus from the response to crisis using securitization discourses to prevention, promoting, for example, the right to health, including reproductive health and education, in areas most affected by identified or presumed ECEs. As we are going to see in the following chapters,[94]

[92] Minamata Convention on Mercury (adopted 10 October 2013, entered into force 16 August 2017) 3202 UNTS, C.N.560.2014, point 1, (i) Annex C.

[93] Otto, 'Remapping crisis through a Feminist Lens' (n 38).

[94] See in that respect, Björnstjern Baade, 'Due Diligence Obligations and Chronic Emergencies'; Martina Sardo, 'The Duty to Cooperate in Addressing the Adverse Impact of Environmental Chronic Emergencies: Ensuring Gender-Sensitive Responses'; Francesca Tammone, 'Transforming *Slow Violence* into

the obligation to respond to ECEs must be characterized by gender sensitivity and by an approach that, while valuing women's participation and gender mainstreaming, does not stop there but embraces intersectional concerns and shapes States' obligations. The issue of reparation is possibly the most challenging one because it means gradually acknowledging – and human rights jurisprudence can help in that respect – that despite the absence of clear causality, the violation of human rights stemming from ECEs deserves a gender-sensitive response.

7. CONCLUSION

This chapter aims to provide the theoretical and methodological basis of our project, using ecofeminism as a method of international law and as the foundation of the concept of ECE. A social movement, an approach, a form of political inquiry with different nuances, ecofeminism, when used in international law, does not replace the more 'classic' methods in international legal analysis, but it interacts with them, disrupting consolidated categories of international law and questioning a legal language that perpetuates discrimination on multiple and intersecting grounds, even when it seems to be prone to gender equality. As we said at the beginning, ECEs are around us; they disproportionately affect women and girls, particularly those at the intersection of different grounds of discrimination, not because they are inherently vulnerable but because of power dynamics that disadvantage them. We can resist the law, or we can comply with it. We situate our project in between, using ecofeminism to break the silences of international law on ECEs and resisting anthropocentric and androcentric expressions of our beloved discipline.

Social Justice: The Quest for Reparation for Environmental Chronic Emergencies' in this Volume.

2. Moving beyond an approach based on crisis and disasters to address environmental chronic emergencies

Deborah Russo

1. INTRODUCTION

For a long time, human beings have used and exploited natural resources in the absence of any significant international legal restraint. Rather, at the time of colonial and post-colonial expansionism, international law authorized the unlimited use of natural resources of other countries together with the imposition of an unequal and unjust model of economic development, based on the exploitation of local populations, women and nature, which ultimately resulted in the separation of the international community between a rich minority and a poor and disadvantaged majority of people. At that time, international rules legitimized a set of dominant interests, hierarchies and hegemonies that reflected the imperialist aims of western States but also established imbalanced power relations at different interrelated levels: inter-state, inter-human, especially between men and women, and between humans and the rest of the environment.[1] Prompted by economic globalization, the Western model of economic development has been spreading to a wide number of developing States, changing to a certain extent the geopolitical balance of international society and increasing the related environmental impact. While the environmental degradation caused by the unsustainable exploitation of natural resources still disproportionately impacts on a part of the world, it is progressively expanding everywhere.

---

[1] Antony Anghie, 'The Evolution of International Law: Colonial and Postcolonial Realities' (2006) 27 (5) *Third World Quarterly* 739; Irene Watson, *Aboriginal Peoples, Colonialism and International Law* (Routledge 2015); Susan Harris Rimmer and Kate Ogg (eds), *Research Handbook on Feminist Engagement with International Law* (Edward Elgar Publishing 2019).

Under the pressure of scientists and a worried public opinion, States made some first attempts to slowly elaborate a few international legal norms for the protection of specific aspects of the global environment and to foster international cooperation in times of disasters. This chapter aims to demonstrate that these rules, comprehensively considered, albeit extremely important, focus on the more striking and flashy effects of the environmental degradation process, without holistically addressing environmental chronic emergencies (ECEs), which develop slowly and silently and harm the environment regardless of their resulting in disasters. These days, States are discussing how to translate the ILC Draft Articles on the Protection of Persons in the Event of Disasters (hereinafter 'Draft Articles on Disasters') into a general treaty.[2] While this development would represent a desirable step forward for international cooperation and humanitarian assistance in the case of calamitous and disrupting events, there is more to do to prevent chronic emergencies and protect the environment, including human beings and animals.[3] Similarly, as this chapter will discuss in the next paragraphs, international courts and human rights monitoring bodies are paying increasing attention to the relationship between the environment and human rights, but they still mostly imply a limited conception of ECEs, which does not sufficiently consider their disproportionate impact on women. In our view, this approach reflects the prevailing conception that it takes a disaster to catalyze an international legal response. As reminded by Sara De Vido's quotation by Hilary Charlesworth in the first chapter, international law has been traditionally conceived as the law of crisis.[4] This statement illustrates how States are cooperating to respond to disasters and major environmental damages, disregarding the structural causes and discriminatory societal patterns that provoke them. In tune with Hilary Charlesworth's view, this chapter advocates a more effective and proactive role for international law and investigates how international law could move beyond an approach based on crisis and disaster to become the law of everyday prevention of chronic emergencies. In particular, this chapter will focus on the concept of 'ECEs' in order to discuss what responding to chronic emergencies entails and why this concept is useful to shape the international law of tomorrow. Although part of this discussion could also be relevant for social chronic emergencies, such as

---

[2] ILC, 'Draft Articles on the Protection of Persons in the Event of Disasters, with Commentaries' (2016) 2 (Part Two) *Yearbook of the International Law Commission* 26.

[3] On the concept of 'environment' that this chapter adopts, see in more detail Sara De Vido, 'Feminist Legal Methods and ECEs: Challenging the Anthropocentric and Androcentric International Legal System' in this Volume.

[4] Hilary Charlesworth, 'International Law: A Discipline of Crisis' (2002) 65 (3) *Modern Law Review* 377, 382.

poverty or unemployment, this book (including the present chapter) will focus on ECEs only. Thus, the analysis of the international legal response to social chronic emergencies exceeds the scope of the present book and will hopefully be addressed by future research. Furthermore, this book (and chapter) will not deal with those chronic emergencies, including ECEs, that derive from armed conflicts and entail, *inter alia*, the application of international humanitarian law. The factual and legal peculiarities of chronic emergencies related to armed conflicts would deserve special research that could in the future be developed, taking inspiration from the change of perspective and approach advocated by this book.

2. THE THEORETICAL DIFFERENCE BETWEEN DISASTERS AND ECEs

This book defines as chronic emergencies the multiple phenomena of slow and silent environmental degradation caused by human exploitation of natural resources in the extractive, agricultural, and intensive animal farming sectors, deforestation, pollution and urbanization which may result, *inter alia*, in air, water, and soil contamination, sea level rise, global warming, acidification of oceans, land and forest degradation and loss of biodiversity. These phenomena, whose peculiarity is to develop gradually and silently, are likely to result in disasters in the long run, with a risk rate that increases in combination with the vulnerabilities of the territory and the human and non-human species involved.[5] Although they are extremely dangerous for the ecosystem and the life of human and non-human animals, regardless of their transformation into disasters, international rules pay attention to them mainly if and to the extent that they result in disasters.

International law does not provide a general definition of 'disaster but the latter can be easily drawn from the whole body of rules called the international law of disasters. This field of international law has developed since the beginning of the twentieth century. In 1927, a first international agreement, the now-terminated Convention establishing an International Relief Union, aimed at coordinating humanitarian assistance to the victims of disasters and encouraged studies on preventive measures against disasters.[6] After the Second World War, the international law of disasters experienced a fragmented process of development, which resulted in the adoption of a sum of bilateral and

[5] On the impact of chronic emergencies on women, see in more detail Enzamaria Tramontana, 'ECEs, Women's Inequality, and International Law' in this Volume.

[6] Convention and Statute Establishing an International Relief Union (adopted 12 June 1927, entered into force 23 March 1976) 135 LNTS 247.

multilateral agreements with different scopes and contents, as well as soft law documents.[7] At the universal level, one of the most well-known treaties is the 1998 Tampere Convention on the Provision of Telecommunication Resources for Disaster Mitigation and Relief Operations, and there are also a few regional agreements, such as the 1991 Agreement Establishing the Caribbean Disaster Emergency Response Agency. Among the soft law documents, one of the more authoritative and comprehensive is the Sendai Framework for Disaster Risk Reduction.[8] In an attempt to codify such a fragmented body of practice, the International Law Commission adopted the 2016 Draft Articles on Disasters[9] and, on 15 November 2024, the Sixth Committee of the UN General Assembly decided to elaborate and conclude a legally binding instrument for the protection of persons in the event of disasters by the end of 2027 at the latest.[10] While these instruments provide for diverse definitions of disaster, they share a common understanding, at least of some qualifiers, that deserves a rapid illustration.

The majority of international instruments on disasters have overcome the distinction between natural and human-made events. Accordingly, the ILC draft article 3(a) provides: '“disaster” means a calamitous event or series of events resulting in widespread loss of life, great human suffering and distress, mass displacement, or large-scale material or environmental damage, thereby seriously disrupting the functioning of society'. As the ILC clarified in the Commentary, the provision does not introduce any limitation concerning the

---

[7] Joseph F. Hutchinson, 'Disasters and the International Order II: The International Relief Union' (2001) 23 (2) *The International History Review* 253; Andrea De Guttry, 'Surveying the Law' in Andrea de Guttry, Marco Gestri and Gabriella Venturini (eds), *International Disaster Response Law* (Springer 2012) 3.

[8] UNGA Res 69/283 (3 June 2015) UN Doc A/RES/69/283 (Sendai Framework for Disaster Risk Reduction). See also: UNGA Res. 43/131 (8 December 1988) UN Doc A/RES/43/131 (Humanitarian Assistance to the Victims of Natural Disasters and Similar Emergency Situations); UNGA Res 45/100 (14 December 1990) UN Doc. A/RES/54/100 (Humanitarian Assistance to the Victims of Natural Disasters and Similar Emergency Situations); UNGA Res 46/182 (19 December 1991) UN Doc A/RES/46/182 (Strengthening of the coordination of humanitarian emergency assistance of the United Nations).

[9] ILC, 'Draft Articles on the Protection of Persons in the Event of Disasters, with Commentaries' (n 2).

[10] UNGA, 'Protection of Persons in the Event of Disasters' (15 November 2024) UN Doc A/C.6/79/L.16. For an early comment on this, see Giulio Bartolini, 'Toward a Universal Treaty on “Protection of Persons in the Event of Disasters”', in (*EJIL:Talk!* 17 December 2024) <https://www.ejiltalk.org/toward-a-universal-treaty-on-protection-of-persons-in-the-event-of-disasters/> accessed 9 April 2025.

origin of the event, that is, whether it is natural or human-made, in recognition of the fact that disasters often arise from a complex set of causes that may include both wholly natural causes and contributions from human activities. This conceptualization implies that the relevant notion includes the events caused by the human exploitation of natural resources that may arise from 'chronic emergencies'. However, by disregarding the causes of disasters, this definition entails an equally neutral responsive approach. Indeed, despite the draft articles aiming at managing the overall operational process of humanitarian assistance, including even disaster prevention, the strategy of prevention is limited to requiring that States introduce managerial rules for preparation for disasters, such as early-warning mechanisms, and does not address the structural conditions and human behaviours that cause the process of environmental degradation.[11] The same logic applies to the humanitarian principles enshrined in draft article 6, which establishes that the 'response to disasters shall take place (. . .) on the basis of non-discrimination, while taking into account the needs of the particularly vulnerable'. The provision prohibits any discriminatory policies and measures in the operational response to disasters, but does not address the structural discrimination that lies at the heart of ECEs and that makes women, in all their differences, more vulnerable. It is valuable that the ILC commentary mentioned that the principle of non-discrimination includes within its scope the States' duty to adopt positive obligations to protect the more vulnerable groups.[12] However, it does not provide any further indication about what the positive obligations necessary to realize substantial equality in prevention, response and reconstruction policies are. This ambiguity is one of the weaker aspects of the international legal frameworks on disasters.[13]

---

[11] See, for example, article 9 of the Draft articles, entitled 'Reduction of the risks of disasters', according to which:

> 1. Each State shall reduce the risk of disasters by taking appropriate measures, including through legislation and regulations, to prevent, mitigate, and prepare for disasters. 2. Disaster risk reduction measures include the conduct of risk assessments, the collection and dissemination of risk and past loss information and the installation and operation of early warning systems.

[12] ILC, 'Draft Articles on the Protection of Persons in the Event of Disasters, with Commentaries' (n 2), para. 7.

[13] Elaine Enarson, Lourdes Meyreles, 'International Perspective on Gender and Disasters: Differences and Possibilities' (2004) 24 (10–11) *International Journal of Sociology and Social Policy* 49; Maureen Fordham, 'Gender, Sexuality and Disaster', in Ben Wisner, Jean-Christophe Gaillard and Ilan Kelman (eds), *Handbook of Hazards and Disaster Risk Reduction* (Routledge 2012) 424; Gabrielle Simm, 'Disasters and Gender: Sexing International Disaster Law' (2019) 2 (1) *Yearbook of International Disaster Law Online* 144.

Furthermore, according to the majority of international instruments, disasters are described as calamitous and extreme events that result in widespread loss of life or otherwise seriously affect people, property,[14] and the environment, causing large-scale human, material or environmental damage. While the relevant threshold has been left uncertain, the definition predicates that disasters 'seriously disrupt the functioning of society'. It is even true that the most recent instruments, including the ILC Draft articles and the Sendai Framework, do not limit the definition of disasters to 'sudden-onset events' such as floods or earthquakes, but include 'slow-onset events', such as droughts.[15] But these types of events differ only in the kind of insurgency and, in the end, both are meant to cause calamitous effects that seriously disrupt the functioning of society in order to catalyze the application of international rules.[16] Differently from slow-onset events, chronic emergencies are legally relevant regardless of the verification of any disastrous event and entail a responsive approach that addresses the structural and systemic causes of the environmental degradation process. Therefore, although 'slow-onset events' and chronic emergencies have in common their slow emergence, the regulatory focus of 'slow-onset events' is on the management of the effects, disregarding the causes.

The conceptualization of what we call ECEs is still largely underestimated. The International Law Commission Study Group on Sea Level Rise in relation to international law recently defined sea level rise as a 'permanent threat' and suggested that 'while the sea level rise phenomenon might not be fully classified as a disaster, within the meaning of the draft articles, many of its

---

[14] Some instruments also refer explicitly to the cultural heritage, such as Article 2 of the 1998 'Agreement among the Governments of the Participating States of the Black Sea Economic Cooperation on Collaboration in Emergency Assistance and Emergency Response to Natural and Man-Made Disasters' (15 April 1998).

[15] As the commentary to the draft art. 3 (a) stresses: 'The draft articles apply equally to sudden-onset events (such as an earthquake or tsunami) and to slow-onset events (such as drought or sea-level rise), as well as frequent small-scale events (floods or landslides)' (ILC, 'Draft articles on the Protection of Persons in The Event of Disasters, with Commentary' (n 2), para. 4). According to the Sendai Framework: 'The present Framework will apply to the risk of small-scale and large-scale, frequent and infrequent, sudden and slow-onset disasters caused by natural or man-made hazards, as well as related environmental, technological, and biological hazards and risks' (UNGA Res 69/283 (3 June 2015) UN Doc A/RES/69/283 (Sendai Framework for Disaster Risk Reduction), para. 15).

[16] Giulio Bartolini, 'The project of articles of the International Law Commission on "protection of persons in the event of disasters"' (2017) 100 (3) *International Law Review* 689; Id., 'A Taxonomy of Disasters in International Law', in Flavia Zorzi Giustiniani, Giulio Bartolini, Emanuele Sommario *et al.* (eds), *Routledge Handbook on Human Rights and Disasters* (Routledge 2018) 18.

manifestations did fall under such a category. Therefore, such manifestations, including the consequences of sea level rise, could be considered a disaster on a case-by-case basis'.[17] This sentence clarifies that sea level rise, which may occasionally result in disasters, is something different from a disaster. However, it is not clear what this difference is, and it is still too early to predict whether the International Law Commission will adopt an innovative conceptual approach based on the chronic emergency nature of sea level rise.

Recently, the notion of 'slow-onset events' has been developed even by some technical and political papers on climate change at the UN level. For example, in the framework of the Convention on Climate Change, a technical paper adopted under decision 1/CP.16 of the Conference of the Parties included within the notion of 'slow-onset events' some of those phenomena that we also define as chronic emergencies (namely sea-level rise, global warming, ocean acidification, desertification...). The paper, which is meant to suggest innovative approaches to manage slow-onset events, focuses on adaptation strategies and tools that do not address the conditions that cause chronic emergencies, including structural discrimination and social injustice. Similarly, the UN policy briefing called 'OCHA and slow-onset emergencies', in spite of mentioning some of the emergencies that we conceptualize as 'chronic emergencies',[18] focuses on early management processes and planning strategies necessary to grant efficient humanitarian assistance in the strict contingency of a disaster or to prevent the effects of disasters. It does not entail a chronic emergencies approach. This shows that the enlargement of the notion of disaster to include 'slow-onset events' does not change the nature of the latter as disasters or the responsive approach of international law. Even the response to 'slow-onset events' aims to grant humanitarian assistance in the immediate aftermath of a disaster and to increase the preparedness level for possible future calamitous events. This 'disaster-based approach' has too limited a scope. It is insufficient to arrest and regress

---

17 ILC, 'Report of the Study Group on Sea-Level Rise in Relation to International Law' (15 July 2024) A/CN.4/L.1002, paras 71, 75.

18 OCHA *Occasional Policy Briefing Series – Brief No. 6: 'OCHA and slow-onset emergencies'* (April 2011) <https://www.unocha.org> accessed 9 April 2025, para. 13: 'It is widely recognized that some of the world's worst humanitarian situations are not transitory problems but long-term chronic emergencies which continue to exist even in the absence of shocks like drought'. See also para. 15:

> This issue reaches to the heart of the definition of 'humanitarian emergencies It is no longer possible to equate humanitarian emergencies solely with short, sharp disasters. Human suffering, when measured by the most agreed indicators such as acute malnutrition (wasting) or excess mortality, is often higher in situations of chronic vulnerability than in situations in which there is a clear trigger for humanitarian action.

the phenomena that precede and cause disasters, which have profound roots in the power dynamics and the discriminatory patterns of society.

From a certain point of view, the 'disaster or crisis-based approach' influences the international legal framework outside the law of disasters. The next paragraphs will focus on the approach taken by the international agreements in the field of environmental law and human rights in responding to the ongoing process of environmental degradation process.

3. THE LACK OF RECOGNITION OF ENVIRONMENTAL CHRONIC EMERGENCIES IN THE CURRENT FRAMEWORK OF INTERNATIONAL ENVIRONMENTAL LAW

Since the 1970s States have started to cooperate in the field of environmental law through treaties and soft legal instruments designed to cope with some of the more drastic effects of certain environmental crises. The first international agreements in this field aimed at preventing and regulating the risk of transboundary environmental damage and were premised on the traditional interstate logic. They aimed to manage national unilateral interests and to prevent and regulate the consequences of territorial damage between neighbouring States. Over time, States have progressively become aware of the global externalities of their economic activities and have started to consider the protection of the environment as a global concern. However, even the agreements concluded to protect the global environment are rigorously premised on the principle of the sovereign freedom of each State to exploit the natural resources within its territory and on the acceptance of common (even if differentiated) responsibilities to adopt adequate measures of mitigation and adaptation.[19] While there are many international treaties that follow this model,[20] the agreements concluded to address the effects of climate change are the best-known ones. The 1992 United Nations Framework Convention on Climate Change, for example, pursues 'the stabilization of greenhouse gas concentrations in the atmosphere at a level that would prevent dangerous anthropogenic interference with the climate system. Such a level should be achieved within a time frame sufficient to allow ecosystems to adapt naturally to climate change, to ensure that food production is not threatened and to enable economic development to

[19] For a comprehensive account of the underlying principles and regulatory approaches of International Environmental Law, see Philippe Sands, Jacqueline Peel, Adriana Fabra *et al.* (eds), *Principles of International Environmental Law* (4th edn, Cambridge University Press 2018).

[20] See for a general recognition: <https://guides.ll.georgetown.edu/InternationalEnvironmentalLaw/treaties> accessed 9 April 2025.

proceed in a sustainable manner'.[21] Although extremely important as the first step for the international protection of the environment, this approach aims at limiting the effects of climate change without addressing the structural causes that provoke them and their disproportionate impacts on women intersecting different grounds of vulnerabilities. Even the 2015 Paris Agreement aims to limit the temperature increase to a certain level and establishes a legal normative framework that does not challenge the causes of the slow and silent environmental degradation that leads to climate change. Other multilateral environmental agreements deal with different phenomena of slow and silent environmental degradation, such as the normative framework for the protection of biodiversity, which is mainly composed of the Convention on Biological Diversity, the Cartagena Protocol on Biodiversity and the Nagoya Protocol on Access and Benefit-sharing, the Stockholm Convention on Persistent Organic Pollutants (Stockholm Convention) and the Minamata Convention on Mercury (Minamata Convention). The approach resulting from their original texts is mostly effect-driven and not sufficiently focused on the disproportionate impact of ECEs on women and other groups of disadvantaged human groups.[22]

Improving the focus on the structural causes of environmental degradation in the reading of these agreements could contribute to better tackling the features of ECEs and increase the understanding that most ECEs are chronic and laced with well-rooted dynamics of power based on alterity, superiority and anthropocentrism.[23]

Yet, there are signs of a rising awareness in some technical papers adopted within the framework of environmental agreements. Documents such as the 'Study on the Differentiated Impacts of Desertification, Land Degradation and Drought on Women and Men', adopted in the context of the United Nations Convention to Combat Desertification and the guide 'Addressing Gender Issues and Actions in Biodiversity Objectives', in the context of the Convention on Biological Diversity, offer interesting insights.[24] These documents recommend

---

21 Article 3 of the United Nations Framework Convention on Climate Change (adopted 9 May 1992, entered into force 21 March 1994) 1771 UNTS 107.

22 For a more extensive and detailed critical gendered analysis of these treaties and their relationship with ECEs, see Tramontana (n 5).

23 For a theoretical insight into such ideologies from a feminist perspective, see more in detail De Vido (n 3).

24 UNCCD, 'Study on the Differentiated Impacts of Land Degradation, Desertification, and Drought on Women and Men' (2022) and CBD, 'Addressing Gender Issues and Actions in Biodiversity Objectives' (2019).

interpreting international obligations by looking at the structural nodes of gender inequality and fostering a holistic strategy to reverse the phenomenon.[25]

An interesting development has also been taking place within the framework of the Convention on Biological Diversity, where an open-ended working group established by the Conferences of the State Parties has adopted a strategic plan to implement broad-based action for a transformation of society's relationship with biodiversity-[26] This strategy, called 'theory of change' advocates a change of economic, social and financial models in order to stabilize and reverse the process of deterioration of biodiversity and acknowledges the need for appropriate recognition of gender equality and women and youth empowerment.[27]

4. THE APPLICATION OF HUMAN RIGHTS IN TIME OF EMERGENCIES: THE STATES' POWER OF DEROGATION . . .

A responsive approach based more on effects than on causes of ECEs may also influence the interpretation and application of certain provisions for the protection of human rights. Although most of the treaties bind States to protect individual rights and do not explicitly deal with the environment, they have been progressively constructed in a wider way in order to protect the life and health of the victims of the most striking effects of the environmental crisis and disasters.[28] More specifically, most human rights monitoring bodies have interpreted the States' obligations to respect and protect human rights, especially the right to life, to health and to respect one's family and private life, as including environmental concerns. However, some authors criticized that the perspective adopted by most human rights bodies was anthropocentric and mainly premised on the recognition that States are entitled to respond to environmental crises and disasters in order to protect the life and health of human beings.[29] To this end, States are allowed either to adopt measures of derogation

---

[25] Mary B. Anderson, 'Understanding the Disaster-Development Continuum. Gender Analysis Is the Essential Tool' (1994) 2 (1) *Focus on Gender* 7.

[26] CBD, 'First Draft on the Post-2020 Global Biodiversity Framework' (5 July 2021) CBD/WG2020/3/3.

[27] *Ibid.*

[28] Giovanna Adinolfi, 'The Right to a Healthy Environment: Delineating the Content (and Contours) of a Slippery Notion', in Flavia Zorzi Giustiniani, Giulio Bartolini, Emanuele Sommario, et al. (n 16) 211.

[29] On ecocentrism as opposed to anthropocentrism, see Sara De Vido, 'A Quest for an Eco-centric Approach to International Law: the COVID-19 Pandemic as Game Changer' (2021) 3 (2) *Jus Cogens* 105; Francesca Cerulli,

of non-mandatory human rights in times of emergencies,[30] or due diligence measures to prevent individuals at risk from becoming victims of disasters.[31]

Regarding the States' power of derogation, some human rights treaties embody 'emergency clauses' that allow States to declare the existence of an exceptional situation of crisis and to adopt non-discriminatory measures of derogation to those provisions that do not grant absolute and mandatory human rights. In so doing, human rights treaties reflect the dichotomous conceptualization of reality as an opposition between normality and exceptions. Although the notion of 'emergency' may relate to the environment, it refers to calamitous and disruptive events that conceptually identify with disasters and do not accommodate the more complex concept of ECEs.[32] In most cases, these public emergencies trigger a state of exception entailing the suspension of certain fundamental rights and the concentration of powers in the government to the extent necessary to ensure the survival of the State and the security of citizens.[33] Derogations normally concern civil and political rights, unless they are absolute and mandatory rights, such as the prohibition of torture and inhuman and degrading treatment. Instead, the protection of economic and social rights should be preserved and even strengthened in the event of a crisis that impacts the economic and social conditions of people, especially vulnerable

'Antropocentrismo vs ecocentrismo nella giurisprudenza della Corte interamericana dei diritti umani' (2023) 17 (2) *Diritti umani e diritto internazionale* 259; Vito De Lucia, 'Anthropocentrism and International Environmental Law' in Vincent Chapaux, Frédéric Mégret and Usha Natarajan (eds), *The Routledge Handbook of International Law and Anthropocentrism* (Abington 2023) 84.

30 Anna-Lena Svensson-McCarthy, *The International Law of Human Rights and States of Exception: With Special Reference to the Travaux Preparatoires and Case Law of the International Monitoring Organs* (Martinus Nijhoff 1998); Jaime Oraa, *Human Rights in States of Emergency in International Law* (Clarendon Press 1992); Joan Fitzpatrick, *Human Rights in Crisis: The International System of Protecting Rights During States of Emergency* (University of Pennsylvania Press 1994).

31 *Social and Economic Rights Action Center (SERAC) and Center for Economic and Social Rights (CESR) v Nigeria*, 'Communication 155/96' (ACHPR, 27 October 2001), para. 51; *López Ostra v Spain* App no 16798/90 (ECtHR, 9 December 1994), paras 51, 55 and 58; *Guerra and Others v Italy* App no 14967/89 (ECtHR, 19 February 1998), paras 57, 58 and 60; *Hatton and Others v The United Kingdom* App no 36022/97 (ECtHR 8 July 2003), paras 96, 98, 104, 118 and 129.

32 Oraa (n 30); Emanuele Sommario, *Stati d'emergenza e trattati a tutela dei diritti umani* (Giappichelli 2018).

33 Mark Klamberg, 'Reconstructing the Notion of State Emergency' (2020) 52 (1) *The George Washington International Law Review* 53.

groups.[34] For this reason, the International Covenant on Economic, Social and Cultural Rights, the European Social Charter and the Additional Protocol to the American Convention on Human Rights in the Area of Economic, Social and Cultural Rights ('Protocol of San Salvador') do not contain emergency clauses. However, some specific provisions of these treaties allow States to adopt measures of limitation, provided that the restrictions are prescribed by law, pursue a legitimate aim (i.e., the protection of national security, public order, public health or public morals), are proportionate to the aim pursued, and are not incompatible with the nature of the rights at stake, that is, do not impair their minimum core or minimum essential levels.[35] The UN Committee on Economic, Social and Cultural Rights, for example, has affirmed that the core obligations regarding economic and social rights cannot be derogated during emergencies.[36] The concept of 'core protection' is strictly linked to the prohibition of discrimination. Policies and procedures that disproportionately impact women or other groups impair the core of social rights protection and are unreasonable.[37]

Similarly, the UN Convention on the Elimination of All Forms of Discrimination against Women (CEDAW) does not allow for derogation, and the CEDAW Committee has specified that treaty obligations do not cease in times of emergency resulting, *inter alia*, from natural disasters.[38]

---

[34] Andrea Broderick, Jennifer Sellin, *Socio-economic Rights, Inequalities and Vulnerability in Times of Crises. Building Back Better* (Edward Elgar Publishing 2024).

[35] Amrei Müller, 'Limitations to and Derogations from Economic, Social and Cultural Rights' (2009) 9 (4) *Human Rights Law Review* 557.

[36] UN Committee on Economic, Social and Cultural Rights (CESCR), 'General Comment No. 14: The Right to the Highest Attainable Standard of Health (Art. 12 of the Covenant)' (11 August 2000) UN Doc E/C.12/2000/4, paras 43 and 47; Id., 'General Comment No. 18: The Right to Work (Art. 6 of the Covenant)' (24 November 2005) UN Doc E/C.12/GC/18, para. 31; Id., 'General Comment No. 13: The Right to Education (Art. 13)' (8 December 1999) UN Doc E/C.12/1999/10, para. 57.

[37] Enzamaria Tramontana, 'Women's rights and gender equality during the COVID-19 pandemic' (2021) 87 *QIL, Zoom-in* 5. CESCR, 'General Comment No. 20: Non-Discrimination in Economic, Social and Cultural Rights (Article 2 (2) of the International Covenant on Economic, Social and Cultural Rights) (2 July 2009) UN Doc E/C.12/GC/20, para. 13.

[38] CEDAW Committee, 'General Recommendation No. 28 on the Core Obligations of States Parties under Article 2 of the Convention on the Elimination of All Forms of Discrimination against Women' (16 December 2010) UN Doc CEDAW/C/GC/28, para. 11.

When treaties contain emergency or limitation clauses, they entail a restrictive understanding of emergencies that identifies with crises and disasters. Accordingly, they focus on the power of derogation without, on the contrary, affirming the States' duty to adopt positive measures necessary to address the special needs of women and vulnerable groups and to dismantle the structural discrimination embedded in society.[39]

A similar restrictive logic permeates other bodies of international law, such as international trade law. In particular, WTO agreements allow states to restrict trade under specific conditions when they aim at protecting the environment.[40] However, environmental concerns in trade agreements are addressed under the dichotomous alternative international rules/national exceptions and are not comprehensively and holistically integrated into the international normative framework. International environmental law and trade regimes have developed in autonomous treaty regimes and have ultimately become separate and fragmented bodies of law.[41] In recent years, states have been debating the need to bring more coherence between trade and environmental rules and have coined the notion of sustainable development as a possible synthesis. However, the concept of sustainable development, whose normative meaning is vague and susceptible to different interpretations, risks supporting an anthropocentric and androcentric conception of human development premised on the instrumentalization of natural resources for all human needs and preferences.[42]

5. . . . AND THE SHAPING OF 'POSITIVE OBLIGATIONS'

The inclusion of environmental concerns within the scope of certain human rights has also led some human rights bodies and courts to shape positive obligations to protect the victims of environmental degradation.

---

[39] See also Deborah Russo, 'The Istanbul Convention in Times of Emergency', in Micaela Frulli and Sara De Vido (eds), *Preventing and Combating Violence Against Women and Domestic Violence: A Commentary on the Istanbul Convention* (Edward Elgar Publishing 2023) 22; Id., 'Gender equality in the context of recovery plans after the Covid-19 pandemic' (2021) 87 *QIL, Zoom-in* 29.

[40] <http://www.wto.org/english/tratop_e/envir_e/envir_e.htm> accessed 9 April 2025.

[41] ILC, 'Fragmentation of International Law: Difficulties Arising from the Diversification and Expansion of International Law' (18 July 2006) A/CN.49/L.702.

[42] Chris Speed, 'Anthropocentrism and sustainable development: oxymoron or symbiosis?' (2006) 93 *WIT Transactions on Ecology and the Environment* 323 <www.witpress.com/Secure/elibrary/papers/SC06/SC06031FU1.pdf> accessed 9 April 2025.

In a set of cases addressing the relationship between the protection of the environment and human rights, for example, the European Court of Human Rights condemned the respondent States for the failure to adopt adequate preventive measures, such as the failures to implement an emergency plan in the presence of a documented risk to health in a certain territorial area and to provide adequate information about the risks faced by the local population.[43] However, in this line of cases, the positive obligations concerned types of measures designed to prevent and prepare for the harmful effects of pollution and environmental degradation, without including a more comprehensive intervention on their causes. A slight change of perspective can be noticed in a couple of recent cases concerning chronic emergencies. In the *KlimaSeniorinnen* case, in particular, the Court emphasized that 'decarbonisation of the economies and ways of life can only be achieved through a comprehensive and profound transformation in various sectors (. . .). Therefore, policies to combat climate change inevitably involve issues of social accommodation and intergenerational burden-sharing, both in regard to different generations of those currently living and in regard to future generations'.[44] While recognizing a margin of discretion to States in the choice of the mitigation strategy and mostly deferring to the international framework designed by the Paris Agreement, the Court made clear that States must follow a transformative approach. In the context of a different chronic emergency addressed in the *Cannavacciuolo* case, the European Court criticized the respondent State for the lack of a systemic, coordinated and comprehensive response to an environmental emergency that had been well known for decades by the national authorities.[45]

A progressive emergence of positive obligations to respond to ECEs is also traceable in the practice of the UN Human Rights Committee and particularly in the more recent reading of the right to life. In its General Comment No. 36, for example, the Human Rights Committee emphasized that environmental degradation, climate change and unsustainable development constitute some of the most pressing and serious threats to the ability of present and future generations to enjoy the right to life. Thus, States parties are bound to implement positive measures 'to ensure sustainable use of natural resources, develop and implement substantive environmental standards, conduct environmental impact assessments and consult with relevant States about activities likely to have a significant impact on the environment, provide notification to other

[43] *Guerra and Others v Italy* (n 31), paras 58–60.

[44] *Verein KlimaSeniorinnen v Switzerland,* App no 53600/20 (ECtHR, 9 April 2024), para. 419.

[45] *Cannavacciuolo v Italy,* Apps nos 39742/14, 51567/14, 74208/14, (ECtHR, 30 January 2025), para. 384.

States concerned about natural disasters and emergencies, and cooperate with them, provide appropriate access to information on environmental hazards and pay due regard to the precautionary approach'.[46] Despite these indications, which may still appear wide and generic, they entail a more advanced approach that moves beyond the urgency to respond to disasters. A similar rationale has been applied to the reviewing of individual communications. In the *Tetiota* case, for example, the Human Rights Committee affirmed that art. 6 of the International Covenant on Civil and Political Rights binds States to adopt positive measures to protect the right of individuals to enjoy a dignified life and to be free from acts or omissions that would cause their unnatural or premature death. Accordingly, the obligations to respect and ensure the right to life extend to all reasonably foreseeable threats and life-threatening situations that can result in loss of life, including environmental degradation, climate change and unsustainable development, which threaten the ability of present and future generations to enjoy the right to life.[47]

Although the Committee recognized that environmental degradation and climate change constitute serious threats to the ability of present and future generations to enjoy the right to life, in the end, it found that the applicant had not provided evidence that he faced any real chance of being harmed in a land dispute. However, in *Billy,* the Committee came to a different conclusion and found that Australia failed to adopt adequate measures to respond to climate change. From the perspective of positive obligations, it is remarkable that the Committee emphasized that States parties should take all appropriate measures 'to address the general conditions in society' that may give rise to direct threats to the right to life or prevent individuals from enjoying their right to a dignified life.[48]

Although the Human Rights Committee did not elaborate more extensively on the types of measures that States should adopt, it is remarkable that States are called to address the general and structural conditions of society.

On these aspects, the more advanced approach stems from the jurisprudence of the Inter-American Court of Human Rights. In particular, since the adoption of its Advisory Opinion OC-23/17, the Court recognized the right to a healthy environment as an autonomous right under Article 26 of the American

46 UN Human Rights Committee, 'General Comment No. 36 on article 6: Right to Life' (3 September 2019) UN Doc CCPR/C/GC/36, para. 62.

47 UN Human Rights Committee, *Daniel Billy et al. v Australia* (22 September 2022) UN Doc CCPR/C/135/D/3624/2019, para. 8.7. See also Id., *Ioane Teitiota v New Zealand* (23 September 2020) UN Doc CCPR/C/127/D/2728/2016, para. 9.4.

48 *Daniel Billy et al. v Australia* (n 47), para. 8.12.

Convention and attributed to it even a collective and ecocentric dimension.[49] Read in this perspective, everyone enjoys a right to a healthy environment even in the absence of evidence of a risk to human beings.[50] As far as the positive obligations of States are concerned, the Inter-American Court stressed that States must take into account the differentiated impact of environmental degradation on the population, and they must ensure access to food, water and basic public services to all without discrimination.[51] The Inter-American Court developed this approach in the *La Oroya* case, where it spelt out that States must comply with a set of procedural and substantial standards.[52] While the former requires the duty to grant access to information, equal participation and access to justice, the latter includes the obligation to adopt laws, regulations and policies to identify the maximum level of tolerance for environmental degradation and to enforce and monitor these standards.

Increased attention to the structural conditions that cause chronic emergencies, including the gender dimension, can also be drawn from the Joint Statement of five human rights bodies on human rights and climate change. Despite focusing only on climate change, the Joint Statement pays attention to the role of women as agents of change and the need to address and regress structural social inequalities.[53] An interesting contribution can also be inferred from the interpretation of the UN Special Rapporteur on human rights and the environment, which considered mandatory for States to enact measures to ensure women's and girls' right to environmental information and participation, to eliminate environmental and gender-based violence, to regulate toxic substances and air pollution, and to grant equitable access to water and sanitation. More recently, the UN Special Rapporteur on the implications

---

49 *The Environment and Human Rights (State Obligations in Relation to the Environment in the Context of the Protection and Guarantee of the Rights to Life and to Personal Integrity – Interpretation and Scope of Articles 4(1) and 5(1) of the American Convention on Human Rights)*, Advisory Opinion OC-23/17, Inter-American Court of Human Rights Series A No 23 (15 November 2017), para. 59. See for a comment on this opinion Monica Feria-Tinta, Simon C. Milnes, 'The Rise of Environmental Law in International Dispute Resolution: The Inter-American Court of Human Rights Issues a Landmark Advisory Opinion on the Environment and Human Rights' (2018) 27 *Yearbook of International Environmental Law* 64.

50 *Ibid.*, para. 61.

51 *Ibid.*, para. 68.

52 *Case of La Oroya Population v Peru*, Preliminary Objections, Merits, Reparations and Costs, Inter-American Court of Human Rights Series C No. 511 (27 November 2023).

53 UN Treaty Bodies, 'Five UN human rights treaty bodies issue a joint statement on human rights and climate change' (14 May 2020) UN Doc HRI/2019/1.

for human rights of the environmentally sound management and disposal of hazardous substances and wastes issued a report on 'gender and hazardous substances'.[54] Considering that women are especially affected by toxic exposures both for biological reasons and because they do more caregiving work, the report called for States to adopt adequate measures to grant maternal and other reproductive health services and to improve social and environmental determinants of health.[55]

Speaking about sexual and reproductive health rights, the UN working group on discrimination against women and girls also recommended that States prioritize sexual and reproductive rights, particularly in times of emergencies.[56]

A particular field where the strengthening of positive obligations is evident concerns the duty to ensure equal participation of women in all phases of the decision-making process aimed at responding to disasters. In general, the equal participation of women in all aspects of political and public life is provided for by all treaties that deal with the protection of civil and political rights.[57] This requirement is gaining increasing attention in the context of response and recovery from disasters.[58] Recently, the CEDAW Committee has

---

[54] UN Special Rapporteur on Human Rights and the Environment, 'Women, Girls and the Right to a Healthy Environment: Good Practices. Supplementary information to the report of the Special Rapporteur, David R. Boyd, on the issue of human rights obligations relating to the enjoyment of a safe, clean, healthy, and sustainable environment' (3 March 2023). Annex to UN Doc A/HRC/52/33.

[55] UN Special Rapporteur on the Implications for Human Rights of the Environmentally Sound Management and Disposal of Hazardous Substances and Wastes, Marcos Orellana: Gender and Hazardous Substances (16 July 2024) UN Doc A/79/163.

[56] UN Working Group on Discrimination Against Women and Girls Report, 'Women's and girls' sexual and reproductive health rights in crisis' (28 April 2021) UN Doc. A/HRC/47/38.

[57] *Mathieu-Mohin and Clerfayt v Belgium* App no 27129/95 (ECtHR, 2 March 1987); UN Human Rights Committee, 'General Comment No 25: Article 25 (Participation in Public Affairs and the Right to Vote, The Right to Participate in Public Affairs, Voting Rights and the Right of Equal Access to Public Service)' (12 July 1996) UN Doc CCPR/C/21/Rev1/Add.7; CEDAW Committee, 'General Recommendation No 23: Political and Public Life' (1997) UN Doc A/52/38, para. 17.

[58] CEDAW Committee, 'General Recommendation No 37 on Gender-related Dimensions of Disaster Risk Reduction in the Context of Climate Change' (7 February 2018) UN Doc CEDAW/C/GC/37, para. 8; CEDAW Committee, 'Concluding Observations on the Sixth Periodic Report of Seychelles' (12 November 2019), UN Doc CEDAW/C/SYC/CO/6, para. 45; CEDAW Committee, 'Concluding Observations on the Ninth Periodic Report of Cabo Verde' (30

released its General Comment No. 40 (2024) on the equal and inclusive representation of women in decision-making systems,[59] which develops the analysis provided by General Comment No. 37 (2018) on the gender-related dimension of disaster risk reduction in the context of climate change.[60] According to General Comment No. 40, research shows that women's participation in decision-making leads to a heightened level of attention to environmental issues. Hence, countries with more women parliamentarians are more likely to adopt policies and ratify treaties for the protection of the environment. Similarly, when women participate equally on corporate boards, business results in more energy efficiency improvements and a reduced environmental footprint. However, given that the goal of equal participation worldwide is far from being implemented, the CEDAW Committee urges the State parties to adopt positive obligations to achieve this target in all decision-making systems across all sectors. In particular, the Committee considers that to achieve systemic change, States must ensure fifty-fifty parity between women and men in all their diversity and in all formal and informal decision-making processes.

Despite being an incomplete process, the evolution from a responsive approach focused on crisis and disaster to an increasing concern toward the structural and systemic causes of environmental degradation is coherent with the progressive recognition of the peculiarities of chronic emergencies in human rights law.

July 2019) UN Doc CEDAW/C/CPV/CO/9, paras 36–7; CEDAW Committee, 'Concluding Observations on the Combined Eighth and Ninth Periodic Reports of Haiti' (9 March 2016) UN Doc CEDAW/C/HTI/CO/8–9, paras 39 and 40; CEDAW Committee, 'Concluding Observations on the Sixth Periodic Report of Cambodia' (19 November 2019) UN Doc CEDAW/C/KHM/CO/6, para. 42; UN Human Rights Council Advisory Committee, 'Final Research-based Report of the Human Rights Council Advisory Committee on Best Practices and Main Challenges in the Promotion and Protection of Human Rights in Post-disaster and Post-conflict Situations', (10 February 2005) UN Doc A/HRC/28/76, para. 69. It is also worth reminding that in the aftermath of the Covid-19 pandemic, Resolution No. 2532 of the UN Security Council called on States to ensure the 'full, equal, and meaningful' participation of women in the development and implementation of an adequate and sustainable response to the pandemic. Similarly, UNGA Res 75/216 (21 December 2020) UN Doc A/RES/75/216, para. 41.

59 CEDAW Committee, 'General recommendation No. 40 on the Equal and Inclusive Representation of Women in Decision-Making Systems' (25 October 2024) UN Doc CEDAW C/GC/40, 5.

60 CEDAW Committee, 'General recommendation No. 37 on the gender-related dimensions of disaster risk reduction in the context of climate change' (n 58).

6. CONCLUDING REMARKS

This chapter has highlighted that the international normative framework has so far mostly aimed to respond to crises and disasters, considered as exceptionally disruptive events that require a coordinated management strategy among States to assist the victims and to mitigate the effects. By clarifying the conceptual difference between disasters and ECEs, this chapter has underlined the need to overcome the radical dichotomy of exception/normality, which mystifies the reality of everyday ECEs. Despite being as destructive as disasters, chronic emergencies are silent and slow, and have their causal roots in the structural imbalances of power, hierarchies and hegemonies embedded in society. Preventing chronic emergencies requires much more than coordinated humanitarian efforts, operational preparedness and mitigation tools. It implies the rereading of the existing international obligations and the rethinking of the future normative strategy in order to address the systemic and chronic dimensions of ECEs and dismantle the structural conditions that cause an otherwise endless spiral of environmental degradation. Enhancing the more advanced knowledge of different sciences, the international law of everyday prevention of chronic emergencies should promote a precautionary and gender-based legal approach. This may be possible, for example, by prohibiting activities that are overly risky for the environment and by shaping positive obligations that regress the structural intersectional discrimination of women, ensuring their full protection of economic and social rights, including sexual and reproductive rights, freedom from violence, access to justice and equal participation in all decision-making procedures.

3. Environmental chronic emergencies, women's inequality and international law

Enzamaria Tramontana

1. INTRODUCTION

During the last decade, international legal scholars have increasingly explored the ways in which international law engages with women's inequality in the context of the prevention of, response to and recovery from disasters, including natural disasters such as earthquakes, hurricanes, tsunamis, or bushfires.[1]

On the contrary, less attention has so far been dedicated to exploring the state of international law on women's inequality and 'environmental chronic emergencies' ('ECEs'), that is to say, according to the definition proposed by this Volume, long-term, gradual environmental phenomena caused by the unsustainable extraction and use of natural resources, pollution and urbanization – such as, for example, air, water and soil contamination, increasing temperatures, sea level rise, loss of biodiversity and desertification – whose adverse impacts on nature and human beings, especially women and other disadvantaged groups, are far less visible than those of disasters but no less pervasive.[2]

---

1 See, for instance, Monika Mayrhofer, 'Gender (In)equality, Disaster and Human Rights – The CEDAW Committee and General Recommendation No. 37' (2018) 1 *Yearbook of International Disaster Law* 233; Marie Aronsson-Storrier, 'Gender, International Law, and Disasters', in Sarah Bradshaw, Maureen Fordham, Jean-Christophe Gaillard *et al.* (eds), *Oxford Research Encyclopedia of Natural Hazard Science* (Oxford University Press 2024).

2 See Sara De Vido, 'Feminist Legal Methods and Environmental Chronic Emergencies: Challenging the Anthropocentric and Androcentric International Legal System'; Deborah Russo 'Moving Beyond an Approach Based on Crisis and Disasters to Address Environmental Chronic Emergencies' in this Volume.

This chapter aims to fill this gap, building upon (and trying to contribute to) a flourishing literature that examines the complex interconnections between gender inequalities and environmental degradation through an ecofeminist lens.[3] To this end, the analysis is organized as follows. Section 2 and Section 3 set the scene by, respectively, illustrating ECEs' disproportionate gendered impacts on women and introducing ecofeminism as a particularly suitable theoretical framework for understanding their root causes and devising adequate legal responses. Section 4 then draws on ecofeminist insights to offer a critical analysis of how current international law, particularly human rights and environmental law, engages with women's inequality in the context of ECEs. It shows that, while noticeable progress has been made in acknowledging the particular challenges that slow environmental degradation poses to women, weaknesses and limitations still remain – due to the conceptual architecture underlying relevant norms, processes and solutions – in how these challenges are currently addressed. Finally, Section 5 briefly summarizes the analysis and provides some concluding observations.

2. THE DIFFERENTIATED AND DISPROPORTIONATE IMPACTS OF ECEs ON WOMEN

Increasing research indicates that the adverse effects of rising temperatures, salinification, desertification and other phenomena falling under the notion of ECEs are felt more keenly by women than by men.

This is not due to the biological difference between males and females. Rather, it is the result of gender stereotypes, norms and practices existing within societies, which render women far more exposed and, at the same time, far less resilient to the hazardous effects of slow environmental degradation, in comparison to men. ECEs creep into long-standing cultural, social, legal and economic inequalities between men and women, intersect and exacerbate their harmful effects and contribute, in a vicious circle, to the perpetuation of their root causes.

---

[3] As a way of example, across different fields of international law, see: Karen Morrow, 'Integrating Gender Issues into the Global Climate Change Regime', in Susan Buckingham and Virginie Le Masson (eds), *Understanding Climate Change Through Gender Relations* (Routledge 2017) 31; Sara De Vido, 'A Quest for an Eco-centric Approach to International Law: the COVID-19 Pandemic as Game Changer' (2021) 3 (2) *Jus Cogens* 105; Meghan Campbell, 'A Greener CEDAW: Adopting a Women's Substantive Equality Approach to Climate Change', in Cathi Albertyn, Meghan Campbell, Helena Alviar García, et al. (eds), *Feminist Frontiers in Climate Justice – Gender Equality, Climate Change and Rights* (Edward Elgar Publishing 2023) 90.

Three main interrelated reasons account for ECEs' distinct and disproportionate harms to women.

First, due to gender discrimination within households and workplaces, women are far more exposed than men to the risks and losses provoked by slow environmental degradation.

It is well known that, owing to stereotyped roles, women carry out much more unpaid housework than their male counterparts. In rural areas, this means that women disproportionately bear the burden of securing food, water, and wood for their families.[4] Drought and biodiversity loss force them to walk longer distances to secure these resources, losing time that they could otherwise spend on education, income-generating activities and leisure, and putting themselves in danger of being attacked on the way.[5] River and lake pollution exposes them to higher risks of developing diseases such as diarrhoea and cholera that thrive in degraded water.[6]

Much about paid work is likewise gendered, with almost a quarter of employed women globally confined within sectors that are significantly exposed to the impacts of environmental degradation, with roles and working conditions that render them more vulnerable than their male counterparts. An estimated 45 million women, for instance, are employed in small-scale fisheries globally.[7] Although the decline in coastal resources due to salinization or eutrophication affects everyone in the sector, women face higher risks than men of losing their income as a consequence thereof, since, due to their concurrent responsibilities for home and child care, they are more likely to practice near shore fishing than men.[8] Approximately 36 percent of working women, to make another example, are employed in the agricultural sector.[9] Although they are engaged in pesticide application to a lesser extent than their male counterparts, they are more severely hit by the adverse health impact of soil pollution, for they tend to be the first to enter fields after chemicals have

4 UN Women, *Unpacking the Care Society: Caring for People and the Planet* (28 November 2023).

5 UN Women, *The Climate–Care Nexus: Addressing the Linkages Between Climate Change and Women's and Girls' Unpaid Care, Domestic, and Communal Work* (November 2023).

6 Global Development Policy Center, *The Gendered Impacts of Climate Change* (17 May 2022).

7 FAO, *The State of World Fisheries and Aquaculture 2022: Towards Blue Transformation* (2022).

8 UN Women, *Gender and Biodiversity: A Data Brief* (20 October 2024).

9 FAO, *The Status of Women in Agrifood Systems* (2023).

been applied and remain there for long hours, with personal protective equipment designed for male workers and therefore less effective for them.[10]

Second, as a result of gender norms, stereotypes and biases, women have fewer means than men to adapt to the impacts of ECEs and are more likely than they are to suffer from the consequences of (negative) coping family and community strategies. This is exacerbated for women who find themselves at the intersection of different and multiple grounds of discrimination because they are, for example, Indigenous, Afro-descendant, older, unmarried, widowed, LGBT+ or because they have disabilities or live in poverty.

Available data indicate that women face disproportionate barriers to owning assets and, as a consequence, have less responsive capacity than men in the face of slow environmental degradation.[11] In many parts of the world, for instance, they have limited or no land rights and, as a consequence, are excluded from credit, extension and advisory services that would allow them to learn about and invest in strategies and technologies to offset the negative impacts of land degradation, drought and desertification.[12] Women have, furthermore, limited chances to participate in and influence the outcomes of environmental policy and decision-making processes and face significant obstacles in claiming and obtaining effective reparations to mitigate losses due to environmental degradation.[13] They are also particularly disadvantaged with respect to access to basic services, including adequate health care: lack of knowledge about the specific health needs of women, coupled with dismissive and misogynistic attitudes, means, for instance, that women suffering from illnesses caused or exacerbated by ECEs, such as those associated with female reproductive health as a result of long-term toxic exposure, do not often receive correct diagnoses and treatments.[14]

Gendered negative coping strategies complete the picture. Several studies, for example, show that women are last in household hierarchies and, as a consequence, when food and water become scarce due to environmental degradation, they are compelled to ensure that men's eating and drinking needs are met before their own.[15] It has been demonstrated, as well, that complex interactions of cultural and social factors put women living in areas affected

---

[10] FAO, *Addressing Gender Issues in Pesticide Management* (2022).

[11] OECD, *Gender and the Environment: Building Evidence and Policies to Achieve the SDGs* (2021).

[12] FAO, *The Gender Gap in Land Rights* (2018).

[13] IUCN, *Women's Participation in Global Environmental Decision Making* (2015).

[14] WHO, *Gender, Climate Change, and Health* (1 December 2014).

[15] UNICEF, *Undernourished and Overlooked: New Report Reveals Global Nutrition Crisis for Women and Girls*, (2023).

by ECEs at greater risk of experiencing gender-based violence. The loss of jobs and livelihoods tied to slow environmental degradation is reported to be associated with rising rates of women victims of intimate partner abuse and women forced into sexual exploitation in exchange for food and natural resources.[16]

Third, slow environmental degradation is connected to the rise of gendered processes and contexts. This is the case, for instance, with migrations and internal displacements driven by loss of livelihoods and depletion of natural resources due to drought, desertification, and sea level rise. Several studies illustrate that distinct and disproportionate adverse impacts exist both for women who 'move' to seek new livelihood and employment opportunities, typically subject to sexual exploitation, harassment and abuse during transit and in destination countries, and for women who 'stay behind', left alone to handle domestic and care responsibilities within households and exposed to increased risks of sexual and physical abuse outside homes.[17]

3. ECOFEMINISM AND ITS RELEVANCE IN ADDRESSING THE GENDERED IMPACTS OF ECEs UNDER INTERNATIONAL LAW

To the extent that the gendered impacts of ECEs result from the intersections between environmental degradation and pre-existing structural patterns of disadvantage for women, ecofeminism is a natural candidate as a theoretical framework to conceptualize and address them under international law.

Ecofeminism is not a single strand of thought but refers to a broad spectrum of views that see the oppression of women and the natural environment as intimately and inextricably entangled.[18] In essence, it focuses on dominant Western conceptual dualisms such as male/female, reason/emotion, mind/body, culture/nature and posits that the oppositional and hierarchical thinking

---

16 IUCN, *Gender-Based Violence and Environment Linkages: The Violence of Inequality* (2020).

17 IOM, *Gender, Migration, Environment, and Climate Change* (2022).

18 Although the term 'ecofeminism' was coined in 1974 (see the seminal text: Françoise d'Eaubonne, *Le Féminisme ou la mort* (Pierre Horay 1974), ecofeminism did not emerge as a distinct strand of philosophical thought until the mid-1980s. For an overview of the main schools of ecofeminism, its basic tenets, as well as the charges of gender essentialism that have been moved against it, see Greta Gaard, 'Ecofeminism Revisited: Rejecting Essentialism and Re-Placing Species in a Material Feminist Environmentalism' (2011) 23 (2) *Feminist Formations* 26. See also Charis Thompson, Sherilyn MacGregor, 'The Death of Nature. Foundations of Ecofeminist Thought', in Sherilyn MacGregor (ed.), *Routledge Handbook of Gender and Environment* (Routledge 2017) 43.

that they entail – in which the former term, associated with maleness and masculinity, is set against and subordinated to the latter, associated with femaleness and femininity – is what have historically enabled and justified both the subordination of women and the exploitation of the environment. It then deconstructs the ways in which existing social norms and political institutions incorporate this dualistic ontology of intra-human and human-nature relationships and encourages its replacement with holistic, non-hierarchical thinking, which recognizes the inherent value of all human and non-human beings.[19]

International legal scholars have increasingly used ecofeminism as a theoretical lens through which to engage with issues concerning gender and the environment.[20] For the purposes of the present analysis, four key insights from the work of ecofeminist scholars are especially noteworthy.

First, by addressing the full web of connections existing between women and the natural environment, ecofeminism sheds light on how multiple factors including (but not limited to) geographical location, socioeconomic status, race, disability and age combine with gender to place women among the most affected by environmental degradation and, at the same time, among the most powerful agents of environmental change.[21] In that, it offers valuable insights into the importance of, on the one hand, identifying and grasping the complexities of the structural causes of women's (intersectional) disadvantage in the context of ECEs; on the other hand, appreciating the contribution that,

---

[19] Just to mention some of the most representative positions: Ynestra King, 'The Ecology of Feminism and the Feminism of Ecology', in Judith Plant (ed.), *Healing the Wounds: The Promise of Ecofeminism* (New Society Publishers 1989) 18; Karen J. Warren, 'The Power and Promise of Ecological Feminism' (1990) 12 (2) *Environmental Ethics* 125; Val Plumwood, *Feminism and the Mastery of Nature* (Routledge 1993).

[20] See, for example, Kate Darling, 'A Weight for Water: An Ecological Feminist Critique of Emerging Norms and Trends in Global Water Governance' (2012) 13 (1) *Melbourne Journal of International Law* 1; Kate P. Wilkinson Cross, 'Comparing the Transformative Potentials of the FCCC and the CCD: an Ecofeminist Exploration' (2018) 30 (1) *Denning Law Journal* 5; Sara De Vido, 'Sea Level Rise as a Form of Gendered Climate Violence: International Legal Implications for Migration', in Elisa Fornalé (ed.), *Sea Level Rise – Implications for Human Rights, Security and Peace*, Springer (forthcoming). For an analysis of the ecofeminist jurisprudence in the context of a broader discussion on the feminist methods of international law, Sara De Vido, 'Approcci giuridici femministi al diritto internazionale: Verso un diritto eco-femminista e post-umano?' (2023) LXXVIII (3) *La Comunità Internazionale* 453.

[21] See, for example, the analysis in Karen J. Warren, 'Taking Empirical Data Seriously: An Ecofeminism Philosophical Perspective', in Karen J. Warren (ed.), *Ecofeminism: Women, Culture, Nature* (Indiana University Press 1997) 3.

thanks to their situated environmental knowledge, women can make to address the root causes of ECEs, avoiding their traditional (gender-based) stereotyped depiction as 'helpless, disempowered victims or as nurturing caregivers of the environment'.[22]

Secondly, by providing a deep understanding of how women's structural disadvantage exacerbates the impacts that environmental degradation has on them, ecofeminism brings to the fore the need to dismantle long-standing discriminatory social norms and institutional structures.[23] As such, it encourages a transformative approach to the gendered impact of ECEs that fully appreciates how women's situational vulnerabilities disproportionately affect the enjoyment of their human rights in the context of slow environmental degradation and conceptualizes the State's obligations accordingly, in order to tear down the patriarchal power dynamics that lie behind these vulnerabilities, redistribute responsibilities and resources and ensure real equal opportunities for everyone.[24]

Thirdly, ecofeminism criticizes mainstream scientific knowledge for being informed by a mechanistic analysis of reality that legitimizes the instrumentalization of non-human nature and human 'others' associated with it, and advocates for the 'alternative' experiential knowledges and views of traditionally marginalized communities, including women, to be fully integrated into environmental governance.[25] In this perspective, its insights are decisive in emphasizing the importance not only of overcoming the existing barriers to

---

22 Campbell (n 3) 104. See also Cathi Albertyn, Helena Alviar García, Meghan Campbell et al., 'Introduction – Feminist Frontiers in Climate Justice: Gender, Equality, Climate Change and Rights', in Cathi Albertyn, Meghan Campbell, Helena Alviar García, et al. (eds) (n 3) 1.

23 See, for example, the analysis in Bina Agarwal, 'The Gender and Environment Debate: Lessons from India' (1992) 18 (1) *Feminist Studies* 119.

24 Karen J. Morrow, 'Ecofeminist Approaches to the Construction of Knowledge and Coalition Building – Offering a Way Forward for International Environmental Law and Policy', in Andreas Philippopoulos-Mihalopoulos and Victoria Brooks (eds), *Research Methods in Environmental Law: A Handbook* (Edward Elgar Publishing 2017) 298. See also Annie Rochette, 'Transcending the Conquest of Nature and Women: A Feminist Perspective on International Environmental Law', in Doris Buss and Ambreena Manji (eds), *International Law – Modern Feminist Approaches* (Hart 2005) 203.

25 See the incipient analyses in Vandana Shiva, *Staying Alive: Women, Ecology and Development* (Zed Books 1989) and, more recently, Val Plumwood, *Environmental Culture: The Ecological Crisis of Reason* (Routledge 2002). See also Betty Wells, Danielle Wirth, 'Remediating Development through an Ecofeminist Lens', in Karen J. Warren (ed.), *Ecofeminism: Women, Culture, Nature* (n 21) 327.

women's pluralistic participation at all levels of ECEs-related decision-making and implementation, but also, and more importantly, of adopting a 'fresh approach to participation' that makes authentic room for women's voices in a bottom-up perspective.[26]

Fourthly, and finally, through its sophisticated comprehension of how the oppression of women and nature are interconnected and mutually reinforcing, ecofeminism spotlights the need for addressing issues of women's rights and environmental protection in a synergistic manner.[27] This implies the understanding that no attempt to redress women's inequality in the context of ECEs will be successful without a concurrent effort to avert the latter's occurrence by identifying – and dismantling – conceptual apparatus, norms and socio-political structures that devalue the natural environment and instrumentalities it to the needs of humanity (or, better to say, to the needs of that particular portion of it that has historically oppressed and exploited both other humans and the non-human world), spawning slow environmental degradation and (further) reinforcing women's marginalisation.[28]

4. WOMEN'S INEQUALITY AND ECEs IN INTERNATIONAL LAW: THE STATE OF PLAY

The issue of the gendered impacts of slow environmental degradation lies directly at the intersection of two main fields of international law: international

---

26 Morrow (n 3), 36–37.

27 As Greta Gaard puts it clearly: 'Drawing on the insights of ecology, ecofeminism's basic premise is that the ideology which authorizes oppressions such as those based on race, class, gender, sexuality, physical abilities and species is the same ideology that sanctions the oppression of nature. Ecofeminism calls for an end to all oppressions, arguing that no attempt to liberate women (or any other oppressed group) will be successful without an equal attempt to liberate nature' (Greta Gaard, 'Living Interconnections with Animals and Nature', in Greta Gaard (ed.), *Ecofeminism: Women, Animals, Nature* (Temple University Press 1993) 1). See also, extensively, Val Plumwood, 'Androcentrism and Anthropocentrism: Parallels and Politics', in Karen J. Warren (ed.), *Ecofeminism: Women, Culture, Nature* (n 21) 327–55.

28 See De Vido (n 2). See also Kate P. Wilkinson Cross, 'A Critical Evaluation of Inter-Generational Equity and Its Application in the Climate Change Context', in Cathi Albertyn, Helena Alviar García, Meghan Campbell et al. (n 3) 40, 66; Karen J. Morrow, 'Towards an Ecofeminist Critique of International Law?' in Vincent Chapaux, Frédéric Mégret and Usha Natarajan (eds), *The Routledge Handbook of International Law and Anthropocentrism* (Routledge 2023) 183, 193.

human rights and international environmental law.[29] It is to them, therefore, that the following subsections respectively turn to critically assess, drawing on ecofeminist insights, the way in which international norms and practice currently engage with women's inequality in the context of ECEs.

4.1 International Human Rights Law

Recent years have witnessed growing attention by UN human rights bodies towards the impacts of ECEs on human rights generally, and on women's rights in particular.

Although the major contribution in this latter respect has come from the Committee on the Elimination of Discrimination against Women (CEDAW Committee), other gender specialized bodies (such as the Special Rapporteur on violence against women and girls) and non-gender specialized bodies (including the Special Rapporteurs, respectively, on the right to food, on the right to water and sanitation, on the human rights of migrants and on the human rights of internally displaced persons, on toxics and human rights and on the human right to a healthy environment) have also played an increasing role in the field.

These monitoring mechanisms have recognized the gendered consequences of several ECEs, such as climate change, land degradation, water pollution, desertification and loss of biodiversity, showing a deep understanding of how they both exacerbate pre-existing forms of disadvantage and compound intersecting forms of discrimination.[30] On this basis, they have identified several

---

[29] As ECEs are likely to result in natural disasters in the long run, another field of international law may indirectly come into play: international disaster law. For a relevant analysis, see the authors cited above, in footnote 1.

[30] See CEDAW Committee, 'General Recommendation No 37 on the Gender-Related Dimensions of Disaster Risk Reduction in the Context of Climate Change' (13 March 2018) UN Doc CEDAW/C/GC/37, paras 2–5; Special Rapporteur on Violence against Women and Girls, its Causes and its Consequences, 'Violence against Women and Girls in the Context of the Climate Crisis, Including Environmental Degradation and Related Disaster Risk Mitigation and Response' (11 July 2022) UN Doc A/77/136, paras 23–56; Special Rapporteur on the Right to Food, 'Integrating a Gender Perspective in the Right to Food' (29 December 2015) UN Doc A/HRC/31/51, paras 54–5, 63–7; Special Rapporteur on the Human Rights to Safe Drinking Water and Sanitation, 'Special Thematic Report on Climate Change and the Human Rights to Water and Sanitation – Part 2' (January 2022), paras 31–33; Special Rapporteur on the Human Rights of Migrants, 'The Impact of Climate Change on the Human Rights of Migrants' (19 July 2022) UN Doc A/77/189, paras 46–9; Special Rapporteur on the Human Rights of Internally Displaced Persons, 'Report on Internal Displacement in the Context

rights that are disproportionately affected by the encounter between gender discrimination and ECEs, including the right to live free from violence, and the rights to health, food, water, employment and education, and required States to eliminate the structural barriers that render women more vulnerable to the adverse impacts of ECEs by, *inter alia*, (a) removing the root causes of gender-based violence against women; (b) addressing gender-based discriminatory laws and practices in relation to ownership and use of land and natural resources, as well as barriers that impede women's equal access to water and food; (c) ensuring women access to gender-sensitive health care; and (d) guaranteeing women's equal access to employment opportunities and addressing their unequal burden of unpaid domestic work and care.[31] They have also underscored the need to provide access to 'gender-transformative remedies' and procedures to hold those responsible for environmental harms fully accountable.[32]

---

of the Slow-Onset Adverse Effects of Climate Change' (21 July 2020) UN Doc A/75/207, para. 32; Special Rapporteur on the Implications for Human Rights of the Environmentally Sound Management and Disposal of Hazardous Substances and Wastes, 'Gender and Hazardous Substances' (16 July 2024) UN Doc A/79/163, paras 14–17, 22, 50; Special Rapporteur on the Issue of Human Rights Obligations Relating to the Enjoyment of a Safe, Clean, Healthy and Sustainable Environment, 'Women, Girls and the Right to a Clean, Healthy and Sustainable Environment' (5 January 2023) UN Doc A/HRC/52/33, paras 5–9, 12–37, 70–71, 75–81.

[31] CEDAW Committee, 'General Recommendation No. 37 on the Gender-Related Dimensions of Disaster Risk Reduction in the Context of Climate Change' (n 30), paras 57, 60, 64, 68, 72 and 78; Id., 'General Recommendation No. 34 (2016) on the Rights of Rural Women' (7 March 2016) UN Doc CEDAW/C/GC/34, paras 57–59; Id., 'General Recommendation No. 39 on the Rights of Indigenous Women and Girls' (31 October 2022) UN Doc CEDAW/C/GC/39, para. 56; Special Rapporteur on Violence against Women and Girls, its Causes and Consequences, 'Violence against Women and Girls in the Context of the Climate Crisis, Including Environmental Degradation and Related Disaster Risk Mitigation and Response' (n 30), paras 78, 85–6; Special Rapporteur on the Right to Food, 'Integrating a Gender Perspective in the Right to Food' (n 30), paras 84 and 86; Special Rapporteur on the Human Rights of Migrants, 'The Impact of Climate Change on the Human Rights of Migrants' (n 30), para. 80; Special Rapporteur on the Issue of Human Rights Obligations Relating to the Enjoyment of a Safe, Clean, Healthy and Sustainable Environment, 'Women, Girls and the Right to a Clean, Healthy and Sustainable Environment' (n 30), paras 61–4.

[32] Special Rapporteur on the Issue of Human Rights Obligations Relating to the Enjoyment of a Safe, Clean, Healthy and Sustainable Environment, 'Women, Girls and the Right to a Clean, Healthy and Sustainable Environment' (n 30), para. 70. See also CEDAW, Committee, 'General Recommendation No 37 on the Gender-Related Dimensions of Disaster Risk Reduction in the Context of Climate

Commendably, in their analyses, all these bodies have stressed the importance of prioritizing the needs of those groups of women who are at the intersection of multiple grounds of discrimination[33] and have emphasized the important contributions that women, in all their diversity, make to confront slow environmental degradation, thereby avoiding their negative gender stereotype as 'helpless victims' in need of protection.[34] In this perspective, they have called on States to guarantee women's meaningful and equitable participation in environmental decision-making and implementation, redesigning decision-making institutions to overcome gender barriers to women's participation and adopting special measures to place them as fundamental 'agents of change in leadership positions across all sectors of environmental governance.[35] Recently, furthermore, some of these bodies have shown signs

---

Change' (n 30), para. 26 (c); Id., 'General Recommendation No. 39 on the Rights of Indigenous Women and Girls' (n 31), para. 61 (d); Special Rapporteur on Violence against Women and Girls, its Causes and Consequences, 'Violence against Women and Girls in the Context of the Climate Crisis, Including Environmental Degradation and Related Disaster Risk Mitigation and Response' (n 30), para. 89. See, more in depth, Francesca Tammone, 'Transforming *Slow Violence* into Social Justice: The Quest for Reparation for Environmental Chronic Emergencies' in this Volume.

33 Special Rapporteur on Violence against Women, its Causes and Consequences, 'Violence against Indigenous Women and Girls' (21 April 2022) UN Doc A/HRC/50/26, para. 28; Special Rapporteur on the Implications for Human Rights of the Environmentally Sound Management and Disposal of Hazardous Substances and Wastes, 'Gender and Hazardous Substances' (n 30), paras 13, 19, 23, 26, 46, 113; Special Rapporteur on the Issue of Human Rights Obligations Relating to the Enjoyment of a Safe, Clean, Healthy and Sustainable Environment, 'Women, Girls and the Right to a Clean, Healthy and Sustainable Environment' (n 30), paras 82–6.

34 CEDAW Committee, 'General Recommendation No 37 on the Gender-Related Dimensions of Disaster Risk Reduction in the Context of Climate Change' (n 30), para. 7; Special Rapporteur on Violence against Women, its Causes and Consequences, 'Violence against Indigenous Women and Girls' (n 33), para. 47; Special Rapporteur on the Right to Food, 'Interim Report' (5 August 2015) UN Doc A/70/287, para. 37; Special Rapporteur on the Human Rights of Internally Displaced Persons, 'Report on Internal Displacement in the Context of the Slow-Onset Adverse Effects of Climate Change' (n 30), para. 37; Special Rapporteur on the Issue of Human Rights Obligations Relating to the Enjoyment of a Safe, Clean, Healthy and Sustainable Environment, 'Women, Girls and the Right to a Clean, Healthy and Sustainable Environment' (n 30), paras 4, 56–60.

35 CEDAW Committee, 'General Recommendation No. 40 on the Equal and Inclusive Representation of Women in Decision-Making Systems', (25 October 2024) UN Doc CEDAW/C/GC/40, paras 8 and 66(m); Special Rapporteur on the

of a synergistic understanding of (and engaging with) women's inequality and environmental degradation: a tendency has started to emerge, in their practice, to address the root causes of ECEs, calling on States to revise environmentally harmful policies and practices, such as mining or fracking, identified as having disproportionate adverse impacts on women, and to regulate and monitor business activities to prevent actions that may undermine women's rights.[36]

These positive developments, however, do not represent the whole picture: the nexus between women's inequality and ECEs remains a largely overlooked or inadequately addressed issue in the practice of several other human rights monitoring mechanisms, both at the UN and at the regional level.

Some of these bodies, for instance, have recognized the nexus between women and environmental degradation, but have limited themselves to addressing gender inequality in the context of crisis situations, neglecting the importance of understanding the distinctive impacts of slow environmental degradation on women's rights and reconceptualizing State obligations accordingly. Based on Article 11 of the Convention on the Rights of Persons with Disabilities, as a way of example, its monitoring Committee has drawn attention to the increased risks faced by women with disabilities in situations of natural disasters, stopping short of broadening its analysis to include, as well, the

Right to Food, 'Integrating a Gender Perspective in the Right to Food' (n 30) para. 76; Special Rapporteur on the Human Rights of Migrants, 'The Impact of Climate Change on the Human Rights of Migrants' (n 30), para. 91; Special Rapporteur on the Issue of Human Rights Obligations Relating to the Enjoyment of a Safe, Clean, Healthy and Sustainable Environment, 'Women, Girls and the Right to a Clean, Healthy and Sustainable Environment' (n 30), paras 68–9, 79.

36 CEDAW Committee, 'General Recommendation No. 37 on the Gender-Related Dimensions of Disaster Risk Reduction in the Context of Climate Change' (n 30), para. 46, 51; Id., 'Concluding Observations on the Sixth Periodic Report of Namibia' (12 July 2022) UN Doc CEDAW/C/NAM/CO/6, para. 51; Id., 'Concluding Observations on the Tenth Periodic Report of Norway' (2 March 2023) UN Doc CEDAW/C/NOR/CO/10, paras 48–9; Special Rapporteur on the Human Rights of Internally Displaced Persons, 'Report on Internal Displacement in the Context of the Slow-Onset Adverse Effects of Climate Change' (n 30), para. 68; Special Rapporteur on the Implications for Human Rights of the Environmentally Sound Management and Disposal of Hazardous Substances and Wastes, 'Gender and Hazardous Substances' (n 30), e.g., para. 118 (d)–(f) and (h); Special Rapporteur on the Issue of Human Rights Obligations Relating to the Enjoyment of a Safe, Clean, Healthy and Sustainable Environment, 'Women, Girls and the Right to a Clean, Healthy and Sustainable Environment' (n 30), paras 87–88.

widely documented disproportionate impact that ECEs have on these women, finding themselves at the intersection of different grounds of discrimination.[37]

Others have focused on the human rights impact of ECEs and on their corresponding State obligations, but have failed to incorporate in their analysis a gender perspective. The Human Rights Committee, for instance, has recognized that environmental degradation, pollution and climate change constitute some of the most serious threats to the ability of present and future generations to enjoy the right to life, and in particular life with dignity, and called on States to ensure the sustainable use of their natural resources.[38] However, it has disregarded the differentiated gendered impact that these phenomena have on women.[39] The Committee on Economic, Social and Cultural Rights has engaged with the human rights aspects of ECEs and acknowledged that women generally face heightened barriers to the enjoyment of their rights due to multiple and intersecting forms of discrimination, but it has failed to grasp the interconnectedness between ECEs and gender inequality. It has, for example, recognized the severe impact that rising temperatures, land degradation and desertification have on access to land, stressed that women have traditionally been discriminated against in terms of enjoyment of land rights, but disregarded the disproportionate impact that these phenomena have on them as a consequence of their intersection with long-standing gender inequalities.[40]

Still other bodies have addressed the human rights impact of ECEs and recognized the unequal harms that women suffer as a consequence thereof, but have fallen short of carefully addressing the root causes of gender disadvantage and drawing appropriate legal consequences from them. The Committee on the Rights of the Child, as an example, has acknowledged that unsustainable extraction and use of natural resources, combined with widespread contamination through pollution and waste, adversely affect the enjoyment of children's rights, particularly those in especially vulnerable situations, and urged States

---

37 UN Committee on the Rights of Persons with Disabilities, 'General Comment No. 3 on Women and Girls with Disabilities' (25 November 2016) UN Doc CRPD/C/GC/3, paras 49–50.

38 UN Human Rights Committee, 'General Comment No. 36: Article 6: Right to Life' (3 September 2019) UN Doc CCPR/C/GC/36, para. 62.

39 *Ibid.* See also the Committee's decision in *Ioane Teitiota v New Zealand*, (23 September 2020) UN Doc CCPR/C/127/D/2728/2016 with the critical comments of Sara De Vido, 'Sea Level Rise as a Form of Gendered Climate Violence: International Legal Implications for Migration' (n 20).

40 E.g., UN Committee on Economic, Social and Cultural Rights, 'General Comment No. 26 (2022) on Land and Economic, Social and Cultural Rights' (24 January 2023) UN Doc E/C.12/GC/26, paras 13–15 and 56–7.

to adopt decisive measures to tackle them.[41] Nonetheless, the Committee has only cursorily referred to the gender-differentiated impact of environmental degradation, without engaging with the patriarchal structures that make girls more vulnerable than boys in the context of ECEs.[42] At the regional level, the European Court of Human Rights has ruled that the Convention encompasses a right for individuals to effective protection from serious adverse effects of climate change on their life, health and well-being, to which corresponds a State obligation to prevent or minimize the causes of climate change and mitigate its adverse effects.[43] Although it has recognized the disproportionate burden that, especially when finding themselves at the intersection of different grounds of discrimination, women might bear as a consequence of climate change, it has failed to engage with it for the purposes of determining legal standing in climate change litigation or take them into account to shape States' relevant obligations.[44] The Inter-American Court of Human Rights, in the context of its far-reaching 'environmental jurisprudence has acknowledged the gendered impact of air, water and soil pollution.[45] However, it has packaged gender with other determinants of vulnerability, overlooking the complex ways through which it intersects with toxic exposure to create distinctive harms to women

---

41 UN Committee on the Rights of the Child, 'General Comment No. 26 on Children's Rights and the Environment, with a Special Focus on Climate Change' (22 August 2023) UN Doc CRC/C/GC/26.

42 *Ibid.*, paras 35, 57, 101–102. See also, e.g., UN Committee on the Rights of the Child, 'Concluding Observations on the Combined Fifth and Sixth Periodic Reports of Togo' (11 October 2023) UN Doc CRC/C/TGO/CO/5–6, para. 41; Id., 'Concluding Observations on the Combined Fifth and Sixth Periodic Reports of the Congo' (1 March 2024) UN Doc CRC/C/COG/CO/5–6, para. 42.

43 *Verein KlimaSeniorinnen Schweiz and Others v Switzerland*, Appl. no 53600/20 (ECtHR, 9 April 2024), paras 544–554. See Björnstjern Baade, 'Due Diligence Obligations and Chronic Emergencies' in this Volume.

44 As a result, the Court rejected the argument of the applicants – four women over the age of 75 and an association of elderly women, who complained about the disproportionate adverse impacts of global warming on their living conditions and health – that the combination of gender and age had made them uniquely at risk of the adverse effects of climate change and in pressing need of individual protection, so as to meet the conditions set forth under Article 34 of the ECHR (*ibid.*, paras 477–488). For a critical perspective, see also: Dina Lupin, Maria Antonia Tigre, Natlia Urzola Gutiérrez, '*KlimaSeniorinnen* and Gender' (*Verfassungsblog* 9 May 2024) <https://verfassungsblog.de/klimaseniorinnen-and-gender/> accessed 7 April 2025.

45 *Case of La Oroya Population v Peru*, Preliminary Objections, Merits, Reparations and Costs, Inter-American Court of Human Rights Series C No. 511 (27 November 2023), para. 264.

and failing to order remedies tailored to redress these harms or aimed at challenging their structural causes.[46]

Overall, therefore, apart from an extensive recognition of the distinctive and disproportionate impacts of ECEs on women, progress in the context of international human rights law remains quite uneven. This, from an ecofeminist standpoint, both in terms of the recognition of the urgent need to dismantle long-standing norms, practices and systems that cause women's inequality and render them, especially those with intersecting identities, more exposed to (and less able to cope with) the impacts of slow environmental degradation and in terms of the consequential reconceptualization of legal categories so as to ensure an effective and comprehensive response to the various forms of gender disadvantage that are exacerbated in the context of ECEs.

Furthermore, despite a noticeable trend to challenge existing practices that cause slow environmental degradation, the human rights discourse on ECEs has mostly remained within a narrow anthropocentric perspective, according to which, rather than for its own sake, the environment is protected for the benefit of human beings, because (and to the extent that) it represents a necessary precondition for the full enjoyment of their human rights.[47] No real progress has thus been made on challenging the conceptual 'separation and hierarchical ordering of the human and non-human worlds'[48] that, in the perspective of

---

46 *Ibid.*, para. 231, where the Court briefly sketched the reasons for the disproportionate effects of environmental pollution on women, children, and the elderly, with a general reference to pre-existing situations of 'poverty, discrimination, and systemic marginalization'. This, notwithstanding expert witness testimony showing, for example, that the caregiving work unequally assigned to women had been made more burdensome in *La Oroya* (para. 232). As for reparations, see *ibid.*, paras 377–78 (where the IACtHR limited itself to awarding women higher compensation 'due to their special condition of vulnerability and the differentiated effects arising from this') and para. 348 (where a specific order was made by the Court to provide differentiated health care only for pregnant women).

47 A significant exception to this prevailing anthropocentric paradigm is represented by the recent approach taken by the Inter-American Court to the conceptualization of the right to a healthy environment under the American Convention on Human Rights. See, e.g., *Case of La Oroya Population v Peru* (n 45), para. 118, with the comments of Maria Feria-Tinta, 'Environmental Chronic Emergencies, Slow-onset Events and Other Anthropocentric Dilemmas in Times of Climate Crisis: The Need for a Re-conception' in this Volume. On the anthropocentric stance of international human rights law see, generally, Frédéric Mégret, 'The Anthropocentrism of Human Rights', in Chapaux, Mégret and Natarajan (eds) (n 28) 35.

48 Kate P. Wilkinson Cross, 'A Critical Evaluation of Inter-Generational Equity and its Application in the Climate Change Context' (n 28) 65.

ecofeminism, traditionally sanctions the exploitation of the natural environment and thereby perpetuates the root causes of ECEs.

4.2 International Environmental Law

Just as ECEs have increasingly, though indirectly, entered the realm of international human rights law, women's inequality has progressively found its place in the most significant multilateral environmental agreements (MEAs) dealing with phenomena of slow environmental degradation: the three 'Rio Conventions' on Biodiversity, Climate Change and Desertification, the Stockholm Convention on Persistent Organic Pollutants (Stockholm Convention) and the Minamata Convention on Mercury (Minamata Convention).

The United Nations Convention to Combat Desertification (UNCCD) and the United Nations Convention on Biodiversity (UNCBD) were among the first MEAs to incorporate in their texts an express reference to women and – based on the acknowledgment of the differentiated impacts that environmental degradation has on them and, at the same time, their crucial role in promoting environmental protection – to make gender an established agenda item for their governing bodies.[49]

While at the beginning their engagement with women was limited to promoting gender mainstreaming at all stages and levels of policies, programmes

---

[49] The text of the UNCCD contains several references to women. See, for example, para. 20 of the Preamble (stressing 'the important role played by women in regions affected by desertification and/or drought (. . .) and the importance of ensuring the full participation of both men and women at all levels in programmes to combat desertification and mitigate the effects of drought') and Article 5, para. (d) (establishing the States' duty to 'promote awareness and facilitate the participation of local populations, particularly women and youth, (. . .) in efforts to combat desertification'). In 2017, the Parties adopted a Gender Action Plan for the Convention: UNCCD, (3 July 2017) ICCD/COP (13)/19. The text of the UNCBD, on the other hand, contains only one relevant reference, in para. 13 of its Preamble (recognizing 'the vital role that women play in the conservation and sustainable use of biological diversity' and affirming 'the need for the full participation of women at all levels of policy-making and implementation for biological diversity conservation'). The Parties to the Convention adopted its first Gender Action Plan in 2008 and updated it twice, in 2014 and 2022. See CBD, 'The Gender Plan of Action Under the Convention on Biological Diversity (23 May 2008) UNEP/CBD/COP/9/INF/12/ Rev.1. They updated it in 2014; Id., 'Decision Adopted by the Conference of the Parties to the Convention on Biological Diversity' (17 October 2014) UNEP/CBD/COP/DEC/XII/7; and Id., 'Decision Adopted by the Conference of the Parties to the Convention on Biological Diversity' (19 December 2022) CBD/COP/DEC/15/11.

and projects, the two conventions' regimes have progressively acknowledged the structural inequalities embedded in the social, political, economic, cultural institutions, norms and practices that cause environmental degradation's disproportionate impacts on women, and have recognized the need to address them.[50] Throughout the years, however, their approach to the women-environmental degradation nexus has remained strongly instrumental, conceiving the promotion of women's equality, rather than as a value per se, as a way to ensure their full participation in efforts to achieve sustainable development as strategic 'agents of change'. As such, their strategy has been limited in scope, with a focus only on two key objectives: on the one hand, building capacities and increasing opportunities to ensure women's equal and balanced participation in the conventions' decision-making and implementation processes, including by working with and through women's organizations, in order to enable the experiences, needs and values of women to inform all relevant actions, plans and programmes; and, on the other hand, ensuring women equal rights to ownership and control over land and natural resources, as well as equal access to education, training, technologies and financial services in order to support their empowerment in affected areas and, thereby, foster their active engagement in the governance, conservation and sustainable use and management of land and biodiversity.[51]

The Framework Convention on Climate Change (UNFCCC) was slower than the UNCCD and the UNCBD in integrating a gender perspective.[52]

---

[50] See, e.g., UNCCD, 'Study on the Differentiated Impacts of Desertification, Land Degradation and Drought on Women and Men' (2022) and CBD 'Addressing Gender Issues and Actions in Biodiversity Objectives' (2019).

[51] For the developments within the UNCCD's regime, see: UNCCD, 'Gender Equality and Empowerment of Women for Enhanced and Effective Implementation of the Convention' (23 October 2017) UN Doc Decision 30 COP13-ICCD/COP(13)/21/Add.1; Id., 'Gender Equality Policy and Plan 2024 to 2030' (10 September 2024). As for the UNCBD, see: 'Towards A Gender-Responsive Post-2020 Global Biodiversity Framework: Considerations for Gender Mainstreaming' (27 July 2019) UN Doc CBD/WG2020/1/INF/1 and '2015–2020 Gender Plan of Action Pocket Guide: Summary and Examples' (14 April 2020) UN Doc CBD/SBI/3/2/Add.3.

[52] The original text of the UNFCCC did not include any references to gender issues. In 2015, the Paris Agreement referred to gender equality in its Preamble (recognizing that 'Parties should, when taking action to address climate change, respect, promote and consider their respective obligations on human rights, (…) as well as gender equality [and] empowerment of women'), Article 7 and Article 11 (requiring a gender-responsive approach, respectively, to climate adaptation and capacity building). In 2015, the Conference of the Parties (COP) established the first Lima Work Programme on Gender (LWPG) (2 February 2015) Decision 18/

Throughout the years, three main themes have emerged from the UNFCCC gender policies: the need to ensure a systematic integration of gender concerns and perspectives into all climate policies and actions; the importance of engaging women in relevant decision-making processes, at all levels, and promoting capacity-building for women, including Indigenous women and women from local communities, in negotiations and the Convention's processes; and the urgency of promoting gender-responsive technological solutions to address climate change, by mobilizing financial resources and fostering women's full participation and leadership in science, technology, research and development.[53]

Overall, the UNFCCC gender strategy replicates the other two Rio Conventions' instrumental perspective on the promotion of women's equality as a means to enhance their role as 'agents of change' for sustainable development. Its approach, however, is even narrower than that developed within the UNCCD and the UNCBD, with no engagement at all with the underlying gender (and other social) inequalities that cause climate change's disproportionate impact on women and no recognition of the need to dismantle existing socio-cultural and economic barriers to their active participation in public life. The measures put forward are nothing but 'quick win' solutions, such as raising awareness of good practices for women to access climate finance, promoting travel funds to support their participation in national delegations or organizing and conducting capacity-building training to promote their leadership and negotiation skills.[54]

Finally, gender features as an important cross-cutting issue in the implementation of the Stockholm Convention and the MCM, based on the shared recognition that women and men are affected differently by the multifaceted harmful impacts associated with POPs and mercury exposure.[55] However, a

CP.20 UN Doc FCCC/CP/2014/10/Add.3, and in 2018 the first gender action plan (GAP) under the UNFCCC was established (8 February 2018) Decision 3/CP.23 UN Doc FCCC/CP/2017/11/Add.1. In 2020, Parties agreed to a 5-year Enhanced Lima Work programme on Gender and its Gender Action Plan (16 March 2020) Decision 3/CP.25 UN Doc FCCC/CP/2019/13/Add.1, and in 2024 they decided to extend the Enhanced Lima Work Programme on Gender for 10 years: see 'Gender and Climate Change' (23 November 2024) Draft Decision-/CP.29 UN Doc FCCC/CP/2023/L.12.

[53] Lima Work Programme on Gender and its Gender Action Plan (n 52) B.1, B.2, and D.2.

[54] See also, from a critical perspective, Wilkinson Cross, 'Comparing the Transformative Potentials of the FCCC and the CCD: An Ecofeminist Exploration' (n 20) 26.

[55] See, respectively, Stockholm Convention, 'Gender: Overview' (2020) and UNEP and Minamata Convention on Mercury, 'Gender Equality and Mercury' (May 2021). The Stockholm Convention, in its 2023 revised text, contains express

significant difference exists between their respective strategies to address gender inequality.

The Stockholm Convention regime has almost exclusively followed a gender mainstreaming and participatory approach. Based on the assumption that women's involvement in environmental decision-making is essential for promoting gender equality and achieving sustainable development, it has merely focused on ensuring gender-balanced participation in the Convention's processes and fully integrating women's perspectives into the design, implementation, monitoring and evaluation of its decisions and activities.[56]

The Minamata Convention, on the other hand, has adopted a more comprehensive strategy which, in addition to mainstreaming gender and ensuring equal opportunities for participation in the Convention's processes, including by supporting women's organizations, groups and networks, aims to address the causes of the disproportionate impact of mercury use on women, especially in the artisanal and small-scale gold mining (ASGM) sector, and eliminate the intersectional barriers to their full agency.[57] Measures adopted to these ends, however, are far from comprehensive.[58] Their focus is merely, on the

---

reference to women in its Preamble (noting the Parties' awareness 'of the health concerns, especially in developing countries, resulting from local exposure to persistent organic pollutants, in particular impacts upon women'), Article 7 (requiring States to consult women's groups in order to facilitate the implementation of the Convention) and Article 10 (requiring States to promote the development, especially for women, of educational and public awareness programmes on the health and environmental effects of persistent organic pollutants and their alternatives). The Minamata Convention, for its part, pays specific attention to women in its Preamble (noting 'the Parties' awareness of health concerns (. . .) resulting from the exposure to mercury of vulnerable populations, especially women and children'). It prioritizes the needs of 'vulnerable' groups, including women, in several of its provisions, including Article 18, on public information and education, and Article 19, on research, development and monitoring.

56 See BRS Gender Action Plan, in Report on Gender-Related Activities Implemented by the Secretariat (23 May 2023) UNEP/CHW.16/INF/42/Rev.1, UNEP/FAO/RC/COP.11/INF/25/Rev.1, UNEP/POPS/COP.11/INF/47/ Rev.1. This text has updated the previous 2016 and 2019 versions.

57 See UNEP and Minamata Convention on Mercury, 'Gender Action Plan for the Minamata Convention on Mercury' (4 July 2023) UNEP/MC/COP.5/INF/10.

58 Subparagraph 1 (i) of Annex C to the Convention – which addresses ASGM as the largest source of mercury emissions and releases and requires Parties who have ASGM to take steps to reduce and, where feasible, eliminate mercury use from such mining and processing – limits itself to stating that national action plans to address ASGM are to include strategies to prevent mercury exposure of vulnerable populations, including women of childbearing age, especially pregnant women.

one side, on promoting economic empowerment initiatives, such as ensuring equal access to or control over land, water, technologies and markets so as to provide women with independent sources of income and thereby avoid their being driven by poverty into mining; and, on the other side, on ensuring that capacity building, technical assistance and technology transfer to developing country Parties are delivered in ways that support gender equality, including by involving women in the introduction of technically and economically viable alternatives to mercury-added products and processes in which mercury is used or that release it.[59]

In sum, international environmental law has broadly recognized both the gendered impacts of ECEs and the contribution that women can make to address them as key actors in the conservation of the environment and natural resources all over the world. Yet, if looked at through an ecofeminist lens, the approach chosen to address the women-environmental degradation nexus – aimed mostly at promoting women's full involvement across all areas of environmental governance – appears severely limited.

First of all, this approach relies on a paradigm of 'formal' equality, which promotes equal rights and opportunities to participate in environmental practices and decision-making, both at the local and international levels, but glosses over the prevailing, deeply embedded gendered roles and relations that may make it practically difficult or impossible for women to take advantage of their enjoyment.[60] As such, it fails to challenge the entrenched social gender inequalities that render women more exposed and less able to cope with ECEs, let alone address the special vulnerability that some of them experience owing to the intersection of gender with other inequalities. The result is that women

---

For an overview of gender issues in the ASGM sector, see UNEP, *Incorporating Gender Dimensions into National Strategy Setting in Chemicals Management for Minamata Convention National Action Plans for Artisanal and Small-scale Gold Mining and Stockholm Convention National Implementation Plans* (2021) 19–27.

59 UNEP and Minamata Convention on Mercury (n 57) and 'Gender Priority Activities for the Biennium 2024-2025' (24 November 2023) UNEP/MC/COP.5/Dec.15.

60 Marsha A. Freeman, Christine Chinkin, Beate Rudolf, 'Article 1', in Marsha A. Freeman, Beate Rudolf and Christine Chinkin (eds), *The UN Convention on the Elimination of All Forms of Discrimination Against Women: A Commentary* (OUP Oxford 2012) 51, 56. The formal equality paradigm, as is well known, has long been the subject of feminist critiques. See, with particular regard to the environmental governance context, Annie Rochette, 'Stop the Rape of the World: An Ecofeminist Critique of Sustainable Development' (2002) 51 *University of New Brunswick Law Journal* 145; and, previously, Dianne Otto, 'Holding Up Half the Sky, but for Whose Benefit? A Critical Analysis of the Fourth World Conference on Women' (1996) 6 (1) *Australian Feminist Law Journal* 7.

are (further) burdened with an instrumental role as responsible actors for environmentally sustainable management of natural resources, without being freed from their already stretched gendered workloads, in a continuing perpetuation of the so-called 'feminization of responsibility'.[61]

Secondly, the adopted approach embeds women into existing normative and institutional frameworks, which promote sustainable development through technological innovation as the response to current global environmental challenges.[62] The notion of sustainable development, however, reflects an anthropocentric and androcentric perspective that justifies the commodification of natural resources to meet human demands and builds upon the dominant, neoliberal economic paradigm that has fuelled, and continues to inflame, social, including gender, inequalities.[63] Consequently, norms and institutions that are

---

[61] Serene J. Khader, 'Global Gender Justice and the Feminization of Responsibility' (2019) 5 (2) *Feminist Philosophy Quarterly* 1.

[62] An express mention of 'sustainable development' – that is, as famously defined in 1987 by the World Commission on Environment and Development, 'development that meets the needs of the present without compromising the ability of future generations to meet their own needs' – as the paradigm inspiring and underpinning policy responses to current global environmental challenges is contained, for instance, in the Introduction to the UNCBD, in the Preamble of the UNCCD, in Article 3 of the UNCCC, in the Preamble and in Article 2(1), 4(1) and 6 of the Paris Agreement, in Article 7 and Annex F of the Stockholm Convention. The Minamata Convention, for its part, recalls in its Preamble the Rio Declaration on Environment and Development, which consecrated sustainable development as 'the conceptual epicentre of global environmental governance' (see Jorge E. Viñuales, 'Sustainable Development', in Lavanya Rajamani and Jacqueline Peel (eds), *The Oxford Handbook of International Environmental Law* (2nd edn Oxford University Press 2019) 285. All these instruments include provisions encouraging technology transfer and scientific cooperation as means to achieve environmental protection. See, e.g., UNBDC, Articles 12 and 16; UNCCD, Articles 16–18; UNFCC, Articles 4 (c) and (g); Paris Agreement, Article 10; Stockholm Convention, Articles 11 and 12; Minamata Convention, Article 14.

[63] Louis Jacobus Kotzé, Duncan French, 'The Anthropocentric Ontology of International Environmental Law and the Sustainable Development Goals: Towards an Ecocentric Rule of Law in the Anthropocene' (2018) 7 (1) *Global Journal of Comparative Law*, 5; Vito De Lucia, 'Anthropocentrism and International Environmental Law', in Chapaux, Mégret, Natarajan (eds), (n 28) 84. Grear notoriously explains the role that legal subjectivity plays in operationalizing the hierarchical order between human beings, as well as between human beings and non-human beings, that is central to 'histories of eco-violation'. See, e.g., Anna Grear, 'The Closures of Legal Subjectivity: Why Examining "Law's Person" is Critical to an Understanding of Injustice in an Age of Climate Crisis', in

informed by it end up perpetuating (and even reinforcing) the structural patterns of environmental exploitation and social disadvantage from which ECEs, and their disproportionate impacts on women, ultimately stem. Reliance on technological innovation, for its part, 'institutionalizes a preference for, and deference to, conventional science' in addressing global environmental challenges.[64] As a result, notwithstanding widespread recognition of the importance of integrating into environmental regimes rural women's unique environmental knowledge, little room is left for the latter to truly influence ECEs governance and its outcomes.

5. CONCLUSION

'Environmental chronic emergencies (...) are around us. Hidden in plain sight, one could say.'[65] Their disproportionate impacts on women are not immediately visible, as those of natural disasters, but are no less severe and pervasive.

International law, with its vocation to address problems whose causes and consequences transcend national borders, may certainly represent a fundamental tool to tackle the challenges rising from the gendered impacts of ECEs. Yet, an analysis conducted through an ecofeminist lens shows that significant limits exist in how international law has so far engaged with them.

Ecofeminism, at the same time, sets the stage for a more ambitious way of addressing the nexus between women's inequality and slow environmental degradation, informed by a recognition of the inherent value of both humans and non-humans and a contextual reconceptualization of the relationships between them. This entails a paradigm shift into how to tackle ECEs, which implies, on the one hand, a genuine commitment towards preventing slow environmental degradation, rather than merely decelerating it or redressing its consequences, grounded in the need to respect the ecological limits of the Earth system, for the sake of its own integrity[66]; on the other hand, a comprehensive engagement

---

Anna Grear and Louis J. Kotzé (eds), *Research Handbook on Human Rights and the Environment* (Edward Elgar Publishing 2015) 79.

64 Rochette, 'Transcending the Conquest of Nature and Women: A Feminist Perspective on International Environmental Law' (n 24) 224. See also Wilkinson Cross, 'Comparing the Transformative Potentials of the FCCC and the CCD: An Ecofeminist Exploration' (n 20) 34.

65 De Vido (n 2); Russo (n 2).

66 These ecological limits have been powerfully identified, in environmental sciences, through the concept of 'planetary boundaries', defining a 'safe operating space for humanity with respect to the Earth system' and associated with certain 'thresholds which, if crossed, could generate unacceptable environmental change'. See Johan Rockström, Will Steffen, Kevin Noone et al., 'A Safe Operating Space

with structural forms of (intersectional) gender discrimination and disadvantage, informed by the recognition of the inherent value of women's equality and empowerment.

There is still a long way to go for international law to achieve full equality between men and women in a world where the natural environment is valued and protected for the benefit of all human and nonhuman living beings, but the road is mapped out and its theoretical foundation laid down.

---

for Humanity' (2009) *Nature* 472; and, more recently, Katherine Richardson et al., 'Earth Beyond Six of Nine Planetary Boundaries' (2023) 9 (37) *Science Advances* 1. The notion of 'planetary boundaries' has increasingly been considered a potentially useful tool for international environmental law as well. See, for instance, Rakhyun E. Kim and Klaus Bosselmann, 'International Environmental Law in the Anthropocene: Towards a Purposive System of Multilateral Environmental Agreements' (2013) 2 (2) *Transnational Environmental Law* 285; Kotzé and French (n 63) 9–10; Edgar Fernandez Fernandez and Claire Malwé, 'The Emergence of the 'Planetary Boundaries' Concept in International Environmental Law: A Proposal for Framework Convention' (2019) 28 (1) *Review of European, Comparative & International Environmental Law* 48. For a thorough discussion on how the concept of 'planetary boundaries' could help frame the international legal response to ECEs, see Karen Morrow, 'Taking the Long View: What Environmental Chronic Emergencies Require of States' in this Volume.

4. Taking the long view: what environmental chronic emergencies require of states

Karen Morrow

1. INTRODUCTION

Law provides crucially important mechanisms in social responses to natural events[1] and to anthropogenically driven adverse environmental impacts. There are, however, significant shortcomings in the dominant approaches that the law adopts to these issues. As discussed below, law tends to anatomize environmental harms, treating 'one-off' incidents and underlying conditions as warranting responses that differ significantly in both type and degree. Reality is, of course, much more complex and requires attending to inherent connections and interactions between the underlying state of the environment, pollution, its regulation,[2] 'one-off' incidents and how they interact, causing harm to the environment and humanity. For the purposes of this chapter, climate change will be used as a case in point, the underlying pollution problem of anthropogenic greenhouse gas emissions being problematic in its own right;[3] in causing and/or increasing the frequency and intensity of what have hitherto been considered 'natural' disasters;[4] and in irreversibly shifting the planet from the

[1] Daniel Farber, 'Navigating the Intersection of Environmental Law and Disaster Law' (2011) *Brigham Young University Law Review* 1783, points out that climate change will intensify longstanding linkages between these areas.

[2] Many other areas of law and interactions between them are also potentially implicated here, *ibid.*, 1788, though discussion in this chapter will focus on the most direct linkage between law related to environmental pollution and disaster, *ibid.*, 1793.

[3] Katherine Richardson, Will Steffen, Wolfgang Luch et al., 'Earth beyond six of nine planetary boundaries' (2023) 9 (37) *Science Advances* eadh2458.

[4] WMO Atlas of Mortality and Economic Losses from Weather, Climate and Water Extremes: <https://library.wmo.int/idurl/4/57564> accessed 31 January 2025.

Holocene to the Anthropocene.[5] The chapter adopts an ecofeminist approach to these issues, viewing the entwined consequences of the long-practiced hierarchical dualism and the systemic othering of women and nature that continue to characterize human systems as tools in the hands of a (predominantly male, white and wealthy) privileged minority in the service of instrumentalization and thus exploitation that result in functionally interconnected injustices both between current and future humans and between humans and non-human nature.[6] In regard to climate change and disaster response, the resulting predicament and necessary responses to it are effectively distilled in the Political Declaration of the sixty-ninth session of the Commission on the Status of Women, which includes in its recognition of 'new challenges':

> Mainstreaming a gender perspective into environmental, climate change and disaster risk reduction policies, recognizing the disproportionate effect of climate change and natural disasters on women and girls, in particular those in vulnerable situations, strengthening the resilience and adaptive capacities of women and girls to respond to the adverse impacts of climate change and natural disasters, and promoting women's participation and leadership in decision-making on environmental and climate change issues.[7]

In this context, it is apparent that the conceptual tools that we have used to date are no longer fit for purpose (if indeed they ever were) and that the concept of environmental chronic emergency (ECE), as developed in this project, is necessary to make sense of and respond to both the current situation and to avert a disastrous future. While ECE is not an entirely new idea, having been defined as: 'A long-term situation of risk and injury to a large proportion of the population that may exist even in the absence of shocks . . . '[8] in

---

[5] Andreas Malm and Wim Carton, *Overshoot: How the World Surrendered to Climate Breakdown* (Verso 2024).

[6] Karen Morrow 'Towards an Ecofeminist Critique of International Law' in Vincent Chapaux, Frederic Megret and Usha Natarajan (eds), *The Routledge Handbook of International Law and Anthropocentrism* (Routledge 2023) 183.

[7] ECOSOC, Commission on the Status of Women, 'Draft resolution on the Political declaration on the occasion of the thirtieth anniversary of the Fourth World Conference on Women', (6 March 2025) UN Doc E/CN.6/2025/L.1, para. 15(r).

[8] Inter-agency Network for Education in Emergencies glossary: <https://inee.org/eie-glossary/chronic-emergency#:~:text=A%20longterm%20situation%20of%20risk%20and%20injury%20to,acute%20malnutrition%2C%20persistent%20epidemics%2C%20or%20protracted%20armed%20conflict> accessed 11 February 2025. See also Deborah Russo, 'Moving Beyond an Approach Based on Crisis and Disasters to Address Environmental Chronic Emergencies' in this Volume.

the Anthropocene, this definition, in focusing narrowly on the human dimension, must be deemed dangerously incomplete. The chapter therefore examines ECEs as key elements of the rapidly shifting planetary context in which the triple environmental crisis is playing out. It focuses on the challenges that this poses for the people and planet and the tests this poses for the law. In section 2, it looks first at the framing of harm in law and its limitations in addressing environmental harm and its impact on most humans. In section 3, it considers the Anthropocene, planetary boundaries and tipping points, and their implications for a new composite framing for environmental law, requiring new approaches to better address systems and survival in what will be termed the human-environment nexus.[9] Section 4 examines the contribution and inherent limitations of a disaster-based approach and the need to shift to an ECEs approach in response to the Anthropocene. It goes on to examine the promise and limitations of some recent developments in international soft law in this area, namely: the International Law Commission's Draft Articles on the Protection of Persons in the Event of Disasters; the right to a clean, healthy and sustainable environment; and the Pact for the Future. Section 5 considers how applying a constitutive ecofeminist conception of the ethics of care could help to reframe the treatment of the environment in law, in the imbricated interests of present and future humans and the environment. It posits that adopting this species of relational approach to the environment would enable a fundamental shift in focus to foreground the prevention of harm, better positioning humanity to address ECE in the Anthropocene.

2. LAW, POLLUTION, HARM TO PEOPLE AND THE ENVIRONMENT

When the need for the state to develop environmental law as we understand it today first emerged in domestic law, as for example in England and Wales in the nineteenth century, it was a reactive enterprise, driven by the need to address the pollution problems that emerged pursuant to the industrial revolution. In this, the complexity of the human-environment nexus inherent in industrial development, generating pollution as a by-product of wealth generation, primarily benefiting the privileged, wealthy few at the expense of most other people and the environment, was abundantly apparent early in modernity. In the first instance, civil litigation under the law of nuisance was invoked, not to address changes to the state of the environment as such, but rather, once

---

[9] For a discussion of the use of this term in cognate areas, see, Ronald C. Estoque, 'Complexity and diversity of nexuses: A review of the nexus approach in the sustainability context' (2023) 854 *Science of the Total Environment*, 158612.

property rights had been adversely affected, to address what were deemed actionable adverse impacts on a privileged class of humanity.[10] There is a significant disconnect here between underlying harm to the environment and actionable harm to human beings, which is still evident to a degree in modern statutory pollution control law.[11] When nuisance litigation was pressed into service to address this new situation, it was generally applied after actionable harm had been identified and had a narrow *inter partes* focus. This temporal framing is also limiting as, while nuisance can offer a forward-looking, harm prevention dimension, in the form of injunctive relief, it tends to foreground response to past damage.

The poor and vulnerable too suffered adverse impacts, not least to their health, from pollution, but would have had no practicable access to legal redress in nuisance.[12] It is salutary to observe that, as ecofeminist analysis would later identify, from the very beginning of modern industry, exploitation of and causing harm to the environment on an industrial scale and inflicting harm on vulnerable humans (now understood intersectionally,[13] to encompass shifting constellations of the poor, women, people of colour, Indigenous peoples, people with disabilities, the young, the old, future generations etc.) in the interests of the privileged few has, while not unchallenged, been the norm.[14]

---

10 Sean Coyle and Karen Morrow, *The Philosophical Foundations of Environmental Law: Property, Rights and Nature* (Hart 2004).

11 See, for example, the multi-stranded definition of pollution in s 1(3) of the Pollution Prevention and Control Act 1999.

12 A.I. Ogus and G.M. Richardson, 'Economics and the Environment: A Study of Private Nuisance' (1977) 36 (2) *Cambridge Law Journal* 248–325, little has changed along the have/have not axis in this regard, with age, race and gender among added aggravating factors, see, Farber n 1, Richard J. Lazarus, 'Pursuing "Environmental Justice": The Distributional Effects of Environmental Protection' (1993) 87 *Northwestern University Law* Review 787 and Sherilyn MacGregor, 'Gender matters in environmental justice' in Brendan Coolsaet (ed.), *Environmental Justice: Key Issues* (Routledge 2020) 234, respectively.

13 See, for example, Jennifer A. Thompson 'Intersectionality and water: how social relations intersect with ecological difference' (2016) 23 (9) *Gender, Place & Culture* 1286; Anjal Prakash, Vilina Engheepi and Shivaang Sinha, 'Intersecting pathways: Eco-feminist perspectives on intersectionality, water management, and responsible tourism for gender-inclusive community development' (2024) 7 *Current Research in Environmental Sustainability* 100254; and Gitanjali Nain Gill and Falguni Joshi, 'Environmental public hearings and intersectionality: women's voices from Gujarat' (2024) *India's Journal of Law and Society* 163.

14 Carolyn Merchant, *The Death of Nature: Women, Ecology and the Scientific Revolution* (Harper and Row 1980).

Despite a degree of fluidity in both the social[15] and environmental dimensions[16] in play, the limiting othering of vulnerable humans and the environment has proven remarkably persistent in regard to pollution impacts.

In any event, it soon became clear that the common law was unable to address the scale and complexity of pollution, and that statute law was needed to rise to these challenges. However, in effect, nuisance law has established a threshold-based approach as the norm for statutory legal intervention in this area. Generally, the adoption of new law was triggered not by environmental harm, but by the immediate need to address pollution that interfered with privileged human interests. Furthermore, statute law too was often deployed reactively, in that it was made in response to threats once they became not just obvious, but impossible to ignore either physically (often in causing harm to human health) or due to their economic ramifications.[17] While modern environmental law tends to at least pay lip service to the need to protect the environment in its own right in addition to human interests, the latter continue to dominate legal intervention. Environmental regulation today is generally focused on 'harm prevention or minimization', employing a pairing that remains stubbornly present, yoked and ubiquitous in environmental law despite its inherent compatibility. The approach adopted in domestic law extends to international law in the concept of significant harm.[18] The limited impact of prevention and even meaningful minimization of harm is all too evident in continued and continual environmental degradation,[19] and while it may ameliorate harm to a degree, it falls short of its ostensible ambition.

There is a profound need to think more clearly about areas where prevention in the true sense of the word needs to be the objective of the law[20] (for example, regarding already transgressed planetary boundaries, of which more below) and those where minimization of harm may suffice. This is particularly important in the context of ECEs, where a more active approach to this issue

---

[15] Including decision-making processes, Prakash, Engheepi and Sinha (n 13).

[16] Thompson (n 13) 1296.

[17] Coyle and Morrow (n 10).

[18] Jutta Brunnée, 'Harm Prevention', in Lavanya Rajamani and Jacqueline Peel (eds), *The Oxford Handbook of International Environmental Law* (Oxford University Press 2021).

[19] See, for example, UNEP: Keeping the Promise – Annual Report 2023: <https://wedocs.unep.org/bitstream/handle/20.500.11822/44777/UNEP_Annual_Report_2023.pdf?sequence=19&isAllowed=y> accessed 29 January 2025. See also William Dinan, Victoria Esteves, Steven Harkins et al., 'Climate dissociations: Trade associations, energy policy and climate communications in Europe' (2025) 4 (1) *PLOS Clim.* e0000467.

[20] Farber (n 1) 1787.

is essential to forestall/minimize incidences of acute harm. The current focus of cutting-edge environmental law, responding in part to increasingly sophisticated scientific understanding of less obvious and more intractable forms of pollution, such as poly- and perfluoroalkyl substances (PFAS) (or 'forever chemicals') and microplastics and, of course, the complex and interconnected triple environmental crisis,[21] ostensibly places the need for preventative action to the fore. However, as considered below, the reality is that prevention remains an area where, increasingly urgently, much more needs to be done to match practice to principle.[22] The imperviousness of the triple environmental crisis, which is characterized by ECE, to dominant legal approaches and rapidly emerging science requires us to think about framing responses to environmental harms more efficaciously, ceasing a spurious bifurcation between how law addresses (or fails to address) chronic harmful underlying states of affairs and acute actionable interference with human interests. Failure to address this crucial issue has always limited the efficacy of legal interventions in this area, but now, as the Anthropocene takes hold and we are increasingly forced to recognize the complex nature of environmental problems, it is something that we must urgently address. As discussed below, ecofeminist approaches, in attending to the inherent links between human flourishing and a sustaining and sustainable environment, offer one way of thinking about these issues in a more holistic fashion.

3. ANTHROPOCENE AND ITS IMPLICATIONS

Its recent (highly controversial) rejection by geologists,[23] notwithstanding, the concept of the 'age of humans' is a useful framing to discuss significant anthropogenic impacts on the environment manifesting at a planetary scale.[24] These impacts raise both environmental and human concerns, and it is crucial to note that both responsibility for them and experience of their impacts

21 Encapsulating climate change, pollution, and biodiversity loss, UNFCCC, 'What is the Triple Planetary Crisis?' (13 April 2022): <https://unfccc.int/news/what-is-the-triple-planetary-crisis> accessed 10 February 2025.

22 Ngozi Ole, Opeyemi Omotuyi, Eti Herbert et al., 'Environmental laws and enforcement: Prospects and challenges' in Ronnie Frazer-Williams, Mary B. Ogundiran and Emmanuel I. Unuabonah (eds), *Environmental Pollution and Public Health: Case Studies on Air, Water and Soil from an Interdisciplinary Perspective* (Elsevier 2024) 305.

23 Alexandra Witze, 'Geologists reject the Anthropocene as Earth's new epoch — after 15 years of debate' (2024) 627 *Nature* 249–50.

24 Mark J. Hudson, 'Dark Artifacts: Hyperobjects and the Archaeology of the Anthropocene' (2014) 1 (1) *Journal of Contemporary Archaeology* 82.

are highly unequal[25] and determined by a toxic juxtaposition of privilege and vulnerability.

The Anthropocene is characterized by anthropogenic initiation/acceleration/amplification of changes to the Earth on a global scale, involving a range of ramifications recognized by Earth system science.[26] The latter adopts a complex systems[27] approach, encapsulating the planet's environmental and human components and the interplay between them. This holistic stance to the human-environment nexus chimes strongly with key strands of established ecofeminist thinking, facilitating potential creative and useful cross-pollination of ideas. This is underlined in associated developments, including planetary boundaries[28] thinking, which speaks to the need to secure a continued 'safe operating space for humanity' in line with that enjoyed during the Holocene[29] and raises the possibility of invoking tipping points[30] and associated cascades[31] if the boundaries are transgressed. This framing arguably allows us to characterize the Anthropocene as a pervasive, grounding global chronic emergency, with planetary boundaries representing guardrails for human flourishing and exceeding them, invoking tipping points and cascades as consequent and consequential acute disasters.

The integrated approach invoked in Earth systems thinking promises to improve understanding of the super-wicked problems[32] of environmental

---

[25] Karen Morrow, 'Tackling climate change and gender justice – integral; not optional' (2020) 11 (1) *Oñati Socio-legal Series* 207.

[26] Will Steffen, Katherine Richardson, Johan Rockström et al. 'The emergence and evolution of Earth System Science' (2020) 1 *Nature Reviews Earth & Environment* 54.

[27] *Ibid.*

[28] Richardson, Steffen, Luch et al. (n 3).

[29] Will Steffen, Katherine Richardson, Johan Rockström et al., 'Planetary Boundaries: Guiding human development on a changing planet' (2015) 347 Science, 736; and Johan Rockström, Will Steffen, Kevin Noone et al. 'A safe operating space for humanity' (2009) 461 *Nature*, 472.

[30] David I. Armstrong McKay, Arie Staal, Jesse F. Abrams et al., 'Exceeding 1.5°C global warming could trigger multiple climate tipping points' (2022) 377 *Science*, eabn7950; Timothy M. Lenton, Hermann Held, Elmar Kriegler et al., 'Tipping elements in the Earth's climate system' (2008) 105 *Proceedings of the National Academy of Sciences of the United States of America* 1786.

[31] Nico Wunderling, Anna S. von der Heydt, Yevgeny Aksenov et al., 'Climate tipping point interactions and cascades: a review' (2024) 15 *Earth System Dynamics* 41.

[32] See, for example, Kelly Levin, Benjamin Cashore, Steven Bernstein et al., 'Overcoming the tragedy of super wicked problems: constraining our future selves to ameliorate global climate change' (2012) 45 (2) *Policy Sciences* 123.

harm more effectively in several ways that better fit the research endeavour to real-world needs. First, it is strongly and broadly interdisciplinary in nature, operating across a broad range of hard and social sciences and law,[33] which places it well to interrogate the complexity of environmental systems, interactions between them and the relationship of both to human systems. Second, the scope involved is sufficiently ambitious in extending its spatial reach to the global, and its temporal reach far into the future. Thirdly, it necessitates engagement with the inseparability of planet and people, reflecting on the relationship between human activities and Earth's life support systems in a focused way, using the safe operating space approach to frame analysis around safeguarding crucial functionality, rather than relying on arbitrary thresholds. Tipping points and cascades raise emerging issues tied to the difficult-to-predict, non-linear and potentially irreversible nature of some anthropogenic shifts in Earth systems.

All these developments and our poor progress to date require us to fundamentally rethink our approaches to environmental harm,[34] understanding it as conjoined to human concerns and foregrounding its prevention as the founding response. Reframing our understanding of environmental disasters is a hugely important part of the required paradigm shift.

4. THE NEED TO SHIFT FROM A DISASTER TO A CHRONIC EMERGENCY FRAMING – PROGRESS OR NOT?

Considering the anthropocentric and reactive roots of early environmental law, the appeal and emergence of environmental disaster as a construct is no surprise, though its limited reach and efficacy in the context of the chronic planetary-scale problems of the Anthropocene outlined above increasingly make its longevity difficult to either explain or justify. This is not to say, however, that the established concept of disaster is entirely lacking in useful insights, and it is important to retain them. There is, for example, value in recognizing the intimate connections between the environmental and human systems components of disasters.[35] This in some ways prefigures both ecofeminist approaches

---

33 Louis J. Kotzé, Rakhyun E. Kim, Catherine Blanchard et al., 'Earth system law: Exploring new frontiers in legal science' (2022) 11 *Earth System Governance* 100126.

34 Simon Sharpe, *Five Times Faster: Rethinking the Science, Economics, and Diplomacy of Climate Change* (Cambridge University Press 2023).

35 See Henrik Svensen, *The End is Nigh: A History of Natural Disasters* (Reaktion Books Ltd 2009), and Farber (n 1).

and the changing understanding of anthropogenic environmental impacts in the Anthropocene.

Human actions can no longer be characterized as merely aggravating the impacts of natural events on vulnerable populations through poor responses to them, as they were in the concept of erroneously named 'natural' disasters. This is still undoubtedly relevant, but, as alluded to above, in the Anthropocene, human acts and omissions are now also increasingly understood as driving the conditions that underpin adverse events, cause[36] them, and contribute to their frequency and magnitude.[37] Climate change in particular illustrates the complex, enmeshed human and environmental factors in play, not least in regard to the emerging (but as yet ill-understood) conception of compound events. The attempt to account for the complexity of the interplay between specific disasters and their milieu is not new and finds antecedents in Rob Nixon's scholarly work on 'slow violence'[38] and related operational conceptions such as the UN Office for the Coordination of Humanitarian Affairs (OCHA) idea of 'slow-onset emergency', defined as manifesting: '. . . gradually over time, often based on a confluence of different events.[39] Compound events are attributable to simultaneous or consecutive occurrences at single or multiple locations, consequent on multiple drivers, which: ' . . . exacerbate the societal and ecosystem impacts of individual hazards and hinder the ability of communities, particularly frontline communities, to respond and cope.[40] The impacts of compound events are, as with other disasters, embedded in and amplify long-term structural inequalities, again a phenomenon recognized in ecofeminism. The impacts of compound events are worse for the most vulnerable, who are simultaneously most exposed and least able to respond to them. Compound emergencies thought is of particular interest for present purposes in explicitly

---

36 See, for example, World Weather Attribution: When Risks Become Reality: Extreme Weather In 2024: <https://www.worldweatherattribution.org/when-risks-become-reality-extreme-weather-in-2024/> accessed 7 February 2025.

37 World Meteorological Organization (2023), Status of Mortality and Economic Losses due to Weather, Climate and Water Extremes (1970–2021), online at <https://storymaps.arcgis.com/stories/8df884dbd4e849c89d4b1128fa5dc1d6> accessed 9 January 2025.

38 Rob Nixon, *Slow Violence and the Environmentalism of the Poor* (Harvard University Press 2011).

39 OCHA Occasional Policy Briefing Series Brief No. 6: OCHA and slow-onset emergencies, (2011) para. 2.

40 Deepti Singh, Allison R. Crimmins, Justin M. Pflug et al., 'Focus on compound events', in Allison R. Crimmins, Alexa K. Jay, Christopher W. Avery et al. (eds), *Fifth National Climate Assessment* (U.S. Global Change Research Program 2023) F1,3.

invoking consequent resource allocation responsibilities on governments to act to better address the needs of their most vulnerable citizens.[41] However, while the aforementioned concepts bring welcome and necessary nuance to our understanding of aspects of the complexity of the interplay between harms to the environment and vulnerable humans, they remain limited in their focus, like broader legal thinking on harm and disasters, concentrating on a particular crisis and inadequately addressing the states of affairs that prompt them and perpetuate future peril. A disaster-focused approach, allied to the dominant after the event[42] response of law to environmental problems, is increasingly inadequate both in principle and in practical terms for present, never mind future purposes. Replacing the concept of natural disaster with that of ECE, understood as mandating addressing underlying environmental damage in order (ideally) to forestall acute harms/disasters entirely or at least to ameliorate their consequences for vulnerable populations, would have much to offer in securing more efficacious responses to the perils of what can usefully be termed environmental breakdown. This has been defined as:

> Negative human impacts on the environment . . . [that] encompass most … natural systems, driving a complex, dynamic process of environmental destabilisation that has reached critical levels.[43]

Crucially, in this context, the concept of ECE is capable of explicitly addressing the crucial role of human agency, not just in responding to natural events but, in the Anthropocene, in acting and/or failing to act in ways that actively fuel environmental breakdown. The prospects for bringing about such a shift are, however, not hopeful as emerging developments in international soft law remain lacking in a meaningful response to what current science understands about the human-environment nexus and beyond (at best) paying lip service to this, continuing, as they have always done, to focus myopically on trying to ameliorate the impacts of the Anthropocene on humans. We shall examine three examples illustrative of this approach: the International Law Commission's (ILC) Draft Articles on the Protection of Persons in the Event of Disasters

---

41 *Ibid.,* at F1, 4–5.

42 Pacific Islands Students Fighting Climate Change and World's Youth for Climate Justice: Youth Climate Justice Handbook Summary for Policymakers (2023): <https://static1.squarespace.com/static/5f063a0c8f53b604aed84729/t/645102469f98ac0c5863a6cf/1683030601262/Handbook_Summary_for_Policymakers_EN.pdf>.

43 Laurie Laybourn-Langton, Lesley Rankin, Darren Baxter, *This is a crisis: Facing up to the age of environmental breakdown* (IPPR 2019): < http://www.ippr.org/research/publications/age-of-environmental-breakdown> accessed 4 April 2025, 4.

(2016)[44]; developments in human rights law, including the General Assembly Resolution on the Right to a Clean, Healthy and Sustainable Environment in 2022;[45] and the United Nations Pact for the Future[46] and associated Declaration for Future Generations.[47] The section will conclude by looking at the contrasting approach that characterizes the 2024 report of the Special Rapporteur on the promotion and protection of human rights in the context of climate change.[48]

4.1 The ILC Draft Articles

Almost a decade in the making,[49] the traditionally grounded and bounded ILC Draft Articles on the Protection of Persons in the Event of Disasters were disappointing in numerous ways, not least in failing to look at the structural causes of human vulnerability in this context.[50] Such a framing, drawing interdisciplinary work and extending to social science scholarship, notably political ecology,[51] and ecofeminist analysis, would have facilitated a more contextualized approach to disasters, viewing them as shaped by the human-environment nexus and inter-human interactions, and be more attuned to real-world conditions. However, the ILC's approach may perhaps be viewed instead as being politically realistic, given that, after being 'noted' in General Assembly resolution in 2016[52] there began a lengthy, ultimately inconclusive,[53] period of

---

[44] International Law Commission, 'Protection of persons in the event of disasters' (27 May 2016), UN Doc A/CN.4/L.871.

[45] Human Rights Council, 'Resolution on the human right to a safe, clean, healthy and sustainable environment' (18 October 2021) UN Doc A/HRC/RES/48/RES/13.

[46] UN General Assembly, 'Resolution on the Pact for the Future' (22 September 2024) UN Doc A/RES/79/1.

[47] *Ibid.*, Annex II.

[48] Special Rapporteur on the promotion and protection of human rights in the context of climate change, Scene-setting report, (21 June 2024) A/HRC/56/46.

[49] Report of the International Law Commission on the work of its Fifty-Eighth Session Official Records of the General Assembly, Sixty-First Session, Supp No 10, UN Doc A/61/10 (2006).

[50] Thérèse O'Donnell, 'Vulnerability and the International Law Commission's Draft Articles on the Protection of Persons in the Event of Disasters' (2019) 68 *International & Comparative Law Quarterly* 573.

[51] *Ibid.*

[52] UN General Assembly, 'Resolution on the Protection of persons in the event of disasters' (13 December 2016) UN Doc A/RES/71/141.

[53] Culminating in UN General Assembly, 'Resolution on the Protection of persons in the event of disasters' (4 December 2024) UN Doc A/RES/79/128.

temporizing by that body on the subject. States appear to want to be seen to be acting to address these issues without actually doing so, and the ILC's work has not therefore improved preparedness to respond to disasters, never mind engaged with ECEs.

4.2 Human Rights and the Right to a Clean, Healthy and Sustainable Environment (RCHSE)

On paper, at least, being based on the principles of universality, inalienability and indivisibility, and on being interdependent and interrelated,[54] human rights offer a viable means to redress the imbalance between privileged and non-privileged humanity that could be very relevant to addressing the highly differentiated impacts of environmental degradation. In practice, things are less clear-cut and the notional enjoyment of rights is constrained by numerous social, political and legal factors.[55] Nevertheless, human rights offer something necessary, but not sufficient, in terms of addressing ECEs, in that they essentially conceive the latter as acts of self-harm to current and future humans, areas where states already operate under established and developing legal obligations that apply domestically, vis-à-vis their own citizens and extra-territorially in regard to their relations with other states. By extension, these obligations necessarily apply to ensuring that states operate within planetary boundaries.[56] There has of late been a flurry of development at the global level in human rights law focused on planetary environmental concerns, and we shall now consider what the most prominent of these, the RCHSE, offers to address ECEs – and what it lacks.

Informed by cutting-edge science and work within and across their remits, the UN's human rights bodies are very aware of the intimate links between multiple aspects of environmental breakdown and the ability of vulnerable people to enjoy their human rights, as evidenced by a joint statement in

---

[54] Succinctly states in the United Nations Population Fund, Human Rights Principles (2005): <https://www.unfpa.org/resources/human-rights-principles> accessed 31 January 2025.

[55] See, for example, Julie Fraser, *Social Institutions and International Human Rights Law Implementation: Every Organ of Society* (Cambridge University Press 2020) 1, 1–20.

[56] Karen Morrow, 'The fragility of climate, human responsibility and finding the impetus to act decisively – investigating the potential of the ethics of care' in Jordi Jaria-Manzano and Susana Barràs (eds), *Research Handbook on Global Climate Constitutionalism* (Edward Elgar Publishing 2019) 114.

2020 by five of them on climate change.[57] The concerns expressed centred on the particularly pronounced risk of harm to those already:

> . . . already marginalized or in vulnerable situations or that, owing to discrimination and pre-existing inequalities, have limited access to decision-making or resources, such as women, children, persons with disabilities, Indigenous peoples and persons living in rural areas.[58]

The statement went on to point out that failure by states to act on climate change could constitute a breach of existing human rights obligations[59] and explicitly positioned emission reduction (mitigation) as the highest priority for states. While a start, this is blatantly inadequate to meet the challenges we currently face.[60] However, the statement also pushed for a broader approach, making explicit reference to:

> hydrometeorological disasters, evacuations of areas at high risk of disasters, environmental degradation and slow-moving disasters . . . [61]

among factors driving migration. This multifaceted and temporally flexible framing of disaster is unusual in its depth and nuance. While this is encouraging, the UN human rights institutions do not wield the power to bring about significant change. The seventy-fifth anniversary of the United Nations, also in 2020, provided an opportunity for states, the empowered actors of international law, to reflect on the organization's past experience, present challenges and future priorities. The General Assembly adopted a brief declaration threaded through with references to human rights,[62] which were reaffirmed as one of the UN's central pillars. Tellingly, though, coverage of the dire state of the environment was confined to a single paragraph, which did not mention human

---

[57] Joint Statement by the Committee on the Elimination of Discrimination against Women, the Committee on Economic, Social and Cultural Rights, the Committee on the Protection of the Rights of All Migrant Workers and Members of Their Families, the Committee on the Rights of the Child and the Committee on the Rights of Persons with Disabilities, 'Statement on human rights and climate change' (14 May 2020) UN Doc HRI/2019/1.

[58] *Ibid.*, para. 3.

[59] *Ibid.*, para. 10.

[60] Malm and Carton (n 5).

[61] Joint UN Human Rights Bodies Statement (n 57) para. 14.

[62] UN Assembly General, 'Declaration on the commemoration of the seventy-fifth anniversary of the United Nations' (28 September 2020) UN Doc A/RES/75/1, para. 6.

rights.[63] In many ways, this document represents the current state of affairs as well as any other: we continue to be myopically focused on human concerns and while on one level we grasp that the ability to address those concerns is being dangerously compromised by anthropogenic impacts on the environment; on another this does not provoke a consonant response, recognizing significant constraints on human priorities. So much then for the general position.

Despite an ultimately fruitless attempt by the UN's human rights machinery to launch an environmental human right in the UN in the early 1990s, academic interest in the environmental dimensions of human rights and the 'greening human rights agenda' was sparked and sustained, and, alongside civil society interest, helped to keep the issue alive. In 2012, the Human Rights Council returned to the fray, introducing a new special rapporteur mandate on human rights in the environment. The mandate generated a voluminous and well-informed evidence base, garnering considerable support from states and generating significant outputs, notably the Framework Principles on Human Rights and the Environment, with a strong focus on 'greening' existing human rights.[64] The HRC's sustained activity ultimately culminated in a seemingly more radical approach, the adoption of a strongly supported resolution on the human right to a safe, clean, healthy and sustainable environment in 2021.[65] This was swiftly followed[66] by a similar (though not identical[67]) and almost unanimous UNGA resolution. It is this iteration of the RCHSE that will be the focus here. The resolution is brief, its preamble significantly exceeding its body text,[68] and the considerable fanfare around its adoption notwithstanding,[69] its

---

63 *Ibid.*, para. 8, which further indicates the disconnect referred to *infra.*

64 Special Rapporteur on the issue of human rights obligations relating to the enjoyment of a safe, clean, healthy and sustainable environment, 'Report on the issue of human rights obligations relating to the enjoyment of a safe, clean, healthy and sustainable environment', (24 January 2018) UN Doc A/HRC/37/59.

65 Human Rights Council (n 45).

66 See Marc Limon, 'United Nations recognition of the universal right to a clean, healthy and sustainable environment: An eyewitness account' (2022) 31 (1) *Review of European, Comparative & International Environmental Law*, 153.

67 The GA's version of the RCHSE was, on closer analysis, significantly less ambitious than that of the HRC; see Karen Morrow: 'Will a Human Right to a Clean, Healthy and Sustainable Environment Address the Wrongs of Environmental Degradation?' in Abigail Bakan and Yasmeen Abu-Laban (eds), *Human Rights and the United Nations: Paradox and Promise* (Routledge 2025), 170.

68 *Ibid.*

69 See, for example, UN News, 'UN General Assembly declares access to clean and healthy environment a universal human right', (28 July 2022): <https://news.un.org/en/story/2022/07/1123482> accessed 7 April 2025 and UNEP: <https://

content, far from being ground-breaking, largely reiterates previous UN commitments.[70] While the RCHSE certainly has symbolic and educational significance, which may well assist in better leveraging of human rights law in contexts where people are harmed by environmental degradation,[71] facilitating the current special rapporteur on human rights and the environment's emphasis on implementation, for example,[72] it remains by its very nature anthropocentric. While the RCHSE perpetuates an established human harm-centred approach to addressing the human-environment nexus, it is potentially useful in providing a more coherently packaged approach to addressing the needs of non-privileged humans in this regard. That said, it also reinforces the centring of human needs and fails to address the implications of the knowledge that human flourishing and ultimately existence is at base dependent on the state of the environment.[73]

4.3 The UN Pact for the Future and Declaration for Future Generations

If the promise of human rights approaches, freighted by their conceptualization and history, has, despite high-profile developments, offered less in practice than they promise, what of UN consideration of future generations? In theory, the expanded view of humanity adopted here, by importing a much longer time scale than is usually the case in law and policy, could provide an incentive to rethink the implications of the human-environment nexus as it entails securing the continued ability of the environment to support human existence and flourishing, extending into the future.[74] A concern of international environmental law since the first Earth Summit in Stockholm in 1972, and entering the mainstream in the 1992 Rio Earth Summit, taking action to safeguard the interests of future generations is appealing in theory, albeit

---

www.unep.org/news-and-stories/story/historic-move-un-declares-healthy-environment-human-right> accessed 7 April 2025.

70 Morrow (n 67).

71 Claudia Ituarte-Lima, 'Biosphere Defenders Leveraging the Human Right to Healthy Environment for
Transformative Change' (2023) 53 *Environmental Policy and Law*, 139.

72 Special Rapporteur on the human right to a healthy environment, see 'Special Rapporteur on the human right to a healthy environment': <https://www.ohchr.org/en/special-procedures/sr-environment> accessed 10 April 2025.

73 Morrow (n 67).

74 William MacAskill, *What We Owe the Future: A Million-Year View* (Oneworld 2022).

challenging – though not impossibly so,[75] in practice.[76] While much discussed over the years, the UN Summit of the Future in 2024 brought new focus to this area and its outcome documents, the Pact for the Future[77] and the Declaration for Future Generations[78] are revealing of how far coverage of this issue has come – and how far it has yet to go. While in-depth discussion is not possible within the confines of this chapter, a brief consideration of these documents provides a fascinating snapshot of what may well prove to be a critical juncture in our treatment of the human-environment nexus.

The Pact, for example, badly states that:

> We are confronted by rising catastrophic and existential risks, *many caused by the choices we make*. Fellow human beings are enduring terrible suffering. If we do not change course, we risk tipping into a future of persistent crisis and breakdown.[79] (emphasis added)

Commitments adopted include prioritizing:

> . . . urgent action to address critical environmental challenges and implement measures to reduce disaster risk and build resilience, reverse the degradation of ecosystems and ensure a clean, healthy and sustainable environment . . .[80]

Actions committed to include:

> Leveraging science, data, statistics and strategic foresight to ensure long-term thinking and planning, and to develop and implement sustainable practices and the institutional reforms necessary to ensure evidence-based decision-making, while making governance more anticipatory, adaptive and responsive to future opportunities, risks and challenges.[81]

However, for all of its promise, the Pact for the Future process is taken as a whole, is ultimately crushingly disappointing, in particular in its overtly technocratic bent. This is far from inadvertent. The Anthropocene here is ultimately presented not so much as a threat to the biosphere and, in consequence, an existential threat to much of humanity, but as a further opportunity for

---

75 Edith Brown Weiss, 'Our Rights and Obligations to Future Generations for the Environment', (1990) 84 (1) *American Journal of International Law*, 198.

76 Richard P Hiskes, *The Human Right to a Green Future: Environmental Rights and Intergenerational Justice* (Cambridge 2009).

77 Human Rights Council (n 45).

78 UN General Assembly (n 46).

79 Human Rights Council (n 45), para. 2.

80 *Ibid.*, para. 18.

81 *Ibid.*, para. 24.

commodification, profit and the consolidation of control by the already powerful. Law in this register is all too easily pressed into the service of those who benefit from a commodified response to how we understand crisis, assisting in perpetuating (and indeed augmenting) a 'business as usual' approach. While achieving any agreement in a fragmented and fractious international polis is an achievement of sorts, it is difficult not to regard the process as a squandered opportunity and one where our generation's responses will be found horribly wanting – not least in addressing environmental breakdown and the many faces of inequality, gender among them.[82]

4.4 The 2024 Report of the Special Rapporteur on the Promotion and Protection of Human Rights in the Context of Climate Change[83]

If the Pact for the Future process was underwhelming, new special rapporteur Elisa Morgera's report offers a much more humane approach to chronic emergency in its thematic inclusion of intersectionality, threading through her analysis of the unequal experience of adverse climate impacts and climate justice and applying it to adaptation and mitigation. Originating in Kimberle Crenshaw's groundbreaking work on feminist legal scholarship on intersectionality,[84] centred on the core recognition that:

> … forms of subordination and privilege intersect in people's lives in complex and mutually reinforcing ways …[85]

has become a hugely influential idea across multiple areas of social inquiry on equality – including broader human rights law. Morgera makes an important contribution in bringing intersectionality analysis so firmly front and centre in the work of the HRC. However, intersectionality is usually predominantly focused on the social sphere, which, while undoubtedly hugely important, as

82 See, for example, Marides Santos: 'Civil Society Organizations React to the "Pact for the Future": A Call for Accountability and Ambition': <https://www.vivatinternational.org/blog/2024/09/30/civil-society-organizations-react-to-the-pact-for-the-future-a-call-for-accountability-and-ambition/> accessed 7 April 2025.

83 UN General Assembly (n 47).

84 Kimberle Crenshaw, 'Demarginalizing the Intersection of Race and Sex: A Black Feminist Critique of Antidiscrimination Doctrine, Feminist Theory and Antiracist Politics' (1989) 1989 (1) *University of Chicago Legal Forum*, 139.

85 Johanna Bond, *Global Intersectionality & Contemporary Human Rights* (Oxford 2021) 6.

Thompson observes, is inadequate to account for the role of environmental factors and the interplay between them.[86] These latter dimensions are increasingly to the fore in respect of the triple environmental crisis, not least climate change and in other ECEs. Thus, an ecofeminist reading of intersectionality is beneficial in that it understands it as having not only social and environmental dimensions but also manifesting at nexus areas between them.

5. USING ECOFEMINIST THINKING TO ENGAGE MORE EFFECTIVELY WITH CHRONIC EMERGENCIES

There is significant common ground between scientific understandings of the Anthropocene, as considered above, encapsulating environmental breakdown and consequent threats to human flourishing (and if unaddressed, extending to an existential threat to our species). In response, it is imperative to shift our thinking and action beyond a narrow concept of disaster and its limited, reactive conception of harm, to embrace the broader idea of ECE and a proactive/preventative approach to harm driven by our understanding of the nuanced nature of human responsibility, vulnerability, and agency (the latter not being viewed as by any means mutually exclusive).[87] To this end, this section discusses what an ecofeminist approach could bring to the table to facilitate the type and scale of change required. As discussed above, ecofeminism[88] is best known for providing a species-critical framing to identify and interrogate the impacts of hierarchical dualism as a categorical approach that enables and fuels the systemic exploitation of the other by the otherer. In this regard, male/female and human/environment dualisms can be understood as sharing salient features that facilitate the application of a common conceptual framing to address them. This section, however, builds on ecofeminist critique, arguing that used in conjunction with feminist ethics of care thinking, it can perform a constitutive function in building a different ethical response to dualism, based on constructive relationality, rather than destructive hierarchy. Taking the view

---

86 Thompson (n 13).

87 National Academies of Sciences, Engineering, and Medicine, *Strengthening Indigenous America: Building Resilience Through Disaster Preparedness, Response, and Recovery: Proceedings of a Workshop in Brief* (The National Academies Press 2024).

88 For a flavour of the vibrant and diverse ecology of ecofeminism, see Karen Morrow; Ecofeminism and International Law, Oxford Bibliographies (2022): <www.oxfordbibliographies.com/display/document/obo-9780199796953/obo-9780199796953–0237.xml?rskey=P558KO&result=1&q=ecofeminism#firstMatch> accessed 12 April 2025.

that, while humans are both in and of nature and thus part of the environment rather than separate from it, the Anthropocene, as considered above, requires us to make a reckoning with our unique status as a planet-shaping creature.[89] There is a dualism here – no other creature is in a position analogous to that of human beings, but the self-generated Anthropocene threat to the environmental conditions that promoted human flourishing in the Holocene negates the illusion of hierarchy and instead requires a relational framing of the ecological reality of human dependence on the biosphere. Our response to Earth systems science and its implications must therefore be an interdisciplinary endeavour that melds hard science with social sciences, humanities and law,[90] and also, as a real-world undertaking, draws on ecofeminism's grasp of the imperative need to combine academic knowledge with lived experience to better grasp the fullness of the human-environment nexus.[91]

Crafting the required relational approach to the human-environment nexus can be achieved by adopting an ecofeminist-infused conception of the ethics of care.[92] Ethics of care approaches, rooted in Carole Gilligan's groundbreaking work in psychology,[93] start from the premise that: 'as humans we are inherently relational, responsive beings and the human condition is one of connectedness or interdependence.[94] Subsequent work by Joan Tronto expanded the analysis of the relational core of the ethics of care in the form of 'caring virtues', namely: attentiveness, responsibility, competence, responsiveness and solidarity and justice.[95] Ethics of care approaches were conceived by Gilligan as an adaptable frame for promoting moral action that did not rely on the enjoyment of rights or entitlements by the subject of care, but rather were founded on the responsibility of the caregiver. Having originated in regard to interpersonal (often familial) relationships, the ethics of care as an approach

---

[89] Karen Morrow, 'Ecofeminist approaches to the construction of knowledge and coalition building – offering a way forward for international environmental law and policy' in Andreas Philippopoulos-Mihalopoulos and Victoria Brooks (eds), *Research Methods in Environmental Law* (Edward Elgar Publishing 2017) 289.

[90] Matt Edgeworth: 'Archaeology of the Anthropocene – Introduction', (2014) 1 (1) *Journal of Contemporary Archaeology* 73, 74.

[91] Morrow (n 89).

[92] Morrow (n 56).

[93] Carole Gilligan, *In A Different Voice* (Harvard University Press 1982).

[94] 'Gilligan Interview', (21 June 2011): <https://ethicsofcare.org/carol-gilligan/> accessed 7 April 2015.

[95] For a succinct synthesis of the development of Tronto's approach see, Tessa Bergman, Nora Lize, Sandra Beijer, et al., 'A care ethics approach to a reduced ability to eat' (2024) 31 (4) *Nursing Ethics* 420, 424.

has subsequently been applied to the caring professions and offers sufficient flexibility to extend to care for the environment.[96] The ethics of care is also open to spatially and temporally expansive framings[97] that make them a good fit for application in and to the Anthropocene.

If we view the planet as a complex system, as discussed above, in addition to offering advantages over an atomized approach, allowing a more realistic analysis of environmental issues, which facilitates:

> identifying mutual links between the individual subsystems and hence . . . improving the physical understanding of how these components interact with each other on various temporal as well as spatial scales and how the corresponding interactions determine the dynamics of the full system.[98]

this also offers a good fit for an ecofeminist infused ethics of care approach, both in terms of how we understand the Earth system and humanity's relationship to it. In accessible terms, as explicitly alluded to in planetary boundaries thinking, systems approaches exhibit some similarities to the intricate functions of self-regulation of living systems, and importantly bring the interplay between social/human and environmental systems firmly to the fore.[99] This is crucial for this chapter as this analysis echoes the true nature of 'natural' disasters, which, far from being 'acts of God/nature, rather occur as:

> . . . consequences of encounters between nature and society, the extent of which depends on how well people have managed to adapt to dangers.[100]

Furthermore, a living systems lens provides a helpful way to think about systemic environmental issues and their manifestation using the terminology drawn from a well-developed field of care: medicine. The categorization of chronic and acute medical conditions and their relation to one another in

[96] Morrow (n 89), expanding on Helena Olofsdotter Stensota, 'Public Ethics of Care – A General Public Ethics', (2015) 9 (2) *Ethics and Social Welfare* 183.

[97] See, for example, Morrow (n 89); Marian Barnes *Care in Everyday Life: An Ethic of Care in Practice* (The Policy Press 2012), in particular, Chapter 6; and Elena Pulcini: *Care of the World: Fear, Responsibility and Justice in the Global Age* (Springer 2009).

[98] Relk V. Donner, Susana Barbosa, Juergen Kurths, and Norbert Marwan, 'Understanding the Earth as a Complex System – recent advances in data analysis and modelling in Earth sciences' (2009) 174 (1) *The European Physical Journal Special Topics* 1.

[99] Rockström, Steffen, Noone et al. (n 29) 475.

[100] Svensen (n 35) 14.

comorbidities is helpful here. In this context, the dictionary definitions are instructive:

> chronic illness is defined as: '. . . lasting a long time, long-continued, lingering, inveterate; opposed to acute';
>
> acute illness is defined as: '. . . coming quickly to a crisis or conclusion; of rapid onset and short duration; of recent or sudden onset; contrasted with chronic' and additionally as 'severe; critical'; and
>
> comorbidity is defined as: 'The coexistence of two or more diseases, disorders, or pathological processes in one individual, esp. as a complicating factor affecting the prognosis or treatment of a patient'.[101]

A responsible medical practitioner would not regard or treat such conditions in isolation from one another but would instead care for the whole patient in order to optimize outcomes. These terms are useful for the current discussion of ECEs in that chronic disease parallels the underlying damaged state of the environment consequent on anthropogenic impacts; acute disease offers parallels with specific disasters; and comorbidities invite us to eschew an overly simplistic view of the relationship between the two, instead seeing their profound and complex imbrication. This approach offers a much more realistic and potentially efficacious approach to understanding the multi-layered nature of harm than that presently used in law, and one that fits much better with the complex systems involved.

6. CONCLUDING THOUGHTS – NOW OR NEVER?

As is apparent from the discussion above that while international law is paying lip service to environmental breakdown and what it means for people and planet, the current trajectory, despite ostensibly attractive repackaging by the United Nations, remains largely one of consolidation – more of the same – rather than instituting the necessary paradigm shift required to engage meaningfully with the impacts of the Anthropocene, not least ECEs. We can no longer afford to accept this for current and future generations.

ECEs are still ill-covered in law, and to even begin to adequately address their impacts on the biosphere, which is also necessary to deal fully with their human impacts, requires fundamentally reconfiguring how the law comprehends anthropogenic harm and damage to the environment. The advent of the Anthropocene means that the game has already changed; how humanity is playing it, however has not, and it must urgently do so. An ecofeminist-infused ethics of care offers a way forward, inviting an expansive, relational view of interactions between humanity and the environment, which would be capable

---

101 Definitions from the Oxford English Dictionary, <https://www.oed.com>.

of encapsulating both its necessary human-environment and inter-human dimensions.[102] What ECEs reveal is the urgent need for a deep re-education of how we understand what it is to be human in the Anthropocene. If we are to tackle environmental breakdown and ensure human flourishing and ultimately the survival of our species, we must grasp and act on the new three 'Rs': a relational and ecologically realistic understanding of the human-environment nexus, adopting a care-based approach to human responsibility grounding ethics, law and praxis.

102 Morrow (n 56).

PART II

Environmental Chronic Emergencies Across Time

5. A fear of falling? The mineshaft as an 'environmental chronic emergency' in modern Cornwall

Timothy Cooper

1. INTRODUCTION

This chapter seeks to provide an overview of the historical applicability of the concept of environmental chronic emergency (ECE). As this book as a whole argues, the idea of ECE develops along socio-legal lines the concept of slow violence proposed by Rob Nixon as an analytic frame through which to engage with the differential temporalities encountered in the politics of environmental justice movements.[1] In his highly influential work, Nixon juxtaposes 'spectacular and unspectacular time' and the inequalities of representation and legal and political action that circulate around the necessary 'adjustment of our rapidly eroding attention spans to the slow erosion of environmental justice.'[2] For Nixon, a literary scholar, this raises the question of representation and how to bring into vision the ways in which localized, unfolding, invisible disasters persist unseen, especially in the Global South. His response, in *Slow Violence and the Environmentalism of the Poor*, is to bring to the fore writer activism in the post-colonial space and its work of visibility and memory.

However, the analytical predisposition of 'slow violence' is not one delimited to a postmodern condition, or to the Global South. Slow violence was, I would argue, presupposed within the very structures of early industrial capitalism itself and was a subject of early legislative concern and social struggle. It is important to remember, as historians of global empire have, that the extractive impulse of modern imperialism and its tendency to accelerate the time of modernity at the expense of the colonial margin is hardly something

[1] Rob Nixon, *Slow Violence and the Environmentalism of the Poor* (Harvard University Press 2011).

[2] *Ibid.*, 6–8.

new, or confined to the oilfield age that is the focus of Nixon's book.[3] In this sense, then, we might think of the industrial age as beckoning a moment of chronic temporal disjunction between the accelerating temporal and spatial accumulation of wealth and the never-ending transformation, poisoning and abandonment of the extractive frontier. This, then, may be the utility of the analytics of ECE, to return us to the historical time of industrial, fossil capital and its already long-standing history of temporal violence.[4]

Rather than a general outline of the instances of ECE that could no doubt be multiplied manifold, in this Chapter I use an example close to (my) home. This chapter is a story of the extinction of the mining industry in Cornwall (UK) and its impact on land and people in the years since. It reflects on the temporality of this phenomenon and its significance for present and future generations, as well as the often neglected lasting effects on the environment and the population. An industry characterized by dangerous but productive labour, often involving a great deal of women's labour, masculinities declined to leave a deep fracture in both society and in nature. Closure of this industry was not the end, but paved the way for new dangers. In its aftermath, it left a risky and unpredictable landscape that was no respecter of either the class or the gender order of society, presenting a mortal risk to man, woman and child alike in a radically unpredictable way.[5] This state of affairs was tolerated for decades until a new productive landscape finally demanded action to reduce the risk to the casual tourist. I begin with two encounters with the post-industrial Cornish landscape, taking place nearly a century apart.

2. TWO STORIES

Walking home across the moors one evening in January 1858, John Berryman had spent the evening at the 'Engine Inn' in Towednack in west Cornwall. Now

---

3 Richard H. Grove, *Green Imperialism: Colonial Expansion, Tropical Island Edens and the Origins of Environmentalism*, 1600–1860 (Cambridge University Press 1995); Richard Drayton, *Nature's Government: Science, Imperial Britain, and the 'Improvement' of the World* (Yale University Press 2000); Fabien Locher and Jean-Baptiste Fressoz, 'Modernity's Frail Climate: A Climate History of Environmental Reflexivity' (2012) 38(3), *Critical Inquiry*, 579.

4 Andreas Malm, *Fossil Capital: The Rise of Steam Power and the Roots of Global Warming*, (Verso Books 2016); David Bond, *Negative Ecologies: Fossil Fuels and the Discovery of the Environment*, (University of California Press 2022).

5 Rossana Barragán Romano and Leda Papastefanaki, 'Women and Gender in the Mines: Challenging Masculinity Through History: An Introduction' (2020) 65(2), *International Review of Social History*, 191.

his, perhaps unsteady, journey took him along a trackway through the disused Reeth Consols mine. Immersed in the shadow of a winter's night, Berryman somehow strayed from what was the 'direct path'.[6] Disoriented, Berryman stumbled towards the edge of a hole in the ground, an old air shaft, and fell. Although he survived a descent of some sixteen fathoms (about 96 feet), with no companion to report him missing, he was left to call for help 'till his strength was exhausted and his voice failed.' There he remained, stuck, for three days in what the *West Briton* rather laconically described as 'that distressing situation'. Eventually, through pure fortune, he was discovered, 'by a person throwing a small stone in the shaft, which attracted his notice.' Dehydrated and bruised, Berryman emerged otherwise intact from this subterranean adventure.

The second story takes place on an autumn day in November 1957. Nearly a century after John Berryman's unfortunate experience, Irene Berryman left her home in Camborne along with her dog, Mark, for their daily walk. The pair were crossing an old mine waste tip when, it was reported, 'the ground beneath her gave way,'[7] Mark 'jumped to safety,' but Mrs Berryman slid down the shaft. At this point, newspapers later dramatically reported, Mark 'stood firm and the lead held' while his companion hung from it above a chasm of 'hundreds of feet'. With her dog's aid, Irene Berryman 'managed to get a grip on the sloping side of the shaft and crawl back to safety. Then she collapsed.'[8] The terrifying story was of such interest that it appeared over the following days on the front pages of both the national newspapers, the Daily Mirror and the *Daily Express*.[9] While these newspapers focused on Mark's supposed role in pulling an unfortunate Irene Berryman to safety, a family tradition remembers this incident rather differently. Instead of an immediate 'chasm of hundreds of feet', a relative later recalled that, 'She fell into what we assume was an adit, which according to her description dropped vertically for maybe 9 or 10 feet before carrying on at an angle. This saved her, as she caught herself on the angle, with the dog still on the ground above. She said she was so glad he didn't jump down to her! Anyway, she edged herself back up the side of the hole using elbows and heels until she came up onto solid ground. I guess from there she walked back home, pretty shaken up I should imagine!'[10]

---

6 Rita Margaret Barton, *Life in Cornwall in the Late Nineteenth Century: Being Extracts from The West Briton Newspaper in the Two Decades from 1855 to 1875* (Bradford Barton 1972) 41.

7 'Woman Saved By Dog's Lead', *The Manchester Guardian*, 22 November 1957, 1.

8 *Ibid.*

9 'Dog "Digs In" Saves Mrs B', *Daily Mirror*, 22 November 1957, 1; 'Spaniel Saves His Mistress from Death Fall', *Daily Express*, 22 November 1957, 1.

10 Private correspondence with Viv Broadhurst, 23 June 2022.

In the century separating these two namesakes' close encounters, Cornwall's metalliferous mining industry had gone from leading world production to practically complete extinction. John Berryman traversed a landscape that still hummed with extractive labour. His world had been forged by the great copper mining boom of the eighteenth and nineteenth centuries.[11] It was a landscape crafted by capitalism at its most unashamedly rapacious. For outsiders, unfamiliar with the brute realities, both human and natural, of this extractive regime, Cornwall was, as Bernard Deacon puts it, a 'landscape of fire'.[12] Even those most impressed by its remarkable industrial achievements viewed Cornwall's mining districts in almost apocalyptic terms. James Watt, whose high-pressure engine designs enabled the expansion of deep-level mining, described the fields around Redruth where:

> The earth has been burrowed in all directions for miles upon miles in search of ore, principally copper—the surface presenting an unnaturally blasted and scarified appearance by reason of the 'deads' or refuse run out in heaps from the mine-heads. Engine-houses and chimneys are the most prominent features in the landscape, and dot the horizon as far as the eye can reach.[13]

These smoking chimneys, arsenic-burned moors and scattered, overflowing burrows were, Deacon writes, 'striking evidence that west Cornwall was leading the way into the fossil-fuel-driven industrialization that has since revolutionized the world'.[14] It has become usual in Cornish self-perception and myth to celebrate and to regret the passing of this extractive history, but mining in Cornwall arguably had much in common with the exploitation of other colonial resource frontiers. An 'internal colony' whose people and wealth were,

---

11 Bernard Deacon, *A Concise History of Cornwall* (University of Wales Press 2007) 104–11; Roger Burt and M. Timbell, 'Multiple Products and the Economics of the Mining Industries: The Case of Arsenic Production in South-West England, 1850-1914', (1991) 20, *Journal of European Economic History*, 379; Peter Joseph, 'The Arsenic Industry at Botallack Mine, Cornwall and Its Archaeology: A Story of Early 20th Century Adaptive Re-Use' (2012) 93, *British Mining*, 50; John F. M. Clark, *Bugs and the Victorians* (Yale University Press 2009), 149.

12 Bernard Deacon, '"The Hollow Jarring of the Distant Steam Engines": Images of Cornwall Between West Barbary and Delectable Duchy', in Ella Westland (ed.), *Cornwall: The Cultural Construction of Place*, (Patten Press 1997), 7–24.

13 James Watt quoted by Samuel Smiles in *Lives of the Engineers: The Steam-Engine. Boulton and Watt* (J. Murray 1874) 176.

14 Bernard Deacon, *The Real World of Poldark: Cornwall: 1783–1820* (Cornish Social and Economic Research Group 2021) 6; Martín Arboleda, *Planetary Mine: Territories of Extraction under Late Capitalism* (Verso Books 2020).

Deacon argues, 'locked into metropolitan-dominated circuits' of capital, making a small few extravagantly wealthy.[15] The lush gardens of this ruling class dotted the countryside, surrounded by stands of trees that obscured a ravaged land beyond. Adam Sharpe has calculated that during the period of the most intense exploitation from c.1750 to c.1850, perhaps as much as one-eighth of the entire land surface of Cornwall was turned over to deep-level excavation.[16] The driver of this extractive revolution was deep-level mining, a development demanded by the geology of copper ores and the progressive exhaustion of accessible surface deposits. The 'Cornish engine' and the productive reorganisation of labour around the 'tribute' system were an outcome of this need to dig deeper and deeper holes.

The 'prosperity' of metalliferous mining proved impermanent. And despite the occasional rags-to-riches story, the Cornish miner was rarely the largest beneficiary of his labours, an early death being a much more likely reward than a windfall.[17] Ultimately, in the 1860s and 1870s, imperial competition put an astonishingly sudden end to copper production.[18] The result, as for other Victorian resource frontiers, was social, cultural *and* environmental catastrophe.[19] In the century after 1860, Cornwall's population fell. At first, calamitously, then more slowly but consistently.[20] Exhausted copper mines closed. A

---

15 Bernard Deacon, *Industrial Celts: Making the Modern Cornish Identity, 1750–1870* (Cornish Social and Economic Research Group 2018) 114; John F. Richards, *The Unending Frontier: An Environmental History of the Early Modern World* (University of California Press 2003).

16 Adam Sharpe, 'The Evolution of the Cornwall and West Devon Landscapes as a Result of Industrialization from the Mid-Eighteenth Century to the Early Twentieth Century', (2005) 27, *Landscape History*, 65.

17 John Rule, 'Risky Business: Death, Injury and Religion in Cornish Mining c. 1780-1870', in John Rule, *Cornish Cases: Essays in Eighteenth and Nineteenth Century Social History* (Clio 2006), 70–97.

18 Deacon (n 15) 138–43.

19 John Bellamy Foster, 'Marx's Theory of Metabolic Rift: Classical Foundations for Environmental Sociology' (1999) 105(2) *American Journal of Sociology*, 366; John Tully, 'A Victorian Ecological Disaster: Imperialism, the Telegraph, and Gutta-Percha' (2009) 20(4), *Journal of World History*, 559; Gregory Rosenthal, 'Life and Labor in a Seabird Colony: Hawaiian Guano Workers, 1857–70' (2012) 17(4) *Environmental History*, 744; Hendrik Snyders, 'From Peru to Ichaboe: The Dynamics of a Shifting Guano Frontier, 1840–5', (2016) 48 (2) *African Historical Review*, 1.

20 Bernard Deacon, 'Deindustrialisation and Depopulation: The 1860s to the 1950s', *Cornish Studies Resources*, (2013) <https://bernarddeacon.com/demography/deindustrialisation-and-depopulation-the-1860s-to-the-1950s/> accessed 26 October 2022.

rural population sustained by combining mining and subsistence farming and fishing was uprooted to find employment in new operations overseas that only further accelerated Cornwall's decline.[21] Between the censuses of 1871 and 1881, the population of the Redruth sub-district, the heart of Cornwall's central mining district, fell by over 7,000.[22]

As this resource frontier faded, the chronic environmental legacies of extraction started to emerge. A landscape cluttered with derelict buildings, rivers and estuaries encumbered with sediment, poisoned agricultural land, and, of course, hundreds of poorly protected, now disused, shafts.[23] When Irene Berryman stepped foot outside her home, the years of Cornwall's mining riches were little more than memory. But beneath ever-shifting burrows of 'halvans', 'mundic' and 'deads', lay countless abandoned shafts: many rudimentarily 'sollared-over' with wooden planks in expectation of later re-opening. In 1961, when the Falmouth borough surveyor J.H.D. Penhale conducted a survey of dangerous shafts in the mid-Cornwall region, he identified 648 shafts, at least 300 of which 'could be considered sufficiently dangerous to require some form of attention.'[24] Identification was far from simple, however. The disused shaft was a weird type of ruin, quite unlike the derelict factory that has attracted most recent scholarly attention.[25] The derelict mine and its diverse entryways presented those traversing it with undetectable dangers. Even for local communities, dangerous shafts might be little more than a rumour or tradition, a secret kept among more adventurous young people.[26] The chronic danger of the shaft was embodied in a very *lack* of presence.

Disused shafts may have been difficult to see, but they were far from inert. In Cornwall's wet, humid climate, ground shifts, rainwater trickled through the earth, and wooden boards and supports rapidly rotted. Old workings continued

---

21 Philip J. Payton, *The Cornish Overseas: A History of Cornwall's 'Great Emigration'* (University of Exeter Press 2020).

22 Parliament. House of Commons, *Census of England and Wales 1881. Preliminary Report and Tables of Population and Houses enumerated in England and Wales, and Islands in British Seas*, Cmd.2955, vol XCVI, 1, 36.

23 Daniel R.S. Middleton, et al., 'Arsenic in Residential Soil and Household Dust in Cornwall, Southwest England: Potential Human Exposure and the Influence of Historical Mining', (2017) 19(4) *Environmental Science: Processes & Impacts*, 517.

24 *Scrapbooks on Mining Industry*, (1927–1970) 1, 61, ICS/JB, Box 42, University of Exeter Special Collections.

25 For an exception see Anna Storm, *Post-Industrial Landscape Scars* (Palgrave Macmillan 2014).

26 Hilary Orange, *Cornish Mining Landscapes: Public Perceptions of Industrial Archaeology in a Post-Industrial Society*, (PhD diss., University of London 2012) 250.

to entropically evolve long after their abandonment, embedded within a landscape itself changing with depopulation, deindustrialization, and the rise of tourism and leisure as trade. The abandoned shaft is a kind of 'hybrid object', a relic of human industry continually being worked upon by the persistent forces of decay.[27] Figure 5.1 gives a sense of just how thoroughly forgotten entryways might be overgrown and obscured when worked upon by ferns, gorse and the ever-present blackberry, in Edensor's words, 'erasing those edges which could be felt and looked at', which 'suggested the object was inviolable as a discrete entity'.[28] However, such object-oriented approaches tell us only so much. Disused shafts continued to evolve in the context of Cornwall's changing society and economy. There was also a powerfully social dimension to the 'fear of falling' that often overrode the physical materiality of the dangers posed by these uncanny objects. It is this social context that I explore in the rest of this paper. The 'risks' posed by these invisible dangers were not just determined by inhuman forces, but also by the social and economic afterlife of the post-extractive landscape. It is a story that, while intensely particular to Cornwall, is also universal, as the world comes to terms with the geophysical legacies of extractivism.

3. DANGER AND DECAY

As mines closed, the public danger of abandoned shafts was brought into clearer focus. In 1860, John Symonds wrote in the *Royal Cornwall Gazette* regarding a recent fatal encounter between a John Letcher of St Agnes and an abandoned shaft. Symonds wanted to alert the public to the 'great danger' associated with open shafts 'in mines that have ceased working.[29] Like John Berryman, Letcher, a member of the Board of Guardians, had been walking home on a dark winter night when he 'walked direct into a shaft 28 fathoms deep'. That such an accident could befall a respectable local notable underscored how the dangers of dereliction were distinct from those of producing mines. Accidents and disease were regarded as unremarkable commonplaces among working miners, in a culture marked by fatalism and the consoling rituals of large neighbourhood funerals.[30] Disused shafts, however, were no respecters of class differences. They imposed dangers at random, across class, across gender, across species and, most alarmingly, across time. These were

27 Jane Bennett, *Vibrant Matter: A Political Ecology of Things* (Duke University Press 2010).

28 Tim Edensor, *Industrial Ruins: Spaces, Aesthetics, and Materiality* (Berg 2005), 114.

29 'Open Shafts', *Royal Cornwall Gazette*, 24 February 1860, 5.

30 Rule (n 17), 80–85.

Source: Photo copyright Cornwall Council. Taken by Ken Quimby. Image courtesy of Kresen Kernow, Mine Shaft Capping AD2428/1/12/33.

Figure 5.1 *The 'industrial ruin' as invisible danger*

public, as opposed to specifically industrial risks, threatening any being traversing the land in a time and place when movement on foot remained the primary means of getting about, even for the well-off. What could be regarded in a *working* mine as an inevitable industrial accident, *abandonment* and the withdrawal of continuous labour turned into an unpredictable and inexplicable end to any passing unfortunate. The dangers of the mine were thus transferred from men at work to any man, woman or child, of any class who happened to stumble upon an industrial remnant. In democratizing risk across class, the mine shaft proved particularly transgressive. As Richard Newton, the coroner examining Letcher's demise, put it, his loss was a 'lamentable forfeit of a *valuable* [my emphasis] life only for the sake of a paltry sum of a half a crown's labour, which would have built a sufficient fence for the protection of everything.' The paradox of a 'valuable life' destroyed through a failure to apply a tiny amount of cheap labour reveals the way in which the chronic nature of the hazard measured and made visible differences of class in the post-productive landscape. A working mine might, over time, consume countless working-class bodies for the sake of paltry sums, but that it should consume a 'valuable' member of the Board of Guardians was intolerable.[31]

Newton's words also reveal the temporal implications of the disused shaft. Especially the way in which, in its very embodiment, in which rights of property intersected with the rights of the future and the agencies of nature created a *chronic* temporal problem. Only permanent periodic *future* additions of labour and materials could ultimately secure the public from these dangers. But this relied on the willingness of private owners to meet an unforeseen externality of the extractive industry; in short, their willingness to pay the permanent future price of past profits. Once capital had moved on from Cornwall's resource frontier, along with whatever profits it had managed to make, on whom should the responsibility and the cost of public safety pass? Who was to bear the ongoing costs of a past process of production when there were no more 'adventurers' willing to invest to call upon? The issue clearly perplexed the coroner, who asked: 'To whom must we direct attention to have this evil redressed? Is it the Lords of the land, or the adventurers who last wrought the mine? Are there any stipulations in the deeds or sets granted to adventurers to compel them for the protection of the public?'[32] His question

---

31 Catherine Mills has argued that, perhaps paradoxically, as the mining industry declined it simultaneously became more capital-intensive, and that occupational risks associated with new machinery *increased* occupational health risks in the later nineteenth century. See Catherine Mills, 'A Hazardous Bargain: Occupational Risk in Cornish Mining 1875–1914', (2005) 70(1) *Labour History Review*, 53.

32 'Open Shafts' (n 29).

reflected a remarkable bourgeois naiveté. If rights of property did not protect the lives of working miners, why expect them to rescue 'respectable' members of the public long after capital had fled? It was a question that would remain unresolved for a century.

By the third quarter of the nineteenth century, fatal or near-fatal encounters with abandoned shafts had become commonplace. In 1864 alone, the *West Briton* newspaper recorded a remarkable litany of deaths in the central mining district around Redruth and St Day. The victims included: several children playing among the old workings; a woman out for a walk; a 'respectable farmer' who happened to be blind, as well as one Mr Skewes of Gwennap who was 'supposed to have fallen into a shaft one fair night between Redruth and St Day but whose 'body has never been found It was claimed that outside one public house in Gwennap, there was a shaft that had claimed *eighteen* lives over the years, including two victims on the same night! This latter story was likely a myth, the product of the perverse fantasies of Cornwall's temperance culture. Nonetheless, that the tale was considered believable is a marker of just how common this kind of accident was becoming as copper mining declined. Even old workings at the remaining mines were dangerous. In 1864, two children, Frederick Charles Gill, 14, and Edwin Harris, 10, were both killed at Wheal Grambler, near St Day, when an old shaft, long forgotten, suddenly opened beneath them. The coroner decried the 'crying evil' and demanded that 'some steps should be taken for the protection of the public'.[33] He also referred to a previous case in February that year of one Mary Bawden, killed at Chacewater.[34]

The dangers of the abandoned shaft embodied an increasingly visible contradiction between what was presented as a 'public' need for safe movement and the rights of private property. In 1866, at an inquest into Timothy Collin's death at a disused East Polberro Mine, near St Agnes, this contradiction between public safety and private liability came into full view. The mine had recently been brought back into operation after many decades of closure, an instance, perhaps, of the forms of speculative investment that characterized Cornwall's mining industry in this period.[35] Remarkably, in this case, we hear the voice of Peter Rowse, a former miner, who was able to recall the history of the offending shaft's earlier life:

---

[33] 'Open Mine Shafts', *Royal Cornwall Gazette*, 20 May 1864, 6.

[34] *Ibid.*

[35] Gillian Burke and Peter Richardson, 'The Decline and Fall of the Cost Book System in the Cornish Tin Mining Industry, 1895–1914' (1981) 23(1) *Business History*, 4.

> I worked on the engine house when the shaft was sinking; the mine was then called Blue Hills; it is 44 years ago; the mine was knocked in 1825; the engine remained on this shaft some years after; when it was taken away. I took down the engine house; the shaft was then covered over by me; it remained covered over until about ten years ago, when it fell in.[36]

Rowse's memory encompassed enough time not only to cover his own work in closing up the shaft but also the work of nature that had undone this. No one appeared at all surprised that a solar in Cornwall's humid climate would fail; the quality of Rowse's work was not questioned; it was the way of things. Instead, the inquest offered a stage on which a three-way drama of responsibility played out between the mineral lord, the mine operator and the public authorities. James Daniel, surveyor for the Local Board of Highways, testified that the lessees' agent, Arthur Gripe, had refused to fence the offending shaft, saying that 'he did not consider it the duty of the adventurers to do it, or to be at the expense of securing the same, as they had never used that shaft.'[37] Gripe, a local man whose father had also been the previous mine agent, now found himself under the shadow of a manslaughter charge and remained silent, but his protection of the adventurers' interests was only in accord with the expected responsibilities of a mine 'captain' in this context. Unfortunately for Gripe, the coroner seemed primarily concerned to ensure an outcome that absolved the mineral lords, the Duchy of Cornwall, of responsibility for the offending pit. At the inquiry, he proudly flourished a letter from the Duchy's agent claiming that it had, in fact, instructed its lessees to enclose the shaft. Whether this 'letter' established any kind of formal covenant covering the lease of East Polberro was disputed. The jury asked to see a copy of the lease, but were prevented from doing so by the coroner. In this moment, the tensions between the coroner and the jury revealed the antagonism between the privileges of Crown property and the concerns of the local community, represented by the jury, to protect a local notable. Mine captains were important figures in the paternalist relations of small Cornish mining towns and villages of this period. Undoubtedly aware of where community sympathies lay, the coroner insisted that it was the jury's duty 'to consider, however painful it might be to their feelings, whether he [Gripe] had not opened himself up to a verdict of manslaughter' on account of the fact that 'although the managing agent of the mine did not take the grant or hold the lease, he had it in his power; he considered it the duty of the agent to secure those shafts'.[38] Ultimately, and at

---

36 'Unprotected Mine Shafts', *Royal Cornwall Gazette*, Thursday 27 September 1866, 8.

37 *Ibid.*

38 *Ibid.*

the coroner's barely concealed urging, a verdict of manslaughter was returned against the unfortunate captain.

Gripe's unfortunate encounter with the law reveals how local elites were trying to navigate the contradictions between public safety and private property. These carried peculiar sensitivities in a social context defined by the 'dispersed paternalism of Cornwall's peculiar industrial geography, accentuated by industrial decline.[39] Unsurprisingly, one response by Cornwall's elite was to look to Parliament, and particularly the putative Mines Regulation Bill, to take responsibility out of their hands and clarify responsibility for the safety and protection of disused sites. In 1872, John Waters, a boy of ten, was killed after falling ten fathoms at the then, still-operating, South Condurrow mine, at Beacon near Camborne: another reminder that even working mines were riddled with old, unused shafts.[40] At the subsequent inquest, the coroner's jury 'censured the manager of the mine for permitting the shaft to remain unsecured'. The *Royal Cornwall Gazette* reported that the accident 'shows the necessity of a speedy passing of the Mines Regulation Bill.[41] Stimulated by the Kinnaird Commission's investigation into workplace safety in the metalliferous mines, the Metalliferous Mines Regulation Act was finally enacted by Parliament in 1872, albeit in the face of much self-interested opposition from well-represented owners of mineral rights. The Act originated in the well-meaning intention of industrial safety, but with the decline of metalliferous mining in Cornwall, it ultimately had a more important legacy in the county as the only legislation covering the safety of derelict mines until it was superseded by the Mines and Quarries Act, 1954. The 1872 legislation required appropriate 'fencing' of any abandoned shaft that lay within fifty yards of a highway, and as Mills has observed in her thorough account of the Act, most of the earliest prosecutions brought under the legislation were for failures to secure abandoned shafts.[42]

The years after the Act's passing were remarkable for the degree of resistance from private landowners to enforcement of the legislation. Given middle-class concern in the 1860s over the dangers presented by shafts, both landowners and local authorities exhibited an incredibly persistent tendency to regard enforcement as a matter of private privilege rather than a public responsibility imposed by national legislation. Their resistance is revealed in the continual frustration expressed by the local Inspectors of Mines. In 1880, for example, HM Inspectors, Clement Le Neve Foster and Robert James Frecheville,

---

39 Deacon (n 14), 167–95.

40 'Unprotected Mine Shafts', *Royal Cornwall Gazette*, April 13, 1872, 5.

41 *Ibid.*

42 Catherine Mills, *Regulating Health and Safety in the British Mining Industries, 1800–1914* (Routledge 2016) 153.

reported the 'persistent disregard to repeated notices' by the Liskeard Board of Guardians respecting shafts near a highway, first reported in 1877. Despite subsequent complaints of inaction, 'up to the middle of June 1879, nothing had been done direct interventions by the Home Office and the Local Government Board brought no improvement and the inspectors complained that 'at the end of July the shafts were still unfenced The Liskeard Board reported in 1880 that the shafts were 'filling up' yet a further complaint was made 'by a person that he had fallen into one of the shafts on 8th January but had luckily escaped with a severe shaking and some bruises. Upon inspection, Le Neve Foster observed, 'it appeared that his story was correct; the shafts were neither filled up nor fenced; and the Liskeard Rural Sanitary Authority had been led into making an erroneous statement owing to a false report from their late inspector.[43] In August, the Board of Guardians again notified the Local Government Board that the work of fencing 'was finished', but the Inspectors asserted, with understandable frustration, that 'we are still unable to confirm the correctness of this statement, as the shafts are not securely fenced even at the present time.' While unclear how far this incompetence was intended or inadvertent, the exchange is a revealing insight into the reluctance of a public authority to accept the ratepayers' responsibility for a danger they had not created. Indeed, the owner of the property on which the offending shafts were located was alleged to be 'a bankrupt, who had absconded, and was thought to be living somewhere in America.'

Resistance to compliance with the 1872 Act reflected the continuing weakness of the British state in late nineteenth-century Cornwall. Local oligarchic control of local boards and Unions remained strong in the Duchy, whose working-class communities were also notable for a popular libertarian suspicion of agents of the crown.[44] The Fortescue family, who owned the Boconnoc Estate, which held considerable mining and quarrying rights in the east of the county, appear to have been particularly persistent resisters to the implementation of public safety at private expense. Between 1876 and 1879, the energetic Le Neve Foster tackled the Fortescues' agent, William Pease, over unfenced shafts at setts including Blencowe Consols, Tregardock Mine, Stenna Gwyn Mine, Cromwell Mine, Tin Hill, Dowgas Mine and Wheal Fortescue.[45] A particular source of frustration was the evident insistence on the part of the Boconnoc Estate that its lessees alone were liable to fence dangerous shafts. Le Neve

---

43 'The Fencing of Abandoned Mine Shafts', *Royal Cornwall Gazette*, 8 July 1881, 7.

44 Edward P. Thompson, 'The Moral Economy of the English Crowd in the Eighteenth Century' (1971) 50 *Past & Present*, 76.

45 Clement Le Neve Foster to Captain Fortescue, 8 September 1877, F/3/17/48, Kresen Kernow.

Foster was persistent that Mr Pease was 'very evidently mistaken about the liability incurred by you [the Boconnoc Estate] under the Mines Regulation Act', and that 'it is your duty to see that your lessees do the work'. His frustration was plain in a letter eventually addressed directly to Captain Fortescue himself, that Pease 'ought to have attended to the matter long ago … I write plainly,' he continued, 'as I do not wish there to be any misunderstanding on the subject'. Though, whether the work was ever completed to Le Neve Foster's satisfaction is unclear.[46] Le Neve Foster's letters reveal how properties' interests could exploit a supposed ambiguity in liability between mineral lords, the lessees or former lessees of mining rights to overburden and confused attempts by public authorities to secure dangerous shafts. In 1917, the Atlas Boring Company of London was fined £5 for their failure to protect an open shaft at Breage, and the Inspector of Mines, Mr Boydell, reported 'a great deal of correspondence with the Company, in the course of which they had promised to do what was necessary to protect the shaft but they clearly had not done so.[47] As late as 1962, local authorities were still complaining of obstructive disputes between landowners and the owners of mineral rights over responsibility for trivial precautions such as signage.[48] For over a century, and despite legislative efforts to secure public safety, the dangerous shaft lingered, a menace that private property was reluctant to acknowledge and for which local government was equally reluctant to take public responsibility.

4. MONSTERS IN THE LANDSCAPE

Cornwall's political economy was reconstituted at the end of the nineteenth century. Changing the county's image as a landscape was a key part of this transformation. Cornwall's reputation as a destination for walkers stretched back to at least the mid-nineteenth century, when the railways began opening the county to direct access from London. This was the era in which Wilkie Collins undertook his walks that would reach a popular audience in the popular *Rambles Beyond Railways*.[49] Cornwall's peculiar ecology and numerous footpaths also appealed to a new breed of 'peripatetic natural historians' and collectors.[50] In their wake, a new mode of extracting value from the landscape

46 *Ibid.*

47 'Dangerous Mine Shaft at Breage', *The Cornishman*, Thursday 27 September 1917, 5.

48 'Dangerous Mineshafts to Have Notices', *The Cornishman*, 11 January 1961; *Scrapbooks on Mining Industry* (n 24).

49 Wilkie Collins, *Rambles beyond Railways* (R. Bentley 1865).

50 Harvey Taylor, *A Claim on the Countryside: A History of the British Outdoor Movement* (Keele University Press 1997).

developed, a product of a coalition of urban commercial interests eager to cash in on the sudden popular fascination with this land of 'druid relics' and ancient, exotic ferns. Alongside, the Great Western Railway's own commercial interests in encouraging long-distance journeys into the South West, the late-nineteenth century saw hoteliers, tradespeople and political elites seek to valorize this emerging environmental imaginary of Cornwall as a place of 'sub-tropical climate and clean air', a world away from the 'landscape of fire'.[51] Seaside towns like Penzance and Newquay emerged as centres for a new brand of 'green tourism', nodal points in a network of footpaths stretching along the coast as well as further inland across moors and dunes.[52]

For Wilkie Collins, the working mine was still part of the landscape of a 'celebrated mineral country'.[53] Dereliction made post-industrial dangers a matter of life and death to those who came after. In 1893, a popular guidebook, the *Handbook for Travellers in Cornwall*, published by John Murray, felt it necessary to offer a 'Caution to Pedestrians' that 'a certain danger attends a walking tour in the mining district of Cornwall from the unprotected pits of abandoned mines, too often left open as pitfalls in the way of unsuspecting travellers, and either unguarded or insufficiently fenced round.'[54] The dangers were very real. In 1875, George Robinson wrote to the *Cornish Telegraph* to express his 'mingled feeling of awe and thankfulness' that he and a party of family and friends 'in their rambles after wildflowers' near Cape Cornwall had been spared a terrible fate when discovering 'half hidden by furze, bushes and fringed with ferns . . . several deep pits probably air shafts to the mines.' This near miss had had a powerful impact on Robinson, as the 'feeling of horror at the possibility of some fatal catastrophe arising from the unprotected condition of these yawning pits of destruction is yet very strong upon me.'

It is perhaps a later dispute over rights of access to the Perran Sands on the North Coast of Cornwall that offers the deepest insight into how a changing landscape imaginary intersected with the chronic dangers of disused shafts. The setting of a small early medieval oratory, supposed to have been built by the fifth-century Irish saint, St Piran, the sands gathered significance in the wake of the late-Victorian 'Celtic Revival' as a supposed site of early

[51] Richard Harris, 'Building Regional Identity: Social and Cultural Significance of Railways for Cornwall in the Late Nineteenth and Early Twentieth Centuries' (2020) 41(2) *The Journal of Transport History*, 254.

[52] David Prynn, 'The Clarion Clubs, Rambling and the Holiday Associations in Britain Since the 1890s' (1976) 11(2) *Journal of Contemporary History*, 65; Melanie Tebbutt, 'Rambling and Manly Identity in Derbyshire's Dark Peak, 1880s-1920s' (2006) 49(4) *Historical Journal*, 1125; Taylor (n 50), 95.

[53] Collins (n 49), 155.

[54] *A Handbook for Travellers in Cornwall* (John Murray 1893) 12.

Celto-Cornish Christianity. St Piran, somewhat appropriately, is the patron saint of tinners, and the sands surrounding the oratory have been subject to extensive historic mining. The sets of Budnick Mine, Wheal Vlow, Gravelhill, Phoenix and Penhale Mines all lie within or border the sands. By the end of the nineteenth century, all were abandoned. One commentator estimated that between 150 and 200 shafts were hidden among the sands' reedy, undulating mounds.[55]

In the early twentieth century, the area became a focus of a temperamental dispute between at least one 'rambler' and local property owners. We can trace the dispute through a series of letters written by 'Rambler' to the *Western Morning News* in 1915. Observing that, 'At the present time one may easily find in the above district a considerable number of open unfenced and insecurely fenced mine shafts, some of which are distinctly dangerous', one local walker argued that they prevented free movement across the sands, as well as access to the oratory. However, it was the continuing presence of the danger that sparked controversy, as it was claimed by free access proponents that the dangers were being cynically tolerated by property owners as a deliberate means of deterring walkers from exercising rights of access. It was also argued that compliant local authorities were deliberately 'apathetic with regard to these public dangers.[56] The access rights activist's intervention sparked a brief but fiery exchange. 'Resident' replied that: 'As a matter of fact, the Sandhills are *private property* [my italics] in the occupation of tenants who, together with those connected with the mining rights, alone have any business there and that 'the public who leave the paths and wander into danger are trespassers and do so at their own peril.'[57] S. Clark, agent for one of these owners, wrote, asserting that 'Rambler had no right to trespass on what is private property and thereby no business complaining [that] shafts were a public danger.'[58] This hardly refuted 'Rambler's' claims, and he soon returned to the fray, suggesting that this was 'a strange way of attracting the public to what might be made a popular health and holiday resort', adding for good patriotic measure the story of a young soldier of the Devon and Cornwall Light Infantry, who had suffered serious injury falling down a pit near Lostwithiel during night operations.[59] The participants in this struggle revealed very different perceptions of the

---

55 Barton (n 6), 239.

56 'Discarded Mine Shafts in the Helston District', *Western Morning News*, 19 April 1915, 6.

57 'Undefended Mine Shafts in the Perranporth District', *Western Morning News*, 1 May 1915, 3.

58 'Undefended Mineshafts in the Perranporth District', *Western Morning News*, 8 May 1915, 7.

59 *Ibid.*

rights of property, access, and risk in Cornwall's landscape. An advocate for private property, 'Occupier', opined that 'If the beach, cliffs, paths, roads and lanes will not accommodate them [i.e., tourists], they ought to be otherwise looked after.[60] 'Resident', framed dangerous shafts as a bizarre kind of conservation measure, protecting the Oratory from what he called 'unscrupulous marauders'.[61]

Retrospectively, this insistence that tourists be kept to beaches and cliff paths may now appear hopelessly naïve, but it is possible that the defenders of property had an eye on the prospect of reopening former mines. What, though, are we to make of 'Rambler's' attack on the abandoned shaft as a kind of wilful sabotage? The deliberate reproduction of a chronic danger as a protection of property rights and privacy. His assertion that rural councils have 'only quite recently' begun to realize that they had statutory powers to address the danger, perhaps signalled a wider shift amongst local political elites.[62] We have seen that property owners actively resisted statutory protection of the public at the end of the nineteenth century. But as local authorities deepened their interests in tourism, protecting the rights of a defunct industry must have seemed increasingly antediluvian. The powers of the 1872 Act were now something that the access activist could exploit. 'FRGS', wrote how: 'I and others have reported such death-traps occurring on private property and it had been not little satisfaction to note the impotent rage of one owner when he received orders from H.M. Inspectors and found that he was forced to comply with them to the great amusement of his neighbours.'[63] Yet, despite this clear turn towards a recognition of the law and of the chronic risks of the mine shaft to public safety, abandoned shafts remained a stubborn presence in the landscape well into the twentieth century. The combination of legislation and public complaint could only achieve so much against the resistance of private property and the increasing seclusion of the mine shaft's own presence.

5. PAST, PRESENT, FUTURE?

Despite the very real dangers of disused shafts, what is most remarkable is how the danger was *tolerated* for so long. If the disused shaft represented an ECE, then it was an ECE imposed in part as the result of a social and political choice to ignore and circumvent legal responsibility and public safety. Only at the end of the twentieth century was any coordinated effort to make former

60 'Unprotected Mine Shafts', *Western Morning News*, 22 May 1915.

61 *Ibid.*

62 'Correspondence', *Western Morning News*, Tuesday 25 May 1915.

63 'Undefended Mineshafts in the Perranporth District', *The Cornishman*, 13 May 1915, 5.

mining sites safe finally attempted. In the 1980s, Carrick District Council finally commissioned a report into dangerous shafts in its area. Written by Cornwall Mining Services Limited, it began with a nod to the chronic nature of the extractive past's legacies in the present.

> The danger of old and forgotten mine workings and the related subsidence damage to property and injury to persons has existed for many centuries in Cornwall and seems to have been accepted and regarded as a local nuisance rather than a real hazard. Besides the known cases of injuries or fatalities it is considered a statistical certainty that a significant percentage of missing persons have fallen down shafts while being alone. The public knowledge and awareness of the dangers associated with mine workings is probably less than at any time in the past, especially to the large annual influx of tourists.[64]

As Rambler's intervention in the 1910s showed, it was not the case that this hazard had just been 'accepted' by local people. In 1898, an exasperated 'Father' had written to *The Cornishman* to 'express, for others as well as self, our anxiety for the safety of children who have to be, or will get near, mine-shafts 'It is a lamentable sight,' he wrote, 'to see so many of the circular stone hedges, which should protect people from these death traps, partly torn down, so damaged, at any rate, that a child can walk inside the enclosure with ease, and should he fall down the fearful chasm he would never more be seen.'[65] He suggested instead the provision of a modern, if intrusive, 'protective concrete wall seven or eight feet high, so that no boy or girl can stick their toes into it, as they do into the interstices of roughly built stone hedges, to search for birds' nests, or mundic-pickers to search for mundic, till, probably, some loved one is lost.' He hoped that 'some authority' or 'legally bound person' would put an end to the 'shilly-shally' and address the problem.

As we have seen, this did not happen, and it might be more accurate to conclude with 'Rambler' that the dangers of the disused shaft had, for different reasons, been tacitly colluded in by both local authorities and private property owners. By the 1980s, the mine shaft danger had endured for over a century. Carrick Council's investigation, which revealed over 2,800 shafts of concern, signalled the beginning of a change in official attitudes. During the 1980s, 'Operation Minecap', a project partially funded by the government's Manpower Services Commission, initiated a process of sealing open shafts, in which private property owners were financially relieved by direct government subsidy of the responsibility for former mineral workings. This project was made technically feasible, not by concrete walls but by the 'Clwyd Minecap'

64 Cornwall Mining Services Limited, 'Report on Survey of Mine Shafts, Carrick Area', 1980, AD2428/1/1, Kresen Kernow.

65 'Correspondence', *The Cornishman*, 17 March 1898, 6.

system. A steel mesh plug filled with concrete that acted as a self-righting 'plug' to a shaft.[66] Many shafts have now been closed up, but uncapped shafts still exist on private property across Cornwall to this day.[67] Such remaining open shafts are sought out by 'urban' explorers seeking access to the industrial past hidden within.[68]

In the early twenty-first century, Cornwall faces the prospect of a resurgence of mining.[69] It is therefore timely to reflect on the chronic environmental consequences of historic extractive processes. In this essay, we have peered into the disused shaft as a remarkably persistent chronic danger. Insofar as the hazards of former mine workings offered a lasting challenge to establishing a sense of distance from the industrial 'past', they call to mind precisely the 'open temporality' which literary scholar Elizabeth Miller has argued characterizes the 'undead futures' left by extractive capital. Forms of exhaustion that deny 'the possibility of futurity' while paradoxically also refusing an 'ending or closure'.[70] It is perhaps this 'undead futurity' that characterizes the temporality of specifically ECEs, the way in which the zombie forms of past extractive or exploitative processes stumble into the present and the future in unforeseeable ways. The disused shaft uncannily connected the worlds of Irene and John Berryman across decades. Their near misses offer a haunting insight into the bodily terrors experienced by others who were not so lucky. The post-extractive afterlife of Cornwall's land surface illustrates the real importance of more-than-human terrestrial forces in everyday life: an array of actants, from blackberry bushes and fences to rotting planks and the subsiding collars of the shafts themselves, which consistently threatened to unmake

---

66 North Cornwall District Council, Leaflet, 'Free Disused Mineshaft Capping Project', 1984, PCTEA/3/71/2, Kresen Kernow.

67 B. Gamble, M. Anderson, and J. S. Griffiths, 'Hazards Associated with Mining and Mineral Exploitation in Cornwall and Devon, SW England' (2020) 29(1) *Geological Society, London, Engineering Geology Special Publications*, 321.

68 Bradley L. Garrett, 'Urban Explorers: Quests for Myth, Mystery and Meaning' (2010) 4(10), *Geography Compass*, 1448.

69 'Mining Firm Hopes to Extract Lithium from Cornwall's Hot Springs', (*The Guardian*, 19 January 2017) <http://www.theguardian.com/uk-news/2017/jan/19/cornwall-mining-firm-extract-lithium> accessed 29 May 2020; Jasper Jolly, '"The Part of Cornwall Nobody Ever Sees": The Hi-Tech Future for Lithium and Tin Mining', (*The Guardian*, 20 October 2022) <https://www.theguardian.com/business/2022/oct/20/the-part-of-cornwall-nobody-ever-sees-the-hi-tech-future-for-lithium-and-tin-mining> accessed 25 October 2022.

70 Elizabeth Carolyn Miller, 'Drill, Baby, Drill: Extraction Ecologies, Open Temporalities, and Reproductive Futurity in the Provincial Realist Novel' (2020) 48(1) *Victorian Literature and Culture*, 42.

the 'modernity' of the Cornish landscape. However, the same history shows how firmly those dangers remained embedded in social, economic and legal relationships, most especially in the struggle between public safety and private property. As Cornwall looks ahead to the possible continuation of its history as a resource frontier, this time in the extraction of lithium and other 'strategic minerals', it becomes urgently necessary to ask who should bear the *unforeseeable* costs of any renewal of Cornwall's history as an extractive frontier.

6. Minamata disease as an environmental chronic emergency: institutional failures and global lessons

Shuichi Furuya

1. INTRODUCTION

Minamata disease remains one of the most devastating environmental and public health disasters of the twentieth century, exposing the long-term consequences of industrial pollution and the systemic failures in governance, legal accountability and human rights protections. Officially identified in 1956 in Minamata City, Japan, the disease resulted from chronic exposure to methylmercury-contaminated fish and shellfish, a consequence of industrial wastewater discharged by the Chisso Corporation.[1] The poisoning led to severe neurological disorders, congenital disabilities and multi-generational health impacts. However, it was not until 1968—more than a decade after the first cases were reported—that the Japanese government officially acknowledged the cause of the disease, reflecting a prolonged period of denial, scientific controversy and corporate resistance.

Minamata disease is more than a historical case of industrial pollution; it exemplifies what this book qualifies as an 'Environmental Chronic Emergency' ('ECE'). Unlike acute environmental disasters such as oil spills or chemical explosions, ECEs unfold gradually, often evading immediate legal and policy responses. These prolonged crises challenge traditional legal frameworks, which prioritize sudden and spectacular events over slow-moving environmental harms that accumulate over generations. The protracted nature of Minamata disease underscores the dangers of regulatory inertia, where delayed recognition and inadequate response mechanisms exacerbate long-term human suffering. This case demonstrates how environmental

1 House of Representatives Research Bureau, Environment Research Office, *Overview of the Minamata Disease Issue* (in Japanese) (2015), 13.

degradation, when compounded by political inertia and corporate influence, can create enduring public health crises that disproportionately affect marginalized populations.

One of the defining characteristics of Minamata disease is its deeply gendered impact. Women, particularly those of childbearing age, bore the brunt of mercury poisoning due to biological susceptibility and social roles that placed them at heightened risk. Mercury exposure during pregnancy led to congenital Minamata disease, which affected children from birth, demonstrating the intergenerational consequences of industrial pollution. Additionally, women in affected communities played crucial roles as caregivers for victims, shouldering the emotional, physical, and economic burdens of the crisis. Despite their central position in the struggle for recognition and justice, women were largely excluded from decision-making processes, compensation schemes and legal redress mechanisms. Their experiences exemplify broader patterns of environmental injustice, where the voices of women remain marginalized in both policy responses and historical narratives.

Understanding Minamata disease through the lens of 'slow violence' provides a critical framework for analyzing its long-term effects. Created by environmental scholar Rob Nixon, slow violence describes harm that is incremental, invisible and temporally dispersed,[2] often escaping media attention and legal accountability. In the case of Minamata, the invisible accumulation of mercury in the food chain and the delayed onset of symptoms made it difficult to establish causality and mobilize timely legal interventions. Moreover, the slow and contested recognition of victims—many of whom struggled for decades to receive official acknowledgement and compensation— reflects the persistent failures of legal and political systems to address human rights violations with long-term consequences. Compared to sudden industrial disasters that capture immediate media attention, Minamata disease illustrates how environmental harm that unfolds over decades often lacks the urgency needed to prompt swift regulatory action.

This article situates Minamata disease within international human rights law, emphasizing the obligations of states to prevent, mitigate, and remedy environmental harm. The Minamata Convention on Mercury, adopted in 2013, represents a critical step toward global mercury regulation, yet its effectiveness hinges on how well it incorporates gender-sensitive approaches to environmental governance. While the Convention focuses on mercury regulation, it falls short in addressing gender-specific vulnerabilities, making the Gender Action Plan (GAP) a crucial supplement. The Plan, adopted in 2023, seeks to fill this

---

2 Rob Nixon, *Slow Violence and the Environmentalism of the Poor* (Harvard University Press 2011) 2.

gap by ensuring that women's rights and roles are integrated into mercury governance through measures such as gender-disaggregated data collection, targeted health interventions and economic support for women in affected communities.

The present article argues for a more nuanced legal and policy framework that recognizes chronic environmental harm as a human rights issue.[3] By analysing Minamata disease through the intersecting lenses of gender, slow violence and international legal obligations, this article highlights the urgent need for a legal paradigm shift—one that moves beyond reactive responses to immediate disasters and instead fosters proactive, gender-responsive mechanisms for addressing long-term environmental injustices. The lessons of Minamata must serve not only as a warning but also as a foundation for strengthening international commitments to environmental justice, public health and human rights protection.

2. UNRAVELING MINAMATA

2.1 Delayed Response and Institutional Failures

Minamata disease is a severe neurological disorder caused by methylmercury poisoning. Symptoms include numbness in the hands and feet, tremors, muscle weakness, loss of coordination and impairments in speech and vision. In extreme cases, it leads to paralysis, coma, and death.[4] One of the most devastating consequences was the emergence of congenital Minamata disease, where fetuses were exposed to methylmercury in utero via the placenta when pregnant women consumed contaminated seafood. Infants born with congenital Minamata disease suffered from cerebral palsy-like symptoms, severe developmental impairments and lifelong disabilities.[5]

---

3 Marcos Orellana, Special Rapporteur on the implications for human rights of the environmentally sound management and disposal of hazardous substances and wastes, points out that 'A human rights-based approach to confront the global toxic tide is indispensable. It calls for scrutinizing not only direct impacts on individuals but also inequities affecting persons and groups that suffer disproportionate impacts because of marginalization, persecution and colonization and, additionally or specifically, due to their sex or gender (UNGA, Gender and hazardous substances [16 July 2024] Report of the Special Rapporteur on the implications for human rights of the environmentally sound management and disposal of hazardous substances and wastes, Marcos Orellana, UN Doc A/79/163, para. 2).

4 House of Representatives Research Bureau (n 1) 1.

5 Masazumi Harada and Masami Tajiri, 'A Clinical Epidemiological Study on Congenital and Fetal Minamata Disease: An Analysis of the Effects of

Despite the official confirmation of Minamata disease in 1956, the actual contamination and human exposure had begun decades earlier. Methylmercury was a byproduct of acetaldehyde production, which Chisso Corporation had been manufacturing at its Minamata plant since 1932. Later research suggested that the first unrecognized cases of Minamata disease likely appeared as early as 1941, meaning that exposure had been occurring silently for at least 15 years before authorities officially acknowledged the disease.

In fact, concerns over industrial pollution from Chisso predated Minamata disease itself. In 1942, a large-scale fishery collapse occurred in Minamata Bay, severely impacting local fishermen's livelihoods. While this event was not recognized at the time as being linked to mercury, it was clear that the factory's wastewater was harming the marine ecosystem. The following year, Chisso compensated the affected fishermen, yet continued to deny any responsibility for the contamination.[6] Had Chisso, or the government, responded to this earlier environmental crisis with stringent wastewater regulations, the conditions leading to Minamata disease might have been mitigated or even prevented. This represents one of several missed intervention points where effective governance could have halted the crisis before it escalated into a full-scale ECE.

In the early 1950s, observable signs of mercury poisoning began appearing in animals before the disease was formally recognized in humans. In 1953, residents noticed that local cats were exhibiting abnormal behaviours, including seizure-like movements and erratic running before sudden death. This condition became known locally as 'dancing cat disease'. By 1955, entire cat populations in the coastal villages were wiped out.[7] At the time, these mass die-offs were dismissed as a curiosity, but in retrospect, they were clear indicators of an escalating environmental disaster.

Meanwhile, in 1956, doctors at Chisso's own company hospital observed severe neurological symptoms in local residents, leading them to report the outbreak to public health authorities. Yet, despite early warnings, both the company and government displayed a pattern of denial, deflection and minimal intervention. In 1957, preliminary investigations identified contaminated seafood as the probable source of poisoning, prompting local fishery cooperatives to self-impose fishing bans in Minamata Bay. However, rather than

---

Methylmercury Contamination on Fetuses and Infants' (2009), 14 *Syakai Kankei Kenkyu [Social Relations Study],* 2–5 (in Japanese).

[6] Interview of Professor Mika Hirose, Kokugakuin University, 'Reasons Why the Ashio and Minamata Incidents Became Major Environmental Disasters Over Several Decades' (2018), <https://jbpress.ismedia.jp/articles/-/53852> (in Japanese).

[7] House of Representatives Research Bureau (n 1) 3.

implementing official preventive measures, the national government refused to prohibit fishing, citing a lack of definitive scientific proof.

By 1959, researchers at Kumamoto University had identified organic mercury as the toxic agent, strongly implicating Chisso's wastewater as the cause of the disease. Yet, the company, rather than implementing pollution controls, continued to deny responsibility outright. Chisso's corporate leadership actively dismissed the findings, with its CEO publicly rejecting the mercury poisoning theory.[8] This institutionalized denial was not merely corporate defiance—it reflected deeper political and economic structures that shielded Chisso from accountability.

Chisso was not just another industrial corporation—it was a central pillar of Japan's post-war economy. Originally a key player in Japan's military-industrial complex before World War II, the company suffered massive losses after the war, but reestablished itself as a major force in Japan's chemical industry during the post-war economic boom. During the 1950s and 1960s, Japan's rapid industrialization was heavily reliant on chemical production, with Chisso pioneering the domestic manufacture of vinyl chloride and octanol, both of which required acetaldehyde, a process that produced methylmercury as a byproduct.

At the time, Japan's industrial policy strongly prioritized economic growth over environmental and public health concerns. Chisso's tax contributions accounted for over half of Minamata City's municipal revenue, effectively making the city economically dependent on the company. This created a situation where local government officials were reluctant to take action that could threaten Chisso's business operations. Residents who criticized the company were sometimes met with hostility from their own communities, as their protests were perceived as threats to local jobs and economic stability.[9]

This economic entanglement contributed to the government's hesitation to hold Chisso accountable, despite the availability of legal mechanisms to do so. In 1958, Japan passed the Water Pollution Control Laws, which empowered authorities to regulate factory effluents. Similarly, Kumamoto Prefecture had Fisheries Adjustment Regulations that could have been used to restrict Chisso's wastewater discharge. Yet, neither law was enforced against Chisso, illustrating how political and economic considerations took precedence over public health and environmental protection.

As pressure mounted over mercury contamination in Minamata Bay, Chisso responded not by stopping production, but by relocating pollution to new

8 Ministry of the Environment, *The Origin of Environmental Issues: 50 Years of Minamata Disease* (2006), 41–4 (in Japanese).

9 Interview of Professor Mika Hirose (n 6).

areas. In 1958, Chisso modified its wastewater disposal system, redirecting factory effluents from Minamata Bay to the Minamata River under the pretense of improving conditions. This merely transferred the contamination further downstream, leading to new cases of poisoning in previously unaffected regions.[10]

This act of pollution displacement represents a classic tactic in ECEs, where industrial actors prioritize short-term economic stability over long-term health and ecological security. By failing to implement pollution controls and instead shifting waste disposal sites, Chisso prolonged exposure and expanded the affected areas, worsening the crisis.

2.2 Gendered Dimensions of Exposure

In 1965, nine years after the first outbreak, a second outbreak of Minamata disease occurred in Niigata, demonstrating that the crisis was not an isolated event but a systemic industrial hazard. Unlike in Minamata, Niigata University Medical School conducted more structured epidemiological studies, leading to the first public acknowledgement of the link between mercury levels in pregnant women and foetal health risks. The findings of the epidemiological studies were alarming. On July 22, 1965, researchers tested the hair mercury levels of seventy-eight women of childbearing age in affected districts, revealing that more than half of the women had levels of more than 50 ppm.

In response, the Niigata local government issued an emergency directive on July 23, 1965, outlining a series of coercive reproductive measures under the pretext of 'public health protection': (a) Mandatory medical testing for pregnant women—those with high mercury levels were pressured into terminating their pregnancies; (b) Recommendations for sterilization and birth control—women with mercury levels above 50 ppm were strongly encouraged to undergo sterilization; and (c) Breastfeeding restrictions—mothers with high mercury levels were prohibited from breastfeeding and instructed to switch to artificial formula.[11]

---

10 Ministry of the Environment, *Lessons from Minamata Disease and Japan's Mercury Policy* (2013), 3 (in Japanese).

11 Sayaka Satoho, 'A Problem of Pregnancy Regulation in Niigata Minamata Disease: From the Perspective of Eugenics and Feminist Ethics' (2020), 38 *Igaku Tetsugaku Igaku Rinri [Journal of Philosophy and Ethics in Health Care and Medicine]*, 15–16 (in Japanese); Sadako Urasaki, 'A Gender Perspective on Niigata Minamata Disease: Examination and Analysis of "Pregnancy Regulation" and "Breastfeeding Prohibition" (2005) 34 *Gendai Shakai Bunka Kenkyu [Contemporary Socio-Cultural Studies]*, 108–111 (in Japanese).

Notably, Minamata disease is neither an infectious disease nor genetically inherited, yet its intergenerational transmission through maternal exposure to environmental contaminants raises profound reproductive rights concerns. The fact that women unknowingly passed mercury poisoning to their children, who were subsequently born with irreversible neurological damage, underscores a violation of their right to a safe and healthy pregnancy. This failure to prevent exposure, despite early warnings, constitutes an environmental reproductive injustice, depriving women of informed choices regarding their pregnancies and undermining their bodily autonomy.

Instead of ensuring women's reproductive autonomy and protecting them from further mercury exposure, these measures placed the burden of response on women's bodies, reinforcing state control over their reproductive choices.[12] The Japanese media exacerbated public anxiety, publishing headlines such as 'Mercury Detected in Healthy Women's Hair', 'Fetal Deformities Expected' and 'Government Advises Against Pregnancy'. The sensationalized coverage coerced women into reproductive decisions they did not fully consent to, thereby compounding state-imposed reproductive injustices.

The full extent of these coercive measures remains unclear, but court testimonies from the Niigata Minamata disease trials revealed that at least seven women underwent forced sterilization or coerced abortions between August 1965 and June 1967. These women later filed lawsuits arguing that state policies had violated their reproductive rights and bodily autonomy, seeking damages for the irreversible consequences imposed upon them.[13]

From a human rights and legal standpoint, these actions constitute a direct violation of reproductive freedom. Instead of implementing policies to prevent mercury exposure and hold industrial polluters accountable, the Japanese government intervened only to regulate women's fertility, effectively blaming women for potential future cases of congenital Minamata disease. This gendered form of slow violence—where women's bodies became sites of both environmental harm and legal control—demonstrates the intersection of reproductive injustice and state neglect in ECEs.

12 *Ibid.*, at 119.

13 *Sakutaro Ohno v Showa Denko*, Judgment by the Niigata District Court (29 September 1974), In 22 *Kakyu Saibansyo Minji Saibannreisyu [Lower Court Civil Case Reports]*, Nos. 9 and 10, Supplement, 1.

3. JUDICIAL AND GOVERNMENTAL RESPONSES TO MINAMATA DISEASE

3.1 The Protracted Struggle for Victim Redress

The history of Minamata disease victim redress is characterized by a complex interplay of litigation, political settlements and legislative measures, none of which have resulted in a comprehensive resolution. Even after nearly seventy years since the official recognition of the disease, a significant number of victims remain unrecognized or uncompensated. The fragmented and incremental nature of redress efforts has created a recurring cycle in which lawsuits challenge restrictive recognition criteria, political agreements attempt to settle disputes, and new legislative measures extend reparations to previously excluded groups, only for another wave of unrecognized victims to emerge. This process underscores the necessity of providing early, broad-based recognition and remedies to victims of environmental disasters in order to prevent prolonged legal and social struggles.

Following the official recognition of Minamata disease in 1956, initial redress efforts were limited in scope. The Chisso Corporation, responsible for the mercury pollution, denied liability but agreed in 1959 to a compensation scheme that took the form of a 'sympathy payment'. This agreement provided one-time payments to affected individuals, but it was highly inadequate, offering meager financial support and including clauses that prevented victims from seeking further compensation should the causal link to Chisso's pollution be scientifically confirmed. The inadequacy of this measure led to increasing pressure on the government to take further action, culminating in the enactment of the Special Measures Law for the Remedy of Health Damage due to Pollution in 1969. This law provided a government-led framework for victim recognition but did not impose legal liability on Chisso, forcing many victims to seek justice through the courts.[14]

Legal challenges against Chisso escalated as victims sought formal recognition and reparation. In 1969, lawsuits were filed in both Niigata and Kumamoto, leading to landmark judicial decisions in the early 1970s. In 1971, the Niigata District Court held Showa Denko liable for Niigata Minamata disease, setting an important precedent for corporate accountability. Two years later, the Kumamoto District Court ruled against Chisso, ordering the company to compensate Minamata disease patients. In response to this ruling, Chisso entered into a compensation agreement with recognized patients, which provided

[14] Minamata Disease Municipal Museum, *Minamata Disease: Its History and Lessons 2022*, 19–20 (in Japanese).

lump-sum payments and lifelong medical support. However, the agreement applied only to officially recognized patients, leaving many others without redress. The challenge of victim recognition persisted as government authorities sought to establish standardized diagnostic criteria for Minamata disease.

In 1977, the Japanese government introduced new Recognition Criteria, which outlined strict diagnostic criteria requiring a combination of severe symptoms, including sensory impairment, ataxia and visual field constriction.[15] This restrictive standard excluded many individuals who exhibited symptoms of mercury poisoning but did not meet the full set of criteria. As a result, numerous victims were denied recognition, prompting a new wave of lawsuits throughout the 1980s. In response to continued legal pressure, the Kumamoto District Court ruled in 1987 in favour of a group of unrecognized patients, awarding partial compensation. However, this decision did not fundamentally alter the restrictive framework governing Minamata disease recognition, and many individuals remained without legal or financial redress.

By the 1990s, the unresolved status of many Minamata disease victims had become a major political and social issue. In 1995, the Japanese government and ruling parties proposed a political settlement aimed at providing reparations to individuals who had been excluded from earlier compensation measures. Under this agreement, eligible victims received a one-time payment of 2.6 million yen and were provided with medical support, but they were required to abandon any pending lawsuits against the government or Chisso.[16] While this settlement expanded redress to some previously unrecognized victims, it failed to resolve the fundamental issue of exclusion, as thousands of individuals who exhibited symptoms remained ineligible for compensation under the government's restrictive criteria.

In 2004, a significant turning point occurred when the Supreme Court of Japan ruled that the government and Kumamoto Prefecture bore partial responsibility for the spread of Minamata disease due to their failure to prevent mercury pollution (described in the next section). The ruling also recognized a broader definition of eligible victims, leading to a surge in new recognition applications and lawsuits. This decision once again highlighted the inadequacy of prior settlements and underscored the persistent failure of governmental and corporate actors to provide comprehensive redress to all affected individuals.

In response to the renewed legal challenges following the Supreme Court decision, the Japanese government enacted the Special Measures Law for the

---

15 Director, Environmental Health Department, Planning and Coordination Bureau, Environment Agency: Notification on the Criteria for the Diagnosis of Acquired Minamata Disease (1 July 1977), *included in* House of Representatives Research Bureau (n 1) 3.

16 Ministry of the Environment, *The Origin of Environmental Issues* (n 8) 47.

Remedy of Minamata Disease Victims in 2009, followed by a 2010 Cabinet Decision aimed at expanding reparations to previously unrecognized victims. However, the implementation of this law was far from comprehensive. Of the more than 40,000 applicants who sought recognition, approximately 20% were denied, leading to yet another wave of lawsuits filed by rejected claimants.[17] Despite repeated attempts to broaden eligibility criteria, the cycle of exclusion and legal contestation has persisted.

Even after the implementation of the 2010 remedy measures, over 9,500 applicants were denied recognition, prompting additional legal challenges. Lawsuits continue to be filed under initiatives such as the 'No More Minamata' movement, in which plaintiffs seek broader recognition criteria and full reparations for all affected individuals. The restrictive nature of government-defined eligibility standards remains a central point of contention, as many victims suffer from significant health impairments but fail to meet the rigid diagnostic thresholds required for official recognition.

The prolonged struggle for Minamata disease victims' redress highlights the fundamental shortcomings of Japan's approach to environmental health crises. The repeated cycle of litigation, political settlements and legislative measures has failed to deliver a truly comprehensive solution, instead offering temporary redress to certain groups while leaving others to seek justice through continued legal battles. The history of Minamata disease demonstrates the critical importance of early and broad-based recognition of victims. Had the government established an inclusive system of recognition and reparation from the outset, the decades-long struggle for justice could have been mitigated. Instead, thousands of victims have been forced to endure prolonged suffering and uncertainty. This case serves as a stark reminder that in environmental and public health disasters, delayed and piecemeal responses only perpetuate harm, creating a legacy of unresolved grievances and continued legal conflict.

3.2 Ruling of the Supreme Court

The 2004 ruling of the Supreme Court on Minamata disease marked a critical moment in the legal history of environmental justice in Japan.[18] The case centred on the government's responsibility for failing to prevent the spread of methylmercury poisoning despite having the regulatory authority to do so. The ruling held that both the national government and Kumamoto Prefecture had acted unlawfully by neglecting to exercise their regulatory powers in a

17 Minamata Disease Municipal Museum (n 14) 26.

18 *Saikousai Minji Hanreisyu,* Judgment of the Supreme Court, Second Chamber, (15 October 2004), In 58 *[Supreme Court Civil Case Reports]*, No. 7, 1802.

timely manner, thereby exacerbating the suffering of thousands of victims. This decision not only acknowledged the state's legal liability but also highlighted broader lessons regarding governmental obligations in environmental health crises.

The lawsuit was filed under Article 1(1) of the State Redress Act, which establishes the government's liability for damages caused by its officials' unlawful actions or omissions in the course of their duties. This provision is comparable to tort liability in common law jurisdictions, imposing an obligation on the government to compensate individuals harmed by state negligence or inaction. In the Minamata case, the plaintiffs argued that the government had failed to exercise its regulatory authority under Japan's water pollution laws, thereby allowing Chisso Corporation to continue discharging methylmercury into Minamata Bay long after the dangers had become apparent.

The Supreme Court found that by November 1959, the government had sufficient scientific evidence to conclude that methylmercury discharged from Chisso's Minamata factory was the cause of Minamata disease. By this time, the government was aware that the disease had led to numerous deaths and severe neurological impairments, particularly among fishing communities that relied on contaminated seafood. Despite this knowledge, the government failed to take decisive regulatory action to halt the discharge of toxic effluents.

Under Japan's Water Pollution Control Laws at the time, the government had the authority to set water quality standards, designate specific water bodies for environmental protection and regulate pollutants discharged from industrial facilities. These laws provided mechanisms to: establish water quality standards and identify specific facilities responsible for discharging wastewater; impose restrictions on facilities whose effluents did not meet designated water quality standards; and order improvements in wastewater treatment, temporary shutdowns of polluting facilities, or other necessary measures to protect public health.

The Supreme Court determined that by late 1959, the government should have exercised these regulatory powers to designate Minamata Bay as a protected water body and impose strict limitations on industrial effluents containing mercury. The ruling stated that the failure to implement these measures was not merely a policy choice but an unlawful dereliction of duty. If the government had taken action in 1959, subsequent cases of Minamata disease could have been prevented. Instead, because regulatory intervention was delayed, mercury contamination continued, leading to a prolonged and avoidable public health disaster.[19]

19 *Ibid.*, 1814–5.

This decision reinforced a crucial legal principle: when faced with emerging environmental hazards, governments have an obligation to act swiftly and decisively to protect public health. The ruling also underscored the consequences of regulatory inaction in the face of scientific uncertainty. The Japanese government had cited the lack of absolute scientific proof as a justification for delaying intervention, but the court rejected this reasoning, emphasizing the necessity of precautionary measures in public health crises. This principle aligns with what is now recognized in international environmental law as the precautionary principle, which obligates states to take preventive action even in the absence of complete scientific certainty about environmental harm.

Beyond its implications for Japanese administrative law, the Minamata ruling contributed to the global discourse on environmental governance. The legal and policy failures exposed by the case influenced the adoption of the Minamata Convention on Mercury[20] in 2013, an international treaty aimed at preventing mercury pollution and protecting human health. The convention reflects many of the lessons from the Minamata case,[21] emphasizing the need for stringent environmental regulations, continuous monitoring of hazardous substances and early intervention to prevent toxic exposure.

The ruling also serves as a cautionary tale about the limitations of ex-post compensation as a remedy for environmental disasters. Even though the Supreme Court recognized the government's liability, the litigation process was long and arduous, with many victims passing away before they could receive justice. This reinforces the importance of establishing proactive regulatory frameworks that prevent harm before it occurs, rather than relying solely on legal remedies after the damage has been done.

Ultimately, the Minamata case illustrates the dangers of regulatory complacency and the human costs of delayed environmental action. Governments must ensure that environmental protection laws are not only enacted but also effectively enforced. The failure to act decisively in the face of known health hazards can constitute a violation of fundamental human rights, leaving affected communities in a perpetual struggle for justice.

---

[20] Minamata Convention on Mercury (adopted 10 October 2013, entered into force 16 August 2017) 3202 UNTS, C.N.560.2014. See also UN Environment Program, *Minamata Convention on Mercury Website*, <https://minamataconvention.org/en>.

[21] Its preamble explicitly provides that '[r]ecognizing the substantial lessons of Minamata Disease, in particular the serious health and environmental effects resulting from the mercury pollution and the need to ensure proper management of mercury and the prevention of such events in the future (*Ibid.*, Preamble, para. 7).

4. FROM CRISIS TO COMMITMENT: MINAMATA CONVENTION AND GENDER ACTION PLAN

4.1 Obligations of State Parties Under the Convention

The Minamata Convention on Mercury establishes legally binding obligations for State Parties to control mercury emissions, manage mercury waste, and protect human health from the harmful effects of mercury exposure. The Convention was adopted as a response to the devastating consequences of mercury pollution, exemplified by the Minamata disease disaster in Japan. In light of the Japanese government's delayed and fragmented approach to Minamata disease illustrates the potential consequences of failing to implement early and effective regulatory measures, the Convention seeks to address such failures by imposing proactive obligations on State Parties to prevent future mercury-related health and environmental crises. These obligations reflect broader principles of international human rights law, particularly the rights to health, environmental protection and public participation in environmental governance.

One of the key obligations under the Minamata Convention is the regulation of mercury supply, trade and storage. The Convention prohibits new primary mercury mining and establishes a fifteen-year phase-out period for existing mining.[22] It also imposes restrictions on international trade, requiring written consent from importing State Parties and limiting exports to non-Parties.[23] These provisions recognize that unregulated mercury trade contributes to environmental contamination and human exposure, particularly in vulnerable communities. Japan's historical failure to control industrial mercury discharge highlights the necessity of such regulations; the lack of early restrictions allowed mercury pollution to persist for decades, exacerbating human suffering.

The Convention also mandates the elimination of certain mercury-added products and the restriction of industrial processes that rely on mercury.[24] The manufacturing of products such as batteries, thermometers and certain types of lamps is gradually phased out, and industrial processes such as chlor-alkali production and acetaldehyde production must transition to mercury-free alternatives.[25] The inclusion of acetaldehyde production in these regulations is particularly significant given that Minamata disease was directly linked to

---

22 *Ibid.*, Article 3 (3) and (4).

23 *Ibid.*, Article 3 (6)-(9).

24 *Ibid.*, Article 4 (1) and Annex A, Part I; Article 5 (2) and Annex B, Part I.

25 *Ibid.*, Article 5 (3) and Annex B, Part II.

mercury discharges from Chisso Corporation's acetaldehyde production facility. If such international standards had been in place and enforced earlier, the Minamata disaster might have been prevented. These obligations reflect the broader principle of corporate responsibility for environmental and human rights harms, a principle that has been increasingly recognized in international human rights law.[26]

State Parties are further obligated to control mercury emissions and releases into the air, water and land by employing the best available techniques and environmental practices. These measures should be implemented as soon as practicable, but no later than five years after the entry into force of the Convention for the respective Party.[27] Furthermore, State Parties must develop a national plan to reduce emissions and establish an inventory of major emission sources.[28] These provisions recognize that mercury pollution is not confined to localized areas; it disperses through air and water, impacting populations far beyond the immediate vicinity of the source. This situation reflects Japan's failure to implement early emission controls at Chisso Corporation, which led to the widespread bioaccumulation of methylmercury in fish and prolonged human exposure. The requirements set forth in the Convention align with the international human right to a healthy environment, compelling States to take preventive actions to avert large-scale environmental damage.[29]

Artisanal and small-scale gold mining (ASGM) is also a major focus of the Convention, as it is one of the largest global sources of mercury pollution. If ASGM is significant in a State Party, that country must develop a national action plan to reduce mercury use and submit progress reports every three years.[30] The Convention further encourages international cooperation

---

26 Guiding Principles on Business and Human Rights: Implementing the United Nations 'Protect, Respect and Remedy' Framework, *annexed to* the Report of the Special Representative of the Secretary-General on the issue of human rights and transnational corporations and other business enterprises, John Ruggie, (21 March 2011), UN Doc A/HRC/17/31; Committee on Economic, Social and Cultural Rights, 'General comment No. 24 (2017) on State obligations under the International Covenant on Economic, Social and Cultural Rights in the context of business activities' (10 August 2017) UN Doc E/C.12/GC/24.

27 Minamata Convention (n 20), Article 8 (4)-(5) and Annex D.

28 *Ibid.*, Article 8 (3) and (7).

29 Committee on Economic, Social and Cultural Rights, 'General Comment No. 15 (2002): The right to water (Articles 11 and 12 of the International Covenant on Economic, Social and Cultural Rights)' (20 January 2003) UN Doc E/C.12/2002/11, para. 8; Committee on the Rights of the Child, 'General comment No. 26 (2023) on children's rights and the environment, with a special focus on climate change' (22 August 2023), UN Doc CRC/C/GC/26, para. 65.

30 Minamata Convention (n 20), Article 7 (3) and Annex C.

to support mercury-free mining alternatives.[31] These provisions align with human rights principles by addressing the disproportionate impact of mercury pollution on low-income and Indigenous communities that rely on small-scale mining for their livelihoods. The Minamata disease crisis similarly demonstrated the unequal distribution of environmental harm; marginalized fishing communities were the primary victims of mercury exposure, while corporate and government actors prioritized economic growth over public health.

In addressing mercury waste and contaminated sites, the Convention mandates that State Parties ensure the environmentally sound management of mercury waste, in line with the provisions of the Basel Convention.[32] The transport of mercury waste across borders is prohibited, except when it is destined for environmentally sound disposal.[33] Furthermore, State Parties are required to identify and remediate mercury-contaminated sites.[34] These obligations hold particular significance for Japan, where the cleanup of Minamata Bay took decades to complete, and mercury contamination continued to impact successive generations. The Minamata case underscores the critical need for comprehensive site remediation policies that not only eliminate toxic substances but also facilitate the restoration of communities affected by environmental disasters.

The Convention also recognizes the importance of protecting human health from mercury exposure. State Parties are required to promote healthcare services for mercury-affected populations, develop public awareness programs on the risks of mercury exposure and support scientific research on mercury's health and environmental effects.[35] These provisions emphasize the right to health, which is enshrined in international human rights treaties.[36] Japan's handling of Minamata disease demonstrated severe shortcomings in this regard; for years, victims were denied access to adequate medical care, and many were forced to engage in prolonged legal battles to obtain recognition and treatment. The Convention's health-related obligations seek to prevent such injustices by

---

31 *Ibid.*, Article 7 (4).

32 *Ibid.*, Article 11 (3)–(5).

33 *Ibid.*, Article 11 (3)(c).

34 *Ibid.*, Article 12 (1)–(2).

35 *Ibid.*, Article 16 (1)(c), Article 18 (1)(b) and Article 19 (1)(c).

36 Committee on Economic, Social and Cultural Rights, 'General Comment No. 14 (2000): The right to the highest attainable standard of health (Article 12 of the International Covenant on Economic, Social and Cultural Rights)' (11 August 2000), UN Doc E/C.12/2000/4; Committee on the Elimination of Discrimination against Women, 'General recommendation No. 24: Article 12 of the Convention (women and health)' (2 February 1999), UN Doc. A/54/38/Rev.1.

ensuring that mercury-affected populations receive timely and appropriate medical support.

While the Minamata Convention does not explicitly reference human rights, many of its provisions align with human rights principles. The preamble recognizes the need to protect vulnerable populations, such as women, children and Indigenous communities.[37] The right to a clean and safe environment is embedded in the Convention's objectives in Article 1 and its requirements for pollution control and waste management.[38] Additionally, the Convention mandates public participation and access to information on mercury-related risks,[39] reinforcing the principle of environmental democracy.

4.2 Gender Action Plan for the Minamata Convention and Its Impact

While, as examined in the previous section, the Convention imposes obligations on State Parties to mitigate mercury exposure, particularly among vulnerable populations, it does not explicitly address gender-specific risks or adopt a human rights-based approach to gender equality. The Gender Action Plan (GAP), adopted at the fifth Conference of the Parties in 2023, supplements and enhances the Convention's framework by mainstreaming gender considerations in its implementation.[40] The GAP strengthens the State Party's obligations under the Minamata Convention, particularly in protecting the rights of women and children, who face disproportionate risks from mercury exposure due to biological susceptibility and socioeconomic roles.

A core contribution of the GAP is its role in integrating gender perspectives into national policies and implementation strategies mandated by the Convention. Under Article 7, State Parties engaged in ASGM must develop national action plans to reduce mercury use. The GAP reinforces this obligation by requiring gender-sensitive approaches in ASGM strategies, recognizing that women play significant roles in small-scale mining but often lack

---

[37] Minamata Convention (n 20), Preamble, para. 5: 'Aware of the health concerns, especially in developing countries, resulting from exposure to mercury of vulnerable populations, especially women, children, and, through them, future generations'.

[38] *Ibid.*, Article 11 (3) and Article 12 (2).

[39] *Ibid.*, Article 18 (1)(a).

[40] Gender action plan for the Minamata Convention on Mercury (4 July 2023), UN Doc UNEP/MC/COP.5/INF/10 (here in advance, 'GAP'); Decisions adopted by the Conference of the Parties to the Minamata Convention on Mercury at its fifth meeting (24 November 2023) UN Doc UNEP/MC/COP.5/Dec.15.

access to resources, training and protective measures.[41] It urges State Parties to ensure women's active participation in the formulation of ASGM policies, provide gender-specific training on mercury-free mining technologies and support alternative livelihoods for female miners. By doing so, the GAP enhances the Convention's objectives by addressing the intersection of environmental protection and gender equality.

Similarly, the GAP strengthens the State Party's obligations in the domain of mercury waste management and public awareness initiatives, aligning with Articles 11 and 18 of the Convention.[42] Women, particularly those in marginalized communities, often bear the brunt of hazardous waste exposure due to their roles in informal labour sectors such as waste picking and subsistence fishing. The GAP mandates the incorporation of gender-responsive strategies in national mercury waste management policies, ensuring that women are adequately informed about the dangers of mercury exposure and provided with protective measures. Moreover, it calls for the collection of gender-disaggregated data on mercury exposure and health impacts,[43] a critical step in developing targeted interventions that address the specific vulnerabilities of women and children.

The lessons from Minamata disease, particularly the historical exclusion of affected women from decision-making processes and medical support, underscore the importance of these provisions. Women in Minamata played critical roles in advocating for recognition and compensation, yet they often faced systemic barriers to justice. The GAP aims to rectify such historical gender imbalances by institutionalizing women's participation in environmental governance and ensuring they have access to necessary health interventions.

From a human rights perspective, the GAP compensates for the Convention's lack of explicit gender protections by reinforcing women's and children's right to health. While Article 16 of the Convention recognizes the need for health-based interventions, it does not include provisions that account for gender-specific health risks. The GAP fills this gap by urging State Parties to implement gender-sensitive healthcare services for populations affected by mercury poisoning.[44] By emphasizing these protections, the GAP ensures that State Parties fulfil their obligations in a manner that aligns with international human

---

[41] GAP, para. 9 (b)(i): Bring gender into the development and implementation of ASGM NAPs.

[42] *Ibid.*, para. 9 (b)(ii): Support and develop gender integration in programmes and projects.

[43] *Ibid.*, para. 9 (b)(iv): Incorporate gender-disaggregated data throughout activities.

[44] *Ibid.*, para. 7 (e).

rights standards, particularly the principles outlined in the Convention on the Elimination of All Forms of Discrimination Against Women.[45]

In addition to health protections, the GAP advances women's participation in environmental decision-making, an area where the Minamata Convention remains underdeveloped. While Article 18 encourages public awareness and education, it does not mandate the inclusion of women in mercury policymaking at the national or international levels. The GAP rectifies this omission by urging State Parties to promote gender-balanced leadership in their delegations to COP meetings, national regulatory bodies and ASGM policy formulation processes.[46] Furthermore, it calls for capacity-building initiatives that empower women's organizations, Indigenous groups and grassroots activists to participate meaningfully in mercury-related governance.[47] By institutionalizing women's involvement in decision-making, the GAP enhances the legitimacy and effectiveness of mercury control policies, ensuring that they reflect the lived experiences of those most affected by mercury exposure.

The Minamata disaster also demonstrated that marginalized communities, particularly women in fishing villages, were disproportionately affected by mercury contamination. Many women engaged in subsistence fishing were exposed to high mercury levels but lacked access to health screenings and economic alternatives. The GAP's emphasis on gender-sensitive training and alternative livelihoods for women mirrors the lessons from Minamata, highlighting the necessity of integrating gender considerations into environmental health policies.

Another significant contribution of the GAP is its role in addressing gender-based socioeconomic disparities, which influence mercury exposure patterns. Women in ASGM communities, fishing sectors and informal labour markets often experience economic marginalization, increasing their reliance on hazardous mercury-related activities. The GAP calls upon State Parties to develop economic empowerment programs that offer alternative livelihoods for women engaged in mercury-intensive industries.[48] These initiatives include financial assistance for transitioning to mercury-free technologies, vocational training for women in affected communities and the establishment of social safety nets for those vulnerable to mercury exposure.[49] By integrating economic justice

---

45 Committee on the Elimination of Discrimination against Women, 'General recommendation No. 24' (n 36).

46 GAP (n 40), para. 9 (b)(ii).

47 *Ibid.*, para. 9 (a)(iv): Promote meaningful, inclusive, and gender-balanced participation in Secretariat processes and activities.

48 *Ibid.*, para. 7 (f).

49 *Ibid.*, para. 9 (b)(vi): Ensure funding and resources, including through the financial mechanism of the Convention (SIP and GEF).

with environmental governance, the GAP ensures that State Party obligations under the Convention extend beyond regulatory compliance to encompass social equity and sustainable development.

To sum up, the GAP substantially enhances the obligations of State Parties under the Minamata Convention by integrating gender considerations into mercury regulation, public health initiatives and environmental management. It strengthens protections for women's and children's right to health, promotes gender-balanced participation in decision-making and addresses socioeconomic disparities. While the Minamata Convention provides a foundational framework for mercury control, the GAP ensures that its implementation is inclusive, equitable and aligned with international human rights and gender equality principles. Through the effective adoption of the GAP, State Parties can fulfil their commitments under the Convention in a manner that is both environmentally sustainable and socially just.

5. CONCLUSION

The lessons of Minamata disease extend far beyond a single environmental tragedy; they serve as a stark reminder of the systemic failures in legal, medical and political frameworks to address chronic environmental harm and human rights violations. Minamata disease, as a case of industrial mercury poisoning, underscores the necessity of integrating human rights considerations—particularly gender perspectives—into environmental governance. The disease disproportionately affected women due to their biological susceptibility to mercury exposure and their socioeconomic roles, yet gendered dimensions were historically overlooked in both response measures and policymaking. This exclusion exemplifies broader patterns of environmental injustices, where the burdens of toxic exposure often fall heaviest on marginalized communities, especially women and children.

One of the most crucial lessons from Minamata disease is the need for early intervention and proactive governance. The delay in recognizing the dangers of mercury pollution and responding to its effects highlights the inadequacy of conventional regulatory mechanisms in addressing slow-onset environmental disasters. Traditional legal frameworks tend to prioritize acute and conspicuous environmental crises over prolonged and cumulative harm, leaving victims of ECEs without adequate protection or redress. The persistence of Minamata disease as a public health crisis illustrates the dangers of regulatory inertia and the necessity of incorporating early warning systems into environmental law. Moreover, gender-responsive policies must be embedded in these frameworks to ensure that women, who often serve as primary caregivers and frontline responders in environmental health crises, are adequately informed, protected and empowered.

A second key lesson is the importance of addressing gendered impacts explicitly in environmental policies. Minamata disease revealed how environmental health crises disproportionately affect women, not only in terms of direct health consequences but also through secondary burdens such as caregiving responsibilities, economic marginalization and social stigma. Women in Minamata, despite suffering severe neurological damage and reproductive health issues, were often excluded from compensation schemes and decision-making processes. Their voices were systematically silenced, and their labour—both in domestic care and activism—was undervalued. The GAP of the Minamata Convention seeks to rectify these historical injustices by ensuring that gender perspectives are fully integrated into mercury governance. By incorporating gender-sensitive health advisories, economic support for affected women and increased participation of women in environmental policymaking, the GAP represents a significant step toward more equitable environmental governance.

Moving forward, the effective implementation of the GAP will be crucial in translating these lessons into tangible outcomes. Although the Minamata Convention establishes a legal framework for mercury regulation, its success depends on how well State Parties integrate gender perspectives into their national policies and enforcement mechanisms. The adoption of gender-sensitive approaches to mercury exposure monitoring, healthcare provisions, economic rehabilitation and policymaking will determine whether the lessons of Minamata truly lead to a more just and inclusive environmental governance system.

Ultimately, Minamata disease serves as both a warning and a call to action. It demonstrates the devastating consequences of failing to address environmental health risks in a timely and equitable manner. The GAP ensures that the mistakes of the past are not repeated by embedding gender considerations into mercury governance, thereby fostering a more holistic approach to environmental justice. By embracing the principles of gender equality, human rights and proactive environmental protection, the international community can ensure that the legacy of Minamata is one of progress and reform rather than tragedy and neglect. Through the full implementation of the Minamata Convention and its GAP, the world has an opportunity to transform the lessons of Minamata into lasting protections for vulnerable communities, ensuring that history does not repeat itself.

7. Environmental chronic emergencies and the challenge of temporality

David M. Scott

1. INTRODUCTION

In December 2024, the International Court of Justice held its oral proceedings for the *Advisory Opinion on Obligations of States in respect of Climate Change* (hereafter 'the Advisory Opinion'), with an unprecedented 96 states and 10 international organizations making submissions over the space of two weeks.[1] In their submissions, states repeatedly affirmed the historical significance of the Advisory Opinion: it was possibly 'the most consequential case in the history of humanity' (Vanuatu)[2]: 'one of, if not *the* most consequential opinion the Court has ever been requested to render' (Germany)[3]; arriving at 'a defining moment' whose significance 'cannot be overstated' (Albania)[4]; and tackling 'one of the gravest challenges humanity has ever faced' (USA).[5]

Yet what was expected from the Advisory Opinion was understood differently between states. For some, 'climate change' is a fundamentally unequal

---

1 *Request for advisory opinion submitted by the General Assembly of the United Nations on the Obligations of States in respect of Climate Change*, International Court of Justice, UN General Assembly resolution 77/276 (29 March 2023), hereinafter Advisory Opinion. Written submissions were also received from the Organization of Petroleum Exporting Countries (OPEC), Office of the Parties to the Nauru Agreement, and Madagascar. At the time of writing, the ICJ had not rendered its Advisory Opinion.

2 Advisory Opinion, *ibid.*, Submissions of Vanuatu (2 December 2024), Verbatim record 2024/35, 98, para. 8.

3 Advisory Opinion, *ibid.*, Submission of Germany (2 December 2024), Verbatim record 2024/35, 153, para. 39. [emphasis original]

4 Advisory Opinion, *ibid.*, Submissions of Albania (2 December 2024), Verbatim record 2024/35, 139, para. 18.

5 Advisory Opinion, *ibid.*, Submissions of the United States of America (4 December 2024), Verbatim record 2024/40, 39, para. 2.

process, with certain states bearing the cost of the past and present actions of others. Opening the oral proceedings, Vanuatu stated that it finds itself 'on the frontlines of a crisis we did not create',[6] driven by the actions of 'a handful of readily identifiable States' who have failed 'for over a century, despite increasingly dire warnings, to rein in the emissions from their territories'.[7] Accordingly, Vanuatu asked the Court 'for recognition that the conduct which has already caused immense harm to my people and so many others is unlawful ... and that its consequences must be repaired'[8]—not only through general obligations to protect the environment globally but also in obligations specific to Vanuatu and other presently impacted states, in 'respect [for] the fundamental rights of [Vanuatu's] people to self-determination in [their] own land'.[9] Other states were even more forthright in drawing connections between the historical past and the present of climate change, arguing that 'the injustice of the climate crisis is inseparable from our shared colonial histories' (the Melanesian Spearhead Group),[10] that 'colonialism and racism ... largely inform our level of development and vulnerabilities in the face of climate change' (the Cook Islands)[11]—indeed, that the 'developed' position of industrialized states was 'powered by colonial exploitation' in the first place (Timor-Leste).[12] In order 'to adequately respond' to the request for an Advisory Opinion, these states asked that the ICJ 'address the colonialism and racism that underpins the unlawful conduct and patterns its effects around the world' (the Cook Islands).[13]

By contrast, other states' submissions located climate change at a shared, global scale. In its submissions, the USA cast climate change as a 'quintessential collective action problem', 'global in its causes' and 'global in its effects'.[14] While major greenhouse gas-emitting states may have a 'particular' role in addressing climate change, 'global action and cooperation by all States' is needed to 'deal with this uniquely complex global problem'.[15] Accordingly, the

---

6 Submissions of Vanuatu (n 2) 96, para. 2.

7 *Ibid.*, 97, para. 4.

8 *Ibid.*, 98, para. 7.

9 *Ibid.*, 100, para. 3.

10 Advisory Opinion (n 1), Submissions of the Melanesian Spearhead Group (2 December 2024), Verbatim record 2024/35, 102, para. 7.

11 Advisory Opinion (n 1), Submissions of the Cook Islands (5 December 2024), Verbatim record 2024/42, 11–2, para. 9.

12 Advisory Opinion (n 1), Submissions of the Democratic Republic of Timor-Leste (12 December 2024), Verbatim record 2024/51, 25, para. 13.

13 Submissions of the Cook Islands (n 11) 16, para. 28.

14 Submissions of the United States of America (n 5), 39, paras 3 and 2.

15 *Ibid.*, 39–40, para. 3.

USA's submissions focused solely on the UN climate change regime, beginning with the 1992 United Nations Framework Convention on Climate Change, as the solution that 'States collectively designed' to tackle climate change, with no other obligations to be found in customary international law or international human rights law.[16] Similar statements can be found from other high-polluting nations, such as Australia,[17] France,[18] Russia[19] and the UK,[20] all positioning the 'crisis' of climate change in the future, as something to avoid.

These two positions reveal a particular dynamic within international law's apprehension of climate change: that the core question before the Court was not *if* climate change is occurring, but *when it began*. For states like Vanuatu, there is a continual link drawn between the past harm caused to their state and the future hopes for humanity as a whole. Existing climate change has not only 'already resulted in injury to Vanuatu', but 'threatens the survival of my people and of humanity as a whole'[21]; and similarly, looking to the future, the Advisory Opinion 'will reverberate across generations, determining the fate of nations like mine and the future of our planet'.[22] States like the USA, however, position the ICJ as only a present guide for future 'urgent action [to be

---

[16] *Ibid.*, 44–7, paras 22–32.

[17] Advisory Opinion (n 1), Submissions of Australia (2 December 2024), Verbatim record 2024/36, stating that the UN climate treaties are 'the central instruments that provide the framework for international co-operation' (36, para. 5) and denying the application of customary international law or the UN Convention on the Law of the Sea (UNCLOS) on the basis of insufficient causation (40–52).

[18] Advisory Opinion (n 1), Submissions of France (5 December 2024), Verbatim record 2024/41, 14–5, para. 26, noting that awareness of climate change, for the purposes of international law, would begin with the UN General Assembly's resolution on the 'Protection of global climate for present and future generations of mankind' and the 1992 Rio Declaration on Environment and Development.

[19] Advisory Opinion (n 1), Submissions of Russia (4 December 2024), Verbatim record 2024/40, stating that '[g]lobal challenges require global solutions' (51, para. 1) and distinguishing international human rights law, UNCLOS, and customary international law obligations (55–61).

[20] Advisory Opinion (n 1), Submissions of the United States (10 December 2024), Verbatim Record 2024/48, 43–4, para. 13, describing the Paris Agreement as 'not only, as a matter of international law, the most relevant applicable international instrument for addressing the challenge, but also, as a matter of fact, the most realistic framework for the concerted action necessary to respond to the crisis'.

[21] Submissions of Vanuatu (n 2) 96, para. 3.

[22] *Ibid.*, para. 1. See also *ibid,* 98, para. 8: the Court must not 'allow future generations to look back and wonder why the cause of their doom was condoned'.

taken] *in this critical decade* ... to *avoid* the most catastrophic impacts of the climate crisis'.[23] The relevant timeframe, then, lies not over centuries, but only in decades, beginning with the UN climate change treaties starting in 1992, 'the clearest, most specific and the most current expression of States' consent to be bound by international law in respect of climate change'.[24] Delimited in this way, past conduct is bracketed out from the Advisory Opinion, with the Court asked only to provide a 'forward-looking response to guide the General Assembly and United Nations Member States on their future conduct'.[25]

This question brings to the fore the idea of environmental chronic emergencies (ECE) as entrenched, structural and embedded within historical inequalities, rather than spectacular or instantaneous disasters that can be solved and overcome in the present.[26] Rather than parsing the specific temporalities attributed to climate change in the submissions of individual states,[27] in this chapter I want to unravel this temporal conflict at a very broad level, by showing the particular demand made on international law in digesting the complexities of ECEs. Building on existing critical scholarship that has critiqued international law's unequal distribution of the responsibility for climate change in the past, present and future,[28] this chapter looks to assess why international law as a discipline or mode of thought appears to struggle so much with integrating

---

[23] Submissions of the United States of America (n 5) 40, para. 4 [emphasis added].

[24] *Ibid.*, 40, para. 8.

[25] *Ibid.*, 47, para. 34.

[26] See in more detail Sara De Vido, 'Feminist Legal Methods and Environmental Chronic Emergencies: Challenging the Anthropocentric and Androcentric International Legal System' and Deborah Russo, 'Moving Beyond an Approach Based on Crisis and Disasters to Address Environmental Chronic Emergencies' in this Volume.

[27] For a preliminary sketch of such an approach, see David M. Scott, 'Time and Temporality before the ICJ in the Advisory Opinion on Obligations of States in Respect of Climate Change' (*EJIL: Talk!* 14 February 2025) <https://www.ejiltalk.org/time-and-temporality-before-the-icj-in-the-advisory-opinion-on-obligations-of-states-in-respect-of-climate-change/> accessed 17 February 2025.

[28] Julia Dehm, 'Carbon Colonialism or Climate Justice? Interrogating the International Climate Regime from a TWAIL Perspective' (2016) 33 *Windsor Yearbook of Access to Justice* 129; Julia Dehm, 'Climate Change, "Slow Violence" and the Indefinite Deferral of Responsibility for "Loss and Damage"' (2020) 29 *Griffith Law Review* 220; Stephen Humphreys, 'Against Future Generations' (2022) 33 *European Journal of International Law* 1061; Eliana Cusato, 'Progress and Linear Time: International Environmental Law and the Uneven Distribution of Futurity' (2025) 84 *Zeitschrift für ausländisches öffentliches Recht und Völkerrecht/Heidelberg Journal of International Law* 865.

ECEs into its work. It does so by locating this difficulty in a particular temporal orientation that undergirds international legal thought and, using parallel debates within historiography, aims to grasp the challenge that our increasing awareness of our climate presents to the 'modern' time in which international law works.

The chapter unspools its critique by working through two notions of 'crisis'—that of international law as a 'discipline of crisis', as famously outlined by Hilary Charlesworth; and that of 'crisis' as a historiographical category, as set out by German historian Reinhart Koselleck—in order to position international law's traditional attachment to crises within a wider temporality of modernity. The chapter then turns to how the temporality of modernity has come under challenge in the climate crisis, demonstrating a disjunction between international law's sense of time and the stakes of the contemporary time of our climate. From this disjunction, the chapter concludes by reflecting on how the meeting point of these two times can be located and brought forward as a disciplinary question within contemporary international legal thought.

While by no means the sole determiner of international law's difficulties in conceptualizing and engaging with ECEs, the background, near-imperceptible influence of our disciplinary assumptions about time makes it all the more important to identify their role in shaping our thought.[29] As the conclusion will reflect, international law's time remains flexible—indeed, international law deals everywhere with time without noticing.[30] But that flexibility is only

---

29 In this, I share André Nollkaemper's assessment that the barriers to international law mitigating climate change are 'mainly historical, political, economic, and societal', but nonetheless also encounter 'principles and processes internal to international law that complicate the effective use of international law to address climate change': André Nollkaemper, 'Causation Puzzles in International Climate Litigation' (2023) 33 *Italian Yearbook of International Law* 25, 25. International law's sense of time, then, would be one part of these unacknowledged 'principles and processes' that structure the discipline's limited response to climate change. My thinking here is also guided by Akbar Rasulov's work on the ideological trope of 'utopianism' versus 'professionalism' in international law discourses: see Akbar Rasulov, 'The Utopians' in Jean d'Aspremont and Sahib Singh (eds), *Concepts for International Law: Contributions to Disciplinary Thought* (Edward Elgar Publishing 2019); Akbar Rasulov, '"From the Wells of Disappointment": The Curious Case of the International Law of Democracy and the Politics of International Legal Scholarship' (2021) 32 *European Journal of International Law* 17.

30 Although not directly referenced below (in part because this would involve unpacking the distinctions between international legal thought and the largely domestic focus of the following works), my thinking on the malleability of legal

helpful if we are first aware of how to recognize and reshape it. Placing time on the table therefore helps to make visible the blind spots of our disciplinary assumptions, not only in dealing with environmental crisis, but other forms of chronic emergency, such as the cyclical and embedded nature of patriarchal violence.[31] While the focus of this chapter is on the temporality of ECEs, then, my hope is that its reflections speak more broadly to aspects of international law's rigidity as a mode of thought and its perceived difficulties in overcoming other forms of structural violence that do not fit its presumption of an open and linear temporality.

2. INTERNATIONAL LAW'S TIME

International law is a discipline of crisis, as Hilary Charlesworth famously set out in 2002.[32] Charlesworth's article analyzed the mode in which international lawyers come to apprehend a problem before them in order to draw out the limits, blind spots and disciplinary biases created by their crisis-centred approach. The argument runs like this. When confronted with a new 'crisis', international lawyers will rush to shape its facts into a legal problem that international law can solve, generating 'the sense that [international lawyers'] work is of immediate, intense relevance'.[33] In so doing, the crisis is disciplined into a particular order upon which international law can begin to work. First, international lawyers will break down the crisis into 'bite-size pieces', looking to find relevant legal obligations in the past that can govern the facts before them.[34] The 'Kosovo crisis', for example, became intelligible to international lawyers through questions drawn from different legal regimes: is 'Kosovo' a breach of the UN Charter or a defence of international human rights? Is it a breach

---

time is influenced here by, among others, Paul W. Kahn, *The Cultural Study of Law: Reconstructing Legal Scholarship* (University of Chicago Press 1999) chapter 2; Emily Grabham, *Brewing Legal Times: Things, Form, and the Enactment of Law* (University of Toronto Press 2016); Tanzil Chowdhury, *Time, Temporality, and Legal Judgment* (Routledge, 2020); Paul Linden-Retek, *Postnational Constitutionalism: Europe and the Time of Law* (Oxford University Press 2023).

31 The editors' description of this book project to contributing authors cites Cynthia Cockburn, 'The Continuum of Violence: A Gender Perspective on War and Peace' in Wenona Giles (ed.), *Sites of Violence: Gender and Conflict Zones* (University of California Press, 2004) as stressing 'the *cyclical* nature of patriarchal violence, drawing connections across different forms of manifestations of unequal power relations between women and men'. [emphasis added]

32 Hilary Charlesworth, 'International Law: A Discipline of Crisis' (2002) 65 *Modern Law Review* 377.

33 *Ibid.*, 377.

34 *Ibid.*, 384.

of international criminal law or a protective measure for refugees displaced by armed conflict? Having determined the regime(s) to be applied in the present, international lawyers then propose a solution to the crisis. In the case of Kosovo, this meant that the intervention was either affirmed as evidence of a new principle of humanitarian intervention or criticized as a breach of international law (albeit one that may be morally justifiable). Each regime narrows the meaning of 'Kosovo' into a certain set of facts that that regime can 'see', so that a solution can then be chosen from within those legal rules.[35]

Underlying Charlesworth's critique is a challenge to the sense of time produced by this focus on crisis. In the rush to create an 'immediate, intense relevance' in the present, international lawyers neglect the past. In seeking to break down a crisis according to the dictates of the discipline, with the need to make the facts 'fit' the legal obligations we seek to apply to the crisis, international lawyers fail to acknowledge that they 'are not trained to reflect on the politics of their choice of facts or the nature of the facts' sources'.[36] In this way, international law's 'cultivated astigmatism', as Michael Reisman (positively) puts it, can end up reproducing and entrenching an 'inaccurate or partial' history,[37] leading the discipline to overlook or oversimplify the structural (and often legal) processes that produce these crises.[38] The endless movement from one crisis to the next also produces a lack of analytic progress within the discipline itself. Because crises are such powerful opportunities for providing 'performances of our art',[39] international lawyers continually rush from one crisis to another, apprehending each new crisis with the same sense of anxiety and haste, 'reporting on a phenomenon before it goes stale and disappears from our radar screens'.[40] As such, each crisis produces an analysis that is 'very specific and tailored to particular immediate circumstances', leading international lawyers to 'rediscover an issue constantly', leaving no sense of historical continuity beyond the crisis's value as a legal precedent for future disputes.[41]

The rush to treat each new crisis in this way also hampers the ability of international lawyers to think cogently about the future. The need for each crisis to be 'solved' in the present, in order to then move onto the next crisis,

---

35 *Ibid.*, 379–81.

36 *Ibid.*, 383–4.

37 *Ibid.*, quoting Michael Reisman and Andrew Willard (eds), *International Incidents: The Law that Counts in World Politics* (Princeton University Press 1988) 19.

38 Charlesworth (n 32) 384–6.

39 *Ibid.*, 379.

40 *Ibid.*, 384.

41 *Ibid.*

means international lawyers fail to grasp the longer horizons of international law's contribution to the circumstances that produce each crisis: they focus on what the law 'is' at a given time, and trust that the solution of each crisis will serve as 'the engine of [the] progressive development of international law'.[42] Yet here international law's 'astigmatism' strikes again. Presuming that a crisis is 'solved' within the terms international law sets up for it leads to a neglect of the ongoing consequences of that solution. The Dayton Accords, international law's first intervention into the break-up of the former Yugoslavia, explicitly excluded the status of Kosovo, establishing 'a system that ultimately contributed to the persecution of the Albanian Kosovars'.[43] When the 'Kosovo crisis' later broke out, international law's contribution to this crisis was forgotten: as a discipline, '[w]e find it hard to contemplate that an international agreement (the form of international law we know and understand so well) that was meant to have stitched up one set of problems could in turn have nurtured violence and disorder'.[44] The same then occurred in the wake of the NATO intervention, posed as a 'solution' for 'Kosovo': debated only on the spectacular, exciting terms of human rights and the use of force, the lingering consequences of the NATO intervention, such as the destruction of civilian infrastructure, the failure to disarm militants within Kosovo, and the forced return of refugees to their homes, were left unexplored—international lawyers had already moved on.[45] The repetitive focus on crises bars international lawyers from thinking about the future ramifications of a particular solution, resulting in a discipline that 'stays glued to the specific, climactic events and fails to see the larger picture'.[46] In this way, crises narrow the agenda for international law, focusing only on 'a snapshot in time of long-simmering disputes' that consequently 'allows us to present our task as a straightforward, if agonizing, choice between two competing principles'.[47]

Charlesworth's article ends with a call for a reorientation of the discipline away from crisis-thinking and towards 'an international law of everyday life' that resists the heroics of crisis-thinking by taking a long-term, structural view that '[examines] what international law has to offer the person who wants to pollute the environment or violate human rights'.[48] While the identification of

42 *Ibid.*, 391.
43 *Ibid.*, 385.
44 *Ibid.*
45 *Ibid.*, 385.
46 *Ibid.*, 386.
47 *Ibid.*
48 *Ibid.*, 392.

international law's crisis focus has been immensely productive,[49] this attempt to move beyond the frame of crisis-thinking has always struck me as somewhat thin. International law's crisis focus is presented as inexplicable—a regrettable lapse of judgment that international lawyers can simply shift their minds away from, now aware of the risks of its narrow focus. What this fails to consider is any historical reason for *why* international lawyers might think in crises. It is from this question that we can now turn to historiography.

3. TIMING INTERNATIONAL LAW

Although well-known in historical circles, German historian Reinhart Koselleck (1923–2006) has only recently gained attention from international lawyers.[50] Koselleck is perhaps best known for his *Begriffsgeschichte* (conceptual history), a historical method for grasping the transformation in the meaning of concepts in relation to wider social changes,[51] and the concept of 'crisis' was the focus of much of Koselleck's early work,[52] most notably in a famous

---

[49] See, among many other citations, the explicit debt paid to Charlesworth's article in the special issue on 'Crisis and International Law: Decoy or Catalyst?' (2013) 44 *Netherlands Yearbook of International Law*; Dianne Otto, 'Decoding Crisis in International Law: A Queer Feminist Perspective' in Barbara Stark (ed.), *International Law and its Discontents: Confronting Crises* (Cambridge University Press 2015) 115; many of the chapters in Makane Moïse Mbengue and Jean d'Aspremont (eds), *Crisis Narratives in International Law* (Brill Nijhoff 2022); and Ntina Tzouvala, 'International Law as a Discipline in Crisis' (2025) 79 *Australian Journal of International Affairs* 71.

[50] For prior engagements with Koselleck in international legal history, see Matthew Craven, 'Theorizing the Turn to History in International Law' in Anne Orford and Florian Hoffmann (eds), *The Oxford Handbook of the Theory of International Law* (Oxford University Press 2016) 21; Martin Clark, 'Ambivalence, Anxieties/Adaptations, Advances: Conceptual History and International Law' (2018) 31 *Leiden Journal of International Law* 747; Anne Orford, *International Law and the Politics of History* (Cambridge University Press 2021) 299–310; David M. Scott, 'Rethinking the Turn to History as a Turn to Time in International Law' (2024) 9 *Jus Gentium: Journal of International Legal History* 401.

[51] On conceptual history and its underpinning precepts, see Reinhart Koselleck, 'Introduction (*Einleitung*) to the "*Geschichtliche Grundbegriffe*"' (2011) 6 *Contributions to the History of Concepts* 1; Reinhart Koselleck, 'Social History and Conceptual History' in Reinhart Koselleck, *The Practice of Conceptual History: Timing History, Spacing Concepts* (Todd Presner et al. trs., Stanford University Press 2002).

[52] Reinhart Koselleck, *Critique and Crisis: Enlightenment and the Pathogenesis of Modern Society* (MIT Press 2000); Reinhart Koselleck, 'Some

contribution to the *Geschichtliche Grundbegriffe: Historisches Lexikon zur Politisch-sozialen Sprache in Deutschland* (*Basic Concepts in History: A Historical Dictionary of Political and Social Language in Germany*), a seven-volume project (and two further volumes of indexes) on the histories of political and social concepts that Koselleck edited and whose theoretical approach he largely stewarded.[53] In that contribution, Koselleck identified 'crisis' as having a long and varied conceptual history.[54] In classical Greek, 'crisis' meant a final moment of decision: an 'imposed [choice] between stark alternatives—right or wrong, salvation or damnation, life or death'.[55] Its initial meaning was legal, denoting a sense of judgment, and went on to take on a theological meaning in the Jewish and Christian expectation of the Last Judgment, where God would offer salvation to the faithful on Earth. But its predominant use up until the sixteenth century was medical, denoting the point at which it could be determined if a patient would live or die.

Starting in the seventeenth century, however, 'crisis' rapidly changed its meaning. The concept was increasingly applied to political crises of the seventeenth and early-eighteenth centuries, leaning on its theological roots to signify '[changes] of fundamental world-historical significance'.[56] From there, through the experiences of the French and American revolutions, crisis came to signify the 'decisive' or 'critical' point that marks the 'epochal' transition from the past to the future. Through this change, the meaning of 'crisis' temporalized, becoming bound up in conceptualizations of movement through the past, present and future:

> Applied to history, 'crisis', since 1780, has become an expression of a new sense of time which both indicated and intensified the end of an epoch ... Conceptualized

---

Questions Regarding the Conceptual History of "Crisis"' in Koselleck (n 51).

[53] Otto Brunner, Werner Conze, and Reinhart Koselleck (eds), *Geschichtliche Grundbegriffe: Historisches Lexikon zur Politisch-sozialen Sprache in Deutschland*, 9 vols. (Klett-Cotta, 1972–1997). For discussions of the significance of the *Geschichtliche Grundbegriffe* and Koselleck's particular role in its production, see Hartmut Lehmann and Melvin Richter (eds), *The Meaning of Historical Terms and Concepts: New Studies on* Begriffsgeschichte (German Historical Institute 1996); Melvin Richter and Michaela W Richter, 'Introduction: Translation of Reinhart Koselleck's "Krise", in *Geschichtliche Grundbegriffe*' (2006) 67 *Journal of the History of Ideas* 343; Niklas Olsen, *History in the Plural: An Introduction to the Work of Reinhart Koselleck* (Berghahn Books 2012) chapter 4.

[54] Reinhart Koselleck and Michaela W. Richter, 'Crisis' (2006) 67 *Journal of the History of Ideas* 357.

[55] *Ibid.*, 358.

[56] *Ibid.*, 363.

> as chronic, 'crisis' can also indicate a state of greater or lesser permanence, as in a longer or shorter transition towards something better or worse or towards something altogether different.[57]

What Koselleck drives at here, as in all his work on the history of concepts, is the important fissure created by this modern sense of time.[58] Earlier meanings of crisis had little sense of past and future. The eschatology of the Last Judgment, for example, made no distinction between past and present: God's judgment would 'cover everyone, the pious and the unbelievers, the living and the dead'.[59] The future of that Judgment, too, was coeval with the present: 'already anticipated by the certainty of that redemption which grants eternal life ... [t]he Apocalypse ... is experienced as already present'.[60] Crisis in the modern sense, however, responded to the rapid acceleration in social change that outpaced this sense of final expectation. By describing the breakdown of old social orders and the revolutionary movements that sought to instantiate new societies, 'crisis' became a concept for the philosophy of history, pointing towards a past that we leave behind and a future we move towards. Koselleck identifies this use of crisis as first arising in the work of Rousseau:

> Behind the overthrow of monarchs ... emerges a vision of radical transformation encompassing all of society: "*Nous approchons de l'état de crises et du siècle des revolutions*" ("We are approaching a state of crises and a century of revolutions"). There will be many revolutions, leading to the subsequent conclusion that the condition of crisis which opens the nineteenth century will become permanent ... This vision of post-revolutionary society suggests the nullification of all human history to date. Rousseau, in effect, turns an eschatological concept into a philosophy of history.[61]

Accordingly, around the eighteenth century, the past, present and future would continue to differentiate from one another: the past no longer seemed the same as the present, becoming 'historical', while social changes continued to drive society forward into a different, open future.[62] Against this backdrop, crisis

---

57 *Ibid.*, 358.

58 See Koselleck, 'Introduction (*Einleitung*)' (n 51) 11–13, where Koselleck identifies the temporalization of concepts as a key marker of the shifts conceptual history seeks to investigate, where concepts became 'infused with a sense of expectation they had not had before' (11).

59 Koselleck and Richter (n 54) 359.

60 *Ibid.*, 360.

61 *Ibid.*, 372–3.

62 Reinhart Koselleck, 'The Eighteenth Century as the Beginning of Modernity' in Koselleck (n 51); Reinhart Koselleck, '*Neuzeit*: Remarks on the Semantics of

became 'a structural signature of modernity'.[63] It is through the designation of crises that we articulate and 'orchestrate' our modern sense of time, wherein new epochs are declared that are different from the past and present.[64]

I do not wish to get bogged down in the full details of the connections between international law and modernity (such a history would be book-length at least, requiring a more thorough interrogation of what 'modernity' means and how international law fits within it,[65] and attending to all its temporal, spatial and racial limits).[66] For present purposes, I merely want to note the resonances between Koselleck's understanding of 'crisis' as a temporalized concept and international law's crisis focus. Koselleck argues that the critical change that happened around the eighteenth century was the separation of the past, present and future. The past, once seen as coterminous with the present, now became fundamentally different, a place it was not possible to return to. On that basis, the future became the new orientation for society. No longer the site of a Biblical 'end of days', the future became an open horizon, able to be shaped and planned for again and again by man on earth.

Charlesworth's argument helps us identify the similarities with how international lawyers orient themselves in time: past events are excluded in the rush to find an immediate solution to the crisis in the present, while the future

---

Modern Concepts of Movement' in Reinhart Koselleck, *Futures Past: On the Semantics of Historical Time* (Keith Tribe tr., Columbia University Press, 2004).

63 Koselleck and Richter (n 54) 372.

64 I take this phrase from John Zammito, 'Koselleck's Philosophy of Historical Time(s) and the Practice of History' (2004) 43 *History and Theory* 124, 133: 'With concepts like "conjuncture" and "crisis", we can orchestrate the temporal layers of a moment of time to grasp more fully the synchrony of systemic change with short-term happenstance'.

65 For existing work on international law and modernity, see David Kennedy, 'International Law in the Nineteenth Century: History of an Illusion' (1996) 65 *Nordic Journal of International Law* 385; Nathaniel Berman, *Passion and Ambivalence: Colonialism, Nationalism, and International Law* (Brill 2011); Craven (n 50); Rebecca Mignot-Mahdavi, 'Futurism: Neglected Histories of International Law' (2025) 27 *Journal of the History of International Law* 154.

66 For critiques of the blind spots of Koselleck's thought on temporality and on the narration of modernity generally, see variously Shahzad Bashir, 'On Islamic Time: Rethinking Chronology in the Historiography of Muslim Societies' (2014) 53 *History and Theory* 519; Vanessa Ogle, 'Time, Temporality and the History of Capitalism' (2019) 243 *Past & Present* 312; Julia Angster, '"Sattelzeit": The Invention of "Premodern History" in the 1970s' (2025) 51 *History of European Ideas* 337; Anja Rathmann-Lutz, '"Ik Bün All Hier (I'm Already Here)": Modern Pre-Modernity or Premodern Modernity?' (2025) 51 *History of European Ideas* 353.

remains open to the intervention of international lawyers as and when new crises arise. The notion that the past might linger into the present and shape or decisively close off the future cannot easily be reconciled with this crisis focus—international law only works as a discipline if it can posit itself as the repeat solution to new crises.[67] Yet as we shall see, the type of modern temporality Koselleck describes has now itself fallen into 'crisis'—one that is intimately connected to climate change, ECEs, and the threat of environmental collapse. Understanding how historians have characterized this change, in the next section, can help bring into focus the disjuncture between international law and the climate crisis.

4. TIMING THE CLIMATE

In recent decades, historians and cultural theorists have begun to assert a transformation in our present sense of time. Where the present had previously felt transitory, the space from which we planned our future, it now stretches out, a 'broad present' that we are unable to escape or move on from.[68] Rapid social and technological change leaves us unable to grasp the parameters of our own time,[69] leaving us unable to think up new cultural or political forms beyond our present age.[70] In the words of Francois Hartog, today '[i]t is as though there were nothing but the present, like an immense stretch of water restlessly rippling'.[71]

This change in our sense of the present relates to changes in our relationship with the past and future. The future, which had once functioned as 'the end point of our desires, goals, or projections',[72] now appears as a threatening inevitability, 'increasingly closed to all prognoses' but, 'at the same time, [seeming]

---

[67] On the idea of international law as intimately connected to the 'capacity to act upon and fix future crises', see in particular Mignot-Mahdavi (n 65) and Cusato (n 28).

[68] Hans Ulrich Gumbrecht, *Our Broad Present: Time and Contemporary Culture* (Columbia University Press 2014).

[69] Hartmut Rosa, *Social Acceleration: A New Theory of Modernity* (Jonathan Trejo-Mathys tr, Columbia University Press 2013).

[70] Mark Fisher, *Capitalist Realism: Is There No Alternative?* (Zero Books 2009); Mark Fisher, *Ghosts of My Life: Writings on Depression, Hauntology and Lost Futures* (Zero Books 2013).

[71] François Hartog, *Regimes of Historicity: Presentism and Experiences of Time* (Saskia Brown tr, Columbia University Press 2017) 18.

[72] Aleida Assmann, *Is Time Out of Joint?: On the Rise and Fall of the Modern Time Regime* (Cornell University Press 2020) 4.

to draw near as a menace'.[73] Coming to terms with this future, 'perceived not as a promise ... but as a threat', also leads to a change in our relationship to the present and past as well. '[S]ince we are also the cause of this threat', Francois Hartog writes, 'it is accepted that we must take responsibility for it, as from today, since we failed to do so in the past.[74] With our increasing awareness of the impact of our past actions on the environment, our relationship toward the future also shifts, from an open horizon to a sense of preservation. As a result, our sense of time is reordered. The future no longer seems an open horizon, but rather a looming catastrophe which we must prevent; the present becomes a space of preservation rather than action; and the past, long thought to be gone and behind us, crops up again and again, in the ceaseless digital archiving of the past,[75] the memorialization of former injustices,[76] and the materialities of waste which 'clog' our future.[77]

While some decry the end of modernity, others find it a productive space to ask new and different questions. Assessing the work of Hartog, Hans Ulrich Gumbrecht and sociologist John Torpey, Aleida Assmann finds a sense of anxiety around the 'loss of many fundamental securities' which modernity had provided.[78] The crisis of time presents an opportunity, however, to historicize and critique the exclusions of that modern paradigm. 'Only after notions such as Messianism, apocalypse and other forms of metaphysical hope for salvation arose in monotheistic religions like Judaism and Christianity,' Assmann writes, 'did Western cultures begin establishing positive, even hyperbolic expectations for the future'.[79] As these cultures were then secularized, '[t]his modern temporal regime was endorsed, strengthened, and systematically developed not only by the Enlightenment, but also by ideologies like communism or the economic system of capitalism', all with their attendant racialization, colonial

---

73 Gumbrecht (n 68) xiii.

74 Hartog (n 71) 191.

75 Gumbrecht (n 68).

76 Much of this work has centred on questions of memory and public memorialization—as Aleida Assmann terms it, the question of how 'the past—especially a traumatic past—often has the present in its grip': Aleida Assmann, *Shadows of Trauma: Memory and the Politics of Postwar Identity* (Sarah Clift tr, Fordham University Press 2015) 239; and see also Assmann (n 72). For Koselleck's own reflections on war memorials, see Reinhart Koselleck, 'War Memorials: Identity Formation of the Survivors' in Koselleck (n 51).

77 Andreas Folkers, 'Fossil Modernity: The Materiality of Acceleration, Slow Violence, and Ecological Futures' (2021) 30 *Time and Society* 223, 225.

78 Assmann (n 72) 190.

79 *Ibid.*, 194.

domination and ecological extraction.[80] The 'end' of the modern time regime, then, gives us the opportunity to ask who was excluded from the triumphalism of these processes and to begin a new phase where Western thought 'relinquishes some of its arrogance, develops a more receptive attitude towards other cultures, and develops guidelines for a fuller engagement with them'.[81] Read in this way, the crisis of time seems 'less like a dangerous disease of time ... and more like a return and rediscovery of those aspects of time that the modern temporal regime had dogmatically excluded'.[82]

In this light, Andreas Folkers' work on 'fossil modernity' provides perhaps the clearest intervention into the specific challenges and opportunities that ECEs pose to modernity.[83] For Folkers, modernity and fossil fuels are inseparable. Not only did fossil fuels 'literally fuel the tremendous dynamism and speed of modern societies', they also served as markers of our increasing mastery over the planet.[84] Fossilized carbon resources, Folkers writes, 'serve as raw material for petrochemical substances used in fertilizers, pesticides, cosmetics and plastics that not only define modern ways of life but also exhibit a molecular structure unforeseen on this planet before the advent of modernity'.[85] Fossil fuels, in other words, materially marked out the epoch of modernity in the unnatural waste that it left behind on the planet: plastic is 'modernity made durable', with fossil modernity having 'saturated environmental spaces with its residuals'.[86]

As knowledge of the detrimental impact of this waste grows, however—in the 'toxification of bodies and environments, degradation of soils, loss of biodiversity, plastic waste, and, of course, climate change'[87]—our relationship to those materials changes too. '[A]s asset and liability', Folkers writes:

> carbon materialities both underpin and undermine the temporal operations of what I call fossil modernity. They make possible and propel the pace and progressive perspective of modern temporality and by the same token, or rather the same material substratum, confront modern societies with a particular slow time of material durability and ecological degradation.[88]

---

80 *Ibid.*
81 *Ibid.*, 176.
82 *Ibid.*, 197.
83 Folkers (n 77). My thanks to Kasia Mika for drawing my attention to this work.
84 *Ibid.*, 224.
85 *Ibid.*
86 *Ibid.*, 230–1.
87 *Ibid.*, 224.
88 *Ibid.*

Locating the production of time in the materiality of fossil fuels helps bring into focus the deep confrontation ECEs pose not to modernity, which could only come to be by avoiding the consequences of the 'slow time of material durability and ecological degradation'.[89] Now confronted with the 'looming ecological disasters' this avoidance has produced, however, 'modernity seems ever more outdated'.[90] Any future temporality, then, must find a path that takes seriously the slow impact of environmental degradation. Echoing Assmann's discussion, Folkers argues that a focus on 'the carbon substratum of modernity' helps unsettle the 'self-reassuring consciousness of [modern] time', leading to a reordering of our relationship to the past and future:

> Since modern societies are confronted with the accumulated residuals of its fossil-fuelled operations, they cannot fully emancipate from the past to seize an open future of progress and possibility. For the same reason, they cannot separate themselves from nature but become implicated in the timescales of a natural history they have inadvertently created.[91]

In order to 'cope with these afterlives of modernist progress', '[s]ocial transformations can no longer be solely understood as bringing forth the new' but will instead 'have to come back to and emerge from the residual',[92] grappling with the differentiated 'thick tempo-material traces of the inequalities and injustices that structure fossil modernity'.[93] And notably, the example Folkers gives comes from international law: namely those movements who challenge 'the hegemonic climate regime' by placing '"historical justice" on the agenda of international climate summits by calling for fairly sharing mitigation efforts and for compensations for present future loss and damages'.[94]

5. LAW, TIME, AND ENVIRONMENTAL CHRONIC EMERGENCIES

With this picture of our contemporary sense of time set out, let me return again to international law and connect together the argument made across this chapter. The oral submissions of Vanuatu and the USA, I have argued, rest on two different temporalities. For Vanuatu, the focus is on undoing harm already caused in the past in order to avoid a near-certain fate of destruction. For the USA, on the other hand, the focus is instead on the present: climate

89 *Ibid.*
90 *Ibid.*, 238.
91 *Ibid.*, 225.
92 *Ibid.*, 233.
93 *Ibid.*, 236.
94 *Ibid.*

change is something states are now working on, and the ICJ can work best if it guides their actions into a future that (the USA presumes) remains open to change. By turning to history, I have tried to locate this split in a particular historical moment. The emergence of modernity led to the raising of 'crisis' to prime position in delineating our sense of time. That time is now, however, breaking down, and so today we are struggling to reorient ourselves to dealing, first, with a threatening future, and second with the legacies of the past. My aim, then, has been to bring into focus the profound demands ECEs make on international law, precisely because it involves such a radical departure from its underpinning modernism.

But does this make the challenge of time insurmountable? International law has certainly failed to measure up to catastrophic futures before. Like with the *Nuclear Weapons* Advisory Opinion,[95] perhaps the Court will again be 'unable to reach the core of the request—the massive killing of the innocent'.[96] Much of the scholarship surrounding the Advisory Opinion also seems anxious as to the hopes for international law to digest this problem. Even where scholars agree with Vanuatu's case, there is an anxiety that international law cannot provide what is asked of it—that it may fail to 'rise to the occasion' or answer the 'plea' of a world 'burning urgently and irreparably'[97]—or that Vanuatu's claims have to overcome obstacles and 'puzzles' in order to fit into the frame of international law.[98] Assessing the hopes for an advisory opinion on climate change (written before the ICJ request was drafted), Philippe Sands writes that it would not be useful 'to dwell or focus on the past, on issues

---

95 *Legality of the Threat or Use of Nuclear Weapons*, Advisory Opinion, International Court of Justice, ICJ Reports 1996, 226 (8 July 1996).

96 Martti Koskenniemi, 'Faith, Identity, and the Killing of the Innocent: International Lawyers and Nuclear Weapons' (1997) 10 *Leiden Journal of International Law* 137, 140. Cf. the interesting use of the *Nuclear Weapons* Advisory Opinion in Advisory Opinion (n 1), Submissions of the Dominican Republic, 10 December 2024, Verbatim record 2024/48, 23, para. 11–2, noting that the 'fundamental right of every State to survival', affirmed by the Court at para. 96 of the *Nuclear Weapons* Advisory Opinion, should be applied to climate change to ensure the protection of small island states.

97 Tom Sparks, Nataša Nedeski and Gleider Hernández, 'Judging Climate Change Obligations: Can the World Court Rise to the Occasion?: Part I: Primary Obligations to Combat Climate Change' (*Völkerrechtsblog* 30 April 2020) <https://voelkerrechtsblog.org/judging-climate-change-obligations-can-the-world-court-raise-the-occasion/> accessed 26 March 2025; Nataša Nedeski, Tom Sparks and Gleider Hernández, 'The World Is Burning, Urgently and Irreparably – a Plea for Interim Protection against Climatic Change at the ICJ' (2023) 22 *The Law & Practice of International Courts and Tribunals* 301.

98 Nollkaemper (n 29).

of historic responsibility', and so any advisory opinion should instead remain focused on 'workable, effective solutions that have the special authority of the law to back them'.[99] Within this frame of 'workable' and 'effective' solutions, Sands follows a model similar to the US: '[t]he purpose of an advisory opinion, if there is to be one, is surely to benefit the international community as a whole, by looking forward'.[100]

That anxiety can be overcome, however, if we think more deeply about international law's role in the construction of time. If we look beyond the discipline's traditional focus on crises, we can find many different legal times, in many more places than we might think. Writing in 1996, Judge Rosalyn Higgins expressed a 'general fascination with the concept of time', both in its scientific meaning ('I puzzle endlessly over the relationship between time and matter, and the insistence of scientists that before the Big Bang time did not exist') and its social significance ('I am intrigued that our concepts of time came to Australia only with the First Fleet, for aboriginal time was cyclical rather than linear').[101] 'It has therefore been a happy occurrence', Higgins writes, 'that the concept of time plays an important part, too, in international law'.[102] Determining jurisdiction, for example, requires the tribunal to determine the temporal limits of a state's acceptance of jurisdiction, as well as when a particular dispute crystallized, to 'see if it is before the exclusion date or outside the exclusion period'.[103] Preventing the retrospective application of the law, on the other hand, 'is an elementary principle of justice', but one that is 'tested to the limits when there is a strong view within society that the offence concerned is so repugnant that it should long since have been classified as a crime, and that change is on the horizon'.[104] Accordingly, the temporalities that courts and tribunals are able to enforce reflect a belief in how international law should be applied and, in this way, the question of what law *can* regulate becomes conjoined to notions of what law *should* regulate.

---

[99] Philippe Sands, 'Climate Change and the Rule of Law: Adjudicating the Future in International Law' (2016) 28 *Journal of Environmental Law* 19, 30, 32.

[100] *Ibid.*, 30. For a similar critique, suggesting the need for a 'reality check' on the hopes for an Advisory Opinion, see Benoit Mayer, 'International Advisory Proceedings on Climate Change' (2023) 44 *Michigan Journal of International Law* 41.

[101] Rosalyn Higgins, 'Time and the Law: International Perspectives on an Old Problem' (1997) 46 *International & Comparative Law Quarterly* 501, 501. Although published in 1997, the article is based on a lecture delivered in November 1996.

[102] *Ibid.*

[103] *Ibid.*, 502.

[104] *Ibid.*, 508.

A similar analysis has been offered for the ICJ's approach in the recent *Chagos Islands* Advisory Opinion.[105] In that Opinion, the ICJ was called upon to determine whether the detachment of the Chagos Archipelago from Mauritius in 1965, prior to Mauritius' attaining independence in 1968, was an unlawful violation of the right to self-determination. The UK argued that such a right would not have been recognized in 1965 and, following the doctrine of intertemporal law, the right could not be violated at that time. The Court instead held that the norm had crystallized in 1960, with the adoption of General Assembly Resolution 1514 (XV), and that its customary status was later confirmed with the adoption of the 1970 Declaration on Friendly Relations. As Steven Wheatley argues, this demonstrated a particular notion of time: not one where a particular state in the past was affirmed (the right of self-determination 'is' or 'is not' in existence in 1965), but rather one that looks back from the perspective of the present (a right to self-determination 'will be' affirmed as existing in 1970).[106]

These examples are impressionistic at best. But they do point towards an underacknowledged flexibility in how international law engages with time. While the USA may claim climate change only became thinkable for international law with the passage of the UN climate change regime, the *Chagos Islands* opinion shows that the Court could instead frame this regime as *recognizing* a harm already known to be occurring. And with the existential threat posed by ECEs, why should the Court not engage head on with the demands of justice, as international law has previously with crimes against humanity?[107]

The answer is by no means certain. But reflecting more deeply on time and its operation within and behind international law will help it squarely meet the demands made upon it at this juncture in history.

---

105 International Court of Justice, *Legal Consequences of the Separation of the Chagos Archipelago from Mauritius in 1965,* Advisory Opinion, 25 February 2019, ICJ Reports 2019, 95.

106 Steven Wheatley, 'Revisiting the Doctrine of Intertemporal Law' (2021) 41 *Oxford Journal of Legal Studies* 484.

107 This argument is also put forward, in different terms, in Nollkaemper (n 29) 28:

> '[I]n some cases, courts have solved puzzles of factual cause-effect relations by relying on normative standards based on the imperative to prevent global risks combined with evidence of general causation. This presents a significant shift in thinking about causation in international law. While traditionally, legal (or 'normative') causation served to restrict the responsibility consequences of factual causation, in recent climate change practice, normative causation extends rather than narrows responsibility.'

8. Environmental chronic emergencies and future generations

Laura Magi

1. 'ENVIRONMENTAL CHRONIC EMERGENCIES' AND FUTURE GENERATIONS

The expression 'environmental chronic emergencies' (ECEs) may appear an intriguing oxymoron: while in common language an emergency is an event that erupts suddenly and unexpectedly,[1] what is chronic is precisely the opposite, namely something that has been occurring for a very long time. Instead, this book adopts a different concept of emergency that, as already well said,[2] comes from the Latin expression *e-mergere*, which means that an emergency is something that comes to light, that reveals itself. Therefore, ECEs translate perfectly the idea of long-lasting phenomena, which happen because human beings have not worried about it, and which may precede (or not) the explosion of forms of violence, disasters or, more generally, the blowing up of a disruptive force.

The degradation of the environment and climate change, caused by human activities and the absence of adequate preventive policies, are perfect examples of ECEs.

Since their eradicated nature and the difficulties of interrupting them, phenomena like climate change affect humans and non-humans who live today, as well as those who will exist tomorrow. Moreover, the well-known incremental nature of the climate emergency allows us to state with certainty that future generations (FGs) will be more affected by the negative consequences of the increase in global temperature than the present ones. The Intergovernmental

---

1 The Collins Dictionary defines an emergency as an unexpected and serious situation that must be dealt with quickly.

2 See Sara De Vido, 'Feminist Legal Methods and Environmental Chronic Emergencies: Challenging the Anthropocentric and Androcentric International Legal System' in this Volume.

Panel on Climate Change (IPCC) predicts that children in the year 2020 are projected to experience a nearly four-fold increase in extreme events under 1.5°C of global warming by 2100, and a five-fold increase under 3°C warming while such increases in exposure would not be experienced by a person aged 55 in the year 2020 in her/his remaining lifetime under any warming scenario.[3] If this trend will not be interrupted, unborn generations will experience even more extreme events. Therefore, ECEs deeply concern FGs.

1.1 Premises on FGs

To begin with, it is indispensable to clarify the notion of FGs and to take a stance on the question of FGs as right holders.

Two different notions of FGs have been formulated; the first considers FGs as synonymous with unborn children. This is the notion adopted by the UN Declaration for Future Generations,[4] which speaks about future generations as 'all those generations that do not yet exist, and who will inherit this planet'.[5] The same definition is provided in the Maastricht Principles on the Human Rights of Future Generations, adopted in 2023 by a group of international law scholars.[6]

In the same vein, the General Comment No. 26 adopted by the Committee on the Rights of the Child (CRC) in 2023 distinguishes between children who are present on Earth and FGs when it deals with the intergenerational equity (IGE) principle.[7]

The other notion encompasses current children as well.[8] It seems to refer to this latter the Committee on Economic, Social and Cultural Rights (CESCR)

---

3 IPCC, *Climate Change 2022: Impacts, Adaptation and Vulnerability. Working Group II Contribution to the Sixth Assessment Report* (2022).

4 The Declaration on Future Generations is annexed to the Pact for the Future and is one of the outcomes of the Summit of the Future, held on 22 and 23 September 2024.

5 UNGA, Res 79/1 (22 September 2024) UN Doc. A/RES/79/1 (Declaration on Future Generations' annexed to the Pact for the Future).

6 The document is readable at <www.ohchr.org/sites/default/files/documents/new-york/events/hr75-future-generations/Maastricht-Principles-on-The-Human-Rights-of-Future-Generations.pdf> accessed 15 November 2024.

7 UN Committee on the Rights of the Child (CRC), 'General Comment No. 26 on Children's Rights and the Environment with a Special Focus on Climate Change' (22 August 2023) UN Doc CRC/C/GC/26, para. 11.

8 Ie Skogly speaks of FGs as 'referring to the rights of current youth and children when they grow into adulthood, as well as other people who will live in the future': Sigur I. Skogly, 'The Right to Continuous Improvement of Living Conditions and Human Rights of Future Generations: A Circle Impossible to

in a background paper for the preparation of a General Comment on sustainable development, when it states that 'access to effective remedies is often undermined by restrictive rules of legal standing, which do not recognize public interest actions, class actions or representative litigation *on behalf of future generations*', and also claims for the recognition of legal standing for children 'whose future enjoyment of Covenant rights are placed at risk due to climate change and environmental degradation'.[9] Similarly, in *Daniel Billy et al. v Australia*, the petitioners – who acted for themselves and on behalf of their children – complained that Australia had violated Article 24, para. 1.[10] of the Covenant on Civil and Political Rights against the future generations of their Indigenous community, in particular their children.[11] While the former definition may seem to be more adherent to the meaning of the expression 'future generations', this chapter will take into account both notions of FGs since (current) children can reasonably be considered 'close future generations'.[12]

The second point concerns the qualification of FGs as rights holders.

Sometimes national tribunals found that FGs were right holders – this is, for instance, the case of the Colombian Supreme Court's judgment in the Lozano Barragán case –[13] while in other cases it was expressly excluded. A crystal clear statement is illustrated by the German Constitutional Court's judgment in *Neubauer et al.,* where the Court's ruling focused on those alive today. In

---

Square?' in Jessie Hohmann and Beth Goldblatt (eds), *The Right to the Continuous Improvement of Living Conditions: Responding to Complex Global Challenges* (Hart 2021) 65.

[9] UN Committee on Economic, Social and Cultural Rights (CESCR), *Issues Paper on Sustainable Development and the International Covenant on Economic, Social and Cultural Rights* (2021).

[10] Article 24 of the International Covenant on Civil and Political Rights (ICCPR) recognizes the right of every child, without any discrimination, to receive from his family, society and the State the protection required by his status as a minor. The implementation of this provision entails the adoption of special measures to protect children, in addition to the measures that States are required to take under ICCPR Article 2.

[11] UN Human Rights Committee, *Daniel Billy et al. v Australia* (22 September 2022) UN Doc CCPR/C/135/D/3624/2019.

[12] This expression is used by Celine Kermisch, 'Specifying the Concept of Future Generations for Addressing Issues Related to High-Level Radioactive Waste' (2016) 22 (6) *Science and Engineering Ethics* 1797, to distinguish born children from unborn or remote future generations.

[13] Colombian Supreme Court, *Andrea Lozano Barragán et al v President of the Republic et al*, Judgment of 5 April 2018, para. 13.

the Court's opinion, FGs 'either as a whole or as the sum of individuals not yet born, do not yet carry any fundamental rights in the present'.[14]

In this author's opinion, children now alive may definitely be considered rights holders and, therefore, it is acceptable to say that FGs are entitled to rights if this expression is only intended as encompassing and synonymous with current children. On the contrary, considering unborn children (namely, FGs according to the first definition recalled above) as right holders is a fascinating thesis,[15] but it is also extremely unrealistic. While it does not necessarily entail accepting that they are subjects of a legal order – in this Author's opinion an entity may be entitled to an international legal right or holder of an international legal duty even if it is not a subject of international law – asserting that FGs may be right holders requires disrupting an even untouchable rule, namely that a right holder is someone (natural or legal person) that already exists.[16] For this reason, this contribution will take the idea of FGs as rights holders aside and, therefore, will prefer the different perspective that conceives present generations as having responsibilities towards FGs. This seems also to be the approach that States prefer, as it has recently resulted from the preamble of the UN Declaration on Future Generations.[17]

---

[14] German Constitutional Court, *Neubauer et al.*, Order of the First Senate, Case no. BvR 2656/18/1, BvR 78/20/1, BvR 96/20/1, BvR 288/20, 24 March 2021, paras 146 and 109.

[15] In that sense Fons Coomans, 'Towards 2122 and Beyond: Developing the Human Rights of Future Generations' (2023) 41(1) *Netherlands Quarterly of Human Rights* 53, who speaks about the right of FGs to live in dignity.

[16] Humphreys states that FGs is a vague concept because the membership of the group is constantly changing and that it is not a good basis of rights; on this basis, he argues that it is preferable to focus on the impact of climate change on persons alive now; see Stephen Humphreys, 'Against Future Generations' (2022) 33 (4) *European Journal of International Law* 1061. Lawrence replied that the category of FGs is indeterminate as well as other categories of vulnerable persons who have particular rights ascribed to them under human rights law, i.e., children, which constantly changes since people fall within and without the definition; see Peter Lawrence, 'International Law Must Respond to the Reality of Future Generations: A Reply to Stephen Humphreys' (2023) 34 (3) *European Journal of International Law* 669. For a radical position see Wilfred Beckerman, Joanna Pasek, 'The Rights of Future Generations' in Wilfred Beckerman, Joanna Pasek (eds), *Justice, Posterity, and the Environment* (Oxford University Press 2001), 11.

[17] Indeed, the Declaration States recognizes '(. . .) that the decisions, actions and inactions of present generations have an intergenerational multiplier effect' and therefore resolves 'to ensure that present generations act with responsibility towards safeguarding the needs and interests of future generations'.

Refusing to frame FGs as rights holders does not mean that they are not a relevant actor for international law as the law of ECEs. On the contrary, FGs may play an important role by means of the IGE principle.

Recently, the discourse on FGs has been considered useless if not harmful.[18] According to this last view, shifting the focus from the present to FGs might conceal existing responsibilities to the detriment of vulnerable groups, diverting attention away from current inequalities and poverty. This would have the effect of carrying today's structural inequalities into the future.[19]

On the contrary, in this author's view, if it is proved that the interest in protecting FGs is more than an ethical value, namely if it is a general principle of international law (GPIL), invoking the interest in protecting FGs or the IGE principle can be decisive in justifying the decision of national courts to refuse the granting of mining or deforestation licenses as measures intended to prevent the eradication of ECEs, or ordering the adoption of effective mitigation measures, etc. and thus achieving concrete results that will produce benefits for unborn as well as for present individuals (see below, para. 2). This will have the effect of tempering present inequalities and, thus, not projecting them into the future.

1.2 Why Adopt an Intersectional Approach to Study ECEs and FGs?

This chapter, as well as the whole book, adopts an intersectional approach to the study of ECEs. As it is well known, intersectionality is a methodological perspective to the study of discrimination and privilege. It assumes that different factors (like gender, age, race, social origins, citizenships, etc.) can meet at an intersection and affect in a specific way an individual's life, a social group, etc.[20] While forged by a legal scholar,[21] intersectionality has been for long ignored in legal studies, while it has been mainly adopted in sociology

---

18 Humphreys (n 16) 1063.

19 *Ibid.*

20 Kimberle Crenshaw was one of the first scholars to use this approach: Kimberle Crenshaw, 'Demarginalizing the Intersection of Race and Sex: A Black Feminist Critique of Antidiscrimination Doctrine, Feminist Theory and Antiracist Politics' 1989 (1) *University of Chicago Legal Forum* 139.

21 Against an approach that ignores that FGs are likely to vary significantly in terms of wealth and power, see Nicky van Dijk, 'The Capability Approach as a Roadmap for Re-thinking Intergenerational Justice' in Jan Linehan and Peter Lawrence (eds), *Giving Future Generations a Voice. Normative Frameworks, Institutions and Practice* (Edward Elgar Publishing 2021) 42; in this sense also Humphreys (n 16) 1075.

or in the philosophy of law (especially by those who claim a feminist legal methodology).[22] More recently, it has also gained ground in human rights law. A hint to the necessity of this approach seems also to be present in the Preamble of the Paris Agreement where it is acknowledged that the 'Parties should, when taking action to address climate change, respect, promote and consider their respective obligations on human rights, the right to health, the rights of Indigenous peoples, local communities, migrants, children, persons with disabilities and people in vulnerable situations and the right to development, as well as gender equality, empowerment of women and intergenerational equity'.

To adopt an intersectional approach to the discourse on FGs (and ECEs) means firstly looking at FGs as a vulnerable group that may be the object of discrimination because of the behaviour of past and present generations, namely as a result of a structural, well-rooted and silent pattern of conduct dominated by interests of here and now (presentism). Secondly, it means looking at FGs not as a monolith, as it is usually done, but, on the contrary, as an entity that is discernible only by disaggregating it into different and overlapping groups that compose it. Being an unborn child is *per se* an identitarian dimension of a (future) individual, but it does not necessarily exhaust the complex identity of

---

22 In the drawback of an intersectional approach, the ecofeminist theory finds the reasons that link women and nature in the Western ideology and its male bias. It sees women and nature as part of a binary relationship where one part is higher and dominant, and the other is lower, oppressed and discriminated against. According to eco-feminism, the dualism between human and nature, male and female, subject and object, present and future generations etc., legitimizes cultural distancing and exclusion, in simple words, domination by one level against another (Val Plumwood, *Feminism and the Mastery of Nature* (Routledge 1993) 43, 47–8). In this binary relationship, what FGs have in common with women and nature is the fact of being in a subordinated and lower level (*ibid.*, 'no attempt to liberate women (or any other oppressed group) will be successful without an equal attempt to liberalize nature', 36). For an overview of the ecofeminist theory see Maria Mies, Vandana Shiva, *Ecofeminism* (Fernwood Publications 1993); Carolyn Merchant, *Earthcare: Women and the Environment* (Routledge 1996). According to this thought, no attempt to overcome dualism will be successful without an overthrow of the established order to develop an alternative culture that fully recognizes human identity (without gender distinction) as in continuity and unity with nature: see Kate Wilkinson Cross, 'A Critical Evaluation of Inter-Generational Equity and Its Application in the Climate Change Context', in Cathi Albertyn, Meghan Campbell, Helena Alviar García et al. (eds), *Feminist Frontiers in Climate Justice: Gender Equality, Climate Change and Rights* (Edward Elgar Publishing 2022) 49.

that individual, which may be characterized by other identitarian dimensions or distinctive elements like gender, place of birth, citizenship, etc.

2. INTER-GENERATIONAL EQUITY AS A MORAL VALUE AND A GENERAL PRINCIPLE OF INTERNATIONAL LAW

As recalled above, while FGs cannot be considered rights holders, FGs concerns can nevertheless play a role if it is proved that the interest in protecting FGs or the IGE principle is not only moral value but are also GPIL. While the ICJ's Advisory Opinion on FGs is still awaited and it will definitely contribute to clarifying the nature of the IGE principle,[23] it is already possible to assert that IGE is more than an ethical value,[24] it is a GPIL.[25]

---

23 On 29 March 2023 the United Nations General Assembly adopted a resolution asking the Court to adopt an advisory opinion on States' Obligations in Respect of Climate Change (UNGA Res A/77/L.58 (29 March 2023) UN Doc. A/RES/77/276/ (Request for an Advisory Opinion of the International Court of Justice on the Obligations of States in Respect of Climate Change). In its request, the GA asked to Court to clarify the States' obligations 'to ensure the protection of the climate system and other parts of the environment from anthropogenic emissions of greenhouse gases for States and for present and future generations' and the legal consequences of their violations in case of 'significant harm to the climate system and other parts of the environment', especially for 'small island developing States' and 'present and future generations affected by the adverse effects of climate change': for an early comment, Otto Spijkers, 'United Nations General Assembly Request for an Advisory Opinion of the International Court of Justice on the Obligations of States in Respect of Climate Change' (2023) 7 (1) *Chinese Journal of Environmental Law* 13.

24 According to some authors, the principle would only be a moral value: see Lavanya Rajamani, *Differential Treatment in International Environmental Law* (Oxford University Press 2006) 84–5; Catherine Redgwell, 'Principles and Emerging Norms in International Law: Intra- and Inter-generational Equity in Kevin R. Gray, Richard Tarasofsky and Cinnamon P. Carlarne (eds), *The Oxford Handbook of International Climate Change Law* (Oxford Academic 2016) 185–94, 198; Riccardo Pisillo Mazzeschi, Alessandra Viviani, 'General Principles of International Law: From Rules to Values?' in Riccardo Pisillo Mazzeschi and Pasquale De Sena (eds), *Global Justice, Human Rights and the Modernization of International Law* (Springer 2018) 113, 151–5.

25 This is the opinion of Edith Brown Weiss, the author who first studied the IGE principle: Edith Brown Weiss, *In Fairness to Future Generations: International Law, Common Patrimony, and Intergenerational Equity* (United Nations University, Transnational Publishers 1989); Edith Brown Weiss, 'Implementing Intergenerational Equity' in Malgosia Fitzmaurice, David M. Ong

The expression GPIL is used here to refer to principles formed within the international legal system,[26] to distinguish them from the general principles of law derived from national legal systems. This does not mean excluding that IGE may also be qualified as a general principle derived from national laws, but an investigation into it is out of the possibility of this research.[27]

It is beyond dispute that the IGE is first taken into account by soft law instruments and treaties – that refer to it in their preamble[28] – as an ethical imperative. Sometimes it is said expressly.[29]

---

and Panos Merkouris (eds), *Research Handbook on International Environmental Law* (Edward Elgar Publishing 2010) 100; Edith Brown Weiss, 'The Theoretical Framework for International Legal Principles of Intergenerational Equity and Implementation through National Institutions' in Marie-Claire Cordonier Segger, Marcel Szabó and Alexandra R. Harrington (eds), *Intergenerational Justice in Sustainable Development Treaty Implementation* (Cambridge University Press 2021) 20. Other authors favouring this opinion are: Gregory F. Maggio, 'Inter/Intrageneral Equity: Current Applications under International Law for Promoting the Sustainable Development of Natural Resources' (1997) 4 (2) *Buffalo Environmental Law Journal* 162; Lynda M. Collins, 'Revisiting the Doctrine of Intergenerational Equity in Global Environmental Governance' (2007) 1 (1) *Dalhousie Law Journal* 79; Rüdiger Wolfrum, *Solidarity and Community Interests: Driving Forces for the Interpretation and Development of International Law* (Brill Nijhoff 2021) 206–8.

[26] The expression is used by the International Law Commission (ILC) in its work of codification on the topic of general principles of international law: see ILC, 'Draft Conclusions Provisionally Adopted by the Drafting Committee on First Reading' (12 May 2023) UN Doc. A/CN.4/L.982, Draft Conclusion 3.

[27] For a study on it see: Alessandra Gianelli, 'La tutela delle future generazioni nel diritto internazionale: regola, principio o valore?' in Micaela Frulli (ed.), *L'interesse delle generazioni future nel diritto internazionale e dell'Unione europea* (Editoriale scientifica 2023) 19; Francesca Cerulli, 'Safeguarding Future Generations: The Legal Status of Intergenerational Equity in International Law' (2024) 55 *Netherlands Yearbook of International Law* (forthcoming).

[28] For a list of treaties referring to IGE in their preamble see Cerulli (n 27).

[29] I.e., Principle 1 of the 1972 Stockholm Declaration states: '(. . .) [m]an has the fundamental right to freedom, equality and adequate conditions of life, in an environment of a quality that permits a life of dignity and well-being, and he bears a solemn responsibility to protect and improve the environment for present and future generations' (See United Nations Conference on the Human Environment, 'Declaration of the United Nations Conference on the Human Environment' (1972) UN Doc. A/CONF.48/14). In the same way, the 1997 UNESCO Declaration on Responsibilities for Future Generations states that the Organization's ethical mission is to deal with the protection of FGs and that UNESCO has a moral obligation to provide guidelines on it. In its 2013 Report titled *Intergenerational*

Nevertheless, considering IGE as an ethical value does not preclude it from being also a GPIL.

According to international law scholars, general principles of international law 'can be deduced from the various rules by extracting and generalizing some of their most significant common points',[30] and when they are peculiar to a particular branch of international law, 'they are general legal standards overarching the whole body of law governing a specific area'.[31] This is also the opinion of the International Law Commission (ILC). In its *Draft Conclusions on General Principles of Law* provisionally adopted in 2023, the Commission qualified general principles formed within the international legal system as rules that 'the community of nations has recognized (. . .) as intrinsic to the international legal system' (*Draft Conclusion 7*);[32] the Commentary to this provision states that the methodology used for the identification of GPIL consists of an inductive analysis of existing international law norms.[33]

When the values that justified the conclusion of a treaty, perhaps expressed in the preamble, are translated into specific State obligations and in provisions establishing cooperative mechanisms among States, it is reasonable to conclude that we are dealing with values that have also been transformed into a GPIL. This is all the more convincing if there are many treaties supporting these values and translating them into binding provisions, and if they are multilateral treaties.

Solidarity and the Needs of Future Generations, the UN Secretary-General states that inter-generational solidarity is a universal value: UN Secretary-General, 'Intergenerational Solidarity and the Needs of Future Generations' (15 August 2013) UN Doc. A/68/322.

[30] Antonio Cassese, *International Law* (Oxford University Press 2001) 151.

[31] *Ibid.*, 152. See also Georg Schwarzenberger, 'The Fundamental Principles of International Law' (1955) 87 *Recueil des cours de l'Académie de La Haye* 201; Giorgio Gaja, 'General Principles of Law', in *Max Planck Encyclopedia of Public International Law* (Oxford University Press 2012) 370–78, para. 31; Beatrice Bonafé, Paolo Palchetti, 'Relying on General Principles in International Law', in Catherine Brölmann (ed.), *Research Handbook on the Theory and Practice of International Lawmaking* (Edward Elgar Publishing 2016) 160–76, 163.

[32] ILC, 'Report of the International Law Commission on the Work of the 73rd Session' (2022) UN Doc. A/77/10, 320, Draft Conclusion 7.

[33] *Ibid.*, 320, para. 3. Draft Conclusion 2 clarifies that a general principle formed within the international legal system has to be 'generally recognized by [the community of nations]'; its Commentary merely clarifies that 'the term does not seek to suggest that there is a need for a unified or collective recognition of a general principle of law': ILC, 'Report of the International Law Commission on the Work of the 72nd *Session*' (2021) UN Doc. A/76/10, 184, para. 4.

This is certainly the case of the IGE principle since, in concluding treaties in the field of environmental protection, whether or not they expressly refer to the interest of the FGs – States make very specific commitments to prevent certain natural resources from risking extinction or destruction by serious and irreversible forms of exploitation also in the interest of FGs.

The principle of IGE is a principle of social justice between generations. It requires States to adopt measures to ensure equal access to and use of resources (natural, but not only) between generations. In concrete terms, it translates into the imposition on States of the obligation to protect resources – while allowing their exploitation – to prevent their impoverishment by one generation to the detriment of the others. It therefore entails the adoption by States of measures that limit the ability of individuals or legal persons to use the resources currently available without limit, and also imposes a fair distribution of the sacrifices that these limitations will entail between present and future generations.

3. HOW CAN IGE PRINCIPLE HAVE A ROLE TO CONTRAST ENVIRONMENTAL CHRONIC EMERGENCIES?

3.1 At National Level

States' duty to protect nature and biodiversity for FGs is provided in many constitutions,[34] and can be the legal foundation for legal actions claiming the constitutionality of laws that do not duly take FGs interests into account.

It is what occurred in *Neubauer et al.* decided by the German Federal Constitutional Court.[35]

The plaintiffs claimed that the Federal Climate Change Act (Bundes-Klimaschutzgesetz, KSG) was unconstitutional because it was in violation of the State's obligations to protect the fundamental rights to life and health and the right to property, provided in Articles 2, para. 2, and 14, para. 1, of the German Constitution, caused by climate change. The Court admitted that Article 2, para. 2, obliged the State to afford protection against the risks of climate change.[36] It also stated that the fundamental right to property under Article 14, para. 1, included the State's duty to protect property against the

[34] In the list of constitutions that the Centre for International Environmental Law surveyed in 2017, more than sixty refer to FGs; States belonging to different legal traditions are represented, although fewer are the Asian States: <www.ohchr.org/sites/default/files/Documents/Issues/Environment/SREnvironment/Child/CIEL.pdf> accessed 24 October 2024.

[35] German Constitutional Court, *Neubauer et al.* (n 14).

[36] *Ibid.*, para. 144.

risks of climate change.[37] However, the Court excluded a violation of them. It found that, given the leeway afforded to the legislator in fulfilling such duties, the Basic Law was only violated if no precautionary measures had been taken or if the measures adopted had proven to be manifestly unsuitable or completely inadequate for achieving the required protection goal, or if they had fallen significantly short of the protection goal. It excluded that this was the case of the KSG.[38] Nevertheless, the Court found that the KSG violated fundamental rights because it interfered with the freedom protected under the Basic Law. The Court accepted that the interference had a constitutional justification, provided by Article 20a of the Constitution, which provides that the State, '[mi]ndful (. . .) of its responsibility toward future generations', shall protect the natural foundations of life and animals by legislative, executive and judicial action. The Court interpreted this provision as encompassing the State's obligation to take climate action and achieve climate neutrality.[39] Nevertheless, it found that the KSG was unconstitutional to the extent that it created a disproportionate risk that the freedom the Constitution protects would have been impaired for future generations. According to the Court, the fundamental rights the Basic Law protects oblige the legislator to reduce the GHG emissions, as required under Article 20a, in a forward-looking way, so that the reduction burdens are not distributed over time and between generations to the detriment of future generations. In the Court's view, it followed from the principle of proportionality that one generation must not be allowed to consume large portions of the CO_2 budget if this would mean leaving future generations with a drastic reduction burden and exposing their lives to serious losses of freedom.[40]

In other countries, the constitutional relevance of the interest in protecting FGs may bring similar results in the near future. It might occur in Italy after the 2022 amendment of the Constitution, which introduced in Article 9 the provision that 'the Republic safeguards the environment, the biodiversity and ecosystems even in the interest of future generations'. As recently declared by the Italian Constitutional Court, the amended Article 9 provides 'an environmental mandate', imposing on all national authorities the obligation to take actions to protect the environment not only in the interest of present individuals and groups, but also in the interest of FGs, to be intended as those not born yet, because present generations have, in the Court's opinion, a duty to preserve a healthy environment for those that will come after them.[41] The Italian

---

37 *Ibid.*, para. 171.
38 *Ibid.*, paras 142–72.
39 *Ibid.*, paras 183–90.
40 *Ibid.*, para. 193.
41 Italian Constitutional Court, *Judgment No. 105 of 7 May 2024*, para. 5.1.2.

legislator is advised: domestic law will have to take the interests of FGs into account.

In the case mentioned above, the constitutional relevance of the interest in protecting FGs is by itself sufficient to trigger the constitutional legitimacy control of laws that do not protect FGs' interests and, as a consequence, that may perpetuate or even increase ECEs. In such cases, the qualification of IGE as a GPIL is less relevant. Instead, in other cases, lacking a constitutional provision protecting FGs, the qualification of IGE as a GPIL may have important consequences. In domestic legal systems, where general international law has a constitutional rank, the existence of a GPIL such as IGE can be a parameter to assess the constitutionality of a domestic law and, therefore, an instrument, among others, to contrast ECEs.

Moreover, and more generally, the enforcement of a GPIL like IGE may help domestic judges in balancing domestic diverging interests or interpreting domestic laws in favour of FGs' interests and, therefore, resulting in actions ultimately supporting the fight against ECEs, as occurred in the cases mentioned below.

In the judgment of the *Land Court of Queensland in Australia in the Waratah Coal Pty Ltd v Youth Verdict Ltd and Others* case, the monocratic judge used extensively the IGE principle in the balancing of interests he had to do in order to recommend the political authorities not to release a mining lease and an environmental authorization to allow Waratah Coal Pty Ltd to mine thermal coal in the Galilee Basin.[42]

The principle of IGE was also the foundation to admit the legal standing of associations before national judges as representatives of FGs. It occurred in the famous case of *Minors Oposa v Secretary of the Department of Environment and Natural Resources*, decided in 1993 by the Supreme Court of the Philippines.[43] The plaintiffs, a group of children represented by their parents, acted for themselves, as entitled to the full benefit, use and enjoyment of the country's virgin tropical forests, but also in representation of their generation

---

[42] Land Court of Queensland, *Waratah Coal Pty Ltd v Youth Verdict Ltd and Others* (2022), QLC 21, paras 1836–1845. For other cases that refer, even in a more nuanced way, to the needs of FGs see Elizabeth Donger, 'Children and Youth in Strategic Climate Litigation: Advancing Rights through Legal Argument and Legal Mobilisation' (2012) 11 (2) *Transnational Environmental Law* 263; Margaretha Wewerinke-Singh, Ayan Garg and Shubhangi Agarwalla, 'In Defence of Future Generations: A Reply to Stephen Humphreys' (2023) 34 (3) *European Journal of International Law* 651.

[43] Supreme Court of the Philippines, *Minors Oposa v Secretary of the Department of Environment and Natural Resources*, Judgment of 30 July 1993 (1994) 33 ILM 173.

as well as generations yet unborn. They claimed that the Government's licences that authorized deforestation were contrary to the Philippine Constitution, which protected the people's right to a balanced and healthy natural environment (Section 16, Article II). The Court accepted that plaintiffs had standing not only for themselves but also as representatives of current and future generations and based this finding on the principle of IGE. Moreover, it ruled in favour of the plaintiffs.

Finally, in domestic legal systems where the interest in protecting FGs does not have constitutional rank, the nature of IGE as a GPIL may be a solid legal justification for the establishment of institutions like the ombudspersons for FGs, whose monitoring activities on the impact of public policies on the interests of FGs, as well as their recommendatory mandate, may play an important role in the action to respond to ECEs. One significant experiment was the establishment of the Office of Ombudsman in Hungary in 2007,[44] followed in 2015 by the adoption of the Well-being of Future Generations Act by Wales, which provided for the establishment of the Future Generations Commissioner for Wales.[45] Significantly, Article 18 of the Act defines the Commissioner's general duty as that of acting 'as a guardian of the ability of future generations to meet their needs'. P. Lawrence rightly said that 'while (. . .) measuring the effectiveness of such institutions is challenging, it is difficult to understand why such institutions could not play a positive role in fostering longer-term sustainable policy making,'[46] and, I add, even in supporting actions that will have a positive effect in contrasting ECEs.

---

[44] For a synthesis of the Hungarian Ombudsman's function see the document prepared by the Ombudsman Office for the UN Office of High Commissioner for Human Rights at this link: <www.ohchr.org/Documents/Issues/Environment/ImplementationReport/Ombudsman%20for%20Future%20Generations.doc> accessed 3 November 2024.

[45] See the 'Well-being of Future Generations Act', especially Articles 17 to 24, related to the Commissioners' functions, at <www.legislation.gov.uk/anaw/2015/2/contents/enacted> accessed 3 November 2024. For other comparable institutions in other States see the Report of the Secretary-General, 'Intergenerational Solidarity and the Needs of Future Generations' (n 29), paras 39–48.

[46] Lawrence (n 16) 680.

3.2 At International Level

3.2.1 'Inter-generational burden sharing' considerations as a tool to justify judicial review and expand *locus standi* before the European Court of Human Rights

At international level, the IGE principle can be used by the international courts to interpret treaty provisions in order to give voice to and take into account the interests of FGs.

A significant example is the judgment of the European Court of Human Rights in the case *KlimaSeniorinnen et al v Switzerland*, decided in April 2024.[47] The Court never quoted the IGE principle; nevertheless, it referred to burden-sharing considerations among generations either to justify its judicial review or to extend the legal standing before itself.

The Swiss Government claimed that the system of individual applications under the Convention was not the appropriate means to press the national authorities to address climate change. In its view, the Swiss democratic institutions provided sufficient and appropriate means to address concerns relating to climate change, and 'judicialization' of the matter at the international level would have only created tension and would have been contrary to principles of subsidiarity and the separation of powers. [48]

In replying to this claim, the Court noted that unborn generations will likely bear heavier consequences of present omissions to combat climate change, while they have no possibility of participating in the current decision-making processes.[49] In the Court's view, the risk that short-term interests may prevail in the current political decision-making processes at the expense of the interests of FGs – notwithstanding the obligation States have to mitigate the rising of global temperature aimed at protecting FGs[50] – justified the Court's judicial review.[51] In this framework, the Court distinguishes between individuals currently alive and future generations and, therefore, considers FGs as synonymous with unborn children.

---

47 *Verein KlimaSeniorinnen Schweiz and Others v Switzerland*, App No. 53600/20 (ECHR, 9 April 2024).

48 *Ibid.*, para. 338.

49 *Ibid.*, para. 420.

50 Article 3 of the United Nations Framework Convention on Climate Change (UNFCCC) provides the obligation of States Parties to protect the climate system for the benefit of future generations on the basis of equity.

51 *Verein KlimaSeniorinnen Schweiz and Others v Switzerland* (n 47) para. 420.

Moreover, the Court used burden sharing considerations among generations, together with other elements,[52] to accept the legal standing of associations as representatives of those already affected (members or not of an association) by climate change, '*as well as those at risk of being affected*, by the adverse effects of climate change'.[53] Thus, the Court accepted that an association may represent individuals not yet affected by climate change, but that may reasonably be in the future, including FGs. However, the Court's opinion seems to refer only to current children: in fact, it also stated that the legal obligations arising under the Convention only extended to individuals currently alive who, at a given time, fall within the jurisdiction of a given Contracting Party.[54]

The Court was interested in avoiding the lodging of complaints by many individuals as potential victims of the adverse effects of climate change. This is evident in the Court's choice to exclude that individuals may be qualified as 'potential victims' in cases concerning a situation with general effects like climate change is,[55] as well as in the Court's decisions to tighten the requirements individuals must satisfy to be qualified as a victim.[56] Nevertheless, what is relevant for the current analysis is that considerations of burden sharing among different generations brought the Court to 'open the door' to the legal standing of associations in the interest of those at risk of being affected in the future and, therefore, also in the interest of FGs,[57] although limited to born children.

---

[52] The Court fostered a growing *consensus* among State parties to the Convention to admit legal standing of associations in environmental matters before national courts (*ibid.*, paras 494 and 497) and the special feature of climate change as a common concern of humankind (*ibid.*, para. 499).

[53] *Ibid.* See also paras 489 where the Court states that in modern-day societies, when citizens are confronted with particularly complex administrative decisions, recourse to associations may be the only means available to defend their particular interests effectively and that it is more relevant in the context of climate change, where intergenerational burden-sharing assumes particular importance since the associations may give 'voice of those at a distinct representational disadvantage'.

[54] *Ibid.*, para. 420. See also para. 499 where the Court states that 'States should take adequate action notably through suitable general measures to secure not only the Convention rights of individuals who are currently affected by climate change, but also those individuals *within their jurisdiction* whose enjoyment of Convention rights may be severely and irreversibly affected in the future in the absence of timely action' (italics added).

[55] *Ibid.*, paras 485.

[56] *Ibid.*, paras 478–88.

[57] Other applications were pending, at the time of writing, before the Court where associations claimed legal standing on behalf of its members as well as of FGs. The reference is to the legal action brought by Greenpeace Nordic and Young Friends of the Earth (and six affiliated young) against Norway. The complaint

Nine months after the ECHR's judgment in *KlimaSeniorinnen*, the Court decided the case *Cannavacciuolo and Others v Italy*,[58] which concerned a large-scale environmental pollution caused by the illegal dumping, burying and burning of hazardous and toxic waste in Italy's *Terra dei Fuochi* ('Land of Fires'). The First Section dismissed the application lodged by several associations as representatives of their associates: the majority of the Court considered that the conditions set out by the Grand Chamber in the case *KlimaSeniorinnen* were not met due to the specificities of climate change, this latter being different from a large-scale pollution event.[59] The distinction the Court drew is not convincing in light of the IGE principle. It is difficult to see how an ECE like that in the 'Land of Fires' cannot have an impact on FGs, since the environmental contamination here produced will have repercussions on the natural environment and human beings' health for many decades, and

---

concerns the issuing of petroleum production licences on the Norwegian continental shelf in the marine areas of the Barents Sea (*Greenpeace Nordic and Others v Norway*, App No. 34068/21 (ECHR), filed on 15 June 2021). The petitioners claimed that the combustion of fossil fuels extracted from this area has been contributing and will contribute to the climate crisis that affects children and young people. They especially claimed the violation of Articles 2 and 8, both alone and in conjunction with Article 14, of the European Convention on Human Right for the greater impact that climate change will have on FGs and declared to act not only as representatives of their members but also as representatives of FGs, because they are particularly vulnerable subjects who would have no other way of being defended (see at 8 of the Application <https://www.climatecasechart.com/documents/greenpeace-nordic-and-others-v-norway-petition_be52) where applicants expressly declared to act on behalf of its members and also as representatives of FGs. See also *Written Observations on Behalf of Applicants in App. No. 34068/21 Greenpeace Nordic and Others v Norway*, 29 June 2022, paras 41–3. Similarly, the Norwegian Grandparents' Climate Campaign, an organization established in the interest of FGs, with the aim of guaranteeing grandchildren a living environment like the one enjoyed by their grandparents, filed a complaint against Norway for the same reason just mentioned and invoked the violation of Articles 2, 3, 8, 13 and Protocol 1 Article 1. In its Application it declared to act as representatives of their members as well as in representation of FGs and asked the Court to interpret the victim status in harmony with the IGE principle and argued that current generations have a duty to act as stewards of the planet for future generations (*The Norwegian Grandparents' Climate Campaign and Others v Norway*, App No. 19026/21 (ECHR) filed on 26 March 2021). The case was eventually decided, pending the publication of this volume, on 28 October 2025. The Court held that there had been no violation of Article 8 of the Convention.

[58] *Cannavacciuolo v Italy* Apps nos 39742/14, 51567/14, 74208/14, (ECtHR, 30 January 2025).

[59] *Ibid.*, paras 220–22.

the burden of decontamination measures will be paid to present as well as to FGs, this latter being an argument the Court used in its 2024 judgment to admit the associations' *locus standi* as representatives of their members and those affected in the future.

3.2.2 IGE principle as a component of the right to have the child's best interest duly considered

In the petition to the Committee on the Rights of the Child concerning the case *Sacchi and Others v Argentina and Others,* the plaintiffs claimed that the violation of the IGE principle had to be considered as a violation of the right of the children to have their supreme interest duly taken into account.[60] According to the plaintiffs, the late adoption of mitigation measures by the respondent States was in contrast with the IGE principle since it shifted to minors and unborn children the costs of adopting decarbonization measures and, therefore, was contrary to the right to have their best interest taken into account. According to this view, taking the legal interests of FGs into account would be a child's right. The Committee did not take any position on this point since the petition was declared non-admissible on the grounds of not exhausting domestic remedies. Nevertheless, the petitioners' proposal to consider the protection of FGs as part of the right protected by Article 3 of the Convention on the Rights of the Child is an interesting idea and merits further exploration and testing. It might also result in a very effective legal tool to bring States to rightly enforce their obligations to mitigate climate change and, thus, result in effective action to prevent and contrast ECEs.

3.2.3 IGE principle as an interpretative tool to impose on states stricter obligations to protect children

The IGE principle was referred to by the Inter-American Court of Human Rights in the landmark judgment of *La Oroya Population v Peru*,[61] where the Court declared the State of Peru internationally responsible for the violation of several rights, including those of children, protected by Article 19 of the

60 *ChiaraSacchi et al v Argentina, Brazil, France, Germany & Turkey*, Communications to the Committee on the Rights of the Child (23 September 2019), paras 28 and 193, <https://climatecasechart.com/wp-content/uploads/non-us-case-documents/2019/20190923_Communication-No.-1042019-Argentina-Communication-No.-1052019-Brazil-Communication-No.-1062019-France-Communication-No.-1072019-Germany-Communication-No.-1082019-Turkey_petition.pdf> accessed 26 October 2024.

61 *Case of La Oroya Population v Peru*, Preliminary Objections, Merits, Reparations and Costs, Inter-American Court of Human Rights Series C No. 511 (27 November 2023).

American Convention, as a result of the mining and metallurgical activities carried out by a state-owned company and a private company. In regard to the victims who were minors at the time the complaint was lodged as well as to those that were minors at the time Peru ratified the Convention (in 1981) – when, according to the Court, the respondent State was already aware of the negative consequences of the companies' activities on the environment and on human health – the Court pointed out that, under the principle of intergenerational equity, States must comply with their obligations to protect the environment taking into account the effects that environmental damage had on present and future generations. The Court stated that this obligation acquired special importance with respect to children, since they were the ones who may be most affected by the present and future consequences of environmental degradation.[62] Therefore, in the Court's opinion, the IGE principle imposed on the State an '*enhanced obligation* to protect children by preventing harm to their health caused by environmental pollution, and providing subsequent care for the illnesses acquired as a result of it'.[63]

4. CONCLUSION

The brief analysis carried out in the previous paragraphs shows how taking FGs' needs into consideration, and using the IGE principle for this purpose, can play a role in orienting the decisions of domestic and international courts in favour of the recognition of the responsibility of States for the ineffective policies to prevent and combat ECEs. These decisions are only a drop in the sea of what needs to be done to eradicate ECEs; nevertheless, they are a sign that a small movement in this direction is underway and that it could be even more significant. Undoubtedly, there is still much to be done, especially to integrate an intersectional approach into this action. In fact, the jurisprudence cited above shows a good rate of care for FGs, while the same cannot be said for its different dimensions. FGs are usually taken into account as an indistinct group of individuals (present and future), but no attention is paid to the different degrees of vulnerabilities, such as migrant status, gender, sickness, disability etc.

It is not easy to understand whether it is due to the difficulties a new category, such as FGs, has to overcome to be accepted and used by national and international courts or whether other cultural elements influence this result.

Yet, an approach that would take into account different identitarian dimensions as well as different (and intersectional) patterns of discrimination could

---

62 *Ibid.*, para. 242.

63 *Ibid.*, para. 243, emphasis added.

help courts to impose on States the obligation to adopt more targeted measures, which would increase the level of effectiveness in responding to the needs of specific groups. The recommendation, as well as the auspice, is that States' policies will take into account a double layer of concern: one looking at FGs and, within it, a sub-level that cares about different identitarian or distinctive elements, like gender, disability, social and geographical origin, etc.

PART III

Environmental Chronic Emergencies in Context

9. Environmental chronic emergencies, slow-onset events and other anthropocentric dilemmas in times of climate crisis: the need for a reconception

Monica Feria-Tinta

1. INTRODUCTION

With the advent of international human rights treaties, human rights norms emerged as binding rules, following the horrors that humanity had endured during the Second World War. The development of legal, human rights standards, however, marked a separation of what is human from Nature. Environmental law, as an area of law, developed after the emergence of human rights law, somehow self-contained from 'the human', and mostly from the 70s onwards, as soft law, separated from human rights. Whether one is to see in the environmental and climate crisis we observe today an environmental chronic emergency (ECE) or the rise of slow-onset events (as they usually come to the attention of courts in the context of the climate emergency), humanity is coming to realize how vital nature is for human beings. This invites a reconceptualization of the law. The law has to be reframed, rethought. This chapter elaborates on the direction that this rethinking of the law is taking and may take. The chapter is divided into three sections. First, Section 2 discusses two case studies reflecting environmental crises (climate and biodiversity crises) in order to set up practical examples of the environmental challenges facing humanity today. It is submitted that while some examples may fit the characterization of ECEs (and some cases may reach courts as such; see, below, the example of global warming in The Caribbean[1] or the *Atrato* river litigation[2]), it is also the case that aspects of the climate emergency are litigated as specific slow-onset events as well, with specific remedies tailored to provide mitigation, adaptation or compensation measures (see the case of the *Torres Strait Islanders*[3] in the United Nations or the case of *Lliuya v RWE*[4]). With the exception of the *Atrato* case, the above examples of climate and biodiversity emergencies have been dealt with from an anthropocentric perspective, which is the underlying paradigm of current human rights law frameworks. Section 3 of this chapter, however, identifies an evolving trend in the current trajectory of environmental human rights litigation. This I call the '*La Oroya* case'[5] prototype or the expansion of human rights law to protect Nature. It stems from the realization by jurisprudential developments that to protect human beings, there is a need to protect the natural world, to the extent that it is accepted that human beings are part and inextricably connected with nature. Nevertheless, the stretching of anthropocentric approaches has its limits, and this expansion of human rights to protect nature is, for that reason, naturally leading towards a non-anthropocentric model. Section 4 explores the non-anthropocentric model conceived as a new paradigm in international law. It is submitted that this is not a new model within the discourse of international law, but a paradigm which was laid down in the 1982 World Charter for Nature, a fundamentally ecological instrument in the development of international law.

2. ENVIRONMENTAL CHRONIC EMERGENCIES AND SLOW-ONSET EVENTS

It is undeniable that environmental degradation globally arises from an economic model developed from the start of the Industrial Revolution and deeply

---

1 See *Amicus Curiae del Instituto de Pequeños y Micro Estados*, ISMS, during the Advisory Opinion Proceedings on Climate Emergency and Human Rights, before the Inter-American Court of Human Rights (14 December 2023), <https://corteidh.or.cr/sitios/observaciones/OC-32/20_microestados.pdf> accessed 11 April 2025.

2 *Atrato River* Decision, Constitutional Court of Colombia, Judgment T-622/16 (10 November 2016).

3 *Daniel Billy et al. v Australia*, Communication 3624/2019 (21 July 2022), UN Doc CCPR/C/135/D/3624/2019, hereinafter '*Torres Strait Islanders* case'.

4 *Saul Lliuya v RWEAG*, Higher Regional Court of Hamm, Indicative Order and Order for the Hearing of Evidence (30 November 2017).

5 *Case of La Oroya Population v Peru,* Preliminary Objections, Merits, Reparations and Costs, Inter-American Court of Human Rights Series C No. 511 (27 November 2023).

embedded in a post-industrialized world. The accumulation of greenhouse gases in the atmosphere (primarily from the burning of fossil fuels), causing today the climate crisis, is the result of accumulated emissions since the start of the Industrial Revolution in the mid-eighteenth century. Global warming (with the effects on the environment, which include sinking islands, sea level rise, increasing temperatures, flooding, glacier melting and extreme weather events, among others) is thus tied to such an economic model. Seen from that perspective, the environmental emergencies linked to climate change are chronic. By way of additional observation, it is pertinent to note that the same economic model, in essence, treats nature as a commodity. Extensive environmental damage today arises from extractivism, which refers to the intensive exploitation of nature. This section provides two examples of environmental cases by way of illustration of the environmental issues that may reach courts. First, the climate emergency situation in the Caribbean is discussed as presented in the Advisory Opinion proceedings on Climate Emergency and Human Rights before the Inter-American Court of Human Rights. This includes a particular analysis of gender-specific impacts of the situation on women. But while this example corresponds well with the notion of ECEs, the section discusses further examples that have not been brought before courts as 'ECEs' but rather as issues of specific slow-onset events, which the law is capable of redressing to the extent that specific measures can be identified. These are examples of the *Torres Strait Islanders* case and *Lliuya v RWE*.

2.1 Global Warming in the Caribbean: Climate Emergency Case Study

The UN Secretary-General, Mr Guterres, has acknowledged that '[t]he Caribbean is ground zero for the global climate emergency'.[6] Small Island States like the Caribbean countries contribute to only 1% of the global greenhouse gas emissions, yet their populations stand to be disproportionately affected.[7] The main environmental changes expected to affect the Caribbean are rising sea levels, stronger hurricanes, longer dry seasons, and shorter wet seasons. As a result, climate change poses a serious threat to the Caribbean

---

6 See Evan Schneider, 'The Caribbean is 'ground zero' for the global climate emergency: Guterres', (*UN News* 3 July 2022), at <https://news.un.org/en/story/2022/07/1121902> accessed 11 April 2025.

7 Climate Watch Data Explorer, at: <https://www.climatewatchdata.org/api/v1/data/historical_emissions/data_sources> as cited by United Nations Development Programme, 'Building resilient futures in the Caribbean' (14 November 2022) <https://climatepromise.undp.org/news-and-stories/building-resilient-futures-caribbean> accessed 11 April 2025.

economy, environment and population.[8] It is estimated that by 2100, climate change damage in the Caribbean will cost more than 20% of the region's GDP if no action is taken to halt climate change.[9]

2.1.1 Extreme weather

Large proportions of the population in the Caribbean live on the coast, making them particularly vulnerable to hurricane activity.[10] Hurricanes are tropical cyclones. Rising air and sea surface temperatures (due to climate change) are predicted to increase the intensity of tropical cyclones. Key factors driving hurricane development are warm air and sea surface temperatures. Higher temperatures increase the likelihood of a storm becoming a hurricane. This provides the energy for hurricane intensification.[11]

Over a 20-year period from 2000–2019, three Caribbean islands have ranked in the top ten most affected by extreme weather according to the Global Climate Risk Index, with two islands in the top five (Puerto Rico (1) and Haiti (3)).[12] Together, these islands suffered losses estimated at US$4,969.4 million and were impacted by a total of 117 events.[13] These losses are projected to increase as climate change worsens, with extreme weather events becoming more frequent and also more devastating events occurring.[14] In 2017, Dominica, for example, was hit by Hurricane Maria, causing losses of US$1.3 billion or 226% of its GDP.[15] With a temperature increase of 2 degrees, this

---

8 Clinton L. Beckford, Kevon Rhiney, 'Geographies of Globalization, Climate Change and Food and Agriculture in the Caribbean', in Clinton L. Beckford; Kevon Rhiney (eds), *Globalization, Agriculture and Food in the Caribbean* (Palgrave Macmillan UK 2016).

9 Adelle Thomas et al., 'Climate Change and Small Island Developing States' (2020), 45 *Annual Review of Environment and Resources*, 1, 8.

10 Nobuo Mimura et al., 'Small islands' in *Climate Change 2007: Impacts, Adaptation and Vulnerability. Contribution of Working Group II to the Fourth Assessment Report of the Intergovernmental Panel on Climate Change* (Cambridge University Press 2007).

11 Jennifer Wall, 'What are Hurricanes', *NASA*, 9 June 2015. <https://spaceplace.nasa.gov/hurricanes/en/> accessed 14 November 2025.

12 David Eckstein, Vera Kunzel, Laura Schafer, *Global Climate Risk Index 2021: Who Suffers Most from Extreme Weather Events? Weather-Related Loss Events in 2019 and 2000–2019* (2021), 13, <https://www.germanwatch.org/sites/default/files/Global%20Climate%20Risk%20Index%202021_2.pdf> accessed 14 November 2025.

13 *Ibid.*

14 *Ibid.*, 17–18.

15 Daphne Ewing-Chow, 'Caribbean Countries Will Be Seeking Climate Justice At COP27', (*Forbes* 12 October 2022), <https://www.forbes.com/sites/

will make storms that used to occur every 100 years over twice as likely in Puerto Rico, occur once every 30 years in the Dominican Republic and three times as likely in the Bahamas.[16]

2.1.2 Oceans: Rising sea levels and damage to ecosystems (including coral bleaching)

Twenty-eight million out of 40 million inhabitants of the Caribbean live on the coast and are therefore particularly vulnerable to rising sea levels.[17] Rising Caribbean Sea levels are already endangering the existence of some islands; for example, the Panamanian island of Cartí Sugdupu in the Guna Yala archipelago. With approximately 1,200 inhabitants, they have begun to abandon the island due to rising sea levels.[18] It is predicted that a 1m sea level rise will cause the CARICOM nations a loss of 1,300 km^2 of land area (including 1% of agricultural land) while a 2m rise would cause over 3,000 km^2 of land to be lost.[19] By 2080, the cumulative capital GDP loss to CARICOM states from rising sea levels would be between US$68.2 and US$187 billion (8.3% and 19.2% of projected GDP in 2080).[20] This would mean an annual loss of 5% of GDP for countries like Belize, Antigua and Barbuda and the Bahamas.

Coral reefs provide US$6.2 billion of benefits to the Caribbean region,[21] with 41 million people highly dependent on the reefs for livelihood or food.[22]

---

daphneewingchow/2022/10/12/caribbean-countries-will-be-seeking-climate-justice-at-cop27/?sh=3bc3733c41ba> accessed 14 November 2025.

16 E. L. Vosper et al., 'Extreme hurricane rainfall affecting the Caribbean mitigated by the Paris Agreement goals?' (2020), 15 (10) *Environmental Research Letters*, 1, 6.

17 Rueanna Haynes, 'The IPCC has highlighted the Caribbean's vulnerability to climate change: what does this mean for climate justice?' (*The Climate Analytics Blog* 11 July 2022), <https://climateanalytics.org/blog/2022/the-ipcc-has-highlighted-the-caribbeans-vulnerability-to-climate-change-what-does-this-mean-for-climate-justice/> accessed 14 November 2025.

18 Felipe Bedoya, 'Esta es la isla del Caribe que empezó a hundirse', (*Telemedellín*, 6 September 2023), at <https://telemedellin.tv/la-isla-del-caribe-que-comenzo-a-hundirse/666857/> accessed 14 November 2025.

19 Simpson et al., 'Quantification and Magnitude of Losses and Damages Resulting from the Impacts of Climate Change: Modelling the Transformational Impacts and Costs of Sea Level Rise in the Caribbean (Key Points and Summary for Policy Makers Document)' (2010), *United Nations Development Programme* (UNDP), 11–12.

20 *Ibid.*, at 16.

21 Ewing-Chow (n 15).

22 ResourceWatch, 'Coral Reefs: Caribbean' (2020) <https://resourcewatch.org/dashboards/coral-reefs-caribbean> accessed 14 November 2025.

The increased temperatures have caused various bleaching events in the Caribbean, with mass events in 1993, 1998, 2005 and 2010. The 2005 event affected 80% of all Caribbean coral reefs, and up to 40% died.[23] Coral reefs are projected to decline by 70–90% at a warming level of 1.5°C and larger losses (>99%) at warming above 2°C.[24] This will drastically affect the lives of communities reliant on the reefs and the sea as a resource.

2.1.3 Economy

The Caribbean is the most tourism-dependent region of the world,[25] with tourism making up an average of 28% of GDP for Caribbean nations.[26] In some countries in the Caribbean, tourism makes up 79% of their GDP.[27] Tourism and agriculture employ approximately 30% and 13% respectively, of the regional labour force.[28]

Tourism is very climate-dependent, with many countries being popular for their climate. With the changes to temperature and water, this is likely to have a severe effect on tourism.[29] It is estimated that climate change may cause the industry to lose up to US$146 million in revenue.[30]

Fisheries are a key resource for the Caribbean, providing employment for 200,000 fishers and 100,000 people who work in the processing and marketing of fish and supporting the industry in general.[31] Fish also supplies 7% of protein intake in the Caribbean,[32] making it a vital food source. However,

---

23 Nadia Makara, 'Improving Resilience to Climate Change for Caribbean Agriculture and Fisheries Sectors' (2021), *The World Bank*, 1, 9.

24 Thomas et al. (n 9), 8.

25 Davina Layne, 'Impacts of Climate Change on Tourism in the Coastal and Marine Environments of Caribbean Small Island Developing States (SIDS)' (2017), *Science Review* 174.

26 Haynes (n 17).

27 Isavela N. Monioudi et al., 'Climate change impacts on critical international transportation assets of Caribbean Small Island Developing States (SIDS): the case of Jamaica and Saint Lucia' (2018), 18 *Regional Environmental Change*, 2212.

28 Michael A. Taylor, Jhordanne J. Jones, Tannecia S. Stephenson, 'Climate change and the Caribbean: Trends and implications' in Elizabeth Thomas-Hope (ed.), *Climate change and food security: Africa and the Caribbean* (Taylor & Francis 2016) 44.

29 Layne (n 25).

30 Michelle Scobie, 'Accountability in climate change governance and Caribbean SIDS' (2018), 20 *Environment, Development and Sustainability: A Multidisciplinary Approach to the Theory and Practice of Sustainable Development* 769, 771.

31 Makara (n 23), 1.

32 *Ibid.*

climate change could cause up to a 35% decline in maximum sustainable yield in fisheries.[33] This would affect the livelihoods and food sources of many.

In addition, fisheries are badly affected by extreme weather events. For instance, Hurricane Gustavo cost US$14 million in damages to the Jamaican fisheries industry, and Hurricane Erika caused a loss of over US$2million to the Dominican fisheries.[34]

2.1.4 Impact on the most vulnerable populations in the Caribbean

The following are some observations regarding the impact of climate change on the most vulnerable populations in the Caribbean. This is not an exhaustive list of such impacts, but rather an outline of some salient elements.

2.1.4.1 Impact on children: Particularly vulnerable to climate change

According to UNICEF, 'one in four people on the move in Latin America and the Caribbean is a child (including she-child) or adolescent, the highest proportion worldwide'.[35]

In the case of the Caribbean, there has been a six-fold increase in the number of persons displaced (including 761,000 children) due to storms and flooding.[36] In 2017 alone, more than 400,000 children were displaced.[37] Children are particularly vulnerable during displacement due to the risk of disease in overcrowded conditions in emergency shelters, or if their parents are killed, they are at risk of exploitation and trafficking.[38] Furthermore, nearly 90% of the global burden of disease associated with climate change is borne by children under five.[39] Children in the Caribbean are particularly vulnerable to climate change, with nine out of ten children in Latin America and the Caribbean

---

33 *Ibid.*, 10.

34 *Ibid.*, 1.

35 UNICEF (Press release), 'El número de niños, niñas y adolescents en movimiento en América Latina y el Caribe alcanza nuevo record, en medio de la violencia, inestabilidad y cambio climático' (7 September 2023), at <https://www.unicef.org/es/comunicados-prensa/numero-ninos-ninas-adolescentes-movimiento-america-latina-alcanza-nuevo-record> accessed 11 April 2025.

36 UNICEF, *Children Uprooted in the Caribbean: How stronger hurricanes linked to a changing climate are driving child displacement* (December 2019), 1, <https://www.unicef.org/media/62836/file/Children-uprooted-in-the-Caribbean-2019.pdf> accessed 11 April 2025.

37 *Ibid.*, 5.

38 *Ibid.*, 8.

39 UNICEF, *The climate crisis is a child rights crisis: Introducing the Children's Climate Risk Index* (August 2021), 110, <https://www.unicef.org/lac/en/press-releases/children-latin-america-and-caribbean-are-exposed-climate-climate-environmental-shocks> accessed 11 April 2025.

exposed to two climate/environmental shocks and one out of four exposed to at least four shocks.[40] Women are mostly in charge of children in the Caribbean. The following are specific observations in relation to them.

2.1.4.2 Impact on women: Disproportionately affected

Women and men living in the Caribbean region experience the impacts of climate change differently.[41] This is because pervasive gender stereotypes and adherence to traditional gender roles still limit the equal participation of women in society in this region.[42] These gender norms increase vulnerability to the impacts of climate change and also limit participation in resilience-building activities and processes.[43] Women are also disproportionately affected by the roles they actually assume within the family. For example, a study by the Economic Commission for Latin America and the Caribbean (ECLAC) notes:

> Although much has been written about the global adverse effects of climate change in the Caribbean subregion in recent years, very little attention has been directed to the role and function of women in the midst of the climate change crisis.
>
> Among the direct impacts of climate change are the changes in rainfall patterns and the resulting decreased availability of freshwater, the increased fallout from floods and/or droughts and the concomitant effects on agricultural infrastructure and food security.
>
> The stark reality of the decreased availability of water in the Caribbean subregion is the disproportionate impacts on women. It is unfortunate that policymakers

---

[40] UNICEF, *9 out of 10 children in Latin America and the Caribbean are exposed to at least two climate and environmental shocks* (20 Aug 2021), at <https://www.unicef.org/lac/en/press-releases/children-latin-america-and-caribbean-are-exposed-climate-climate-environmental-shocks> accessed 11 April 2025.

[41] Angie Dazé and Cameron Hunter, 'Gender-Responsive Resilience Building in the Caribbean: Understanding the role of knowledge, attitudes, behaviours, and practices in coordination mechanisms for climate change and disaster risk reduction'. (2021), *UN Women and International Institute for Sustainable Development*, 1, <https://wrd.unwomen.org/sites/default/files/2021-11/ENGEND~1.PDF> accessed 11 April 2025.

[42] Organisation for Economic Co-operation and Development, *SIGI 2020 regional report for Latin America and the Caribbean, social institutions and gender index* (2020), <https://doi.org/10.1787/cb7d45d1-en> accessed 11 April 2025, as cited in Dazé and Hunter (n 41), 3.

[43] IDB, *Study of the impacts of climate change on the women and men of the Caribbean. Pilot Programme for Climate Resilience Countries* (2020), <https://publications.iadb.org/publications/english/document/Study-of-the-Impacts-of-Climate-Change-on-the-Women-and-Men-in-the-Caribbean-Pilot-Programme-for-Climate-Resilience-Countries.pdf> accessed 11 April 2025.

tend to ignore and/or overlook the fact that women are the ones with major responsibility for the management of water in the household.

Numerous studies on gender have identified gender biases in the intra-household differences in incomes, which have differential impacts on access to resources for women and men. Despite these findings, the household is still treated as one where the male is the head who takes responsibility for the interests of all its members. The role of women as active decision makers within the household is therefore still not fully acknowledged.

This is very evident in the area of water management, particularly in relation to water for irrigation, which is regarded as a male domain. Consequently, it is wrongly assumed that women do not need independent access or entitlement to water. Women generally tend to crops, particularly for household consumption, and they have the primary responsibility for childcare and other reproductive responsibilities in the care economy, including cleaning, cooking and washing. Lack of access to water, therefore, makes these responsibilities more burdensome, particularly in situations where women do not have access to pipe-borne water.

The status of women and their lack of economic and cultural power may provide some insights into explaining why issues of water access and sanitation do not attract the attention that they deserve. Policies need to be adopted to address the gender issues in climate change with respect to the management of water. In this context, the mainstreaming of gender in policies which aim to assist the subregion in its adaptation to climate change should be seen as a priority, not only in the context of national development planning but more importantly in public and private investment decisions, for example, the privatisation of water.

The fact that it is women who are disproportionately impacted by the trend to privatise water should not be ignored. As a direct result of trade liberalisation, the Caribbean subregion is being targeted by private interests in water [. . .].

The privatisation of water, wherever it takes place, is likely to have serious implications for large sections of the population, particularly female-headed households and the poor, because of increased costs for water supply. In addition to water supply, the other key areas of concern, which are likely to directly impact women at the level of the household, are agricultural development and land use policies, which will also have consequences for food security.[44]

Thus, Caribbean Poverty Assessments (CPAs) over the years have shown that poverty levels are higher in female-headed households, and that women are more likely to live in inadequate housing in urban and rural areas of low land value that are vulnerable to the impacts of climate-related events such as floods, storms, avalanches, earthquakes, landslides and other hazards.[45] Focus

44 ECLAC, Subregional Headquarters for the Caribbean, (produced by Sheila Stuart), *Women and Water* (2008–2009) 1–2, at <https://repositorio.cepal.org/server/api/core/bitstreams/de4fca70-1df7-4d7d-b70a-279d7ce2e973/content> accessed 11 April 2025.

45 ECLAC, *The Caribbean Outlook*, (2018), 50, at: <https://repositorio.cepal.org/server/api/core/bitstreams/06596b00-78a5-46e2-a850-c5545c36e1ef/content> accessed 11 April 2025.

groups held as part of an Inter-American Development Bank Study on the Impacts of Climate Change on the Women and Men of the Caribbean found that in the aftermath of Hurricane Maria in 2017, the livelihoods of urban and rural female participants in Dominica were upended, with most losing their homes, businesses or crops.[46]

Furthermore, Damage and Loss Assessments of hurricanes in the Caribbean carried out by the Economic Commission for Latin America and the Caribbean since 2015 show that women represent the majority of the primarily affected population who had been displaced from their homes and were living in shelters.[47] This accords with the July 2022 report of the UN Special Rapporteur on the rights of migrants, which underscored that 80% of people currently displaced by climate-related events are women and girls.[48]

It is expected, in my view, that the Inter-American Court of Human Rights will consider the gender-specific impacts of climate change on women in the Caribbean, in its analysis of obligations by States under the applicable human rights instruments in the Americas, in its Advisory Opinion on the Climate Emergency.

2.2 Liulya v Rwe: Climate Cases Arising from Slow-onset Events

Even if it is accepted that the climate emergency is an ECE with a multiplicity of effects as seen above, it is often the case, however, that in climate dispute resolution, a particular slow-onset event is brought before the courts (the notion of 'ECE' does not enter into the courtroom in that context). Take the example of the case of *Lliuya v RWE,* a transboundary harm case against energy giant RWE.

Saul Luciano Lliuya, a Peruvian farmer, filed a case in November 2015 against German energy company RWE in the German courts for the costs of preventing the glacial Lake Palcacocha from flooding his hometown of Huaraz,

---

46 Inter-American Development Bank, *Study of the Impacts of Climate Change on the Women and Men of the Caribbean* (December 2020), <https://www.cif.org/sites/cif_enc/files/knowledge-documents/study-of-the-impacts-of-climate-change-on-the-women-and-men-in-the-caribbean-pilot-programme-for-climate-resilience-countries.pdf> accessed 18 April 2025.

47 Economic Commission for Latin America and the Caribbean, *Draft Report: Mainstreaming Gender in Climate Change and Disaster Risk Reduction in the Caribbean* (2017), 9, <https://www.cepal.org/sites/default/files/events/files/draft_-_mainstreaming_gender_in_climate_change_and_disaster_risk_reduction_in_the_caribbean.pdf>, accessed 18 April 2025.

48 UNGA (19 July 2022), *Report of the Special Rapporteur on the human rights of migrants*, UN Doc A/77/189, para. 47.

Peru. The Palcacocha Lake, which sits 4,650 meters above the regional capital Huaraz, has been growing in volume due to meltwater input from receding glaciers. The increased volume, he argues, could cause the lake to overflow and flood his town. In 1941, a huge chunk of glacier fell into the lake, causing the breaking of the moraine walls that limit the lake's downhill. Between 1,800 and 7,000 inhabitants of Huaraz died victims of the avalanche. Lliuya fears, today, that climate change is putting him and Huaraz at a similar risk. Science shows that the melting of glaciers is caused by climate change. RWE, the biggest emitter in Europe, has caused 0.47% of global post-Industrial Revolution carbon emissions. So Lliuya is suing RWE for that proportion of the costs of flood prevention. The case went to trial in 2022, with German judges going to Peru to see first-hand the state of the glaciers and Lake Palcacocha, now posing an imminent risk to Lliuya's house. An evidentiary hearing focusing on flood risk took place recently from 17 to 19 March 2025, with an imminent decision on the case to be delivered by the German courts on 14 April 2025.[49]

It is Lliuya's position that there is environmental damage in his hometown: 'The glaciers are collapsing, they are disappearing, and there are palpable consequences for atmospheric pollution'.[50] In his view, those who pollute are responsible. 'RWE, they produce energy, but all the carbon, the CO_2 that they have burned has been dissipating in the atmosphere and over the years (operating for 130 years), RWE has contributed to climate change by 0.47%' – Lliuya states.[51] RWE's position, by contrast, is that it could not be held accountable for providing electricity to the German people, a lawful act. But the courts in Germany previously held that you can be held accountable if you knew of the deleterious effect, and that since 1958 it has been foreseeable to an optimal observer that increasing CO_2 emissions would lead to global warming with the allegedly associated consequences.[52]

Whilst there are more effects of global warming in Huaraz, which include the drying up of underground water, rising temperatures, emergence of insects that terminate staple agricultural products and others, this case focuses on one aspect of the environmental harm: the melting of glaciers. Similarly, the *Torres Strait Islanders'* case before the United Nations Human Rights Committee did not bring the case of climate degradation in the islands as an 'ECE' but

---

49 Ajit Niranjan, 'Farmer's house in danger from climate change, court told in RWE case' (*The Guardian* 19 March 2025), <https://www.theguardian.com/business/2025/mar/19/farmer-climate-change-legal-case-rwe-peru-germany> accessed 14 November 2025.

50 Author's interview with Saul Luciano Lliuya, 28 February 2025.

51 *Ibid.*

52 Higher Regional Court Hamm Order and reference order, in the legal dispute of Mr Saúl Ananiás Luciano Lliuya versus RWE AG (1 July 2021), 4.

as specific impacts that required specific mitigation and adaptation measures. The impacts raised in said case included slow-onset events such as the fact that the islands, the homes of the petitioners, were sinking.

3. THE 'LA OROYA CASE' PROTOTYPE: THE EXPANSION OF HUMAN RIGHTS LAW TO PROTECT NATURE

Despite the fact that international human rights law follows an anthropocentric model, in recent years, however, there has been an expansion of human rights law to protect nature.

Advisory Opinion 23[53] by the Inter-American Court on Human Rights marked, in my view, a potentially critical turning point in the approach by human rights courts to the protection of nature. The dictum introduced new, non-human elements in the realm of human rights protections. Components of the environment, 'such as forests, rivers and sea', were acknowledged by the Court to be 'legal interests in themselves' (even in the absence of the certainty or evidence of a risk to individuals). The Court declared these components of the environment to be subject to protection of the right to a healthy environment conceived as 'an autonomous right'.[54] From this perspective, the right to a healthy environment 'protects nature and the environment, not only because of the benefits they provide to humanity or the effects that their degradation may have on other human rights, such as health, life or personal integrity, but because of their importance to the other living organisms with which we share the planet' – which in words of the Inter-American Court 'also merit protection in their own right'.[55]

The enunciation of these principles soon found a concrete application in contentious cases. In the *La Oroya*, a case arising from an Andean town contaminated by mining activities, which led to high concentrations of lead in children's blood, the Court found that Peru had violated the residents' right to live in a healthy environment and unequivocally held that 'States are obliged to protect nature not only for its usefulness or effects with respect to human beings, but also for its importance for other living organisms with which the planet is shared'.[56] To put it simply, this is the first clear pronouncement by a human rights court asserting that States are obliged to protect Nature.

---

[53] *The Environment and Human Rights*, Advisory Opinion OC-23/17 Requested by the Republic of Colombia, Inter-American Court of Human Rights, Series A No 23 (15 November 2017).

[54] *Ibid.*, para. 62.

[55] *Ibid.*

[56] *La Oroya* (n 5) para. 118 [Author's translation].

It is the ecological and climatological state of our world that is triggering this adaptation of the law. It is not by chance that the prototypical case reflecting a key expansion of human rights law to protect nature has arisen from *La Oroya*, one of the most polluted places on Earth.

Indeed, precisely because of the ecological and biodiversity crisis we face today, the expansion of human rights to protect the natural world has become a reality in the current evolving human rights case law. I can see this expansion operating in at least two ways: (i) at the international level, in international human rights courts or international quasi-judicial bodies; and (ii) in domestic systems with Constitutional Courts delivering novel jurisprudential developments.

3.1 International Level

The *La Oroya* case is not an isolated example of the expansion of human rights in protecting nature. The Inter-American System is not alone. The recent *Torres Strait Islanders* case before the UN Human Rights Committee, a case arising from the climate change crisis, is another good example of this tendency.[57] Effectively, what the Torres Strait Islanders wanted to do was to save their ancestral territory, their islands, from climate degradation. But their ancestral territory did not stop with the land; it also covered the sea. They denounced that their culture depended 'on the continued existence and habitability of their islands and on the *ecological health of the surrounding seas*'.[58] Their claim aimed to protect the soil of the islands, the coconut trees (today diseased by saltwater invasion), the climate stability, the culturally significant species like crayfish, the dugong, and the many other disappearing species.[59] The Human Rights Committee found violations of Articles 17 (protection of home) and 27 (cultural rights of minorities) of the Covenant, which both protected those ancestral lands.[60]

These developments need not stay within the human rights realm. They are penetrating international law as a whole. The recent ITLOS Advisory Opinion on Climate Change and International Law[61] is an addition to that corpus juris. The marine environment, which contains rare and fragile ecosystems, understood as 'functional units consisting of living organisms, the

57 *Daniel Billy et al v Australia* (n 3).

58 *Ibid.*, para. 3.5 (emphasis added).

59 *Ibid.*, para. 2.5.

60 *Ibid.*, paras 8.12–8.14.

61 Advisory Opinion on Climate Change and International Law, International Tribunal for the Law of the Sea, Case No 31 (21 May 2024).

non-living environment and the interactions within them'[62] has never before received more timely, focused attention by a tribunal and protection than in this ground-breaking dictum.

3.2 National Level

National Courts are also exploring uncharted territories. A constitutional legal action (*Tutela*), filed by *Tierra Digna*, on behalf of a number of Afro-Colombian and other ethnic communities living along the *Atrato*, a very polluted river located in northwestern Colombia, in the Department of Chocó, paradoxically one of the most bio-diverse regions of the planet, gave rise to a landmark ruling T-622/16, delivered by the Constitutional Court of Colombia, on 10 November 2016. This ruling declared that the Atrato River is a subject of rights which entail 'its protection, conservation, maintenance and, in the specific case, restoration'.[63]

The Court provided that the Colombian State, together with the ethnic communities that live on the Atrato river bank in Chocó, were to exercise the guardianship and legal representation of the River. What is interesting about this case is that this was a purely jurisprudential development (it was not implementing a Constitutional provision on rights of nature, unlike other examples in Latin America). In fact, the original claim had not been made on behalf of the river, but it had been advanced on behalf of people's fundamental rights. The pollution of the river by heavy metals such as mercury had contaminated the environment, the soil and the fish, and had entered the organisms of people. In a documentary called *Atrato envenenao: la huella del mercurio* ('Poisoned Atrato: the footprint of mercury'), the level of contamination among people can be seen as including irritation to the eyes, loss of peripheral vision, irritation of skin, stomach pains, coughs and chest pains, or difficulty breathing, insomnia, irritability, indecision, headache, weakness or exhaustion, among others.

The Court had found that the best way to ensure the rights of those living in (and relying on) such a polluted environment was to grant rights to the river itself. A deep consideration of the fundamental human right to water prompted the Constitutional Court to adopt a non-anthropocentric approach to make justice in the case. The Court held that water (the River) is 'an essential part of the environment and is necessary for the life of the multiple organisms and species that inhabit the planet and, of course, for the human communities that develop

---

62 *Ibid.*, para. 169.

63 *Atrato River* Case (n 2), para. 9.32 [Author's translation].

around it'.[64] It granted, as a result, substantive rights to the River. It also granted the river procedural rights: direct standing before the Constitutional Court. The Court provided that the Colombian State, together with the ethnic communities that live on the Atrato river bank in Chocó, were to exercise the guardianship and legal representation of the River. It ordered that this system of guardianship had to become operational within three months of the notification of the judgment and gave a term of one year for the commission of guardians to design a plan to decontaminate the water sources of the Chocó, beginning with the Atrato River basin and its tributaries, the riverside territories, recover its ecosystems and avoid additional damage to the environment in the region. In practice, the communities appointed gender-balanced guardianship representatives.[65]

4. THE NON-ANTHROPOCENTRIC MODEL: NEW PARADIGM

It is clear that today, the protection of components of the environment is moving to a non-anthropocentric model: the granting of legal personhood to forests, rivers, lagoons, and mountains. But as we may perceive from above, a non-anthropocentric protection system parallel to the human rights system is not watertight, separate from a human rights system and vice versa. There is a necessary connection between them.

Of course, what the idea of autonomous protection of the environment may mean in practice, may find its more integral version in this non-anthropocentric approach. This is following three main modalities: (i) through legislation (either at constitutional level or via legislation passed by parliament as in the case of Mar Menor; (ii) through local authorities' own powers (as in the case of Lewes or in the case of the river Magpie in Canada;[66] or (iii) via the work of domestic courts (as in the prototypical case of the *Atrato* river in Colombia).

This, I submit, is a fundamental paradigm shift for humanity. One that ought to be considered against the background of post-industrialization. What is happening merits a revision of the international legal framework of environmental law and a process of taking stock.

---

64 *Ibid.*, 79.

65 Pacifico Task Force, 'Guardianas del Río Atrato: Defensoras del Territorio', (*Las2Orillas* 4 September 2024), <https://www.las2orillas.co/relatos-de-poder-femenino-del-pacifico-guardianas-del-rio-atrato-defensoras-del-territorio/> accessed 11 April 2025.

66 *Reconnaissance de la personnalité juridique et des droits de la rivière Magpie – Mutehejau Shipu* (*Province de Québec*, Minganie Regional County Municipality, Resolution no. 025–21, 17 February 2021).

But what is the ultimate normative value of recognizing ecosystem components (e.g., rivers, oceans, forest cover etc.) as rights-holders? How does this conferral or recognition of rights result in markedly better protection than if public interest claims were asserted for such ecosystem components? It is about how we understand substantive rights, not merely procedural ones. The separation of the protection of the right to life as a notion in international human rights law from the right to exist of other species and Nature was an artificial construction that has led to a wrong anthropocentric vision of the world. Is human life the only and highest value worth protecting in a system of values on earth? This separation, I argue, has failed, demonstrated by the planetary (climate, biodiversity) crises today. Human beings are part of Nature, and Nature, treated merely as a resource to exploit, has now reached tipping points in no longer being able to sustain life as it has been able to do. It is simple. Human life is deeply connected to the lives of other species and the planet itself. Our lives are closely connected to the rights of the trees in the rainforest in the Amazon to exist, deeply connected to the uninterrupted functioning of natural systems surrounding us. It is those natural systems that are in need of urgent protection.

Take the example of a cloud forest that was threatened by a mining project. Under the human rights paradigm, as there were no human inhabitants in this forest, a mine could have gone ahead with a mining license and bulldozed DNA that could not be found anywhere else in the world. There was no 'harm' because no human rights were 'affected'. From the perspective of the rights of nature, the extinction of species in nature is unlawful, therefore such a project could not go ahead. This was the *Los Cedros* case, a case in which I acted and which was examined by the Constitutional Court of Ecuador. It shows the value of a paradigm shift, which I discussed in detail in the forthcoming book, *A Barrister for the Earth* (Faber, 2025).

Environmental law, internationally, grew from sets of principles stated in soft law instruments. The core of environmental principles is found in the 1972 Stockholm Declaration[67] which initiated 'a process of normative development' in the environmental area, as noted by Pierre-Marie Dupuy,[68] and which was expanded and consolidated later with the adoption of the Rio

[67] Declaration on the United Nations Conference on the Human Environment, 11 ILM 1416 (16 June 1972).

[68] Pierre-Marie Dupuy, Ginebra Le Moli, Jorge E. Viñuales, 'Customary International Law and the Environment' (2018), *2 C-EENRG Working Papers*, 1, 9.

Declaration on Environment and Development in 1992.[69] These, in essence, are both anthropocentric instruments.

In between both Declarations, however, lies 'an avowedly ecological instrument which emphasizes the protection of nature as an end in itself'[70]: the 1982 World Charter for Nature.[71] Adopted by a vote of 111 in favour, eighteen abstentions and one vote against (the UK voted in favour of its adoption), the Charter enunciates that '*Mankind is part of nature and life depends on the uninterrupted functioning of natural systems*' and that '*every form of life is unique, warranting respect regardless of its worth to man*'.

Underlying this instrument, one can see a recognition of the inextricable connection between human life and the environment. The kind of recognition that has been appraised in the 2017 Advisory Opinion No. 23 of the Inter-American Court on Human Rights, and that is coming to light in dicta contained in the *Atrato* judgment or the *La Oroya* decision. Have we reached a full circle? Is it time to retake the trajectory recognized by the world with the *World Charter for Nature* in 1982, but then abandoned?

The interconnectedness between mankind and the natural world, reflected in these legal developments, does not belong only to Indigenous peoples living in close harmony with nature. It actually has a profound footing in science and Western tradition, despite what appears on the face of it. Alexander von Humboldt, the eighteenth-century German naturalist and explorer, went to the Americas in 1799 and noted in his diary: '*Alles ist Wechselwirkung*' ('Everything [in Nature] is *interconnectedness')*. I dare say we are currently standing at the very liminal moment in which the law is catching up with such a basic but fundamental truth.

---

69 Rio Declaration on Environment and Development (13 June 1992), UN Doc A/CONF.151/26. Rev.1.

70 Philippe Sands, Jacqueline Peel, *Principles of International Environmental Law*, (4th edn, Cambridge University Press 2018), 37.

71 UNGA (28 October 1982), *World Charter for Nature*, UN Doc A/RES/37/7.

10. States and corporations in the context of environmental chronic emergencies: Responsibility and liability at the crossroads

Patricio Barbirotto

1. INTRODUCTION

The primary responsibility for upholding human rights rests with states. However, there is increasing recognition of the significant role that transnational corporations (TNCs) and, more broadly, private businesses play in ensuring respect for human rights. Since the adoption of the United Nations Guiding Principles on Business and Human Rights in 2011, it has become widely accepted that TNCs exercise considerable influence, and control, over activities affecting human rights. Consequently, they are not absolved of human rights obligations; rather, they are required to take proactive measures to prevent adverse human rights impacts and may be held accountable for any violations resulting from their actions.

In this context, it is necessary to examine the rationale for holding TNCs accountable for human rights violations that are not confined to isolated incidents but instead persist over extended periods, potentially continuing even after the corporation has ceased operations in a specific region. This chapter argues that TNCs actively engage in activities that have far-reaching implications for human rights and the environment, with a particular focus on the disproportionate impact of environmental chronic emergencies (ECEs) on women's rights. The chapter seeks to move beyond the traditional doctrinal perspective, which centres on subjects, rules and individual violations, towards an approach that considers the relational dimensions of transnational corporate activity, which often exploits gaps in international regulation. It examines the interactions between TNCs, states and affected communities, highlighting the social and structural dynamics that underpin transnational business operations. This requires engaging with critical approaches to international law, particularly through the lenses of relational feminism and ecofeminism, to uncover overlooked dimensions of corporate responsibility and integrate them into the legal framework governing TNCs.[1]

The chapter begins by situating TNCs within the broader context of ECEs. It then analyzes their international legal obligations and the mechanisms that allow the victims of human rights violations to access justice, considering the respective roles of both host and parent states. Further, the chapter explores the specific challenges posed by corporate involvement in ECEs. Finally, it evaluates potential legal and policy responses, including the role of soft law transnational mechanisms and the pursuit of judicial remedies through both domestic and international (regional) *fora*.

2. THE PROBLEM OF INVISIBILITY

2.1 Invisibility and Activities of TNCs

In Chapter 2, ECEs are defined as situations that develop slowly, leading to harmful effects over years, if not decades.[2] Consequently, these emergencies may be perceived as somewhat invisible, frequently impacting multiple generations.[3] Moreover, ECEs generate varying effects across diverse social groups, leading to differentiated impacts on the most vulnerable populations. As explained in Chapter 1, the analysis of ECEs necessitates that all stakeholders operating on the global stage adopt an alternative perspective, switching the focus to the process rather than maintaining it on the crisis itself,[4] and this is undoubtedly relevant to the activities of TNCs. This chapter argues that the concept of ECEs is closely connected to the operations of TNCs. It asserts that the relevant international obligations apply to these activities, albeit requiring a shift in perspective to fully integrate this concept into international law. That would, in fact, be impossible unless additional elements are considered: the relational nature of transnational activities, with due regard for the context in which these activities occur; the relations said activities establish with local populations; how these activities have an impact on an intersectional

---

1 See Sara De Vido, 'Feminist Legal Methods and Environmental Chronic Emergencies: Challenging the Anthropocentric and Androcentric International Legal System' in this Volume.

2 See Deborah Russo, 'Moving Beyond an Approach Based on Crisis and Disasters to Address Environmental Chronic Emergencies' in this Volume.

3 Sara De Vido, 'In dubio pro futuris generationibus: una risposta giuridica eco-centrica alla slow violence' in Micaela Frulli (ed.), *L'interesse delle future generazioni nel diritto internazionale* (Editoriale scientifica 2022) 419.

4 See De Vido (n 1).

discriminatory basis, in particular on gender and racial groups; and the relation that human beings, especially those most affected by TNCs' activities, establish with the environment.[5]

The detrimental impacts of transnational corporations' activities, although relatively recent, are not entirely new. The impact of these activities on human rights and the environment has risen to mainstream public attention since notable incidents occurred, such as the Bhopal disaster in 1984 and the child labour cases, revealed in the 1990s.[6] Since the 1970s, there has been a gradual rise in inquiries within the international community concerning the regulation of TNCs. In response, TNCs have begun to adopt more responsible practices, implementing corporate social responsibility (CSR) strategies that demonstrate their commitment to upholding human rights. In their CSR policies, TNCs seek to address societal requirements and expectations, frequently those of wealthy nations where these enterprises maintain their headquarters or generate profits. However, the focus has primarily been on activities with immediate visible effects, overlooking the wider implications of TNCs' activities for future generations. This oversight is particularly evident in instances such as the Minamata disease, where the release of chemicals into water sources did not produce immediate visible consequences. However, it ultimately had profound long-term effects on human health, notably impacting women's reproductive health and foetal development.[7] The Minamata case demonstrates that the invisible effects mentioned earlier can significantly affect individuals who are especially vulnerable. The detrimental nature of a given phenomenon is exacerbated in those who are more susceptible. Increased vulnerability may stem from the social group's inherent connection to societal structures or indicate specific (chronic) emergency situations.[8] In particular, concerning

---

5 *Ibid.*

6 On the Bhopal Case see, among the others, David H. Ott, 'Bhopal and the Law: The Shape of a New International Legal Regime' (1985) 7 (3) *Third World Quarterly* 648; On child labour see for instance the ILO Report Statistics on Working Children and Hazardous Child Labour in Brief (1st edn, 1997) <https://www.ilo.org/publications/statistics-working-children-and-hazardous-child-labour-brief-first-edition> accessed 20 April 2025.

7 Sara De Vido, '"Violenza climatica" e migrazioni di genere nel diritto internazionale' in Angela Di Stasi, Raffaele Cadin, Anna Iermano, Valentina Zambrano (eds), *Donne migranti e violenza di genere nel contesto giuridico internazionale ed europeo* (Editoriale Scientifica 2023) 137.

8 Monika Mayerhofer, 'Framing UN Human Rights Discourses on Climate Change: The Concept of Vulnerability and its Relation to the Concepts of Inequality and Discrimination' (2024) 37 *International Journal for the Semiotics of Law – Revue internationale de Sémiotique juridique* 91.

the activities of transnational corporations, the Minamata case demonstrates a notable gender-based impact, affecting areas like reproductive rights. In other scenarios, it places an extra burden on women due to ECEs disrupting social structures, such as desertification and subsequent migration from sub-Saharan Africa.[9]

2.2 Historical and Contemporary Cases of ECEs

The impact of the activities of TNCs in ECEs is huge, especially on women, but difficult to assess precisely because of its invisibility. Along with the Minamata case, the Love Canal disaster serves as a historical example of the constant existence of ECEs, despite its introduction as a contemporary concept. This incident occurred in the late 1970s in Niagara Falls, New York. Love Canal was initially conceived as a canal for a proposed hydroelectric project in the early 1900s; however, it was subsequently abandoned and repurposed as a dumping ground for chemicals by the Hooker Chemical Company. In 1953, the area was sold for real estate development, and by the late 1970s, inhabitants of the Love Canal community began experiencing health problems, particularly concerning women's reproductive health. Similar to the Minamata case, the region exhibited elevated rates of birth defects, illnesses and miscarriages that surpassed average levels. Local activism facilitated the identification of the correlation between chemical contamination and these health issues, which subsequently resulted in increased pressure on local authorities, the federal government and Hooker Chemical for clarification and accountability.[10] In 1978, Love Canal residents initiated legal action against Hooker Chemical, citing the company's negligent disposal of toxic waste and the subsequent adverse effects on the community's health. In the claim, residents asserted that the company had prior knowledge of the situation at the time of the land sale in 1953. The case centred on strict liability, a concept that is currently recognized in international law, particularly within the realm of international environmental law. This principle states that an entity is accountable for the damage resulting from hazardous activities, regardless of whether the entity acted with malicious intent.[11] In 1980, the US federal government enacted the

---

[9] Jaya Ramji-Nogales, 'Slow-onset Climate Justice and Human Mobility' (2021) 93 *Temple Law Review* 671.

[10] On the *Love Canal* Case see William R. Ginsberg, Lois Weiss, 'Common Law Liability for Toxic Torts: A Phantom Remedy' (1981) 9 *Hofstra Law Review* 860.

[11] Dinah L. Shelton, Alex Kiss, 'Strict Liability in International Environmental Law' in Tafsir Malick Ndiaye and Rüdiger Wolfrum (eds), *Law of the Sea,*

Comprehensive Environmental Response, Compensation, and Liability Act (CERCLA),[12] which facilitated a settlement agreement wherein the company consented to cover a portion of the cleanup costs and aid in relocating affected residents. The United States federal government ultimately assumed responsibility for remediation initiatives in accordance with CERCLA. The Love Canal case underscored critical concerns about environmental contamination and the accountability of corporations in such matters. The situation prompted an examination of the sufficiency of existing environmental regulations and highlighted the necessity for safeguarding victims impacted by the misconduct. The precedents set forth in the Love Canal cases played a significant role in shaping the concept of environmental justice, which seeks to address unequal environmental burdens experienced by more vulnerable populations. In its amended form, this legislation remains crucial in managing hazardous waste sites and ensuring that companies responsible for pollution are held accountable for their environmental impact.[13]

Fast forward to current issues, an instance of activities leading to persistent emergencies can be identified within the extractive sector, specifically in mining operations across the Global South. In this context, considerable media attention has focused on mining operations in the Democratic Republic of Congo (DRC), owing to the critical role these activities play for technological conglomerates.[14] The DRC serves as a significant source of rare earth elements, which are essential for the manufacturing of semiconductors and various electronic devices, such as smartphones, laptops and batteries for electric vehicles.[15] The sector has been the subject of numerous reports by non-governmental organizations (NGOs) that document a range of human rights violations at all levels of operation, from illicit artisanal mining to extensive industrial activities.[16] Reports indicate that the mining industry

---

Environmental Law and Settlement of Disputes: Liber Amicorum Judge Thomas A. Mensah (Brill Academic Publishers 2007).

[12] Comprehensive Environmental Response, Compensation and Liability Act 1980, 42 U.S.C. Chapter 103.

[13] Superfund Amendments and Reauthorization Act 1986.

[14] For an overview on mining in the DRC see Marie Mazalto, 'Governance, Human Rights and Mining in the Democratic Republic of Congo' in Bonnie Campbell (ed.), *Mining in Africa: Regulation and Development* (Pluto Press 2009) 187.

[15] *Ibid.*

[16] See, for instance, the 2023 report of Amnesty International on the situation in the DRC, <https://www.amnesty.org/en/location/africa/east-africa-the-horn-and-great-lakes/democratic-republic-of-the-congo/report-democratic-republic-of-the-congo/> accessed 20 April 2025.

poses significant environmental challenges, primarily stemming from mineral extraction, which leads to deforestation, water pollution and the degradation of ecosystems. Furthermore, this industry directly affects the daily lives of local communities that rely on water sources for drinking, fishing and agricultural activities. The environmental consequences of mining give rise to substantial repercussions that can be accurately characterized as ECEs. The aforementioned effects exacerbate the humanitarian crisis in the DRC, leading to increased food insecurity and the proliferation of waterborne diseases, thereby further harming the most vulnerable segments of society, particularly women and children. Workers in the mines of the DRC frequently endure perilous working conditions. Numerous miners develop respiratory ailments as a result of exposure to harmful dust and toxic substances such as mercury, while lacking access to sufficient healthcare. Furthermore, protections for labour rights are virtually absent. In this context, women engaged in the mining sector encounter especially challenging conditions, with numerous individuals employed in low-wage positions, such as the transportation of minerals. Following years of conflict that altered societal frameworks, resulting in the abandonment of numerous women, mining became one of the few avenues for women, particularly widows, to earn a living.[17] In addition, they remain vulnerable to sexual exploitation and violence, and engagement in sex work represents a means of securing employment opportunities. Sexual violence, especially in the form of rape, is prevalent in mining regions, where women and girls are targeted by both armed factions and local miners, and sexual exploitation, including trafficking, affects a significant percentage of the female population.[18] Children are also obligated to work in the mines, despite existing child labour regulations in the country. Minors, some as young as seven or eight, are engaged in labour under perilous conditions within mining operations, frequently receiving minimal or no compensation for their efforts. They face significant physical dangers while excavating in unsafe environments, as well as being exposed to hazardous chemicals. Children are frequently engaged in labour under coercive circumstances, facing threats of violence or intimidation from armed groups or employers. The issue with TNC operations in the DRC and their contribution to ECEs is not limited to human rights violations supporting

---

[17] Sara Geenen, Gracia Kabilambali, Fiz Mussa Bashizi, Elisa Vanlerberghe, 'Women who "age too fast": Female work, bodies and health in the gold mines of Eastern Democratic Republic of Congo' (2022) 12 (3) *The Extractive Industries and Society* 101138.

[18] Caren Grown, 'How mining affects women in the Democratic Republic of Congo' WEF Report published on 23 September 2015, <https://www.weforum.org/stories/2015/09/how-mining-affects-women-in-the-democratic-republic-of-congo/> accessed 20 April 2025.

the electronics and battery manufacturing industries, but is primarily about the lack of visibility surrounding this phenomenon. TNCs may procure minerals from the DRC via a network of intermediaries that fail to perform due diligence to ascertain that these minerals are not associated with armed groups or exploitative practices. Meanwhile, these enterprises seem disconnected from the abuses, particularly in their target markets, which are the more affluent regions where they distribute their final products.

The scenario is certainly not unique to the DRC, and a similar situation can be found, for example, in Peru, where the extractive industry is responsible for deforestation, water and air pollution and soil contamination. In such contexts, women in mining communities are often more vulnerable to the health – including reproductive health – impacts of environmental pollution, especially as many are responsible for household tasks like collecting water or preparing food. Many women actively participate in the industry, often in the informal mining sector, where they receive lower pay compared to male miners and face harassment, sexual violence and exploitation.[19]

2.3 Response

The brief overview of the impact of TNCs on human rights, particularly women's rights, and their role in ECEs highlights the complexities involved in addressing the negative consequences of their activities. A key factor in this complexity is the often-disproportionate bargaining power TNCs wield in relation to the host states where they operate. This power imbalance can lead to exemptions from national legal frameworks, potentially resulting in adverse effects on local populations.

The challenges posed by ECEs are further exacerbated by the long-standing lack of awareness surrounding these issues. This lack of recognition interacts with structural characteristics of TNCs, allowing for the identification of two interrelated legal dimensions that must be addressed. The first concerns responsibility, understood as the obligation to comply with established legal norms. In this context, responsibility pertains to the international obligations applicable to TNCs and the legal consequences that arise in cases of noncompliance. The second dimension concerns accountability, referring to the mechanisms that ensure the enforcement of responsibility, including the obligation to hold TNCs accountable for violations before courts of justice or through alternative mechanisms that secure access to justice for victims.

---

[19] See, for instance, Araceli Valencia, 'New extractivism, foreign investment and inclusive development: reclaiming participatory gender equality in Perú' (2022) 19 (6) *Globalizations* 876.

Only through a clear distinction between responsibility and accountability can effective measures be implemented to mitigate the adverse impacts of TNCs' activities, ensuring that liability is properly established. The following sections will examine these two dimensions, first by analyzing the existing framework of TNC responsibilities – particularly the obligations applicable to their operations – and then by exploring accountability mechanisms, including the available *fora* for adjudicating wrongful acts. Both aspects will be considered within the specific context of ECEs, beginning with the current legal framework and advancing towards necessary reforms.

3. ISSUES OF LEGAL PERSONALITY AND OBLIGATIONS AT MULTIPLE LEVELS

3.1 Visibilising TNCs as Subjects of International Law

To understand the obligations of TNCs, a brief overview of their international legal personality is essential. The activities of TNCs present a structural challenge to the system of international law. In its traditional conception, international law is established by states and fundamentally connected to concepts of statehood and territoriality. By nature, transnational corporations operate beyond national borders, engaging with diverse societies. They must adhere to the legal regulations of each jurisdiction in which they operate – regulations that may differ significantly worldwide – while also adapting to a range of social and economic contexts and to the varying expectations of local communities. Historically, international law viewed TNCs not as subjects but rather as objects or, possibly, as actors within the international legal framework. However, this viewpoint is outdated. Modern scholarship in international economic law now acknowledges TNCs as legal subjects with an effective yet limited legal persona.[20] They possess the capacity to hold rights and obligations, initiate claims pertaining to their obligations and rights and engage in binding agreements with other entities under international law.

---

[20] On the international legal personality of TNC see, among the many others, Alice de Jonge, 'Transnational corporations and international law: bringing TNCs out of the accountability vacuum' (2011) 7 (1) *Critical Perspectives on International Business* 66; James Crawford, *Brownlie's Principles of Public International Law* (Oxford University Press 2012) 655; Malcolm Shaw, *International Law* (Cambridge University Press 2017) 197; Arno Dal Ri Júnior, Erika Louise Bastos Calazans, 'Transnational Corporations Subjectivity Based on the Criteria of the Bernadotte Case and the Traditional International Law Doctrine' (2018) 18 (1) *Anuario Mexicano De Derecho Internacional* 155; Fabrizio Marrella, *Diritto del commercio internazionale*, (CEDAM 2023) 152.

TNCs' personality is indeed peculiar and presents challenges, as TNCs typically comprise multiple entities, each a separate legal person governed by the laws of various jurisdictions. TNCs can be viewed as collectives of interconnected legal entities operating in national or regional contexts. Every company linked to a TNC aims to maintain its corporate identity while adhering to the operational standards of a unified global enterprise. Yet, some subsidiaries may seem detached from the main group and branded differently, especially when engaged in activities perceived as unethical. This is done in order to manage reputational risks in the TNC's home country,[21] or when the TNC is directly connected to or owned by a state. [22]

Irrespective of the particular configuration of a TNC, contemporary international law regards the TNC as a whole as a subject. Such a subject is given by a collective entity, comprising interconnected companies pursuing a unified objective. This matter is at the core of determining which obligations apply to TNCs and is to be considered in light of how states typically view each individual company that makes up the TNC as a distinct domestic legal person. At this point in the analysis, it is significant to note that the possession of international personality implies that TNCs may be subject to international accountability for any potential violations, including those involving ECEs. Situations such as climate change, rising sea levels, or desertification can be related to the activities of TNCs, particularly in sectors characterized by significant resource consumption, including the extractive and chemical industries, or in less apparent sectors like intensive agriculture or fishing.

3.2 The International Level: International Legal Obligations

The issue of international responsibility of TNCs for misconduct has attracted increasing attention since the late 1970s. Historically, the actions of private entities have been subject to the jurisdiction of domestic law. As discussed above, the recent development is the possibility that TNCs possess international legal personality. This allows them to bear international obligations and be held accountable for violations. The first attempts to influence the activities of TNCs were carried out through soft law instruments, namely the 1976 OECD Guidelines for Multinational Enterprises on Responsible Business

---

21 Terry O'Callaghan, Belinda Spagnoletti, 'Mining, corporate social responsibility, and corporate reputation' in Terry O'Callaghan, Geordan Graetz (eds), *Mining in the Asia-Pacific Region: Risks, Challenges and Opportunities* (Springer 2017) 285.

22 For an overview on TNCs as organs or agents of a state see Deborah Russo, *L'impresa come organo o agente di uno Stato nel diritto internazionale* (Editoriale Scientifica 2023).

Conduct (hereinafter OECD Guidelines)[23] and the 1977 Tripartite Declaration of Principles concerning Multinational Enterprises and Social Policy (hereinafter MNE Declaration).[24] The initial attempt to impose international binding obligations upon TNCs dates back to 2003 with the adoption of the Draft Norms on the Responsibilities of Transnational Corporations and Other Business Enterprises with regard to Human Rights by the UN Subcommission on the Promotion and Protection of Human Rights (hereinafter referred to as 'Draft Norms').[25] Although the Draft Norms did not achieve broad acceptance, the Draft Norms constitute the first formal restatement of the responsibilities of TNCs concerning human rights.[26] In parallel, in 1999, the United Nations launched the Global Compact initiative, whose initial phase culminated in the inaugural Global Compact Summit in 2004.[27] The initiative proposed the Global Compact, a set of ten principles that companies, including but not limited to TNCs, are invited to follow.[28] These principles are designed to enhance human rights and foster sustainable development by engaging private enterprises in the pursuit of the sustainable development goals (hereinafter referred to as SDGs) outlined in the 2030 Agenda,[29] through the reinforcement of CSR. In 2011, the UN Human Rights Council adopted the Guiding Principles on Business and Human Rights (hereinafter 'Guiding Principles'),[30] a comprehensive soft-law framework (non-binding principles and guidelines) designed to tackle the issue of human rights in relation to TNCs. The Guiding Principles are structured around three fundamental pillars: the duty of the state to protect

---

23 OECD Guidelines for Multinational Enterprises on Responsible Business Conduct, adopted on 21 June 1976, last amended on 27 October 2023, OECD/LEGAL/0144.

24 Tripartite Declaration of Principles concerning Multinational Enterprises and Social Policy, approved at the ILO Governing Body 204th Session, 1977, last amended at the ILO Governing Body 346th Session, 2022.

25 Draft Norms on the Responsibilities of Transnational Corporations and Other Business Enterprises with regard to Human Rights, E/CN.4/Sub.2/2003/12.

26 David Weissbrodt and Muria Kruger, 'Norms on the Responsibilities of Transnational Corporations and Other Business Enterprises with Regard to Human Rights' (2003) 97 (4) *American Journal of International Law* 901.

27 United Nations Global Compact, official website <https://unglobalcompact.org/> accessed 20 April 2025.

28 UN Global Compact: Principles, available at <https://unglobalcompact.org/what-is-gc/mission/principles> accessed 20 April 2025.

29 Transforming our world: the 2030 Agenda for Sustainable Development, A/RES/70/1.

30 United Nations Guiding Principles on Business and Human Rights, [ST/]HR/PUB/11/4.

human rights, the responsibility of TNCs to uphold human rights and the access to justice for victims of violations.

In connection with the Guiding Principles, on 6 March 2018, the OECD adopted a non-binding instrument, the OECD Due Diligence Guidance for Responsible Business Conduct (hereinafter Due Diligence Guidelines).[31] This instrument aims at enhancing the Guiding Principles, as well as the OECD Guidelines and the MNE Declaration, by providing unified rules for TNCs to draft self-regulation tools known as codes of conduct, which will be discussed below. In light of the increasing recognition of human rights in business practices, provisions pertaining to human rights have been progressively incorporated into international investment agreements (IIAs), one of the principal instruments governing the operations of TNCs. In fact, TNCs frequently operate through foreign direct investments (FDI), which grant them significant bargaining power in relation to states.

3.3 The Regional Level: EU Obligations and Regulatory Challenges

At the regional level, the EU has adopted legally binding tools aimed at regulating the activities of the TNCs. The EU Corporate Sustainability Reporting Directive, hereinafter referred to as CSRD,[32] and the EU Corporate Sustainability Due Diligence Directive, hereinafter referred to as CSDDD,[33] represent efforts to innovate or, at the very least, to advance in this area, having come into effect on 5 January 2023 and 24 July 2024, respectively. The CSRD and the CSDDD seek to reconcile the regulatory frameworks of both home and host states by imposing obligations on companies incorporated within the EU and on those generating over 150 million euros annually in revenue within EU markets. The CSRD requires TNCs to produce social corporate responsibility reports, holding them accountable for conduct related to their activities throughout the value chain. By contrast, the CSDDD mandates TNCs to identify and address the human rights impact of their activities and value chain, along with implementing a transition plan aligned with the Paris Agreement goals. While both directives are undoubtedly a positive step forward in the context of safeguarding human rights globally, numerous companies have

---

31 OECD Due Diligence Guidance for Responsible Business Conduct, 2018.

32 Directive (EU) 2022/2464 of the European Parliament and of the Council of 14 December 2022 amending Regulation (EU) No 537/2014, Directive 2004/109/EC, Directive 2006/43/EC and Directive 2013/34/EU, as regards corporate sustainability reporting.

33 Directive (EU) 2024/1760 of the European Parliament and of the Council of 13 June 2024 on corporate sustainability due diligence and amending Directive (EU) 2019/1937 and Regulation (EU) 2023/2859.

emphasized the challenges imposed upon them, particularly in maintaining complete oversight over the actions of their partners and managing the butterfly effect of potential human rights violations occurring without the company's knowledge or ability to intervene. Currently, a proposal for amending certain requirements and deadlines is under review by the European Parliament and the Council.

3.4 The Domestic Level: Home and Host States and Corporate Obligations

Moving to the domestic level allows to tackle some of the challenges encountered by international instruments. TNCs have historically evolved by modifying their structures and operations to optimize the benefits associated with operating across various jurisdictions. For this reason, most international legal provisions impact the activities of TNCs through domestic legislation, and the majority of the regulatory framework is derived from domestic legislation, which enacts international inter-state commitments concerning human rights.[34]

Although the TNC is regarded as a subject of international law in its entirety, within the scope of domestic law, each constituent company of the TNC is considered a distinct legal entity. Consequently, from a state's perspective, the issue arises regarding the legal personality of the entity responsible for misconduct, which is frequently incorporated in the jurisdiction where the incidents occur and is legally distinct from the parent company. Assessing the applicability of international obligations is complex, especially for TNCs in sensitive sectors, which are those more prone to induce the subtle repercussions characteristic of ECEs. The principal entity, referred to as the parent company, is established in a jurisdiction known as the home state, while conducting operations globally through a framework of subsidiaries incorporated in diverse jurisdictions, termed host states. Consequently, each subsidiary is governed by a distinct regulatory framework. On the one hand, the parent company is regulated by its home state, which may seek to oversee the entirety of the activities of the transnational entity by regarding it as an integral part of its national framework. This is typically conducted in accordance with the nationality principle of jurisdiction,[35] driven by factors ranging from strictly legal considerations, such as the influence of international obligations imposed on the home state,

---

[34] Guiding Principles (n 30) Principle 1.

[35] Sara L. Seck, 'Conceptualizing the Home State Duty to Protect Human Rights' in Karin Buhman, Mette Morsing, Lynn Roseberry (eds), *Corporate Social and Human Rights Responsibilities: Global Legal and Management Perspectives* (Palgrave Macmillan 2011) 25.

to local pressures stemming from civil society and public opinion. These factors have led home states to adopt unilateral regulatory measures for TNCs. To a certain extent, the home state may view itself as bearing the responsibility for overseeing the activities of TNCs that it deems to fall within its jurisdiction, in accordance with the obligation to protect human rights as articulated in the Guiding Principles.[36] Indeed, presuming that home state regulation is carried out in good faith and with the intention of promoting human rights,[37] it nonetheless retains an extraterritorial nature and could be perceived as interfering with the sovereignty of the host state.[38] The host state bears an equivalent responsibility for safeguarding human rights, just as the home state does. Furthermore, it possesses territorial jurisdiction to govern activities within its borders, thereby theoretically placing the host state in a superior position regarding the protection of human rights. However, host states face constraints in governing the operations of TNCs due to their obligations under international investment agreements. These agreements, and even more so the state contracts concluded directly between the host state and TNCs, grant specific conditions for TNCs investing within the host country, which may clash with the human rights of local communities. TNCs could use these provisions to their advantage in arbitral dispute resolution, as briefly discussed later.[39]

3.5 The Transnational Level: Self-regulation Tools

Before delving into the concept of accountability, referred to in this chapter as access to justice, it is crucial to briefly explore an additional layer of regulation relevant to international and transnational business law. A significant portion of international business practices stems from self-regulation mechanisms and privately initiated regulatory tools. *Lex mercatoria* can even be chosen as the governing law of a contract if arbitration is chosen as a dispute resolution mechanism. In this context, the regulation of business and human rights could rely on measures arising from self-regulation. This can manifest as rules established individually by companies or as collectively developed guidelines through the efforts of pertinent NGOs. As will be shown in the following sections, TNCs may choose to adopt certain behaviours (i.e., rules) not solely due to the influence of domestic or international legislation, but rather in

---

36 Guiding Principles (n 30) Pillar 1.

37 Sara L. Seck, 'Unilateral Home State Regulation: Imperialism or Tool for Subaltern Resistance?' (2008) 46 (3) *Osgoode Hall Law Journal* 565.

38 *Ibid.*

39 Tomer Broude, Caroline Henckels, 'Not all rights are created equal: A loss–gain frame of investor rights and human rights' (2021) 34 (1) *Leiden Journal of International Law* 93.

response to market pressures, which typically exhibit a more rapid reaction to challenges than legal frameworks. Consequently, since the early 2000s, TNCs have implemented strategies associated with CSR, a comprehensive term that encompasses the approaches and self-regulatory mechanisms employed by these entities to promote human rights protection and sustainable business practices.[40] In the context of CSR, a related concept has emerged: sustainable and ethical investment, denoted by the acronym ESG (Environmental, Social and Governance). This approach to business practices is intricately linked to the realization of SDGs and has resulted in the creation of investment funds that exclusively support enterprises committed to sustainable development.[41]

Both the Global Compact and the Guiding Principles acknowledge and address this distinctive aspect of business regulation. The Global Compact initiative encourages participating companies to incorporate the ten principles into their policies, strategies and procedures, particularly in pursuit of the SDGs.[42] This is particularly evident in company regulations informed by codes of conduct which integrate the commitments outlined in the Global Compact.[43] The Guiding Principles advance the involvement of TNCs, allocating the second pillar to the obligation of TNCs to respect human rights, to be implemented through various mechanisms of self-regulation. Companies are urged to implement a policy commitment to respect human rights within their operations[44] and to engage in human rights due diligence.[45] This process necessitates the implementation of a human rights impact assessment aimed at identifying potential adverse impacts on human rights resulting from the company's activities[46] and incorporating the findings of this assessment into their policies.[47] In this context, the Due Diligence Guidelines provide a significant practical resource for TNCs in the realization and execution of due diligence practices.[48] Self-regulatory tools implemented by transnational institutions, particularly codes of conduct, have received commendation for indicating a

---

40 Ilias Bantekas, 'Corporate Social Responsibility in International Law' (2004) 22 *Boston University International Law Journal* 309.

41 Paul Lee, *The Rule of Law and investor approaches to ESG: Discussion paper* (Birmingham Centre for the Rule of Law 2022).

42 UN Global Compact for sustainable development, Business and the Sustainable Development Goals: Acting Responsibly and Finding Opportunities, 3.

43 UN Global Compact (n 28).

44 Guiding Principles (n 30) Principle 16.

45 Guiding Principles, *ibid.*, Principle 17.

46 Guiding Principles, *ibid.*, Principle 18.

47 Guiding Principles, *ibid.*, Principle 19.

48 Due Diligence Guidelines (n 31).

shift in perspective from a narrow focus on financial gain to an emphasis on ethical considerations in profit generation. Nonetheless, such practices have also faced criticism, as companies are purportedly engaging in them for marketing purposes rather than demonstrating a genuine commitment to human rights, with no consequences in case of abuses, and, moreover, created without considering the context, the causes and the process where the investments happen, nor the voices of those affected.

The introduction of transnational regulatory mechanisms, including those related to self-regulation, brings about a unique form of accountability that differs from the conventional notion of access to justice. While accountability may present challenges within judicial contexts, TNCs are undoubtedly answerable, albeit not in the conventional legal sense, to their shareholders and stakeholders, which encompass the target markets. In this context, TNCs face the risk of market sanctions, which may manifest as a decline in market share stemming from consumers' hesitance to purchase goods and services linked to the infringement of the rights of vulnerable groups.[49] TNCs frequently operate in regions with legal ambiguity, where an action may be lawful in the host country but deemed unethical or illegal elsewhere. Bringing attention to this disparity can influence consumer behaviour in the respective markets. For instance, a notable example of this phenomenon is evident in the Nike Sweatshops controversy in Pakistan and Cambodia. Following an initial adverse reaction towards Nike, the company took steps to enhance its practices and codes of conduct related to labour standards.[50] NGOs play a significant role in exposing and highlighting human rights abuses perpetrated by TNCs. In relation to ECEs, a key role is played by those organizations driven by women and advocating for women's rights, turning the light on the invisible phenomena described above.[51] Although this approach depends on voluntary instruments instead of mandatory frameworks, it is evident that stakeholders generally exhibit greater sensitivity or, at the very least, a swifter response to issues associated with ECEs, particularly when compared to the duration of judicial proceedings.

---

[49] Dominique Carreau and Fabrizio Marrella, *Diritto internazionale* (Giuffrè 2023) 659.

[50] Debra Cohen Maryanov, 'Sweatshop Liability: Corporate Codes of Conduct and the Governance of Labor Standards in the International Supply Chain' (2010) 14 *Lewis & Clark Law Review* 397.

[51] For an overview, see the dedicated web page of the OHCHR, <https://www.ohchr.org/en/women/women-human-rights-defenders> accessed 20 April 2025; the Council of Europe entails a mechanism for the participation of NGOs in women's rights related issues, see more at <https://www.coe.int/en/web/ingo/ngos-as-advocates-for-gender-equality-and-women-s-rights> accessed 20 April 2025.

3.6 Conclusive Remarks on the Obligations of TNCs

Despite the mentioned developments, none of the aforementioned tools were designed to address ECEs directly; instead, they were developed from a crisis management perspective. [52] Consequently, the primary issue pertains to the application of the aforementioned tools to behaviours akin to those delineated in section 3.2, which contribute to ECEs. Although heightened awareness at the international level is indeed commendable, it is likely that the initial shift in perspective will originate from the states, encompassing both home and host nations. This change will necessitate a recognition of the previously overlooked issues and a transition from a framework focused on crisis management to one that directly addresses ECEs.[53] The proposed transition may significantly influence the future evolution of international instruments, serving as an initial step towards the formation of customary law that could potentially be incorporated in future endeavours. [54] In this regard, there is currently an initiative proposed by Bolivia and South Africa in 2014 for a binding instrument,[55] aimed at restating the international norms applicable to TNCs, adopting an approach similar to that taken with the Draft Norms. Nonetheless, this instrument appears to be quite distant from becoming an international agreement,[56] even though in 2021 the third draft was adopted.[57]

4. ACCESS TO JUSTICE

4.1 Traditional Paths to Accountability: Access to Courts of Justice

Once the obligations applicable to TNCs have been identified, it remains to ascertain where victims can access justice. Ensuring access to justice, which

[52] See De Vido (n 1).

[53] *Ibid.*

[54] Seck (n 35).

[55] Elaboration of an international legally binding instrument on transnational corporations and other business enterprises with respect to human rights: draft resolution, A/HRC/26/L.22.

[56] The 10th session of the open-ended intergovernmental working group on transnational corporations and other business enterprises with respect to human rights took place on 16–20 December in Geneva, see <https://www.ohchr.org/en/hr-bodies/hrc/wg-trans-corp/session10> accessed 20 April 2025.

[57] Text of the 3rd revised draft legally binding instrument with the textual proposals submitted by States during the 7th session of the Open-Ended Intergovernmental Working Group on Transnational Corporations and Other Business Enterprises with Respect to Human Rights, A/HRC/49/65/Add.1.

is recognized as the third pillar of the Guiding Principles, poses a number of challenges related to certain issues already discussed in the previous sections. Based on the prior discourse, an initial analysis suggests that victims can, in the first instance, seek recourse in the domestic courts of both the home state and the host state.

Domestic courts of the home state may, in principle, exercise what is referred to as justice jurisdiction, thereby providing access to victims of human rights violations perpetrated by a TNC within the territory of the host state.[58] The most apparent benefit of engaging in proceedings before the courts of the host state is that the parent company may be directly subject to prosecution. Nonetheless, courts in the home state have typically exhibited hesitance in this regard, and the application of justice jurisdiction by these courts reinterprets the conflict with the sovereignty of the host state previously highlighted. Conversely, the domestic courts of the host state may lack the capacity to effectively adjudicate such cases and, more critically, to offer the victims appropriate remedies.[59] Particularly, when violations take place in least developed countries, the judiciary in those nations may not be fully equipped to adequately deal with violations committed by TNCs.[60] Additionally, host state courts typically possess jurisdiction solely over the local subsidiary of the TNC, which may lack assets or even be dissolved prior to the conclusion of proceedings. Furthermore, constraints may emerge from IIAs or state contracts that apply to the operations of TNCs, as previously indicated. Typically, disputes between TNCs and states regarding FDIs are submitted to an arbitral tribunal, where an unfavourable judicial decision by the host state can be qualified as interference with the investment.[61]

The perception of TNCs by the state as a group of separate legal entities influences the decision regarding whether to engage the domestic courts of the home state or those of the host state. Identifying the most appropriate court (and the applicable law) is traditionally addressed within the framework of private international law, and it is done through connecting factors. However, in instances of ECEs, an additional complexity arises due to the required shift

---

58 Seck (n 37).

59 Report of the European Law Institute, Business and Human Rights: Access to Justice and Effective Remedies (with input from the EU Agency for Fundamental Rights, FRA) (2022) 43.

60 Lucas Roorda, Cedric Ryngaert, 'Business and Human Rights Litigation in Europe: the Promises Held by Forum of Necessity-based Jurisdiction' (2016) 80 (4) *Rabels Zeitschrift für ausländisches und internationales Privatrecht / The Rabel Journal of Comparative and International Private Law* 783.

61 Francesco Francioni, 'Access to Justice, Denial of Justice and International Investment Law' (2009) 20 *European Journal of International Law* 738.

towards a relational perspective that allows for restructuring and redefining the relationship itself. To do so, connecting factors should be selected on the basis of the structure to be achieved, considering the nature of a given relationship, its context and its values.[62] For instance, by requiring the highest standard of care before the courts (and under the law) of the place where the TNC has its headquarters, rather than where the connected company has acted, people affected by the TNC's activity and its adverse effects may attempt to restructure an investment relationship characterized by inequality and a disproportionate impact on women and children.[63] Indeed, domestic courts in the home jurisdiction may be required to take action against what is, in a technical sense, a foreign entity established in the nation where the infringement occurred, and based on the claims of victims who are likewise foreign nationals to the home jurisdiction. In either scenario—whether involving home state courts and host state courts—it is essential that, alongside the domestic courts' willingness to proceed, the requested courts exhibit a degree of receptiveness and flexibility in their approach. This includes a readiness to consider the often-overlooked adverse effects on victims, in particular on women, resulting from ECEs, which may only become apparent years after the occurrence, particularly when evaluating the strict liability of the TNC. In this context, the direct causal relationship between the operations of the TNCs and the negative outcomes resulting from those operations can become evident only decades after the onset of the event, as shown by the Minamata case.[64]

Additionally, seeking justice for victims can involve pursuing claims against states, particularly targeting the home state, due to its inaction in efficiently regulating the TNCs' activities subject to its jurisdiction. Should domestic courts in the home state decline to address violations, alongside a failure to regulate the actions of TNCs, this scenario may result in the international responsibility of the home state for its inaction in overseeing the conduct of private actors.[65] This development facilitates the possibility of claims being directed towards the home state, as opposed to the TNCs themselves, within the judicial framework of the home state as well as in international judicial bodies – in particular, regional courts such as the European Court of Human Rights (ECtHR) or the Inter-American Court of Human Rights (IACtHR). Transferring the burden from transnational entities to states may enhance the likelihood of judicial rulings that favour victims, as exemplified by the

---

62 Roxana Banu, 'A Relational Feminist Approach to Conflict of Laws' (2017) 24 (1) *Michigan Journal of Gender & Law* 33.

63 Sara De Vido, 'The Privatisation of Climate Change Litigation: Current Developments in Conflicts of Laws' (2024) 6 (1) *Jus Cogens* 65.

64 De Vido (n 2).

65 Seck (n 37).

recent *KlimaSeniorinnen* case.[66] This solution appears to be currently the most immediate and effective way to implement the concept of ECEs in relation to the activities of TNCs.

4.2 International Arbitration

The nature of the activities of TNCs presents unique challenges in terms of regulation and adjudication. Nevertheless, the characteristics of the relations they establish with the host states provide an opportunity to investigate alternative approaches to accountability that diverge from conventional frameworks. In particular, disputes arising in connection with FDI often follow the path of transnational arbitration for their resolution.

What is relevant is the contribution that commercial or investment arbitration can offer in relation to accountability concerning ECEs. In its traditional understanding, transnational arbitration, functioning as a mechanism for private justice, tends to exclude victims of human rights violations, as it is inherently designed to resolve disputes between business partners who have consented to have their dispute decided by the arbitral tribunal. Nonetheless, in recent years, particularly after the adoption of the Guiding Principles, there has been a notable increase in the engagement of transnational arbitration with human rights issues.[67] Following the adoption of the Hague Rules on Arbitration Relating to Business and Human Rights on 12 December 2019,[68] addressing human rights issues in commercial arbitration has been facilitated, particularly concerning community agreements and value chain due diligence.[69] Regarding ECEs, community agreements – that is, agreements between an investor and a local community on how the community should

---

[66] *Verein KlimaSerniorinnen Schweiz and Others v Switzerland* [GC], App. No. 53600/20 (ECtHR 9 April 2024).

[67] Fabrizio Marrella, 'The UN guiding principles on business and human rights as an evolving regime: their contribution to international investment law and arbitration' in Dominique D'Ambra, Peggy Ducoulombier, Gabriel Eckert et al., (eds), *Mélanges en l'honneur de Florence Benoît-Rohmer. Les droits de l'homme, du Conseil de l'Europe à l'Union européenne* (Bruylant 2023) 329.

[68] Hague Rules on Arbitration Relating to Business and Human Rights, adopted on 12 December 2019 at The Hague.

[69] Nathalie Bernasconi-Osterwalder, The Hague Rules on Business and Human Rights Arbitration: What role in improving avenues for victims to access justice? (*IISD Investment Treaty News*, 7 October 2022) <https://www.iisd.org/itn/en/2022/10/07/the-hague-rules-on-business-and-human-rights-arbitration-what-role-in-improving-avenues-for-victims-to-access-justice-nathalie-bernasconi-osterwalder/> accessed 20 April 2025.

benefit from the investor'[70] – hold significant importance, as they are related to investments in the extractive industry and are required in specific jurisdictions prior to approving foreign investments.[71] Local community claims enter the arbitration process when they intersect with the investment, and one party – typically the investor – activates the arbitration clause either because of state actions supporting the local community (viewed as interference with the investment) or due to state inaction, such as failing to halt local protests against the investor.[72] When the community dimension becomes part of the arbitration process, its position can be presented through an *amicus curiae* brief by an NGO advocating for the local community's interests, though this representation may not guarantee full participation. Alternatively, community positions can be represented directly by the state through a counterclaim. Yet, in such instances, the state's interests may diverge from those of the local communities.[73] In addition, representing local communities in arbitral proceedings could be problematic due to currently existing social and economic conditions,[74] in a context where generally diversity and intersectionality are underrepresented – for instance, in the formation of the arbitral panel.[75] Considering the above, arbitration should not be seen as a tool to replace domestic courts but rather as a means to complement them as a valuable mechanism for accountability, subject to the parties' consent.

---

70 World Bank, Community Development Agreements, Responsible Agricultural Investment (RAI) Knowledge Into Action Note no. 18, Brief no. 124293, 15 March 2018 <https://documents.worldbank.org/en/publication/documents-reports/documentdetail/176621521090697239/community-development-agreements> accessed 20 April 2025.

71 See Sondra Faccio, 'Investment Contracts and the Reform of Investment Arbitration: Towards Sustainability' (2023) 38 (3) *ICSID Review – Foreign Investment Law Journal* 625.

72 Lorenzo Cotula and Mika Schröder, *Community perspectives in investor-state arbitration* (IIED 2017) 15.

73 *Ibid.*

74 See Shahla Ali, Filip Balcerzak, Giorgio Colombo et al. 'Reaching Sustainable Diversity in International Arbitration' in Shahla Ali, Filip Balcerzak, Giorgio Colombo et al. (eds), *Diversity in International Arbitration* (Edward Elgar Publishing 2022) 2.

75 Kabir A.N. Duggal and Rekha Rangachari, 'Gender, race, or both? The need for greater consideration of intersectionality in international arbitration' in Shahla Ali, Filip Balcerzak, Giorgio Colombo et al. (eds), *ibid.*, 48.

5. HOW TO DEAL WITH THOSE PROBLEMS?

The issues at hand are not novel; the interconnection of business and human rights has been a matter of discourse for nearly fifty years. Nevertheless, business and human rights are comparatively recent within the realm of international law, a field that has traditionally depended on fixed classifications and categories for centuries. It was only after the Second World War and the process of decolonization that certain foundational aspects began to be gradually challenged and rediscussed. The concept of ECEs and the approach articulated in this book definitely represent a major novelty and a challenge for the international legal order. It is a fact that a revolution does not happen overnight. Therefore, expanding the long-standing traditional approach within courts to encompass the concept of ECEs requires significant effort. Nonetheless, significant progress has been made in upholding human rights concerning the operations of TNCs over the past two decades. In regional contexts, both the ECtHR and the IACtHR have shown openness and engagement towards environmental issues, which, as explained in this chapter, often stem from the specific actions of TNCs. The problematic element of ECEs primarily revolves around methodology and perspective. Although the long-term goal may involve reforming international human rights control mechanisms and setting up an international adjudication forum to address not just traditional business and human rights issues but also ECEs,[76] practical short-term measures should be based on current operational frameworks. States and courts are required to recognize the often-hidden aspects of TNC activities and be open to alternative methodologies like ecofeminism. This involves focusing on the entire process, considering the relational aspect of transnational activities, and incorporating the environment to reveal what may seem invisible. This objective can be achieved within a short period, particularly if civil society increases its awareness of the issue and applies pressure on the state, its institutions and international organizations. A faster approach could entail international courts addressing instances where states have failed to regulate the operations of TNCs. While not the most optimal approach, since it prioritizes

---

76 On the proposal of a 'world court of human rights', see, for instance, Manfred Nowak, 'A World Court of Human Rights', in Gerd Oberleitner (ed.), *International Human Rights Institutions, Tribunals, and Courts. International Human Rights* (Springer 2018) 271.

state responsibilities over those of TNCs, this strategy could initially improve access to justice for victims. Moreover, this could act as a driving force for states to strengthen their regulatory frameworks regarding the activities of TNCs and to tackle potential misconduct, especially with regard to the most affected victims.

11. Due diligence obligations and environmental chronic emergencies

Björnstjern Baade

1. INTRODUCTION

To what extent can the existing human rights framework respond to emergencies? With due diligence obligations, human rights law has developed considerable capacities at addressing acute disasters (see Section 2). But even though this jurisprudence has developed to include systematic, structural human rights problems, it remains uncertain whether human rights law is fit for purpose regarding emergencies that unfold slowly (see Section 3).

Much like the medical concept, the chronicity of societal and environmental emergencies refers to problems that are long-lasting and not easily remedied. Such chronic emergencies not only pose difficulties for democratic processes but also for human rights assessments.[1] Somewhat paradoxically, it turns out to be more difficult to respond to dangers that unfold not suddenly but gradually.[2] Can human rights law play its part in ensuring that chronicity does not come to be associated with hopelessness?[3]

---

[1] Helen Arling and Hani Taghavi, 'KlimaSeniorinnen v. Switzerland – A New Era for Climate Change Protection or Proceeding with the Status Quo?' (*EJIL Talk!* 6 April 2023) <https://www.ejiltalk.org/klimaseniorinnen-v-switzerland-a-new-era-for-climate-change-protection-or-proceeding-with-the-status-quo/>, accessed 12 April 2025.

[2] Cf. Nicole Rogers, 'Climate violence and the word' (2023) 14(2), *Journal of Human Rights and the Environment*, 144, 150. See also Chapters I and II.

[3] Donald Venes (ed.), *Taber's Cyclopedic Medical Dictionary* (20th edn, 2005), 415: 'chronic: 1. Of long duration. 2. Denoting a disease showing little change or of slow progression; the opposite of acute'; *ibid,* 39: 'acute: 1. Sharp, severe. 2. Having rapid onset, severe symptoms, and a short course; not chronic'.

2. HUMAN RIGHTS DUE DILIGENCE AND ACUTE EMERGENCIES

The concept of due diligence has become a fundamental principle in international human rights law. It establishes the standard of conduct that states must adhere to fulfil their duty to protect human rights. This duty, which is derived in connection with the respective human rights treaties' protection clause, e.g. Article 1 ECHR, does not require states to guarantee success in preventing human rights violations but obliges them to take reasonable measures to mitigate certain risks, most notably in acute, immediate emergencies that require instant action.[4]

2.1 The Risks Human Rights Must be Protected From

In principle, due diligence obligates states to take measures to safeguard human rights from infringement. This duty extends beyond violations committed by state agents. States have a responsibility to prevent foreseeable harm no matter where it comes from. One of the most significant applications of due diligence in human rights law is the protection of individuals from harm caused by other private individuals or corporations. First developed in cases of domestic, sexual and other forms of gender-based violence,[5] it was eventually extended to environmental contexts.[6] Such environmental hazards can be directly linked to corporate misconduct, but a connection to a clearly identifiable actor, whose actions cause the risk, is not even necessary. This is significant when it comes to environmental disasters, and the reasoning can be transposed to other risks such as a public health crisis.[7]

---

4 See for more detail on the following: Björnstjern Baade, 'Due Diligence and the Duty to Protect Human Rights' in Heike Krieger, Anne Peters, and Leonhard Kreuzer (eds), *Due Diligence in the International Legal Order* (Oxford University Press 2020), 92–110.

5 *Maria da Penha v Brazil*, Report no 54/01, (IACommHR, 16 April 2000) Case 12.051, paras 55–8; *Opuz v Turkey*, App no 33401/02 (ECtHR, 9 September 2009), paras 183–202.

6 *López Ostra v Spain*, App no. 16798/90 (ECtHR, 9 December 1994), para. 51; *Opinio Consultativa Solicitada por la Republica de Colombia: Medio Ambiente y Derechos*, Advisory Opinion (IACtHR, 15 November 2017), para. 163.

7 *Di Sarno and Others v Italy*, App no 30765/08 (ECtHR, 10 January 2012), paras 107, 113.

2.2 The Necessary Risk Mitigation in Specific Cases

The duty to protect is often divided into substantive and procedural obligations. While the substantive aspect requires states to take preventive action to mitigate risks before the harm occurs, the procedural aspect entails remedial measures after harm is done. In cases of grave interferences by individuals, the latter includes criminal investigations.[8] Both aspects work together to create a comprehensive due diligence framework.

In its substantive as well as in its procedural limb, due diligence operates as a standard of conduct. It is assessed based on three general factors: foreseeability of the risk, significance of the protected interest and countervailing aspects such as the state's capacity to act and others' rights.[9]

In the ecological context under this book's attention, due diligence requires states to implement disaster risk reduction strategies and issue timely warnings to affected populations if necessary. They may be held responsible for failing to take adequate preventive measures against foreseeable natural disasters.[10] A leading case of a state's failure to avert the consequence of a foreseeable natural disaster is *Budayeva and Others v Russia*.[11] In this case, a series of devastating mudslides struck a town in the Caucasus. The authorities had prior knowledge of the high risk of mudslides due to scientific reports and previous incidents, but failed to take sufficient preventive measures. As a result, several people died. The ECtHR found a violation of the right to life under Article 2 ECHR. The case illustrates how due diligence obligations extend to environmental risks, and allow holding states accountable for inaction in the face of known threats.

3. HUMAN RIGHTS DUE DILIGENCE AND ENVIRONMENTAL CHRONIC EMERGENCIES

3.1 Environmental Chronic Emergencies and Systemic Risks

The duty to protect and the due diligence standard that applies as a yardstick have proven useful not only in addressing acute emergencies but also regarding systemic human rights violations. Even though human rights courts mostly

---

8 See e.g., *Salman v Turkey*, App no 21986/93 (ECtHR, Grand Chamber, 27 June 2000), paras 104–5.

9 Baade (n 4), 97.

10 Cf. Leslie-Anne Duvic-Paoli, *The Prevention Principle in International Environmental Law* (Cambridge University Press 2018), 179 et seq.

11 *Budayeva and Others v Russia*, App nos 15339/02 et al. (ECtHR, 20 March 2008).

find concrete violations in individual complaints, they have developed due diligence as a tool that allows addressing broader systemic issues as human rights violations. If due diligence requires states to take appropriate measures to mitigate risks to human rights, this may also mandate addressing structural, institutional problems.

In particular, international human rights courts have recognized that patterns of gender-based violence require a systemic response.[12] Systemic deficiencies, such as a lack of guidelines or proper training for law enforcement personnel, may constitute a violation in the individual case.[13] In environmental contexts, states must regulate industries that pose environmental and health risks through licensing, oversight, environmental impact assessments and enforcement of safety standards.[14]

If due diligence can be a tool against systemic risks, it seems to provide a good basis for addressing environmental chronic emergencies (ECEs) as well. After all, a systemic risk to human rights predictably leads to human rights violations in individual cases – not in each and every case where the risk exists, but expectably again and again. Importantly, it is not necessary to prove causality of systemic deficiencies for individual violations.[15] Even though a person might have been shot anyway if the police had been properly trained and issued human rights compatible guidelines, a lack of guidelines and training nonetheless constitutes a violation of Article 2 ECHR because these safeguards were required to reduce the risk.[16]

Nonetheless, emergencies that unfold slowly over a long time may pose additional challenges for an assessment of the diligent response that human rights require. The way due diligence has been applied thus far might fail to grasp the significance of ECEs. Being hard to see by definition, responding adequately and in time is a challenge. As seen in the examples above, the requirements of human rights due diligence are generally flexible and only become more stringent once the threat becomes sufficiently clear.

---

12 See e.g., *Nachova and Others v Bulgaria*, App nos 43577/98 et al. (ECtHR, Grand Chamber, 6 July 2005), para. 160.

13 *Giuliani and Gaggio v Italy*, App no 23458/02 (ECtHR, Grand Chamber, 24 March 2011), para. 250.

14 *Öneryildiz v Turkey*, App no 48939/99 (ECtHR, Grand Chamber, 30 November 2004), paras 71, 90; IACtHR (n 6), paras 149–52.

15 Cf., critical on that point: Helen Keller and Corina Heri, 'The Future is Now: Climate Cases Before the ECtHR' (2022) 40(1), *Nordic Journal of Human Rights*, 153, 164.

16 *Makaratzjs v Greece*, App no 50385/99 (ECtHR, Grand Chamber, 20 December 2004), paras 56–72.

On an abstract level, many different responses would often be lawful. States' margin of appreciation is particularly wide when it comes to resource allocation.[17] The diligent response required by human rights becomes more stringent only once the risk and its severity have become sufficiently apparent. States cannot and need not prepare for every entirely unlikely or entirely negligible threat to human rights. Under the standards elaborated thus far, diligence duties might become sufficiently stringent only once it is too late. Or these duties might become more stringent so late that, when the threat and its severity are sufficiently clear, they rather suddenly require responses vastly more intrusive, also regarding other human rights, than would have been necessary had the diligent measures been taken earlier. This is where an intertemporal, intergenerational perspective becomes important.

In short, even where due diligence jurisprudence has recognized the systemic dimension of a problem, this recognition was always event-driven. ECEs, as understood in this Volume, pose additional problems. Consisting of long-term, gradual environmental phenomena caused by the unsustainable extraction and use of natural resources, pollution and urbanization, such slow violence develops gradually and thus the responses seem more difficult. Emergencies that are chronic can be hard to see and thus impede not only proper political responses but also an appropriate legal assessment.

3.2 KlimaSeniorinnen Schweiz and Others v Switzerland

The ECtHR case *Verein KlimaSeniorinnen Schweiz and Others v Switzerland*[18] develops the Court's case law to cover climate change, which is 'a global and complex phenomenon'.[19] Its causes accumulate slowly, and their effects have a significant time lag. It may be the paradigmatic case of an ECE.

The Court addresses the interplay between climate change and human rights, primarily with regard to the right to respect for private and family life under Article 8 ECHR. An association of elderly women, *KlimaSeniorinnen*, asserted that Switzerland failed to meet its positive obligations to protect them from the adverse effects of climate change, particularly life-threatening heatwaves exacerbated by insufficient greenhouse gas emission reductions.

Building on the Court's due diligence jurisprudence in environmental matters, the Grand Chamber held that Article 8 imposes positive obligations on states to protect individuals' private and family life from environmental harm,

---

17 *Di Sarno and Others v Italy*, App no 30765/08 (ECtHR, 10 January 2012) para. 110.

18 *Verein KlimaSeniorinnen Schweiz and Others v Switzerland,* App no 53600/20 (ECtHR, 9 April 2024).

19 *Ibid.*, para. 489.

and that includes climate change. The judgment underscores the need for states to take both mitigation and adaptation measures: states need to combat the anthropogenic causes of climate change and adjust to climate change to protect human rights from those negative effects of climate change that cannot be averted. The following analysis will focus on such due diligence obligations under Articles 2 and 8 ECHR.[20]

3.2.1 Mitigation and adaptation

Once a right is affected in a sufficiently serious manner and thus applicable, it has to be determined what, if any, measures to protect it are required. If a sufficiently severe risk has been established that is sufficiently foreseeable, states must make use of their capacities to mitigate that risk. The risks of climate change are generally clearly foreseeable, despite climate change not being a monolithic phenomenon, and are evidently very serious. The Court carefully and convincingly traced this finding in the scientific evidence. Like other courts, it referred in particular to the reports of the Intergovernmental Panel on Climate Change (IPCC). States also have various measures at their disposal to mitigate that risk and/or adapt to it. As with other systemic risks, a legislative and administrative framework meant to protect the rights from that risk must be established and operated effectively.[21]

These general parameters, the Court clarified, must be adapted somewhat for climate change cases, which differ from isolated cases of environmental harm. As in other environmental cases, an effective regulatory and policy framework is necessary, but in the climate context, deficiencies reside particularly at this level. This framework must provide for measures to mitigate the effects of climate change by preventing a further increase in greenhouse gas (GHG) concentrations and thus a rise in global average temperature, which would

[20] The violation of the right of access to a court under Art. 6(1) ECHR, which the Court found, will not be analyzed here. See ECtHR (n 18), paras 594 et seq. Likewise, even though the court asked the participants in the proceedings to comment on it, Art. 3 ECHR was not dealt with, see on this: Corina Heri, 'The ECtHR's Pending Climate Change Case: What's Ill-Treatment Got to Do with It?' (*EJILTalk!* 22 December 2020) <https://www.ejiltalk.org/the-ecthrs-pending-climate-change-case-whats-ill-treatment-got-to-do-with-it/>, accessed 12 April 2025. Or even arguing that climate anxiety violates art. 3 ECHR: Natasa Mavronicola, 'The Future is a Foreign Country: Rethinking State Behavior on Climate Change as Ill-Treatment' (*University of Birmingham New Approaches*, 2021). <www.birmingham.ac.uk/research/climate/climate-publications/new-approaches/the-future-is-a-foreign-country-rethinking-state-behaviour-on-climate-change-as-ill-treatment.aspx> accessed 12 April 2025.

[21] ECtHR (n 18) paras 104–20, 538, 546.

produce 'serious and irreversible adverse effects on human rights'. Adaptation measures must alleviate the most severe or imminent consequences, also considering particular needs for protection, but these were not the focus of this case. Article 8 ECHR, the Court held, requires states to take mitigation measures to substantially and progressively reduce GHG emissions, aiming at net neutrality 'within, in principle, the next three decades'. This conforms to the global aims set out in the Paris Agreement, which the Court took account of by means of systematic interpretation within the meaning of Article 31(3)(c) Vienna Convention on the Law of Treaties.[22]

In environmental matters, states generally enjoy a wide margin of appreciation, and a 'disproportionate burden must not be imposed on the authorities without consideration being given, in particular, to the operational choices which they must make in terms of priorities and resources'.[23] The Court emphasized that it was not its task to determine all necessary measures to combat climate change, but at the same time, it highlighted its subsidiary competence to review such decisions under human rights law. In this review, it plays an important role whether the decision-making process was adequate, in particular whether it took into account all relevant interests. Appropriate investigations by the government are necessary before it can strike a fair balance between various conflicting interests at stake. It must seek to predict and evaluate in advance the effects of activities that might harm the environment and available countermeasures, even though it cannot be asked to provide 'comprehensive and measurable data' for everything. The margin is also wider if individuals were informed and had the opportunity to participate in the decision-making.[24]

Finally, a distinction must be made between a reduced margin for the State's commitment to the necessity of combating climate change and the setting of aims and, on the other hand, a wider margin regarding the choice of means. In general, the choice of means (e.g., which sectors have to contribute to what extent) thus remains within states' margin of appreciation. But taking into account the scientifically known global, severe and potentially irreversible consequences of climate change, in particular adverse effects on human rights, and the corresponding urgency of fighting it, the Court clarified that climate protection must be accorded 'considerable weight' in any balancing with other interests. States' 'generally inadequate track record' in addressing climate change during the past decades, as evidenced by the IPCC's findings, likewise advocates for a reduced margin.[25]

---

22 *Ibid.*, paras 540, 545–8, 478–9.
23 *Ibid.*, para. 538.
24 *Ibid.*, paras 538–9.
25 *Ibid.*, paras 542–3.

In order to reach the goal of GHG reduction and to avoid disproportionately burdening future generations, the Court therefore considered immediate action necessary. It developed important procedural parameters to assess a state's compliance and whether it remains within its margin. National authorities have to have due regard in particular for the need to adopt a timeline for achieving carbon neutrality and reduction targets (e.g., by sector) to meet the overall national GHG reduction goals. States need to provide evidence that they are at least in the process of complying with these goals, update targets based on the best available evidence and, finally, they must act in good time and in an appropriate and consistent manner in devising and implementing the relevant legislation and measures. Compliance with these requirements will be assessed as a whole.[26]

3.2.2 Switzerland's violation

The Court held that Switzerland failed to comply with its positive obligations under Article 8 to implement sufficient measures to combat climate change. Notably, the Swiss authorities failed to quantify GHG emission limitations through a national carbon budget and ensure timely and consistent legislative and administrative measures.

Switzerland had passed legislation to mitigate climate change by reducing GHG emissions by 20%, compared to 1990 levels, by 2020. It missed that target, which was considered to be insufficient anyway to achieve the objective of limiting the temperature rise to 1.5–2.0°C. This, the Court held, 'indicates the insufficiency of the authorities' past action to take the necessary measures to address climate change'. A proposal to revise the climate legislation in order to increase the reduction was rejected in a popular referendum in June 2021. After 2020, a legislative lacuna existed, and only in December 2021 were goals enacted for the years 2021 to 2024. The period after 2024 was left unregulated. These lacunae, the Court held, were incompatible with the requirement for specifying the respondent State's mitigation measures in line with a net neutrality timeline. Switzerland had failed to devise a regulatory framework setting the requisite objectives and goals. It went beyond the state's margin of appreciation to leave this issue unregulated. After all, the latest Synthesis Report of the IPCC had emphasized that the choices and actions implemented in this decade would have impacts now and for thousands of years.[27]

---

26 *Ibid.*, paras 549–1.

27 *Ibid.*, paras 558–9, 560–62. See IPCC, 2023: Climate Change 2023: Synthesis Report. Contribution of Working Groups I, II and III to the Sixth Assessment Report of the Intergovernmental Panel on Climate Change [Core Writing Team, H. Lee and J. Romero (eds.)], IPCC, Geneva, Switzerland.

In September 2022, reflecting the commitments of its updated Nationally Determined Contribution under the Paris Agreement, a new Climate Act was enacted and confirmed in a referendum, envisaging a net-zero emissions target by 2050 by providing that the GHG emissions should be reduced 'as far as possible'. It contains an intermediate target for 2040 (75% reduction compared with 1990 levels) and for the years 2031 to 2040 (average of at least 64%) and 2041 to 2050 (average of at least 89% compared with 1990 levels). It also set indicative values for the reduction of emissions in the building, transport and industrial sectors for the years 2040 and 2050. It did not, however, contain concrete measures. These matters remain to be determined by the Federal Council and proposed to Parliament 'in good time'.[28] This law establishes intermediate targets only for the period after 2031. Given the fact that the 2011 law provided for legal regulation of the intermediate targets only up until 2024, the period between 2025 and 2030 still remains unregulated pending the enactment of new legislation.[29]

In light of the pressing urgency of climate change, the Court had 'difficulty accepting' that the mere legislative commitment to adopt the concrete measures 'in good time' satisfied the State's duty to protect.[30] While acknowledging that 'significant progress' was to be expected from the new Climate Act, the Court concluded that the new legislation was nonetheless insufficient.[31]

The Government argued that Swiss national climate policy could be considered as being similar in approach to establishing a carbon budget and that it was based on relevant internal assessments prepared in 2020 and expressed in its NDCs. Again, however, the Court was 'not convinced' that a regulatory framework could be effective without quantifying the GHG emissions limitations more concretely.[32] Acknowledging that the measures and methods determining the details of the State's climate policy generally fall within its wide margin of appreciation, the absence of any domestic measure attempting to quantify the respondent State's remaining carbon budget, the Court, again, had 'difficulty accepting' that the State could be regarded as complying effectively with its regulatory obligation under Article 8 of the Convention.[33]

---

28 ECtHR (n 18), paras 555–6.
29 *Ibid.*, para. 565.
30 *Ibid.*, paras 555, 567.
31 *Ibid.*, para. 568.
32 *Ibid.*, para. 570.
33 *Ibid.*, paras 572–3.

3.2.3 Critique of the judgment

The legal scholarship largely received the judgment favourably, characterizing it as a 'landmark'[34] or even a 'historic'[35] decision. The Court was praised for assuming a 'strategic role as a norm-setter', offering contracting states 'valuable guidance'.[36]

Some commentators, however, regarded the ruling as a more 'moderate' success, underscoring the persistent difficulties of pursuing climate litigation before the ECtHR.[37] The measures prescribed by the Court were deemed 'unambitious' and even 'modest',[38] with most EU member states already meeting the established requirements.[39]

---

[34] Linos-Alexander Sicilianos and Maria-Louiza Deftou, 'Breaking New Ground: Climate Change before the Strasbourg Court' (*EJILTalk!* 12 April 2024) <https://www.ejiltalk.org/breaking-new-ground-climate-change-before-the-strasbourg-court/>, accessed 12 April 2025.

[35] Charlotte Blattner, 'Warum das KlimaSeniorinnen-Urteil nicht undemokratisch ist: Anmerkungen zu einer Schweizer Debatte' (*Verfassungsblog*, 25 June 2024) <https://verfassungsblog.de/egmr-klimaseniorinnen-gewaltenteilung/>, accessed 12 April 2025.

[36] See Ole W. Pedersen, 'Climate Change Hearings and the ECtHR' (*EJILTalk!* 4 April 2023) <https://www.ejiltalk.org/climate-change-hearings-and-the-ecthr/>, accessed 12 April 2024.

[37] Lea Raible, 'Priorities for Climate Litigation at the European Court of Human Rights (*EJILTalk!* 2 May 2024) <https://www.ejiltalk.org/priorities-for-climate-litigation-at-the-european-court-of-human-rights/>, accessed 13 April 2025; Giorgia Pane, 'Litigating the Climate between National and International Human Rights Regimes: Judicial Complementarity?' (2024) 26, *International Community Law Review 26*, 531, 548; Aoife Nolan, 'Intergenerational Equity, Future Generations and Democracy in the European Court of Human Rights' Klimaseniorinnen Decision' (*EJILTalk!* 15 April 2024) <https://www.ejiltalk.org/inter-generational-equity-future-generations-and-democracy-in-the-european-court-of-human-rights-klimaseniorinnen-decision/>, accessed 12 April 2025: 'work in progress'.

[38] Raible (n 36); Marko Milanovic, 'A Quick Take on the European Court's Climate Change Judgments' (*EJILTalk!* 9 April 2024) <https://www.ejiltalk.org/a-quick-take-on-the-european-courts-climate-change-judgments/>, accessed 12 April 2025.

[39] Ole W. Pedersen, 'Climate Change and the ECHR: The Results Are In' (*EJILTalk!* 11 April 2024) <https://www.ejiltalk.org/climate-change-and-the-echr-the-results-are-in/>, accessed 12 April 2025; Patrick Abel, 'Mixed Signals for Domestic Climate Law: The Climate Rulings of the European Court of Human Rights' (*VerfassungsBlog*, 17 April 2024) <https://verfassungsblog.de/mixed-signals-for-domestic-climate-law/>, accessed 12 April 2025.

From a procedural standpoint, the judgment was also met with criticism. The ECtHR recognized the standing or 'victim status' of the association *KlimaSeniorinnen* under Article 34 ECHR, but declined to extend the same recognition to the individual applicants. Alongside other inadmissibility decisions issued on the same day, this was widely interpreted as evidence of the Convention's structural limitations in addressing 'rampant climate injustice'.[40] Although the Court acknowledged that individuals particularly vulnerable to climate change are often underrepresented in decision-making processes, the Grand Chamber itself, some argue, failed to adequately incorporate their perspective.[41] Achieving meaningful legal protection, these critics say, would require a fundamental reconfiguration of human rights law.[42]

This prevailing strand of academic commentary, which broadly welcomed the ruling but found it insufficiently progressive, largely did not pay much attention to critical perspectives. Even Judge Tim Eicke, who followed in the tradition of British judges who had, since the 1970s, scrutinized the evolution of the Convention in dissenting opinions, received little engagement.[43] Eicke contended that the judgment constituted a departure from established case law without adhering to recognized methodological principles.[44] A former Swiss federal judge went further, accusing the ECtHR of acting ultra vires by interfering in Swiss climate policy, asserting that the 'Rubicon' had been crossed – 'definitively'.[45]

---

40 Raible (n 38).

41 ECtHR (n 18), paras 529–31; Dilruba Begüm Kartepe and Mariia Zheltukha, 'Gender, Climate, and the Illusion of Neutrality: Rethinking Intra- and Intergenerational Equity in the ECtHR's Climate Jurisprudence' (*Völkerrechtsblog* 5 March 2025) <https://voelkerrechtsblog.org/gender-climate-and-the-illusion-of-neutrality/>, accessed 12 April 2025; Corina Heri, 'KlimaSeniorinnen and its discontents: Climate change at the European Court of Human Rights' (2024) 4, *European Human Rights Law Review*, 317, 330–1.

42 Raible (n 38).

43 See already: Tim Eicke, 'Climate Change and the Convention: Beyond Admissibility' (2022) 3, *European Convention on Human Rights Law Review*, 8–16.

44 Partly Concurring Partly Dissenting Opinion of Judge Eicke, paras 1, 2, 4, 10–11, 65.

45 Ulrich Meyer, 'Der Menschenrechtsgerichtshof hat den Rubikon überschritten' (NZZ, 12 April 2024) <https://www.nzz.ch/meinung/egmr-und-klimaseniorinnen-den-rubikon-ueberschritten-ld.1825593>, accessed 12 April 2025.

3.2.4 The case law's adaptability to environmental chronic emergencies

Both the criticism that the Court did not go far enough and the contention that it exceeded its mandate must be assessed within established doctrinal principles. The duty to protect human rights is a well-established part of the Convention.[46] It applies irrespective of whether the threat to human rights originates from private actors, public authorities, or natural phenomena.

Unlike the American Convention on Human Rights and the African Charter on Human and Peoples' Rights, the ECHR does not enshrine a right to a healthy environment.[47] Nevertheless, the ECtHR has consistently acknowledged that environmental hazards can interfere with the right to respect for private and family life under Article 8 ECHR, thereby giving rise to corresponding state obligations. It was on this basis that the Court adjudicated the *KlimaSeniorinnen* case.[48] In the context of climate change, the Court clarified, states are required to implement adaptation measures to address the severe and foreseeable adverse effects of climate change on human rights, which cannot be averted by climate mitigation.[49] Flood protection is a case in point. This entirely aligns with the Court's due diligence jurisprudence as elaborated above.

The obligation of climate mitigation, i.e., to address the root causes of climate change, also builds upon established case law. The duty to protect has always encompassed preventive measures,[50] even in instances where full and definitive protection is unattainable.[51] It suffices that the measures adopted contribute to risk reduction.[52] Consequently, Article 8 ECHR imposes an obligation upon contracting states to substantially and progressively reduce greenhouse gas emissions with the aim of achieving greenhouse gas neutrality

---

[46] See only *Opuz v Turkey*, App no 33401/02 (ECtHR, 9 June 2009), paras 183–202.

[47] Article 26 American Convention on Human Rights; Art. 24 African Charter on Human and Peoples' Rights.

[48] ECtHR (n 18), para. 544.

[49] *Ibid.*, para. 552.

[50] Cf. Evelyne Schmid, 'Victim Status before the ECtHR in Cases of Alleged Omissions: The Swiss Climate Case' (*EJILTalk!* 30 April 2022) <https://www.ejiltalk.org/victim-status-before-the-ecthr-in-cases-of-alleged-omissions-the-swiss-climate-case/>, accessed 12 April 2025.

[51] Cf. Alexander Zahar, 'The Limits of Human Rights Law: A Reply to Corina Heri' (2022) 33 *European Journal of International Law* 953, 954–5, 956–9.

[52] *Finogenov and Other v Russia*, App nos 18299/03 et al. (ECtHR, 20 December 2011) paras 255, 264–265; ECtHR (n 45), para. 136.

'in principle within the next three decades'.[53] The Court anchored this obligation in the scientific consensus, as authoritatively established by IPCC, which enjoys broad political legitimacy, operating under a United Nations mandate.[54] Referencing the emissions reduction targets outlined in the Paris Agreement further bolstered this finding.

Although Article 32 ECHR restricts the Court's jurisdiction to overseeing compliance with the Convention, and – despite repeated calls from the Parliamentary Assembly over the past two decades – no protocol has been adopted to establish a right to a clean environment.[55] But the lack of a more specific right has never precluded the Court from considering the impact on existing rights. The principle of systemic integration, as enshrined in Article 31(3)(c) of the Vienna Convention on the Law of Treaties, allowed the Court to take into account the Paris Agreement, which has been ratified by all Council of Europe member states, in interpreting the Convention.[56]

The United Nations climate protection regime – often criticized as insufficiently robust – was thus imbued with a degree of human rights gravitas. But ultimately, the extent of this influence remains contingent upon the margin of appreciation afforded to states. In that regard, the Court made a significant determination when deciding which rights are applicable. While it acknowledged, in line with scientific evidence, that heatwaves pose a particular health risk to elderly individuals, especially women, the threshold for triggering state obligations under Article 2 ECHR requires the existence of a 'real and imminent risk' in terms of both material and temporal proximity.[57] This high threshold corresponds with higher requirements: under Article 2 ECHR, states are required to undertake 'everything' necessary to safeguard the right to life. The protective measures required under Article 8 ECHR generally require less stringent measures.[58] Historically, the ECtHR has granted states considerable discretion in environmental matters,[59] and has refrained from prematurely

---

53 ECtHR (n 18), para. 548.

54 See UNGA, *Protection of Global Climate for Present and Future Generations of Mankind* (6 December 1988) Res. 43/53, UN Doc A/RES/43/53.

55 Tim Eicke, 'Human Rights and Climate Change: What Role for the European Court of Human Rights?' (2021) 26, *European Human Rights Law Review*, 262, 265.

56 ECtHR (n 18), para. 547.

57 *Ibid.*, paras 511, 513.

58 Similarly, the right to property under Article 1 Protocol 1 must be protected by 'reasonable' measures: ECtHR (n 11), para. 175.

59 Heri (n 41), 327–8.

supplanting national assessments of competing interests. Likewise, the Court refrained from determining each and every climate policy.[60]

The Grand Chamber's sensitivity to the complexity of these issues is reflected in its careful phrasing, even as it ultimately found violations. Given the 'urgent need' for climate action, the Court had 'difficulty accepting' that Switzerland's climate legislation at the time provided effective protection against the adverse effects of climate change.[61] While this finding was largely uncontroversial to many commentators, it raises broader and more contentious questions regarding the trajectory of climate justice. The large-scale transformation required for decarbonizing the economy is inseparable from the equitable distribution of burdens, both between states – acknowledged in the 1992 United Nations Framework Convention on Climate Change (UNFCCC) through the principle of 'Common but Differentiated Responsibilities and Respective Capabilities'[62] – and within states, where mitigation and adaptation policies must balance competing socio-economic interests.

Progress in combating climate change is therefore closely intertwined with broader societal advancement, often in a tension-filled relationship. The tension between decarbonization and economic development is palpable in the Global North, just like in the Global South.[63] Measures of mitigation and adaptation both need to dispense benefits and burdens in a socially acceptable manner.[64] Substantial conflicts must be resolved, and their resolution cannot be entirely deduced from human rights law.[65] The ECtHR judgment rightly distinguishes between the duty to mitigate and adapt, on the one hand, and the specific means states may employ, on the other.[66] Contracting states retain discretion in deciding which sectors contribute to emissions reductions, the extent of such contributions and whether these are achieved through regulatory mechanisms

60 ECtHR (n 18), para. 538.

61 *Ibid.*, paras 555, 567.

62 For an overview: Lavanya Rajamani, Jacob D. Werksman, 'Climate Change', in Lavanya Rajamani, Jacqueline Peel (eds.), *The Oxford Handbook of International Environmental Law* (2nd edn, Oxford University Press 2021) 492, 493–7.

63 Zahar (n 50), 955, 956–9. Alan Boyle, Catherine Redgwell, *Birnie, Boyle & Redgwell's International Law and the Environment* (4th edn, Oxford University Press 2021), 356–7.

64 See e.g., Anika Klafki, 'Klimaschutzrecht und Klimagerechtigkeit' (2023) 56 *Die Verwaltung*, 179, 191.

65 César Rodríguez-Garavito, 'Litigating the Climate Emergency: The Global Rise of Human Rights-Based Litigation for Climate Action' in César Rodríguez-Garavito (ed.), *Litigating the Climate Emergency* (Cambridge University Press 2023), 9, 31: 'minimum fair share'.

66 ECtHR (n 18), para. 543.

or market-based instruments such as emissions trading. However, socio-economic considerations cannot simply override the duty to protect: Given the scientifically documented, severe and potentially irreversible consequences of climate change, the Grand Chamber underscored that climate action must be accorded 'significant weight' in any balancing exercise. The 'generally inadequate track record' of states in addressing climate change, as documented by the IPCC, warrants a narrower margin of appreciation.[67] Immediate action is imperative to achieve emissions reductions and prevent an undue burden on future generations.[68] Such action must also take into consideration patterns of discrimination in our societies that disproportionately affect groups of people. Addressing the root causes of climate change also requires work on structural inequalities that exacerbate the effects of ECEs, including climate change.

While the judgment's substantive part merely continues well-established jurisprudence, a notable doctrinal development emerges at the procedural level. While victim status under Article 34 ECHR for acute emergencies was well established in prior jurisprudence, securing standing for mitigation obligations proved more challenging.[69] The incremental accumulation of risk and the temporal gap between present actions and future human rights violations – the existence of an ECE – posed significant hurdles. Under previous standards, the requisite element of temporal proximity was absent. Moreover, the Court has consistently held that Article 8 ECHR does not extend to general environmental burdens that affect all individuals in modern urban environments.[70] Thus, applicants would have needed to demonstrate particularly severe personal harm. The established requirement that an interference with Article 8 ECHR must reflect a 'pressing need' was transposed to require a pressing need for protection.[71] The individual applicants, though belonging to a demonstrably vulnerable group, failed to meet this criterion.

The Court then went on to apply different criteria for their association. As a legal entity, the association could not invoke rights specific to individuals, such as the right to life or the health-related aspects of Article 8 ECHR.[72] Nor

---

67 *Ibid.*, para. 542.

68 *Ibid.*, paras 549–51.

69 Cf. Rodríguez-Garavito (n 65), 38.

70 *Fadeyeva v Russia*, App no. 55723/00 (ECtHR, 9 June 2009), para. 69.

71 ECtHR (n 18), para. 487.

72 See critically: Brigitte Pfiffner, 'EGMR-Urteil für Grüne Alt-Bundesrichterin «nicht haltbar»' (*Swissinfo* 19 May 2024) <https://www.swissinfo.ch/ger/egmr-urteil-f%c3%bcr-gr%c3%bcne-alt-bundesrichterin-%22nicht-haltbar%22/77962895>, accessed 12 April 2025.

could it act as a representative of its members, given their lack of individual standing.[73]

Judge Eicke argued that – in spite of all denials – this introduced an *actio popularis*.[74] Some scholars countered this with a democratic and intergenerational reading, arguing that the association was not advocating for a general public interest but rather for the rights of future generations who lack representation.[75] That this excludes applicants from the Global South highlights, some argue, the persistence of racist and neocolonial structures within the Convention system, as exemplified by Article 56 ECHR's colonial clause.[76]

In my view, neither interpretation is convincing. While states must consider the interests of future generations in their decision-making, the ECtHR does not conceptualize this obligation as an intertemporal 'interference-like effect' on the right to life, as the German Federal Constitutional Court did in its climate ruling.[77] Instead, this intertemporal effect is understood as part of the public interest within the framework of the state's duty to protect under Article 8 ECHR. It is also questionable whether private organizations should be entrusted with safeguarding the rights of individuals who have not conferred such authority upon them.

The specific criteria established by the ECtHR regarding standing further support this position. To claim victim status, organizations must be founded under the law of a contracting state, possess legal standing within that jurisdiction, and have the explicit purpose of defending the human rights of their members or other affected individuals within the relevant territory. Additionally, they must be deemed 'genuinely qualified and representative' to act on behalf of their members or other affected persons within the jurisdiction, specifically those exposed to distinct dangers or adverse consequences of climate change affecting their lives, health, or well-being.[78]

---

73 ECtHR (n 18), paras 514, 519.

74 Eicke, Diss. Op. (n 44), paras 44–5.

75 George Letsas, 'Did the Court in Klimaseniorinnen Create an *Actio Popularis*? (*EJILTalk!* 13 May 2024) <https://www.ejiltalk.org/did-the-court-in-klimaseniorinnen-create-an-actio-popularis/>, accessed 12 April 2025.

76 Raible (n 36); Helen Keller and Corina Heri, 'The Future is Now: Climate Cases Before the ECtHR' (2022) 40(1), *Nordic Journal of Human Rights*, 153, 162.

77 German Federal Constitutional Court, Order of the First Senate of 24 March 2021, 1 BvR 2656/18 et al., para. 183, English version available at: <https://www.bundesverfassungsgericht.de/SharedDocs/Entscheidungen/EN/2021/03/rs20210324_1bvr265618en.html>, accessed 12 April 2025.

78 ECtHR (n 18), paras 502, 523–24. Cf. Jeremy Letwin, 'Klimaseniorinnen: the Innovative and the Orthodox' (*EJILTalk!* 17 April 2024) <https://www.ejiltalk

In its reasoning, the Court emphasized that it cannot alter the fact that the Convention system does not provide for an *actio popularis*. It underscored that its primary function is to redress human rights violations that have already occurred, rather than to prevent potential future infringements. However, the Court also acknowledged that an overly restrictive interpretation of standing could risk precluding challenges to 'obvious deficiencies and dysfunctions in government action or the democratic process affecting Convention rights'.[79]

The Court thus deliberately refrained from granting standing to individuals on an unrestricted basis. Instead, it conferred standing upon certain NGOs, allowing them to advocate on behalf of individuals who, while not yet experiencing severe harm and therefore lacking individual standing, are nonetheless exposed to specific threats or detrimental consequences of climate change.[80] This doctrinal development can be justified by reference to evolving state practice, which increasingly acknowledges the role of NGOs in national legal frameworks, particularly in environmental matters. The Aarhus Convention, which grants NGOs standing in certain environmental matters, exemplifies this broader trend.[81]

The Court appears to have intentionally adopted a solution that, while breaking new doctrinal ground, ultimately strikes a middle course. From a doctrinal perspective, both a near-complete exclusion of standing in cases concerning mitigation measures and, conversely, the broad recognition that all individuals are affected by the climate crisis would have been easier to justify. The latter approach need not necessarily have been classified as an *actio popularis*, as the fact that the rights of numerous individuals may be infringed does not automatically transform these rights into a matter of general public interest. Acknowledging that certain groups of people are more affected than others by climate change, the Court's approach channels the legitimate demand for legal protection in climate matters into a form of collective complaint, comparable to the mechanism established under the Aarhus Convention. Given the institutional constraints facing the Court, this approach may ultimately prove to be a judicious one.

.org/klimaseniorinnen-the-innovative-and-the-orthodox/>, accessed 12 April 2025: 'loophole'.

79 ECtHR (n 18), para. 484.

80 Foreshadowed by: Keller, Heri (n 76), 157; Corina Heri, 'Climate Cases as Public Interest Litigation before the European Court of Human Rights' in Justine Bendel, Yusra Suedi (eds), *Public Interest Litigation in International Law* (Routledge, 2024), 317, 333: 'some kind of special status'.

81 ECtHR (n 18), para. 601.

4. CONCLUDING OBSERVATIONS

Did the ECtHR have to address climate change to safeguard its legitimacy,[82] or was its intervention in these matters ultimately counterproductive for climate protection?[83] If the Convention were to serve as a 'normative hook' for the reduction targets set out in the Paris Agreement – an interim objective on the path to the overarching goal of climate protection –[84] then the unintended consequences of a potential backlash must also be considered.[85] Those who hope for a 'disruption' of existing legal frameworks by international courts, aiming to adapt the law to societal developments,[86] should not lose sight of the fact that 'society' is not uniformly supportive of the most ambitious climate goals.[87] However necessary they may seem, deducing drastic climate protection measures from human rights[88] could ultimately provoke significant resistance. Some reactions to the *KlimaSeniorinnen* decision substantiate this concern. As expected, the right-wing populist Swiss People's Party (SVP) once again called for Switzerland to withdraw from the ECHR, arguing that the judges in Strasbourg had acted as 'puppets of activists'.[89] Yet, opposition to the ruling was not limited to usual critics: both the Swiss Council of States and the National Council passed resolutions stating that they would not comply with the decision.[90]

---

82 Cf. Keller, Heri (n 76), 170.

83 Eicke, Diss. Op. (n 44), paras 1, 2, 4, 10–11, 65.

84 Stephen Humphreys, 'A Swiss human rights budget?' (*EJILTalk!* 12 April 2024) <https://www.ejiltalk.org/a-swiss-human-rights-budget/>, accessed 12 April 2025.

85 Heri (n 80), 322.

86 See, on the pending ICJ advisory opinion: Jannika Jahn, Marlene Letsch, 'Progress through disruption? What role for the ICJ in the Advisory Opinion on Climate Change' (*EJILTalk!* 22 January 2025) <https://www.ejiltalk.org/progress-through-disruption-what-role-for-the-icj-in-the-advisory-opinion-on-climate-change/>, accessed 12 April 2025.

87 Heri (n 80), 338.

88 In the direction of a prohibition of the extraction of fossil fuels: Andreas Buser, 'Exercising Planetary Jurisdiction: On the Legality and Legitimacy of Unilaterally Mitigating Planetary Ecological Footprints' (2024) 35(4) *European Journal of International Law*, 897, 913.

89 'Inakzeptable Einmischung der Strassburger-Richter: SVP-Fraktion fordert einstimmig die Kündigung der EMRK' (*SVP* 17 May 2024) <https://www.svp.ch/aktuell/publikationen/medienmitteilungen/inakzeptable-einmischung-der-strassburger-richter-svp-fraktion-fordert-einstimmig-die-kuendigung-der-emrk/>, accessed 12 April 2025.

90 See Blattner (n 35).

While some welcome the ruling as a legal breakthrough, others fear its far-reaching implications. Both the media and legal scholars have recognized the decision as a 'powerful precedent',[91] with some predicting entire 'waves' of climate litigation.[92] Just as the ECtHR's ruling heavily relies on the UN climate protection regime,[93] it could, in turn, spark further legal developments at the national level[94] – potentially leading to even more extensive obligations, a prospect that is both anticipated and feared.[95]

The ECtHR's judgment in *KlimaSeniorinnen* has certainly contributed to some degree of progress in the fight against the ECE.[96] The general obligation to implement mitigation measures should not be underestimated, especially given the recent backsliding on climate commitments, particularly – but not exclusively – in the USA. In this regard, the Court's decision undoubtedly serves the purpose of addressing at least 'obvious deficiencies and dysfunctions in government action or the democratic process' concerning human rights. At the same time, concerns that strategic litigation grants NGOs disproportionate influence over policymaking[97] are unfounded. The ECtHR remained well

---

91 'How a group of elderly Swiss women could take the UK out of the European Court' (*Politico* 11 April 2024, <https://www.politico.eu/article/uk-echr-switzerland-climate-ruling-could-blow-up-uk-politics/>, accessed 12 April 2025).

92 Milanovic (n 38).

93 Jannika Jahn, 'The Paris Effect: Human Rights in Light of International Climate Goals and Commitments' (*VerfassungsBlog,* 25 April 2024) <https://verfassungsblog.de/the-paris-effect/>, accessed 12 April 2025; Rajamani, Werksman (n 62), 493–7, 507: 'useful hook'; Rodríguez-Garavito (n 65), 10–11, 14.

94 Pedersen (n 39).

95 See Gerry Liston, 'Reflections on the Strasbourg climate rulings in light of two aims behind the Duarte Agostinho case' (*EJILTalk!* 7 May 2024) <https://www.ejiltalk.org/reflections-on-the-strasbourg-climate-rulings-in-light-of-two-aims-behind-the-duarte-agostinho-case/>, accessed 12 April 2025; Patrick Abel, 'Mixed Signals for Domestic Climate Law: The Climate Rulings of the European Court of Human Rights' (*VerfassungsBlog* 17 April 2024) <https://verfassungsblog.de/mixed-signals-for-domestic-climate-law/>, accessed 12 April 2025; Andreas Buser, 'Exercising Planetary Jurisdiction: On the Legality and Legitimacy of Unilaterally Mitigating Planetary Ecological Footprints' (2024) 35(4) *European Journal of International Law*, 897, 910, 912.

96 Thomas Skouteris, 'The Idea of Progress', in Anne Orford, Florian Hoffmann, Martin Clark (eds), *The Oxford Handbook of the Theory of International Law* (Oxford University Press 2016), 939, 939–40.

97 Thus argued the former German minister of justice: Von Marco Buschmann, 'Klimaneutralität bis 2045? Sie wissen nicht, was sie tun' (*Frankfurter Allgemeine Zeitung*, 20 March 2025) <https://zeitung.faz.net/faz/politik/2025-03-20/c3b4974302ef0fd2847c129a1713ebea?GEPC=s9>, accessed 12 April 2025.

aware of its own limitations. It is noteworthy that, despite criticism of the ruling, Switzerland incorporated new climate targets and measures into its climate law as of January 2025, with a view to 2030. The Committee of Ministers of the Council of Europe, responsible for overseeing the implementation of judgments under Article 46 ECHR, acknowledged this development with approval in early March 2025. However, it also requested additional information on the quantification of these measures, as mandated by the Court.[98]

This more restrained understanding of the Court's function also informs the broader question of whether the increasing complexity of strategic litigation ultimately leads to an ever-expanding body of law without effectively advancing its underlying objectives.[99] The recognition that more international law does not inherently translate into greater progress holds true for climate issues as well. Acknowledging the limits of international law does not, however, imply abandoning it as a tool – contrary to what some proponents of realist international relations theories have recently suggested. Given the current tendency to underestimate the effectiveness of international law – after previous periods of overestimation –[100] international law should not be overburdened with unrealistic expectations that it is bound to disappoint. It can be used, however, in a way that embraces new concerns, shaping due diligence obligations in a way that is relevant for addressing ECEs, including climate change, in a gender-sensitive manner. Disproportionate impacts of climate change on women, especially at the intersection of different grounds of discrimination, must be acknowledged. Just like the Court did regarding systemic risks, it should further adapt its case law to the complex phenomenon of ECEs. Even where disaster is not imminent, mitigation measures might be necessary for that very reason.

The ECtHR can and should take seriously its function to correct 'obvious deficiencies and dysfunctions in government action or the democratic process

[98] Committee of Ministers, 1521st meeting, 4–6 March 2025 (DH), CM/Del/Dec(2025)1521/H46-30.

[99] Cf. Jelena Bäumler, 'Jelena Bäumler Review of Ivano Alogna, Christine Bakker, Jean-Pierre Gauci (eds). Climate Change Litigation: Global Perspectives' (2024) 35(3) *European Journal of International Law*, 763, 771; Relying so much on the law to generate progress might also be a somewhat Western preoccupation: Tilmann Altwicker and Oliver Diggelmann, 'How is Progress Constructed in International Legal Scholarship?' (2014) 25(2), *European Journal of International Law*, 425, 431.

[100] Josef L. Kunz, 'The Swing of the Pendulum: From Overestimation to Underestimation of International Law' (1950) 44(1) *American Journal of International Law*, 135–40.

affecting Convention rights',[101] and that certainly requires a gender-sensitive approach. Just like it referred to the goals of the Paris Agreement, it should take into account, according to the preamble and Articles 7(5) and 11 (2) of the Agreement, any gendered effects of climate change, as well as of the adaptation and mitigation measures adopted to counter it. Just like other human rights bodies, the Court has found that an unresponsive and dismissive attitude that fails to provide women equal protection of the law violates the discrimination clause as enshrined, e.g., in Art. 14 ECHR in conjunction with other affected rights.[102] This holds true in ECEs as well, in which gendered norms, stereotypes, and socio-economic structures work to exacerbate women's exposure to environmental harms, deepening pre-existing disparities and thus creating a feedback loop that sustains systemic discrimination.[103]

101 ECtHR (n 18) para. 484.

102 IACommHR (n 5) paras 45–50, 55–8, 61.4.; ECtHR (n 5), paras. 183–202; *Nachova and Others v Bulgaria*, App. Nos. 43577/98 et al. (ECtHR, 6 July 2005), para. 160.

103 For pertinent examples, see Enzamaria Tramontana, 'Environmental Chronic Emergencies, Women's Inequality, and International Law' in this Volume.

12. The duty to cooperate in addressing the adverse impact of environmental chronic emergencies: ensuring gender-sensitive responses

Martina Sardo

1. INTRODUCTION

International cooperation can be considered essential in addressing environmental chronic emergencies (ECEs), which—as extensively shown in this book—disproportionately impact women.[1] The duty to cooperate in facing events that fall under the definition of ECEs—including environmental degradation, climate change, industrial pollution-related effects and the use of ergotoxins and pesticides—has become a key issue in discussions among UN Member States.[2] An increasing number of countries—both developing and

[1] The impacts of ECEs are not experienced equally by all individuals and communities worldwide, nor do all share the same level of responsibility in causing them. Women bear the disproportionate burdens of ECEs due to structural inequalities and deeply entrenched societal discrimination. Indeed, these factors exacerbate the effects of ECEs on women, highlighting the need for targeted, gender-sensitive approaches to environmental crises. For a more in-depth discussion of this point, see Sara De Vido, 'Feminist Legal Methods and Environmental Chronic Emergencies: Challenging the Anthropocentric and Androcentric International Legal System'; Deborah Russo, 'Moving Beyond an Approach Based on Crisis and Disasters to Address Environmental Chronic Emergencies'; and Enzamaria Tramontana, 'Environmental Chronic Emergencies, Women's Inequality, and International Law' in this volume.

[2] *Statement of the Alliance of Small Island States* (AOSIS, on behalf of its 37 UN Member States), as well as those of Brazil, Croatia, Germany, India, Jamaica, Malaysia, Papua New Guinea, Sierra Leone, the Netherlands and the Small Island Developing States of the Pacific (SIDS, on behalf of its 12 UN Member States), UNGA, *Sixth Committee*, UN *Secretariat summary*, UN Doc. A/C.6/77/SR, 25–9.

developed—are acknowledging the necessity of a comprehensive examination of international cooperation in tackling the consequences of events that can be conceptualized under our framework as ECEs.[3] Indeed, affected States need increased technical, financial and operational support to respond effectively to ECEs, which, in turn, demand a paradigm shift from the traditional international law approach to crises.[4] This shift must account for the structural inequalities and deeply rooted discrimination that contribute to environmental emergencies and their disproportionate impact on specific groups of individuals, especially women.[5]

The present chapter aims to explore how the international legal obligation to cooperate in the context of ECEs is evolving and responding to their unequal effects on women. The analysis is structured as follows. Section 2 begins with a brief overview of the duty to cooperate in international law, followed by an exploration of its role in addressing ECEs across three relevant, interconnected fields: international human rights law (Section 2.1); international disaster law (Section 2.2); and international environmental and climate change law (Section 2.3). Section 3 then investigates whether current international law regulating the duty to cooperate addresses the disproportionate effects of ECEs on women. It evaluates if emerging cooperative approaches incorporate a gender perspective and—from an ecofeminist standpoint, which this book adopts as its legal methodology—examines the extent to which these efforts effectively challenge the deeply entrenched patterns of oppression and

---

Full declarations of States are available at <www.un.org>, accessed 23 April 2025.

[3] See, *inter alia*, *Statement by the Federal Republic of Germany, Sixth Committee - Agenda item 77-II, Sea-level rise in relation to international law* (28 October 2022).

[4] See De Vido (n 1); Russo (n 1); Tramontana (n 1). In the same perspective, see Hilary Charlesworth, 'International Law: A Discipline of Crisis' (2002) 65 (3) *The Modern Law Review Limited* 377–92.

[5] As extensively explained in this book, ECEs derive from Rob Nixon's concept of *slow violence* [Cf. Rob Nixon, Slow Violence and the Environmentalism of the Poor (Harvard University Press 2011)], which challenges traditional international law's understanding of environmental crises [Cf. Hillary Charlesworth (n 3)], emphasizing the gradual, often overlooked nature of environmental impacts. Thus, the concept of ECEs shifts the focus from immediate, dramatic events to the ongoing, cumulative effects of some environmental challenges, including climate change, that disproportionately affect some groups of individuals, especially women. In addition, ECEs extend beyond the notion of slow violence, which had initially only marginally considered structural issues like gender and intersectional dimensions (On this point, see Jenna Marie Christian, Lorraine Dowler, 'Slow and Fast Violence: A Feminist Critique of Binaries' (2019) 18 (5) *ACME: An International Journal for Critical Geographies*, 1066; and De Vido (n 1).

discrimination that shape the disproportionate effects of ECEs on women.[6] Finally, Section 4 concludes by highlighting the need to strengthen the duty to cooperate to more effectively address the gendered effects of ECEs.

2. THE DUTY TO COOPERATE IN ADDRESSING ENVIRONMENTAL CHRONIC EMERGENCIES: BETWEEN VAGUENESS AND RESPONSIVENESS TO SPECIFIC CONTEXTS

To analyze the duty to cooperate in addressing ECEs, it can be useful to first briefly explore the concept of international cooperation and its key developments in international law. The essence of international cooperation can be found in Articles 1(1) and 1(3) of the UN Charter. These articles outline the organization's objectives and principles, including international cooperation for maintaining international peace and security, for solving international economic, social, cultural or humanitarian problems and for promoting respect for human rights and fundamental freedoms.[7] The 1970 *Declaration on Principles of International Law concerning Friendly Relations and Cooperation among States*[8] reaffirmed the UN Charter's commitments and linked cooperation to various areas of international law.[9]

---

[6] See De Vido (n 1). Several studies have highlighted that adopting feminist approaches can drive a paradigm shift from the traditional international law's response to crises by dismantling patriarchal structures and addressing the structural inequalities and discrimination embedded in slow-onset environmental challenges (Dianne Otto, 'Decoding crisis in international law: a queer feminist perspective' in Barbara Stark (ed.), International Law and Its Discontents: Confronting Crises (Cambridge University Press 2015) 115; Charlesworth (n 3);

[7] Charter of the United Nations, Articles 1(1) and 1(3). For the concept of inter-State cooperation, see, *inter alia*, Jost Delbrück, 'Coexistence, Cooperation and Solidarity in International Law: The International Obligation to Cooperate—An Empty Shell or a Hard Law Principle of International Law?—A Critical Look at a Much Debated Paradigm of Modern International Law', in Holger P. Hestermeyer et al. (eds), 'Coexistence, Cooperation and Solidarity: Liber Amicorum Rüdiger Wolfrum' (Brill 2012). Laurence Boisson De Chazournes, Jason Rudall, 'Cooperation', in Jorge E. Viñuales (ed.), The UN Friendly Relations Declaration at 50: An Assessment of the Fundamental Principles of International Law (Cambridge 2020), 105.

[8] UNGA, *Declaration on Principles of International Law Concerning Friendly Relations and Cooperation among States in Accordance with the Charter of the United Nations* (24 October 1970) Res 2625 (XXV), UN Doc A/RES/25/2625.

[9] De Chazournes, Rudall (n 7). On this point, see also Pierre-Marie Dupuy, 'International Law: Torn between Coexistence, Cooperation and Globalization:

Thus, the duty to cooperate has been progressively consolidated and refined within specific contexts and is now applied across different areas, including counterterrorism, peace and security, international economic relations, human rights, environmental protection and disaster risk reduction. However, its precise nature and scope remain difficult to define. Although enshrined in multiple international legal instruments,[10] the duty to cooperate often lacks clear, precise content and retains a predominantly political character, serving as an expression of social necessity or a moral imperative—often framed as a 'matter of equity'. [11]

Nevertheless, in certain key fields of international law relevant to addressing the phenomena that present the particular characteristics of ECEs, international cooperation has begun to take on more specific forms. The duty to cooperate is increasingly recognized in international human rights law, international disaster law and environmental and climate change law, and this supports the delineation of the content of international cooperation within States' efforts to address ECEs. The following sub-sections explore whether and to what extent the cooperation obligations undertaken by States in these areas are effectively responding to the challenges posed by ECEs.

2.1 International Human Rights Law and the Evolving Duty to Cooperate in Responding to Environmental Chronic Emergencies: The Role of Courts and Human Rights Treaty Bodies

The crucial role of international human rights law in protecting people affected by the negative impacts of phenomena conceptualized as ECEs has been progressively recognized by various human rights courts and UN treaty bodies.[12]

General Conclusions' (1998) 9 *European Journal of International Law*, 273, 278.

[10] See, *inter alia*, Article 22 of the 1948 Universal Declaration of Human Rights, stating that everyone is entitled 'to the realization, through national effort and international cooperation [...], of the economic, social and cultural rights indispensable for [their] dignity and the free development of [their] personality'.

[11] *Statement by Antigua and Barbuda on behalf of the Alliance of Small Island States (AOSIS)*(2022) para. 4; UNGA, *In larger freedom; towards development, security and human rights for all*, Report of the Secretary-General (21 March 2005) UN Doc A/59/2005, para. 18.

[12] HRC, 'Human Rights and Climate Change' (25 March 2009) UN Doc A/HRC/RES/10/14; OHCHR, 'Panel Discussion on the Relationship Between Climate Change and Human Rights, Summary of Discussions' (15 June 2009); HRC, 'Human Rights and Climate Change' (15 July 2014) A/HRC/RES/26/27. IHRL has significantly contributed to clarifying the meaning of the duty to

In its 2017 Advisory Opinion on *The Environment and Human Rights*, the Inter-American Court holds that States have a duty to cooperate in good faith to protect the rights to life and to personal integrity from environmental damage and 'environmental emergencies.'[13] In order to comply with this obligation, States must notify the other potentially affected States promptly and in advance when they become aware that a planned activity within their jurisdiction could pose a risk of significant transboundary harm as well as in cases of 'environmental emergencies',[14] and must consult and negotiate, in a timely manner and in good faith, with any States potentially affected by such harm.[15] In addition to the duties of notification, consultation, and negotiation in relation to projects that could entail the risk of transboundary damage, the Court notes that, as part of the duty to cooperate, several international instruments contain provisions aimed at 'facilitating', 'promoting' or ensuring the exchange of information between States[16] concerning 'scientific and technological knowledge', among other matters.[17]

---

cooperate as envisaged by the UN system. This duty is rooted in the concept of international solidarity [HRC, 'Human rights and international solidarity' (22 June 2009) UN Doc A/HRC/12/27, para. 40], which holds that while each State bears primary responsibility for respecting, protecting, and fulfilling human rights within its own territory, this can only be achieved effectively through collaboration with other States, international organizations, and civil society [ECOSOC, 'Human rights and international solidarity', Working paper submitted by Rui Baltazar Dos Santos Alves (15 June 2004) UN Doc E/CN.4/Sub.2/2004/43, para. 35]. In this context, international cooperation serves as a crucial mechanism for the practical realization of international solidarity (*ibid.*).

13 *The Environment and Human Rights (State Obligations in Relation to the Environment in the Context of the Protection and Guarantee of the Rights to Life and to Personal Integrity: Interpretation and Scope of Articles 4(1) and 5(1) in Relation to Articles 1(1) and 2 of the American Convention on Human Rights)*, Advisory Opinion (IACtHR, 15 November 2017), para. 209. The Advisory Opinion was issued in response to Colombia's request of March 14, 2016. Colombia's key inquiries focused on the interpretation of *jurisdiction* under Article 1.1 IACHR and on the scope of State Parties' obligations to respect and guarantee the rights to life and personal integrity in cases of environmental harm; see paras 181–205.

14 *Ibid.*, paras 190 and 196.

15 *Ibid.*, paras 197–205.

16 See, for example, United Nations Framework Convention on Climate Change (UNFCCC), entered into force 21 March 1994, Article 4(1)(h); Convention on Biodiversity, entered into force 29 December 1993, Article 17.1.

17 Cf. Rio Declaration on Environment and Development, adopted at the United Nations Conference on Environment and Development, Rio de Janeiro (14 June 1992) UN Doc A/CONF.151/26 (Vol. I), Principle 9; Stockholm Declaration on the Human Environment, adopted at the United Nations Conference on the

The Human Rights Council emphasized the importance of strengthening and defining the content and the scope of international cooperation in addressing phenomena related to ECEs. In its resolutions 26/27, the Council recognized 'the need to give due consideration [. . .] to the role of international cooperation in relation to the special needs and particular circumstances of developing countries and to addressing the adverse impact of climate change on the full and effective realization of human rights.'[18] For this reason, the Council urged all States to further cooperate in addressing the negative effects of phenomena related to what we define as ECEs, on the enjoyment of human rights, 'including the right to development, particularly in developing countries [. . .] including through dialogue and measures, such as the implementation of practical steps to promote and facilitate capacity-building, financial resources and technology transfer.'[19]

Regarding the specific context of natural disasters and environmental degradation, the Committee on Economic, Social and Cultural Rights affirmed that States and international organizations bear an individual and joint responsibility to cooperate in providing disaster relief and humanitarian assistance in times of emergency.[20] The Committee added that each State should contribute to this task to the maximum of its capacity.[21] It also clarified the nature and content of the duty to cooperate under the ICESCR.[22] According to the

---

Human Environment, Stockholm (5–16 June 1972) UN Doc A/CONF.48/14/Rev.1, Principle 20. On this point, see para. 1.3 of this Chapter.

[18] HRC (n 12, 2014), Preamble. On this point, see also HRC, 'Human rights and climate change' (22 July 2015) A/HRC/RES/29/15, Preamble; CEDAW Committee, 'General recommendation No. 37 on the gender-related dimensions of disaster risk reduction in the context of climate change' (13 March 2018) UN Doc CEDAW/C/GC/37, para. 2.

[19] *Ibid.*, para. 5.

[20] CESCR, 'General Comment No. 14 on Article 12 of the International Covenant on Economic, Social and Cultural Rights, on the right to the highest attainable standard of health' (11 August 2000) UN Doc. E/C.12/2000/4, para. 40.

[21] *Ibid.*

[22] On the nature and content of the duty to cooperate for the realization of economic, social and cultural rights, see, in general, the work of the CESCR: 'General Comment No 3 on the nature of States parties' obligations of 1990'; 'General Comment No 19 on the right to social security (Article 9 of the Covenant)', (4 February 2008), UN Doc E/C.12/GC/19; 'General Comment No 15 on the right to water' (Articles 11 and 12 of the Covenant), (20 January 2003), UN Doc. E/C.12/2002/11; 'General Comment No 14 on the right to the highest attainable standard of health (Article 12 of the Covenant)', (11 August 2000), UN Doc E/C.12/2000/4. For more on this point, see De Chazournes, Rudall, Co-Operation (n 7), 116–20.

Committee, the full realization of the rights enshrined in the Covenant would remain an unfulfilled aspiration in many countries without international assistance and cooperation programs from States in a position to support and promote them.[23] Consequently, international cooperation for the realisation of economic, social, and cultural rights is an obligation for all States, though those that have the capacity to assist others bear a greater responsibility.[24] Understood in this way, the duty to cooperate complements the primary responsibility of States to fulfil their national human rights obligations.[25]

This is particularly important for our analysis, as it provides valuable insights into the scope and impact of phenomena that present the particular characteristics of ECEs, offering a deeper understanding of how these prolonged emergencies can profoundly affect the protection and realization of fundamental rights, while also highlighting the need for assistance and cooperation from non-affected States.

Specifically, in its General Comments, the Committee envisaged that international assistance and cooperation for the realisation of economic, social and cultural rights would mainly take the form of economic and technical support.[26]

More broadly, human rights treaty bodies have progressively examined the obligation of developed States to provide adequate financial resources to protect human rights from the adverse effects of climate change, including through international cooperation.

In 2023, several treaty bodies addressed climate finance and cooperation in their reports and decisions.[27] Among them, the Committee on the Elimination of Discrimination against Women (CEDAW) placed the greatest emphasis on climate finance and cooperation within its state reporting procedure.[28] In its

---

23 CESCR (n 22, 1990), para. 14.

24 *Ibid.*

25 HRC, 'Report of the independent expert on human rights and international solidarity, Rudi Muhammad Rizki' (5 July 2010) UN Doc. A/HRC/15/32, para. 43.

26 See, *inter alia*, CESCR, 'General Comment No 13 on the right to education (Article 13 of the Covenant)', (8 December 1999) UN Doc E/C.12/1999/10, para. 56.

27 HRC, 'Report of the Special Rapporteur on the promotion and protection of human rights in the context of climate change, Elisa Morgera' (24 July 2024) UN Doc. A/HRC/56/46, para. 62.

28 *Ibid.* CIEL, 'States' Human Rights Obligations in the Context of Climate Change. Guidance Provided by the UN Human Rights Treaty Bodies', Synthesis Note (*CIEL*, August 2024), 18–9. In addition to the CEDAW Committee, both the Committee on the Rights of the Child (CRC) and the CESCR have also addressed financial cooperation in the context of climate change (*Ibid.*). See, CRC, 'General

Concluding Observations (COB) on Norway and Timor-Leste, the Committee called on those States to 'actively support and participate in the creation and operation of new funding arrangements for responding to loss and damage'.[29] In a joint statement on human rights and climate change, CEDAW, CESCR, CRC, the Committee on the Protection of the Rights of All Migrant Workers and the Committee on the Rights of Persons with Disabilities emphasized that high-income States should support adaptation and mitigation efforts in developing countries by facilitating the transfer of green technologies and contributing to the financing of climate mitigation and adaptation.[30]

In conclusion, the content and scope of the duty to cooperate in international human rights law remain somewhat vague and largely confined to instruments of a primarily recommendatory nature. Nevertheless, the work of international courts and human rights treaty bodies is gradually clarifying its application, which is crucial for responding to ECEs. This duty encompasses efforts to promote human rights through the allocation of resources, including financial, economic and technical support, from developed to developing countries.[31]

2.2 International Disaster Law and Cooperative Efforts in Preventing Environmental Chronic Emergencies

As extensively explained throughout this book,[32] ECEs develop gradually, shaped by a complex interplay of adverse and overlapping factors. Though often invisible, these environmental phenomena can escalate into large-scale disasters—such as mega-fires and floods—causing severe and widespread damage.[33]

In this context, international disaster law can play a crucial role in preventing ECEs from transforming into disruptive disasters. Indeed, States are increasingly committed to strengthening cooperation in disaster management.[34]

comment No. 26 on children's rights and the environment with a special focus on climate change' (22 August 2023) UN Doc. CRC/C/GC/26.

[29] CIEL (n 28) 18–19.

[30] CEDAW, CESCR, CRC and others, 'Statement on human rights and climate change' (14 May 2020) UN Doc HRI/2019/1, para. 17.

[31] De Chazournes, Rudall (n 7) 120.

[32] See De Vido (n 1); Russo (n 1).

[33] *Ibid.*

[34] There are numerous instruments specifically aimed at protecting individuals during disasters, which highlight the significance of international cooperation in addressing their effects. In bilateral agreements, this is often evident in titles emphasizing cooperation or mutual assistance (Cf., for instance, the Agreement between the Government of the French Republic and the Government of Malaysia

Several instruments and guidelines have been adopted, establishing standards and priorities with an emphasis on prevention.[35]

In particular, the 2016 *Draft Articles of the International Law Commission (ILC) on the Protection of Persons in the Event of Disasters* recognize the central importance of international cooperation, also in the reduction of disaster risk.[36] Draft Article 7 includes a specific formulation of the duty to cooperate in the context of disasters, stating that 'States shall, as appropriate, cooperate among themselves, with the United Nations, with the components of the Red Cross and Red Crescent Movement, and with other assisting actors.'[37] Thus, the Article enshrines a legal obligation to cooperate for all parties concerned.[38]

Under Article 7, the duty to cooperate is enshrined in general terms,[39] providing a framework to guide the actions of States and other stakeholders,

---

on Cooperation in the Field of Disaster Prevention and Management and Civil Security, 25 May 1998, preambular para. 4). The Tampere Convention on the Provision of Telecommunication Resources for Disaster Mitigation and Relief Operations of 1998 explicitly states in its preamble that parties' intent to 'facilitate international cooperation to mitigate the impact of disaster.'

35 Federica Passarini, 'Disaster Risk Reduction in International Law', Doctoral Thesis 2020; Giulio Bartolini, A taxonomy of disasters in international law (Routledge, 2018) 12; Barbara Nicoletti, 'The prevention of natural and man-made disasters: what duties for States', in Andrea De Guttry, Marco Gestri, Gabriella Venturini (eds), International Disaster Response Law (T.M.C. Asser Press, 2012) 177, 195.

36 The Draft articles on the protection of persons in the event of disasters (hereinafter Draft articles) were adopted by the International Law Commission at its sixty-eighth session in 2016 and submitted to the General Assembly as a part of the Commission's report for that session (A/71/10). The report, which also contains commentaries to the draft articles (para. 49), appeared in Yearbook of the International Law Commission, 2016, vol. II, Part Two.

37 For some studies on the work of the ILC in relation to disaster cooperation, see Eduardo Valencia-Ospina, 'The Work of the International Law Commission on the "Protection of Persons in the Event of Disasters"' (2019) 1 *Yearbook of International Disaster Law*, 13–15; Giulio Bartolini, 'A Universal Treaty for Disasters? Remarks on the International Law Commission's Draft Articles on the Protection of Persons in the Event of Disasters' (2017) *International Review of the Red Cross*, 1103; Flavia Zorzi Giustiniani, 'The Works of the International Law Commission on 'Protection of Persons in the Event of Disasters'. A Critical Appraisal'', in Andrea De Guttry, Marco Gestri, Gabriella Venturini (eds), International Disaster Response Law (T.M.C. Asser Press, 2012).

38 Draft articles, commentary to Article 7, para. 6.

39 Giulio Bartolini, 'Il Progetto di articoli della Commissione del diritto internazionale sulla "protection of persons in the event of disasters"' (2017) 3 *Rivista di diritto internazionale*, 677, 699–700.

aligning those actions with their respective roles and capacities, and grounding them in good faith in the implementation of disaster-related measures.[40] The Article includes, at a minimum, the duty of an affected State to notify other States of potential disasters that might affect them, which is considered a norm of customary international law.[41] Indeed, in the case of events that could cause transboundary environmental damage, a customary obligation to cooperate is recognised.[42]

Specific modalities of cooperation are further elaborated in subsequent articles of the Draft, addressing both disaster response and risk reduction.[43] Cooperation in disaster risk reduction, which is particularly significant for preventing ECEs, is outlined in Article 9, stating that: 'Each State shall reduce the risk of disasters by taking appropriate measures, including through legislation and regulations, to prevent, mitigate, and prepare for disasters'.[44] Paragraph 2 of the same article specifies that: 'Disaster risk reduction measures include the conduct of risk assessments, the collection and dissemination of risk and past loss information, and the installation and operation of early warning systems'.[45]

Article 9 makes clear that the duty to reduce disaster risk primarily entails domestic measures.[46] However, when such measures require inter-State cooperation or engagement with other assisting actors, they fall within the scope of Article 7, which mandates States to cooperate in disaster risk reduction.[47]

The Draft Articles' explicit reference to risk reduction highlights the increasing importance of preventing phenomena that could escalate into major

---

40 Draft articles, commentary to Article 7.

41 *Ibid.* Bartolini (n 39), 699–700.

42 *Ibid.* For the existence of a customary duty to cooperate in preventing transboundary environmental harm, see Rüdiger Wolfrum, 'Purposes and Principles of International Environmental Law' (1990) 33 *German Yearbook of International Law*, 308, 313–15; Riccardo Pisillo Mazzeschi, 'Diritti umani e cambiamento climatico: brevi note sulla sentenza KlimaSeniorinnen della Corte di Strasburgo' (2024) 2, *Diritti Umani e Diritto Internazionale*, 383, 396.

43 Draft articles, commentary to article 7, para. 9. The forms of cooperation in the response phase are elaborated in article 8. According to article 8, forms of cooperation in the response to disasters include humanitarian assistance, coordination of international relief actions and communications, and the provision of relief personnel, equipment and goods, and scientific, medical and technical resources. The list is illustrative and not exhaustive (Draft articles, commentary to Article 8).

44 Draft Article 9.1.

45 *Ibid.*, Article 9.2.

46 *Ibid.*

47 Draft articles, 2016, commentary to Article 7, para. 9.

disasters and impact the human rights of affected persons.[48] Consequently, disaster risk reduction has been extensively addressed in various multilateral agreements, with the *Sendai Framework for Disaster Risk Reduction*[49] being the most significant example of this evolving normative trend.

Although not legally binding, the Sendai Framework is usually accorded prominence in promoting and developing international cooperation in disaster risk reduction. The Framework establishes the primary responsibility of States for prevention, including through regional, cross-border, and bilateral partnerships.[50] Paragraph 8 of the Framework emphasizes that international cooperation is vital for reducing disaster risk and supporting States, local authorities and communities. Strengthening existing mechanisms is crucial for effective implementation, especially in developing and most vulnerable countries. These countries need targeted support through bilateral and multilateral channels to enhance capacity-building, financial and technical assistance and technology transfer, in line with international commitments.[51]

One of the Sendai Framework's key priorities, particularly relevant in preventing ECEs, is 'understanding disaster risk'.[52] In this context, the Framework underlines that disaster risk management should be based on a thorough understanding of vulnerability, capacity, exposure, hazards and the environment.[53] This knowledge supports pre-disaster risk assessment, prevention, mitigation, preparedness and effective response.[54] In addition, the Framework outlines the content of cooperation in disaster risk reduction, emphasizing that effective disaster and pre-disaster risk assessment requires promoting the exchange of scientific knowledge, technology and data among States, fostering joint research and capacity-building initiatives, and ensuring access to reliable risk information.[55] Furthermore, at both national and global levels, cooperation should focus on developing and sharing best practices, enhancing disaster risk assessments, and improving early warning systems.[56] Finally, international

---

48 Bartolini (n 39), 700.

49 United Nations Sendai Framework for Disaster Risk Reduction (23 June 2015) UN Doc A/RES/69/283 (hereinafter 'Sendai Framework'). Other examples include the so-called Hyogo Framework for Action, which preceded the Sendai Framework for Disaster Risk Reduction.

50 Sendai Framework, para. 19 (a).

51 *Ibid.*, para. 8.

52 *Ibid.*, para. 23 ff.

53 *Ibid.*

54 *Ibid.*

55 *Ibid.*, para. 24.

56 *Ibid.*, para. 25.

cooperation must support education, training and public awareness campaigns to strengthen disaster preparedness and resilience.[57]

From the above, it emerges that international disaster law embodies a broad expression of solidarity and cooperative action in preventing disasters. Indeed, the current legal framework reflects a growing commitment by States to collaborate in achieving common goals, with an increasing focus on disaster risk reduction. In particular, the *Draft articles* include a duty to cooperate in addressing disasters,[58] including measures related to risk reduction.[59] In this regard, the Draft contains provisions for progressive development, which can contribute to the creation of treaties at various levels and to the emergence of new international norms. The UN General Assembly's decision to 'elaborate and conclude a legally binding instrument on the protection of persons in the event of disasters' exemplifies this trend'.[60]

More broadly, the provisions within the analyzed instruments help define the duty to cooperate in preventing phenomena like ECEs from escalating into disruptive events, even though they fail to capture these events when such consequences have not yet occurred. Cooperation in disaster reduction encompasses information-sharing, communication between States and relevant actors, and the provision of technical and scientific assistance.

While the above-mentioned instruments emphasize disaster risk reduction, they continue to adopt an emergency-oriented approach to pre-disaster risk assessment, largely overlooking the slow onset effects of ECEs and the broader social contexts in which they unfold, thereby failing to address structural inequalities and discrimination rooted in society.[61]

Moreover, these instruments—particularly the Sendai Framework—primarily focus on developing countries that are often labelled as disaster-prone.[62] Though phenomena that fall under the definition of ECEs should not be viewed solely through the lens of developing countries, they must also account for the challenges and issues faced by developed States. Indeed, to prevent ECEs

57 *Ibid.*

58 Cf. Draft Article 7.

59 Cf. Draft Article 9.

60 UNGA, 'Protection of persons in the event of disasters' (14 November 2024) UN Doc A/C.6/79/L.16. In this regard, Giulio Bartolini, 'Toward a universal treaty on "Protection of Persons in the Event of Disasters"', (EJIL:Talk! 17 December 2024) <www.ejiltalk.org>, accessed 24 April 2025.

61 De Vido (n 1). In this perspective, see also Zehra Zaidi, Maureen Fordham, 'The missing half of the Sendai framework: Gender and women in the implementation of global disaster risk reduction policy' (2021) 10 *Progress in Disaster Science*.

62 Cf. for example Sendai Framework, Preamble, para. 4.

from escalating into disruptive disasters, it is crucial that developed countries acknowledge their own risks and take long-term, proactive actions tailored to their specific needs. In this context, disaster risk reduction cooperation efforts should encourage a more comprehensive approach, recognizing that both developing and developed nations share challenges and responsibilities in addressing the root causes and impacts of ECEs.

2.3 The Duty to Cooperate in International Environmental and Climate Change Law: The Pivotal Role of Technical and Financial Support in Facing Environmental Chronic Emergencies

In the context of international environmental and climate law, the duty to cooperate is essential for averting transboundary risks. This duty aligns with the obligation to prevent transboundary environmental harm, recognized as a norm of customary international law.[63]

The duty to cooperate is fundamentally enshrined in both the Stockholm and Rio Declarations. These instruments emphasize the need for cooperation between States, international organizations and private actors to achieve environmental objectives.[64] This duty is also reflected in the case law of various international courts and tribunals.[65]

Over time, the duty to cooperate has evolved to include various forms, such as the exchange of information between States, the conduct of scientific research and systematic observation, consultation and prior notification,[66] and the requirement for prior informed consent or environmental impact assessment.[67]

The duty to cooperate is now embedded in several environmental and climate treaties—relevant in addressing ECEs and their negative effects—and has become increasingly clear and specific over time.

---

[63] Pasquale De Sena, Massimo Starita, Corso di Diritto Internazionale (Il Mulino, 2023) 145–7; Pisillo Mazzeschi (n 42) 396; *Paper Mills on the Uruguay River* (*Argentina v Uruguay*), Judgment on the merits, ICGJ 425 (ICJ, 20 April 2010), para. 77.

[64] Stockholm Declaration on the Human Environment (15 December 1972) UN Doc A/RES/2994, Principle 24; Rio Declaration on Environment and Development (12 August 1992), UN Doc A/CONF.151/26, Principle 7 and 27.

[65] *See, ex multis, MOX Plant Case* (*Ireland v United Kingdom*), Interim Measures, (ITLOS, 3 December 2001), para. 82.

[66] *See, ex multis, Paper Mills on the Uruguay River* (n 63), para. 77.

[67] In this regard, see *Certain Activities Conducted by Nicaragua in Border Areas,* (*Costa Rica v Nicaragua*), Interim Measures (ICJ, 8 March 2011).

According to the 1992 Convention on Biological Diversity, for example, contracting Parties shall, as far as possible and appropriate, conserve and sustainably use biological diversity.[68] This cooperation encompasses various forms of support, including financial and technical assistance for *ex-situ* conservation, particularly in developing countries,[69] and the promotion of collaboration between governmental authorities and the private sector to develop sustainable resource use methods.[70] Moreover, it involves developing educational and public-awareness programmes to foster a deeper understanding of biodiversity conservation.[71] International scientific cooperation is also a key aspect to be enhanced through national and international institutions alongside efforts to support developing countries in capacity building, human resource development and institutional strengthening.[72] Additionally, the Convention emphasizes the importance of establishing mechanisms for knowledge-sharing and promoting collaboration in technology development and transfer, including traditional and indigenous technologies.[73]

The Minamata Convention on Mercury encourages Parties to cooperate with each other, as well as with relevant intergovernmental organizations and other entities, to achieve its objectives.[74] This cooperation includes developing strategies to prevent the diversion of mercury to artisanal and small-scale gold mining; promoting education and capacity-building initiatives; supporting research into sustainable, mercury-free alternatives; and providing technical and financial assistance.[75] The Convention also emphasizes the need to enhance monitoring, assessment and research on mercury emissions, their environmental and health impacts, and the development of non-mercury technologies, while promoting harmonized methodologies and information-sharing to ensure effective global action.[76]

In the more specific context of climate change, the duty to cooperate has developed from the principle of common but differentiated responsibilities.[77]

---

68 Convention on Biological Diversity, Rio de Janeiro, 5 June 1992, Art. 5.

69 *Ibid.*, Article 8.

70 *Ibid.*, Article 12.

71 *Ibid.*, Article 13.

72 *Ibid.*, Article 18.

73 *Ibid.*

74 Minamata Convention on Mercury, Kumamoto, 10 October 2013, Article 4.

75 *Ibid.*

76 See Articles 14, 16 and 19.

77 The principle of common but differentiated responsibilities (CBDR), established at the 1992 United Nations Conference on Environment and Development in Rio de Janeiro, has been pivotal in climate cooperation efforts. This principle underpins the UNFCCC and the broader International Climate Change regime,

This duty has gradually assumed a more defined purpose and content, reflecting the varying capacities and responsibilities of States in combating climate change.

The 1994 Convention to Combat Desertification establishes obligations to cooperate, with a particular focus on Africa.[78] The forms of cooperation include the exchange of information, technology transfer, technical and financial assistance, and capacity-building efforts to support affected regions.[79]

Article 6 of the Paris Agreement provides for voluntary cooperation between Parties so that more ambitious Nationally Determined Contributions (NDCs) can be established,[80] while Article 7 envisages a role for cooperation in strengthening national efforts to *adapt* to climate change. The article emphasizes the importance of providing developing countries with support to implement their adaptation strategies by sharing information and best practices, strengthening institutional arrangements and climate-science knowledge, as well as identifying effective adaptation practices.[81] Both articles are phrased in general, non-binding terms. However, the subsequent articles offer more precise and binding provisions.

According to Article 9 of the Paris Agreement, developed country Parties *shall* provide financial resources to assist developing country Parties with both mitigation and adaptation, as a continuation of their existing obligations under the Convention.[82] Article 10 establishes that the Parties *shall* strengthen cooperative action on technology development and transfer.[83] In other words, the Paris Agreement enshrines a duty to cooperate, which primarily takes the form of technical and financial assistance from developed to developing countries.

Technical and financial cooperation has increasingly evolved and become central through the decisions of the Conferences of the Parties.[84] For example,

---

emphasizing that States must collectively address climate change (Lavanya Rajamani, 'The Changing Fortunes of Differential Treatment in the Evolution of International Environmental Law' (2012) 88 (3) *International Affairs*, 605).

78 Convention to Combat Desertification in those Countries Experiencing Serious Drought and/or Desertification, particularly in Africa, Paris, 14 October 1994, Article 4. About cooperation among African country Parties see Articles 16 and 18.

79 *Ibid.*, Articles 8 and 12.

80 Articles 6, Paris Agreement. On this point, see Jason Rudall, 'The Obligation to Cooperate in the Fight against Climate Change' (2021) 23 *International Community Law Review*, 184, 186.

81 Articles 7, Paris Agreement.

82 Article 9, Paris Agreement.

83 Article 10, Paris Agreement.

84 Established in 2013 under the UNFCCC, the Warsaw International Mechanism (WIM) on loss and damage aims to tackle climate change impacts

at COP27, new financing arrangements were established to help vulnerable developing countries address loss and damage from climate change.[85] At COP28 in Dubai, the new *Loss and Damage Fund* was operationalized to provide financing for climate-related emergencies and to fill gaps in existing funding institutions.[86] The establishment of the Fund marks the beginning of deploying financial instruments to address climate-induced loss and damage,[87] offering additional support and improving access to finance for particularly vulnerable developing countries.[88]

To conclude, it is evident that international cooperation has significantly progressed within international environmental and climate law. The duty to cooperate assumes well-defined forms and operational modalities, manifested primarily through information exchange and, more importantly, through technical and financial support to address the adverse effects of phenomena such as mercury pollution and climate change, both of which our framework considers as ECEs. However, these forms of cooperation—particularly technical and financial support—often prove insufficient to meet the challenges posed by ECEs.[89] For instance, despite being the most responsible for climate change, wealthy countries have so far pledged only a few million dollars to the *Loss and Damage Fund*—an amount vastly inadequate compared to the economic and non-economic losses that developing countries incur each year as a result of global warming.

---

that adaptation and mitigation cannot address alone. See UNFCCC, *Warsaw International Mechanism for Loss and Damage associated with Climate Change Impacts* <www.unfccc.int>, accessed 24 April 2025. On this point, cf. Paris Agreement, Articles 8.3 and 8.4.

[85] UNFCCC, 'Funding arrangements for responding to loss and damage associated with the adverse effects of climate change, including a focus on addressing loss and damage' (20 November 2022) Decision 2/CP.27/2/CMA.4.

[86] UNFCCC, 'Operationalization of the new funding arrangements, including a fund, for responding to loss and damage referred to in paragraphs 2–3 of decisions 2/CP.27 and 2/CMA.4' (13 December 2023) Advance Draft decision -/CP.28-/CMA.5.

[87] UNDP, 'Loss and Damage Fund for Developing Countries' (26 January 2024) <www.undp.org>, accessed 24 April 2024. COP29 took significant steps to ensure the operability of the 'Loss and Damage' Fund. On this point, see 'Historic Decision in Baku: The Loss and Damage Fund fully operationalized' (23 November 2024) <www.cop29.az>, accessed 24 April 2025.

[88] UNFCCC (n 86) Annex I, II, para. 6.

[89] UNGA, 'Violence against women and girls, its causes and consequences' (11 July 2022) UN Doc A/77/136, para. 70; Melanie Pill, Georgia Hammersley, 'A climate loss and damage fund that works' (Policy Brief, September 2024) <www.unfccc.int>, accessed 24 April 2025.

3. INTEGRATING A GENDER PERSPECTIVE INTO EMERGING COOPERATIVE APPROACHES TO ENVIRONMENTAL CHRONIC EMERGENCIES

While emphasizing the need for cooperation and specifying the content of the duty to cooperate in addressing phenomena related to ECEs, both the binding and non-binding instruments discussed above also recognize the disproportionate impact of ECEs on women. Indeed, these frameworks underscore the need to strengthen cooperation among States in reducing disaster and climate risk, including through efforts to eliminate gender discrimination and inequalities.

Regarding international cooperation in responding to ECEs, the CEDAW Committee has emphasized that States must align their human rights obligations with the goals and targets set by the *Sustainable Development Goals* (SDGs), particularly Goal 5 on gender equality and Goal 13 on climate action.[90] States are required to integrate gender perspectives into international cooperation programmes for disaster risk reduction, sustainable development and climate change.[91]

According to the Paris Agreement, all Parties shall cooperate to enhance the capacity of developing countries to implement mitigation and adaptation efforts, ensuring that this process is 'effective, iterative [. . .] participatory, cross-cutting, and gender-responsive'.[92] Thus, the Agreement recognizes the importance of gender equality and women's empowerment in climate action, emphasizing the need to promote women's empowerment and to ensure that women's rights are fully integrated into cooperation efforts to achieve climate goals.[93] However, this remains a rather generic recognition that does not translate into specific cooperation obligations on this matter.

In more general terms, the UNFCCC regime, through its climate treaties and COPs decisions, has been of fundamental importance in recent years for integrating the gender dimension into climate-related participatory and decision-making processes, recognizing women's unique vulnerabilities and highlighting their pivotal role as agents of resilience and recovery. In particular, the UNFCCC *Gender Action Plan* (GAP) underscores women's critical role in climate action and advocates for their full, equal and meaningful participation

---

90 CEDAW Committee (n 18), para. 41; CIEL, 'Women's Rights Obligations of States in the Context of Climate Change' (2019) <www.ciel.org>, accessed 24 April 2025.

91 CEDAW Committee (n 18), para. 41; CEDAW COB to Australia and South Korea.

92 Paris Agreement, Articles 11(3).

93 *Ibid.*, Preamble.

in the international climate process.[94] The plan aims to integrate gender considerations into climate policies and strategies, ensuring that women's contributions are both recognized and supported.[95] It also frames finance for implementation by sharing experiences on gender-responsive budgeting and raising awareness of available financial support, particularly for grassroots women's organizations, Indigenous peoples and local communities.[96] While it highlights the importance of gender mainstreaming, sex-disaggregated data and engagement with gender institutions and women's groups in national climate strategies and NDCs, it does not directly provide funding for gender-responsive implementation or capacity development.[97]

The Convention to Combat Desertification has also adopted the *Action Plan on Gender Equality*, which highlights the importance of Indigenous and rural women in implementation, particularly through strategic partnerships to mobilize women, leverage their knowledge and strengthen women's land rights.[98] However, the connections between women's contributions to implementation, capacity development and financing are only briefly addressed.[99]

Similarly, the Convention on Biological Diversity recognizes the vital role that women play in the conservation and sustainable use of biological diversity and affirms the need for their full participation at all levels of policymaking and implementation for biological diversity conservation.[100] The Convention has developed a *2015–2020 Gender Plan of Action*, aiming at stimulating and facilitating committed, collective action on gender equality in the context of biodiversity and at increasing awareness and understanding, and the capacity to address barriers to equal opportunity.[101] The *UNCBD's Gender Plan*

94 At COP 25, Parties agreed to a 5-year enhanced Lima work programme on gender and its gender action plan (UNFCCC, Decision 3/CP.25), which was amended because of the intermediate review of the implementation of the gender action plan at COP 27 (UNFCCC, Decision 24/CP.27).

95 UNFCCC, 'Five Reasons Why Climate Action Needs Women' (8 March 2023) <www.unfccc.int>, accessed 24 April 2025. At COP 29, Parties concluded the GAP review and decided to extend the enhanced work programme on gender for ten years (UNFCCC, Draft Decision -/CP.29).

96 UN Women, 'Advancing Gender-Responsive Synergies Across the Rio Conventions' (Working Paper, 2024) 10.

97 *Ibid.*

98 Cf. Gender, <www.unccd.int/land-and-life/gender/overview>, accessed 24 April 2025; UN Women (n 96) 10.

99 *Ibid.*

100 Convention on Biological Diversity (n 68), Preamble, para. 13.

101 Cf. Convention on Biological Diversity, 'Gender and Biodiversity, 2015–2020 Gender Plan of Action' <www.cbd.int/gender/action-plan>, accessed 24 April 2025.

of Action strongly advocates for women's and girls' equal access to financial services and credit, as well as for specific funding for gender-responsive implementation and gender-responsive budgeting. While it includes grassroots women, Indigenous peoples and local communities, it calls for a stronger connection between finance, implementation, capacity development and the work of women at the local level, with an emphasis on prioritizing financing for gender-responsive implementation.[102]

In its Preamble, the Minamata Convention on Mercury includes specific recognition of the disproportionate impact of mercury on women—especially pregnant women—children and future generations.[103] The Convention also adopted a *Gender Action Plan*, which 'provides a comprehensive blueprint for actions to promote gender equality.'[104] The Plan identifies 'the enabling conditions as well as specific policy and programmatic steps to mainstream gender and to work effectively towards gender equality and the empowerment of women and girls within all activities under the purview of the Convention'.[105] Despite the explicit recognition of the disproportionate effects of mercury on women and the development of a dedicated action plan, references to women remain limited and are not incorporated into the Convention's operative part, particularly that concerning States' obligations.[106] Furthermore, the vulnerability of women is not solely tied to their reproductive roles but also to the societal contexts in which they live and work—a factor not yet adequately addressed by the Minamata Convention.[107]

The Sendai Framework emphasizes the importance of women in implementing the goals of disaster risk reduction.[108] The Framework states that 'a gender, age, disability, and cultural perspective should be integrated in all policies and practices[109] and that 'women and their participation are critical to effectively managing disaster risk and designing, resourcing and implementing gender-responsive disaster risk reduction policies, plans and programmes'.[110] The Sendai Framework also stresses the importance of 'empowering women and persons with disabilities to take on public leadership roles and advocate for gender-equitable and universally accessible approaches to disaster response,

102 UN Women (n 96) 10.
103 On this point, cf. De Vido (n 1)
104 Conference of the Parties to the Minamata Convention on Mercury, Gender Action Plan (4 July 2023) UNEP/MC/COP.5/INF/10, para. 5.
105 *Ibid.*
106 See De Vido (n 1).
107 *Ibid.*
108 Sendai Framework, Preamble.
109 *Ibid.*, para. 19(d).
110 *Ibid.*, para. 36(a)(i).

recovery, rehabilitation, and reconstruction'. identifying this as a key recommendation to enhance disaster preparedness and ensure effective responses.[111] Finally, women, together with children and youth, persons with disabilities, older adults, Indigenous peoples and migrants, are recognized as key stakeholders in the disaster risk reduction process, whose active engagement must be guaranteed throughout the Framework's implementation.[112] However, while the Framework acknowledges the importance of women's representation and participation in the development and implementation of disaster risk reduction action,[113] it falls short of addressing deeper structural inequalities that exacerbate gendered vulnerabilities in disaster situations.[114] The Framework primarily focuses on short-term disaster impacts such as mortality rates, while overlooking other critical aspects.[115] Notably, it lacks indicators that capture women's contributions to disaster preparedness, response and recovery.[116] Additionally, it fails to include indicators to assess women's access to land, healthcare and financial resources.[117] Furthermore, the Framework lacks actionable strategies or implementation measures to ensure the meaningful participation, leadership and capacity building of women in disaster preparedness within concrete national and subnational planning and programming.[118] This narrow focus perpetuates the stereotype of women as passive victims rather than acknowledging their pivotal role in building resilience.[119] Similarly, the ILC's 2016 Draft Articles do not adequately address women's specific needs.[120] In this regard, the forthcoming treaty on the protection of persons in the event of disasters is expected to give greater consideration to the disproportionate effects of ECEs on certain categories of individuals particularly susceptible to disasters, including women.[121]

111 *Ibid.*, para. 32.

112 *Ibid.*, para. 36(a). Zehra Zaidi, Maureen Fordham, 'The missing half of the Sendai framework: Gender and women in the implementation of global disaster risk reduction policy' (2021) 10 *Progress in Disaster Science*, 3.

113 *Ibid.*, 36(a)(i).

114 Zaidi, Fordham (n 112), 3; Salvano Briceno, 'Looking Back and beyond Sendai: 25 years of international policy experience on disaster risk reduction' (2015) 6 *International Journal of Disaster Risk Science*, 1–7.

115 Zaidi, Fordham (n 112) 3.

116 *Ibid.*

117 *Ibid.*

118 *Ibid.*

119 *Ibid.*, 4.

120 See De Vido (n 1). In this perspective, Zaidi, Fordham (n 112).

121 See De Vido (n 1); Bartolini (n 60).

Based on the analysis conducted so far, it can be affirmed that existing agreements, related decisions and soft-law instruments demonstrate a global commitment to integrating gender perspectives into environmental and climate cooperation efforts and to promoting women's representation and inclusion in decision-making processes.

However, it is essential to highlight, also in relation to emerging cooperative efforts, that formal commitments to addressing gender disparities—and the need to reduce them—are insufficient, since international law itself can perpetuate patterns of discrimination and inequality, thereby contributing to structural violence against women.[122] Indeed, despite the growing recognition of ECEs' disproportionate impact on women and girls, this awareness has not significantly influenced policies at global, regional, or national levels.[123] While women's representation and participation are essential, they are not *transformative* unless dominant analytical categories—including the very concept of 'crisis'—are critically reviewed.[124] True gender-sensitive responses to phenomena exhibiting the characteristics of ECEs require not only short-term, reactive measures but also long-term, proactive strategies that address root causes of inequality, such as unequal access to resources, education and decision-making power. Without this broader perspective, the instruments analyzed above risk reinforcing the *status quo* rather than transforming it.[125]

For this reason, several human rights treaty bodies advocate for responses to ECEs that address intersectionality and women's structural inequalities,[126]

---

122 On this point, see De Vido (n 1).

123 Report of the Special Rapporteur on violence against women and girls, its causes and consequences, Reem Alsalem, 'Violence against women and girls in the context of the climate crisis, including environmental degradation and related disaster risk mitigation and response' (11 July 2022) UN Doc A/77/136, paras 12, 20, 59; Zaidi, Fordham (n 112).

124 See De Vido (n 1).

125 Zaidi, Fordham (n 112) 3.

126 As this book has already underlined, intersectionality is crucial for addressing inequalities, as it reveals how structural barriers and systemic discrimination disproportionately affect certain groups, requiring nuanced and inclusive approaches to justice and human rights. Women, especially those at the intersection of different grounds of discrimination—Black women, displaced women, Indigenous women, women belonging to minorities, low-income women, women with disabilities, girls etc.—are particularly affected by ECEs. In this regard, see De Vido (n 1). About intersectionality cf. Kimberle Crenshaw, 'Mapping the Margins: Intersectionality, Identity Politics, and Violence against Women of Color' (1991) 43 (6) *Stanford Law Review*, 1241; Lorena Sosa, Intersectionality in the Human Rights Legal Framework on Violence against Women (Cambridge University Press, 2017).

rejecting narratives that frame them solely as victims or saviours.[127] CEDAW General Recommendation No. 37 underscores women's role as 'agents of change'[128] advocates for their active participation in decision-making and recognition of their valuable knowledge and calls for addressing stigmatization in climate policies, challenging growth-driven ideologies, dismantling gender and human-nature hierarchies and reinforcing state responsibility and cross-border cooperation.[129] In this sense, from the ecofeminist approach underlying this book,[130] effective responses to ECEs must address gender inequality, the systemic exploitation of nature and the deep-rooted patterns of discrimination within society. This means that emerging cooperative efforts must consider systems of oppression, acknowledge that responsibility for ECEs often rests with specific segments of humanity and go beyond merely ensuring women's representation and participation.

4. CONCLUSION: STRENGTHENING GENDER-SENSITIVE COOPERATION IN ENVIRONMENTAL CHRONIC EMERGENCIES RESPONSES

The analysis conducted so far demonstrates States' increasing recognition of the need to cooperate in responding to ECEs, highlighting how the duty to cooperate has been progressively embedded in human rights, disaster, and environmental and climate change instruments. Recent developments have sought to define the content of this duty, particularly within environmental and climate-change frameworks. However, these cooperative efforts remain insufficient and inadequate in responding to the disproportionate impacts of ECEs on specific groups of individuals, particularly women. A critical aspect of enhancing cooperation in responding to ECEs lies in ensuring gender-sensitive responses, with policies and agreements explicitly and effectively addressing

---

127 Report of the Special Rapporteur on the promotion and protection of human rights in the context of climate change, Ian Fry, 'Exploring approaches to enhance climate change legislation, supporting climate change litigation and advancing the principle of intergenerational justice' (28 July 2023) UN Doc A/78/255; CEDAW Committee (n 18).

128 In this regard, Angela Hefti, 'Intersectional Victims as Agents of Change in International Human Rights-Based Climate Litigation' (2024) 13 (3) *Transnational Environmental Law*, 610.

129 CEDAW Committee (n 18) para. 46. See also Meghan Campbell, 'A Greener CEDAW: Adopting a women's substantive equality approach to climate change', in Cathi Albertyn et al. (eds), Feminist Frontiers in Climate Justice (Edward Elgar Publishing 2023) 90, 114.

130 See, footnote 5 in this chapter.

the unequal effects on women. Therefore, States should further strengthen cooperation by providing targeted education, training and leadership opportunities for women—especially those at the intersection of multiple forms of discrimination—while ensuring their access to climate finance, healthcare and sustainable livelihoods. Cooperation should also focus on improving data collection through the production of gender-specific statistics, including building technical capacity and providing financial support to these initiatives.[131] This would enable a shift in the perception of women from passive victims to active agents of change in decision-making processes, resulting in more effective, targeted and legally binding frameworks. Even more essential for achieving comprehensive, long-term solutions to ECEs is the ability of international cooperation to challenge and address systemic inequalities and deeply rooted power imbalances in society. Without dismantling existing structures of discrimination and oppression, cooperative efforts risk remaining superficial and failing to address the root causes of environmental crises and their disproportionate impacts on the groups of individuals made vulnerable by these schemes of discrimination and oppression.

131 Zaidi, Fordham (n 112).

13. Transforming slow violence into social justice: the quest for reparation for environmental chronic emergencies

Francesca Tammone

1. INTRODUCTION

It is a well-established principle that any breach of international rules gives rise to an obligation to make reparation.[1] Reparation, a corollary of international responsibility, is based on the concept of civil liability and can be considered a 'general conception of law'[2] rooted in ancient legal culture. Its archetype was paradigmatically regulated by Roman Law in the *restitutio in integrum*, an action aimed at *undoing* the effects of a harmful act by restoring the pre-damage condition (*status quo ante*).[3] This narrative, according to which the law—whenever possible—has to re-establish the situation affected by the breach *as if it had never occurred*, has also long permeated international law.[4]

However, the legal understanding of reparation has evolved considerably over time. Under contemporary international law, it should be argued that

[1] This principle is enshrined in Article 31 of the Draft Articles on Responsibility of States of International Wrongful Acts (adopted by the International Law Commission in 2001, with commentaries, UN Doc. A/56/10; hereinafter, 'ARSIWA'), which states that 'The responsible State is under an obligation to make *full reparation* for the injury caused by the internationally wrongful act'.

[2] *Case Concerning the Factory at Chorzów (Germany v Poland)* (Merits) PCIJ Rep Series A No 17, 29.

[3] Fritz Schulz, *Classical Roman Law* (OUP 1951) 65–8.

[4] This is clear from the long-standing international case law, starting with the 1928 leading case *Factory at Chorzów* (n 2). In that case, the Permanent Court of International Justice, while elaborating on the general principles of reparation, held that 'reparation must, as far as possible, *wipe out* all the consequences of the illegal act and *re-establish* the situation which would, in all probability, have existed if *that act had not been committed*' (at 47, emphasis added).

reparation is based on '*new* legal relations that arise from the commission by a State of an internationally wrongful act'.[5] That is, remedies for wrongdoing should aim to establish a new framework of obligations between victim and offender, including the duty to prevent further violations in the future. Such a 'corrective and transformative' function of reparation,[6] which has been mainly examined in studies on transitional justice mechanisms[7] in the aftermath of armed conflict or authoritarian regimes,[8] goes at the same pace as the growing recognition of a victim's rights to reparation in international law.[9]

---

[5] See International Law Commission (2001), p. 31, also cited by Paolo Palchetti, 'A Developing Field of Activity: Reparation for Breaches of Human Rights in the Case Law of the International Court of Justice' in Maren Heidemann (ed.), *The Transformation of Private Law—Principles of Contract and Tort as European and International Law. LCF Studies in Commercial and Financial Law. A Liber Amicorum for Mads Andenas* (Springer 2024) 233; see also, *mutatis mutandis,* Ruth Rubio-Marìn, 'Gender and Collective Reparation in the Aftermath of Conflict and Political Repression', in Ruth Rubio-Marìn (ed.), *The Gender of Reparations: Unsettling Sexual Hierarchies While Redressing Human Rights Violations* (CUP 2009) 383.

[6] Rubio-Marìn (n 5) 384.

[7] Diane Odier Contreras-Garduno, *Collective Reparations. Tensions and Dilemmas Between Collective Reparations and the Individual Rights to Receive Reparation,* (Human Rights Research Series 2019) 252. Coherently with that, literature is abundant on the topic of collective reparation for violations of international criminal law and international humanitarian law in transitional justice contexts. See, among others, Christine Evans, *The Right to Reparations in International Law for Victims of Armed Conflict* (CUP 2021); Jo-Anne Wemmers (ed.), *Reparation for Victims of Crimes against Humanity. The healing role of reparation* (Routledge 2014).

[8] East Timor, Sierra Leone, Morocco, Liberia, Colombia, Guatemala and Peru are examples of countries in which transitional justice programmes, such as the Truth Commission, have been implemented. For an in-depth analysis of the juridical aspects of this experience in Peru and Morocco, see Odier Contreras-Garduno (n 7) 256–60, with bibliography references. See also Julie Guillerot, *Reflections on the Collective Dimension of Reparations: Where We Are? Where To Go* (2022), at <https://reparations.qub.ac.uk> accessed 18 April 2025.

[9] The existence of a victim's right to reparation is now witnessed by several sources of international law, including human rights treaties and extensive practice. See, among others, UNGA, 'Basic Principles and Guidelines on the Right to a Remedy and Reparation for Victims of Flagrant Violations of Human Rights and Serious Breaches of Humanitarian Law', (16 December 2005), UN Doc A/RES/60/147 (here in advance, 'Basic Principles'); Institut de Droit International, 'Resolution on the Immunity from Jurisdiction of the State and of Persons Who Act on Behalf of the State in Case of International Crimes' (10 September 2009); *Legal*

These principles are of utmost importance when reflecting on possible remedies to Environmental Chronic Emergency (ECE), a concept with profound 'transformative' aspiration. As previous pages emphasized, integrating ECEs into international legal discourse calls for a paradigm shift in the way of conceiving international actors, law-making, justice and existing international obligations. This comprehensive and innovative reading of legal categories inevitably involves reparations as an essential means to reinforce rules and address specific victims' needs and concerns. It is, therefore, crucial to ask whether and to what extent reparation could assume a corrective and transformative function, thus contributing to reshaping the unjust power relationship on which ECE is grounded.[10]

In international environmental law, the function of reparation is still underdeveloped, as regulation in this area mainly focuses on primary rules of prevention and the establishment of compliance mechanisms.[11] Similarly, international disaster law, in the absence of a 'flagship treaty', mainly focuses on recovery and relief from disasters and hazards, and still lacks generally accepted specific rules on reparations.[12] In this context, remedial practice before human rights adjudicating bodies, already being tasked to provide remedies for ECEs, has therefore gained traction over the last few years.

Against this background, this Chapter explores recent case law to investigate whether international law is equipped with an adequate remedial toolbox to address ECEs. It mainly focuses on secondary rules, as an in-depth analysis of the primary rules is provided by other contributions in this volume. Liability of corporations and national case law also fall outside the scope of the present analysis.[13]

Consequences of the Construction of a Wall, Advisory Opinion, International Court of Justice (9 July 2004), paras 151–53. On the right to reparation, Riccardo Pisillo Mazzeschi, 'International obligations to provide for reparation claims?' In Albrecht Randelzhofer, Christian Tomuschat (eds), *State responsibility and the individual: reparation in instances of grave violations of human rights,* (Brill Nijhoff, 1999) 149.

10 On the theoretical background of this concept, see Sara De Vido, 'Feminist Legal Methods and Environmental Chronic Emergencies: Challenging the Anthropocentric and Androcentric International Legal System' in this Volume.

11 Pasquale De Sena, Massimo Starita, *Corso di diritto internazionale* (Il Mulino 2023) 352.

12 Giulio Bartolini, 'Il Progetto di Articoli della Commissione del Diritto Internazionale sulla «Protection of Persons in the Event of Disasters' (2017) 100 (3) *Rivista di Diritto Internazionale*, 677–8.

13 On this topic, Patricio Barbirotto, 'States and Corporations: Responsibility and Liability at the Crossroads', in this Volume.

To this end, the chapter is structured as follows. Section 2 first makes some premises on aspects related to international responsibility for wrongdoings related to ECEs and their remedial implications (Subsection 2.1). Specifically, it explains how the specific features of ECEs have legal consequences for quantifying environmental damage and the effectiveness of remedies (Subsection 2.2).

After having demonstrated that some international judges have overcome some hurdles related to international responsibility, Section 3 delves into the specific analysis of selected international remedial practices. It focuses on the latest trends in the right to a healthy environment (3.1) and large-scale, widespread pollution (3.2) to demonstrate that international adjudicating bodies are moving toward a 'transformative' approach to reparations. In light of this analysis, Section 4 engages in some considerations about the strengths and limitations of this case law. Finally, some conclusions are drawn.

2. A CALL FOR A PARADIGM SHIFT: PRESENT CHALLENGES TO THE WELL-SETTLED APPROACH TO INTERNATIONAL WRONGDOING AND REPARATION

When considering the legal consequences of ECEs, it is necessary to consider their scope, the obligations to which they relate, and how to frame the harmful effects they cause.[14] These issues have important implications for international responsibility, and, by extension, for reparations.[15] Some brief premises on contextual international responsibility are therefore appropriate (Subsection 2.1) to explore the features that reparation for ECEs might assume (Subsection 2.2).

2.1 Putting the International Responsibility Requirements to the Environmental Chronic Emergencies Test

The innovative and disruptive concept of ECE does not easily fit into a narrow understanding of international responsibility rules. Indeed, according to international customary law and the *Draft Articles on Responsibility of States for Internationally Wrongful Acts* (from now on, 'ARSIWA'), international

---

[14] In detail, Deborah Russo, 'Moving Beyond an Approach Based on Crisis and Disasters to Address Environmental Chronic Emergencies', in this Volume.

[15] International responsibility is a *sine qua* non for reparation. See *supra* at the Introduction of this Chapter.

responsibility is usually attributed to an identifiable actor[16] when there is a *sufficient* causal link between the wrongful conduct and the ensuing harm.[17] Since ARSIWA does not establish specific criteria to determine causation,[18] standards may vary depending on the context. When dealing with ECEs, the application of the 'condition *sine qua non* causation test', which prevails in the ICJ's case law and is also applied to environmental-related cases,[19] is particularly challenging.[20] Indeed, this requires assessing that the harm would not have occurred without the '*direct* and *certain*' contribution of a single state.[21] The circumstance that ECEs arise from slow, cumulative, and potentially eventless environmental harm presents significant challenges to such a well-settled, long-standing approach. Indeed, when dealing with incremental environmental degradation, emerging 'gradually and *out of sight*, [. . .]' and 'disbursed *across time and space*',[22] it could be difficult—and, sometimes, even impossible—to establish a *direct* causal link between a state and international wrongdoing, as also emerges from climate change disputes.[23]

Moreover, the transboundary effects of ECEs have often challenged the assessment of state jurisdiction over environmental harms. As well known, in this regard, the Inter-American Court of Human Rights (hereinafter, 'IACtHR' or 'San José Court') adopted a broad interpretation of Article 1 ACHR in its Advisory Opinion No. 23, clarifying that state extraterritorial jurisdiction covers environmental harms that occurred outside the state's territory, provided the state exercises effective control over the source of harm.[24] Shortly after, however, subsequent climate case law did not uphold this opinion, favouring instead a case-by-case approach. While some judgments adopt a narrow

---

16 In this regard, see Eliana Cusato, *The Ecology of War and Peace* (CUP 2021) 58.

17 This derives from Article 31 ARSIWA, establishing that states are obliged to make full reparation for the injury *caused* by their internationally wrongful act (n 1) 93.

18 ARSIWA (n 1) 92–3.

19 See, among others, *Certain Activities Carried Out by Nicaragua in the Border Area (Costa Rica v Nicaragua),* Merits, International Court of Justice, ICJ Reports 2015, 665 (16 December 2015).

20 In this regard, see André Nollkaemper, 'Causation Puzzles in International Climate Litigation' (2024), 33 *Italian Yearbook of International Law,* 25, 30.

21 *Ibid.*, 27.

22 Rob Nixon, *Slow Violence and the Environmentalism of the Poor* (Harvard University Press 2013), 2.

23 Nollkaemper (n 20) 27.

24 Advisory Opinion OC-23/17 Requested by the Republic of Colombia, 'The Environment and Human Rights', Inter-American Court of Human Rights Series A No. 23 (15 November 2017).

interpretation of international responsibility requirements,[25] others try to 'render human rights law fit for purpose on climate change'.[26] A recent example of a broad interpretation is provided by the landmark judgment *KlimaSeniorinnen v Switzerland,*[27] the only case in which the court has found a State party to the European Convention on Human Rights in breach of its treaty obligations related to climate change. In the case at issue, the Strasbourg Court had to determine whether Switzerland could be held responsible for the negative effects of pollution caused by the cumulative conduct of multiple 'big emitters'. However, it was found that the 'extraterritorial' aspect inherent to 'shared' greenhouse emissions did not impair Swiss jurisdiction in the case at issue. In fact, despite the negative impact of climate change resulting from the contribution of several states, all the applicants were residents of Switzerland.[28] Moreover, the court's reasoning repeatedly referred to 'the *special features* of the problem of climate change',[29] in light of which the causal link between the source of harm and damage is *necessarily more tenuous* and *indirect* than in cases involving *local sources* of harmful pollution.[30] In these words, some authors read a certain degree of 'attenuation' of the causal link between state conduct and the damage, or risk of damage, produced by that conduct.[31]

This example makes clear that a concrete integration of ECEs into legal discourse is not excluded *per se*, but rather requires an effort of broader and/or innovative interpretation by international courts and bodies. Undoubtedly, this approach is not exempt from risks, such as the withdrawal from the ECHR

---

25 See, for example, the decision of inadmissibility rendered by the European Court of Human Rights in the case *Duarte Agostinho and Others against Portugal and 32 Others,* App. No. 39371/20 (ECtHR 9 April 2024).

26 The expression is taken from the title of the article by Alice Venn, 'Rendering International Human Rights Law Fit for Purpose on Climate Change' (2023) *Human Rights Law Review,* 1.

27 *Verein KlimaSeniorinnen Schweiz and Others v Switzerland,* App No. 53600/20 (ECtHR 9 April 2024), hereinafter 'Klimaseniorinnen'.

28 *Ibid.*, paras 422–40.

29 *Ibid.*

30 *Ibid.*, para. 439. For in-depth reflections on the assessment of causation in this judgment, see Vladislava Stoyanova, '*KlimaSeniorinnen* and the Question(s) of Causation' (*Verfassungsblog* 7 May 2024) <https://verfassungsblog.de/klimaseniorinnen-and-the-questions-of-causation/>, accessed 30 March 2025.

31 Riccardo Pisillo Mazzeschi, 'Diritti umani e cambiamento climatico: brevi note sulla sentenza *KlimaSeniorinnen* della Corte di Strasburgo' (2024) 18 (2) *Diritti umani e diritto internazionale,* 383, 385.

in the face of a very broad expansion of the scope of human rights obligations through a firm stance by the ECtHR.[32]

However, the implications for redress for victims must not be underestimated. In fact, only the assessment of international responsibility opens the possibility of obtaining reparations. In this case, remedies have specific features that deserve further exploration.

2.2 Remedial Implications: Quantification and Effectiveness

Once that international responsibility for wrongdoing has been ascertained, it is up to international adjudicating bodies to determine *how* full reparation can be achieved. Provided that the possible forms of reparation may vary depending on the dispute parties' requests and the powers of the adjudicating body at stake, the ARSIWA established some general rules in this regard. As to the kind of reparations to be awarded, Article 34 ARSIWA mentions restitution, compensation and satisfaction—either singly or in combination. Importantly, restitution—which implies re-establishing, as far as possible, the *status quo ante*—'comes first among the forms of reparation'[33] and must be preferred over compensation or satisfaction, which should be awarded only when restitution is not possible or insufficient for full reparation.[34] While compensation provides a monetary quantification of the harm suffered as a result of wrongdoing, satisfaction consists of 'an acknowledgement of the breach, an expression of regret, a formal apology, or another appropriate modality'.[35]

Two additional forms of reparations, namely rehabilitation and the guarantees of non-repetition, are mentioned by the *Basic Principles and Guidelines on the Right to a Remedy and Reparation for Victims of Gross Violations of International Human Rights Law and Serious Violation of International Humanitarian Law of 2005*[36] and in the *ILA Draft Declaration on Reparation*

---

32 Regarding the position of Switzerland in the case at stake, see Lorenzo Acconciamessa, 'Il contenzioso climatico davanti alla Corte europea dei diritti umani, tra aspettative, rischi e realtà' (2024) 18 (2) *Diritti umani e diritto internazionale,* 369, 381.

33 ARSIWA (n 1) 96. The fact that *restitutio of integrum* is the primary source of reparation is also supported by the case law of human rights courts and treaty bodies, as noted by Giulio Bartolini, *Riparazione per violazione dei diritti umani e ordinamento internazionale* (Jovene 2009) 227–38.

34 Articles 36 and 37 ARSIWA (n 1).

35 Article 37 ARSIWA (n 1)

36 Basic Principles (n 9).

for Victims of Armed Conflict of 2010.[37] While rehabilitation is often referred to as the need for victims to receive medical, psychological, social and legal assistance,[38] guarantees of non-repetition are aimed at preventing further violations in the future, sometimes breaking 'the structural causes of societal violence'.[39] These forms of reparations, although not expressly contemplated by Article 34 ARSIWA, have increasingly gained momentum in the context of human rights reparations over the last years.[40] Especially, the IACtHR has largely applied both rehabilitation and guarantees of non-repetition in its case law.[41]

However, notwithstanding these recent developments, restitution and compensation are largely considered the two main forms of reparation under contemporary international law, even in environmental matters.[42] From the analysis of this practice, restitution measures are far less frequent than compensation measures,[43] although restoring the *status quo ante* is—intuitively—the most appropriate form of reparation for this kind of harm. As an example, restitution may include revegetation in case of deforestation, reintroduction of wild species, repopulation of rivers and so on.[44]

Nonetheless, concretely implementing such measures can be extremely difficult—or sometimes even impossible. Article 35 ARSIWA expressly contemplates this possibility, where it excludes restitution from being awarded when restoring the *status quo ante* is materially impossible or involves a *disproportionate burden* compared to compensation.[45] The practice of international

---

37 International Law Association 'Declaration of International Law Principles on Reparation for Victims of Armed Conflict (Substantive Issues)' (15–20 August 2010), <https://www.ila-hq.org/en_GB/documents/conference-resolution-the-hague-2010-english> accessed 18 April 2025.

38 Odier Contreras-Garduno, *Collective Reparations* (n 7), 87.

39 African Commission on Human and Peoples' Rights, 'General Comment No. 4 on the African Charter on Human and Peoples' Rights: The Right to Reparation for Victims of Torture and Other Cruel, Inhuman or Degrading Treatment or Punishment (Article 5)' (4 March 2017), para. 45.

40 Odier Contreras-Garduno, *Collective Reparations* (n 7) 75.

41 *Ibid.*

42 Saverio Di Benedetto, 'Restitution and Compensation for Environmental Damage in International Law: Towards an Ecological Approach' (2024) 33 *Italian Yearbook of International Law,* 197–9.

43 *Ibid.*, 201.

44 *Mutatis mutandis*, Ann Carette, 'Right to a healthy environment and the remediation of ecological damage: seeking effective remedies?' in Hendrick Schoukens, Farah Bouquelle (eds), *The Right to a Healthy Environment in and Beyond the Anthropocene* (Edward Elgar Publishing 2024) 304–7.

45 Article 35 ARSIWA (n 1).

courts—frequently awarding compensation for environmental-related damages—fully reflects this legal framework.[46] In these cases, one of the main issues in the background concerns the *quomodo* of compensation. In fact, in most disputes, 'environment' is considered a mere 'intermediate' element in the occurrence of damage to other interests.[47] As a result, international law still does not provide a uniform method for calculating 'pure' environmental damage,[48] e.g., damage to the environment *itself*,[49] including harm to environmental resources that have no commercial value.[50] Such uncertainty has had significant practical implications, as recently emerged in the landmark judgment of *Costa Rica v Nicaragua*,[51] when the ICJ's method for calculating damage was deemed 'unclear',[52] leaving many questions unanswered regarding the most appropriate methodology to be used in these cases.

Undoubtedly, such a broader debate on compensation for 'pure' environmental damage inevitably informs legal research on remedies for the harmful effects of ECEs. In particular, this discussion brings to light the necessity of wondering whether and how to provide monetary compensation for damage affecting territories and local communities. However, it needs to be emphasized that dealing with remedies for ECEs implies additional issues in light

---

46 See, among others, *Corfu Channel (United Kingdom v Albania)*, Judgment, Merits, International Court of Justice, ICJ Reports 194, 4 (9 April 1949); *Case Concerning Ahmadou Sadio Diallo*, Judgment on compensation, International Court of Justice, ICJ Reports 2012, 324 (19 June 2012).

47 Carette (n 44) 304.

48 Di Benedetto (n 42) 212.

49 Carette (n 44) 305. As noted by the Author, this kind of damage, referred to as 'ecological damage' [. . .] 'differs from bodily injuries caused by pollution, property damage caused by illegal logging or economic losses suffered by fishermen after an oil spill at sea, making fishing temporarily impossible. The environment only plays an intermediate role in the occurrence of these forms of *personal* damage' (ibid.).

50 Kévine Kindji Gaspard, Michael Faure, 'Assessing reparation of environmental damage by the ICJ: A lost opportunity?' (2019) *Questions of International Law, Zoom-in 57*, 5–7.

51 *Certain Activities carried out by Nicaragua in the Border Area (Costa Rica v Nicaragua)*, Judgment, Compensation owed by the Republic of Nicaragua to the Republic of Costa Rica, International Court of Justice, I.C.J. Reports 2018, 15 (2 February 2018).

52 Elena Fasoli, 'The ICJ and the compensation for environmental damage in the Costa Rica/Nicaragua case: Does the application of equitable principles offset independent technical expertise?' (2019) *Questions of International Law, Zoom-in 57*, 1–3.

of their specific features. From this perspective, at least two aspects warrant particular attention.

First, the cumulative process behind ECEs makes it difficult to determine the apportionment of damage.[53] Given that international responsibility rules require that states must provide full reparation to the extent of the damage they have caused, establishing the *quantum* of reparation of a single state is challenging when causation is blurred.[54]

Second, when reparations for ECEs are at stake, monetary compensation can prove unsatisfactory from a victim-centered perspective. Indeed, compensation can only provide *partial* redress for victims, since while it may restore actual harm, it is unable to capture the structural and systemic nature inherent in the harm suffered, which arises from prolonged and incremental unlawful violence against the environment.

However, current environmental challenges have inevitably compelled international judges to confront these emerging concerns and overcome these hurdles in order to redress victims. This can also be reconducted to applicants' requests in some disputes (like climate ones), which are more often aimed at raising awareness of climate change obligations than at obtaining monetary compensation. As a result, in parallel with some international courts' 'shifting the paradigm' in the legal understanding of international responsibility, a 'modulation' of remedies is also gradually emerging before international courts, as explained in the foregoing.

3. TRANSFORMATIVE REPARATIONS? INSIGHTS FROM A SELECTED PRACTICE

Some recent decisions show an attentiveness to the potential 'corrective' function of reparations, whose purpose may extend beyond the strict necessity of repairing the actual harm to include long-term strategies for the future. For the purposes of this chapter, it can be argued that this type of reparation is 'transformative' in the sense that it sometimes addresses the underlying causes of the wrongful act or has the potential to reshape the relationship between the parties to a dispute. As examples of that, the following subsections are limited to a focus on case law about the right to a healthy environment and on recent practices of the ECtHR.

53 Nollkaemper (n 20) 47–53.

54 See *supra*, para. 2.1.

3.1 Beyond Monetary Compensation: Reparation in the Jurisprudence on the Right to a Healthy Environment

As noted *supra*, the reflection on remedies for 'pure' environmental damages is deeply connected to the legal response to ECEs, underlying slow violence against the environment, understood as a *unicum* comprising humans and non-humans as intertwined elements.[55]

In human rights treaties, the protection of the environment *per se* is currently a widely debated issue. Among human rights treaties, only the African Charter of Human and Peoples' Rights[56] and the San Salvador Protocol to the American Convention on Human Rights[57] enshrine it. By contrast, other treaties, like the European Convention on Human Rights (ECHR) and the International Covenant on Civil and Political Rights (ICCPR), do not expressly address environmental matters.[58] However, the right to a healthy environment has been interpreted as implicit in other rights, like the right to life, as emerging, *inter alia*, from the ECtHR's case law starting with the 1994 *Lopez Ostra* case.[59] The Human Rights Committee has instead only recently recognized the nexus between harm to the environment and the right to life in the case of *Portillo Cáceres v Paraguay*.[60] Just a couple of months later, the Committee confirmed this finding in its first decision on climate migration, *Teitiota v New Zealand*.[61]

Despite not expressly relying on the existence of an autonomous right to a healthy environment, some reparation measures show a broad understanding of the connections between environmental harm, living communities and means to prevent further violations in the future. While specific considerations

---

[55] De Vido (n 10).

[56] Specifically, Article 24 ACHRPR.

[57] Additional Protocol to the American Convention on Human Rights in the Area of Economic, Social, and Cultural Rights ('San Salvador Protocol'), signed at San Salvador, El Salvador (17 November 1988), Article 11.

[58] However, recent climate litigation has reopened discussion about the adoption of an Additional Protocol to the ECHR on the right to a healthy environment: <https://ennhri.org/news-and-blog/ennhri-publishes-paper-on-climate-change-and-human-rights-in-the-european-context/> accessed 30 March 2025.

[59] *Lopez Ostra v Spain*, App. No. 16798/89 (ECtHR 19 December 1994); see also, among others, *Öneryıldız v Turkey* [GC], App no. 48939/99 (ECtHR 30 November 2004), *Guerra and Others v Italy*, Apps 116/1996/735/932 (ECtHR 19 February 1998).

[60] *Portillo Cáceres and Others v Paraguay*, Communication 2751/2016 (25 July 2019), UN Doc. CCPR/C/126/D/2751/2016.

[61] *Ioane Teitiota v New Zealand*, Communication 2728/2016, (24 October 2019) UN Doc. CCPR/C/127/D/2728/2016, para. 9.9.

on the ECtHR's case law will be made in Subsection 3.2, recent trends in the decisions of the Human Rights Committee (hereinafter 'HRC') can be mentioned. For example, the case *Daniel Billy v Australia* (also known as the 'Strait Torres Islanders' case)[62] addressed Australia's failure to adopt adequate measures to prevent and mitigate the detrimental effects of climate change.[63] In recognizing the breach of Articles 17 and 27 of the ICCPR, the HRC asked the Australian government not only to compensate victims for the harm suffered, but also to engage in 'meaningful' consultations with communities to conduct 'needs assessments'.[64] Hence, the effective participation of victims in the reparation process was considered *as part of the reparation as a whole*, and a means to foster prevention and ensure the community continues to survive on its territory.

However, the jurisprudence on an *autonomous* right to a healthy environment undoubtedly provides for an even more progressive approach. The main reference here is the case law of the IACtHR, which, among human rights regional courts, has developed the most articulated approach to remedies for collective claims, with reparation orders designed to meet the collective needs of entire communities.[65] In this context, both satisfaction and guarantees of non-repetition have gained prominence as means of reparations, given their preventive vocation and capacity to meet the needs of entire groups of victims. This is clear, for example, in the copious jurisprudence on Indigenous people's land rights,[66] also regarding the serious effects on the well-being of Indigenous communities caused by illegal infrastructural and exploitative activities (such as the granting of logging and mining concessions) within their traditional territory. In this context, the IACtHR has awarded measures for the rehabilitation of the territory, including the necessary measures to remediate any adverse

---

62 *Daniel Billy et al. v Australia*, Communication 3624/2019 (21 July 2022) UN Doc. CCPR/C/135/D/3624/2019.

63 *Ibid.*, para. 2.3.

64 *Ibid.*, para. 11.

65 Guillerot (n. 8) 8.

66 Among others, *Case of the Saramaka People v Suriname*, Preliminary Objections, Merits, Reparations and Costs, Judgment, Inter-American Court of Human Rights Series C No 172 (28 November 2007); *Case of The Kaliña and Lokono peoples v Suriname*, Merits, Reparations and Costs, Inter-American Court of Human Rights Series C No 309 (25 November 2015); *Mayagna (Sumo) Awas Tingi Community v Nicaragua,* Merits, Reparations and Costs, Inter-American Court of Human Rights Series C No 79 (31 August 2001). On this topic, see Enzamaria Tramontana, 'The contribution of the inter-American human rights bodies to evolving international law on Indigenous rights over lands and natural resources' (2010) 17 *International Journal on Minority and Group Rights*, 241.

effects of exploitative industrial practices or reforestation.[67] In so doing, it also emphasized that several practices, like the forced eviction of local communities from their ancestral lands, relied on structural discrimination.[68] In these stances, the IACtHR seems to have incorporated a transformative conception of reparation, already endorsed in other disputes. In its words, provided that wrongdoings have occurred in the context of *structural discrimination*, '[. . .] reparations must be designed to change this situation so that their effect is not only one of *restitution but also of rectification*. In this regard, the reestablishment of the same structural context of violence and discrimination is not acceptable'.[69]

However, despite addressing the negative impact of natural resources exploitation on local communities, the IACtHR in its case law/jurisprudence on Indigenous Peoples' land rights has rarely framed this human conduct as violence against the environment, whose protection has rather been considered merely 'functional' to the well-being of local inhabitants and the enjoyment of other conventional rights.[70] This 'anthropocentric' approach to environmental-related cases[71] is reflected in the IACtHR's interpretation of the right to live in a healthy environment under Article 11 of the San Salvador Protocol, which is treated as a corollary to the right to property, the right to life and the right to have access to information.[72]

The IACtHR overcame such an interpretation only in 2017, when it recognized the existence of a standalone right to a healthy environment under the scope of Article 26 of the ACHR on states' duty to adopt measures to achieve progressive development of the treaty's social, educational, scientific and cultural standards. The IACtHR first elaborated these findings in Advisory

---

67 See, for example, IACtHR, *Kaliña and Lokono peoples v Suriname* (n 66), para. 290.

68 Tramontana (n 66) 253.

69 *Case of González et al. (Cotton Field) v Mexico*, Preliminary Objection, Merits, Reparations, and Costs, Inter-American Court of Human Rights Series C No. 205 (16 November 2009), para. 450 (emphasis added).

70 Enzamaria Tramontana, 'The Right to a Healthy Environment before the Inter-American Court of Human Rights: Some Remarks in the Aftermath of the Judgment in *Habitantes de La Oroya v Perú*' (2025) 1 *Rivista Giuridica dell'Ambiente*, 125, 135.

71 *Ibid.*

72 The possibility of invoking Article 11 of the San Salvador Protocol had seemed to be prevented by Article 19 (6) of the same treaty, which limits the jurisdiction of the IACtHR only to trade union rights and the right to education. In this regard, see Lucas Carlos Lima, 'The Protection of the Environment before the Inter-American Court of Human Rights: Recent Developments', (2020) 3 *Rivista Giuridica dell'Ambiente*, 495, 496.

Opinion No. 23,[73] and, a few months later, in its judgment in *Lhaka Honhat v Argentina*.[74] In this decision, the IACTHR ordered several measures with a collective impact, such as the creation of an effective mechanism for the demarcation and titling of Indigenous communities' territories, the elaboration of a specific action plan to address their basic needs and the inclusion of Indigenous community victims in policymaking on the utilization of natural resources.[75] However, despite recognizing Argentina's responsibility for breaching Article 26 of the ACHR, the *Lhaka Honhat* judgment did not substantially depart from the anthropocentric approach adopted in the IACtHR's pre-2017 jurisprudence.[76] This emerges not only from the merits of the case decision but also from the reparation order. Parallel to the fact that damage to the natural environment per se was not even considered, reparation measures were limited to addressing the negative impact of environmental degradation on the enjoyment of Indigenous peoples' rights, thus missing the opportunity to grasp and to address the legal consequences of 'pure' environmental damage.

In this perspective, the 2024 judgment *Inhabitants of La Oroya v Peru*[77] represented a landmark milestone for its evolutionary approach to the right to a healthy environment. This judgment, in which the IACtHR directly addressed an environmental emergency not involving Indigenous peoples for the first time,[78] is of utmost importance for this chapter for several reasons.

First, the facts in the *La Oroya* case exemplify ECE, since the IACtHR held Peru responsible for the harmful effects of high-level pollution in La Oroya caused by a metallurgical complex established in 1922. The pollution led to severe environmental damage and health risks for the local population,

---

73 Advisory Opinion OC-23/17 (n 24).

74 *Case of Indigenous Community Members of the Lhaka Honhat (Our Land) Association v Argentina*, Merits, reparations and costs, IACtHR Series C No. 400 (6 February 2020).

75 *Ibid.*, para. 334. Consultation with the Indigenous community was considered crucial also in other judgments, e.g., *Case of Kichwa Indigenous Peoples of Sarayaku v Ecuador*, Merits, Reparations, Costs, Inter-American Court of Human Rights Series C No 245 (27 June 2012), para. 289.

76 Tramontana (n 70) 134.

77 *Case of La Oroya Population v Peru,* Preliminary Objections, Merits, Reparations and Costs, Inter-American Court of Human Rights Series C No. 511 (27 November 2023). Here in advance, 'La Oroya'.

78 José Saldaña, '*People from La Oroya vs Peru*, Inter-American Court of Human Rights: How Effective is International Law to Protect the Environment in Extractive Contexts?' (*EJIL:Talk!* 11 April 2024) <https://www.ejiltalk.org/people-from-la-oroya-vs-peru-inter-american-court-of-human-rights-how-effective-is-international-law-to-protect-the-environment-in-extractive-contexts/> accessed 9 December 2025.

including the 80 applicants, with metals detected in their bloodstream. The IACtHR found violations of multiple rights, including the right to a healthy environment, health, personal integrity, life, political participation, children's rights and progressive development.[79]

In its ruling, the IACtHR upheld an innovative reading of the right to a healthy environment, also reflected in extensive reparations. Having found that this right includes the protection of human health, the San José court stressed that states must prevent environmental damage even in the absence of scientific certainty about the consequences of human conduct on people's health.[80] It therefore reinforced the precautionary principle, according to which states cannot evade their responsibility by relying on uncertain causal links between their conduct and harmful effects on the environment.[81] Such an 'anticipatory' approach is reflected in reparation orders aimed at directly protecting the environment per se, rather than merely serving as an intermediary for human well-being.[82] Among these measures, some non-reparation guarantees deserve mention: the implementation of a plan for the integral recovery of the local ecosystems of La Oroya; the harmonization of legislation on air quality standards to keep the content of polluting metals within the maximum permitted limits so as not to endanger the environment and human health; the monitoring of air quality in La Oroya and the compliance of metallurgical activities with environmental standards; and the training of state agents in environmental matters.[83] Such a broad understanding of reparation makes it clear that the right to a healthy environment should aim not only to protect human health, but also 'the health of the different components of the environment themselves'.[84]

However, the IACtHR's 'transformative' approach to reparation in *La Oroya* can also be read in the order to establish a baseline diagnosis of contamination, develop an action plan to repair the damage within 18 months and prioritize high-risk areas. Moreover, some reparation measures aimed at strengthening local consultation were provided, given that Peru had not informed local

---

79 *La Oroya* (n 77) para. 266.

80 *Ibid.*, para. 133.

81 The precautionary principle was first established in the Rio Declaration on Environment and Development (12 August 1992), UN Doc A/CONF.151/26 (Vol. I) at Principle 15. This principle has then been embodied in other treaties. It is provided, among others, by Article 3(3) of the United Nations Framework Convention on Climate Change, the Preamble of the Biodiversity Convention, Article 3 of the Convention on the Protection and Use of Transboundary Watercourses and International Lakes, and Article 191 TFUE.

82 Tramontana (n 70) 139.

83 *La Oroya* (n 77) paras 342–55.

84 Tramontana (n 70) 139.

communities about the serious risk of high-level pollution in the area, nor had it introduced effective measures to involve the community in environmental decision-making and give the victims a meaningful voice or influence over policy.[85] These reparation measures, by enhancing the cruciality of access to information and political participation in environmental matters,[86] can contribute to remedying the pre-existing exclusionary dynamics embedded in society. Indeed, the court's will to 'rebalance' unjust power relationships in social structures through reparations also emerges in the order to establish specialized medical care for children, pregnant mothers and the elderly. This is clear from the IACtHR's acknowledgement of the disproportionate impact of environmental pollution on some groups and communities that already bear the burden of poverty and environmental degradation,[87] either because they live in environmentally protected areas or because they are economically dependent on natural resources.

Against this backdrop, it is quite surprising that the San José court missed the chance to recognize the unequal impacts of environmental pollution on women,[88] now attested by several international documents[89] confirming the causal link between air pollution and pregnancy risks, or between saline contamination of drinking water and maternal health,[90] with violent repercussions on women's sexual and reproductive rights (including, but not limited to, maternal health). As already underlined in other chapters, the IACtHR could

---

85 *La Oroya* (n 77), paras 253–60.

86 In this regard, see Thalia Viveros-Uehara, '*La Oroya* and Inter-American Innovations on the Right to a Healthy Environment', (*Verfassungsblog* 16 May 2024) <https://verfassungsblog.de/la-oroya-and-inter-american-innovations-on-the-right-to-a-healthy-environment/> accessed 30 March 2025.

87 *La Oroya* (n 77) 252–62.

88 Dina Lupin, Maria Antonia Tigre, Natalia Urzola Gutiérrez, 'KlimaSeniorinnen and Gender' (*Verfassungsblog* 9 May 2024)<https://verfassungsblog.de/klimaseniorinnen-and-gender/> accessed 30 March 2025.

89 See, among others, Gender Responsive Climate Action; Special Rapporteur of Violence the Effects of Climate Change against Women Report on COVID; CEDAW Committee, 'General recommendation No. 37 (2018) on the gender-related dimensions of disaster risk reduction in the context of climate change' (13 March 2018) UN Doc CEDAW/C/GC/37; Human rights of older women: the intersection between aging and gender, UN Doc. A/76/157; Human Rights Council, 'The Impact of Climate Change on the Human Rights of People in Vulnerable Situations', A/HRC/50/57, para. 45.

90 IPFF, The climate crisis and sexual and reproductive health and rights (2021) at <https://www.ippf.org/sites/default/files/2021-03/IPPF%20position%20paper%20The%20climate%20crisis%20and%20sexual%20and%20reproductive%20health%20and%20rights_Jan2021.pdf>, accessed 30 March 2025.

have stressed the interconnections between the exposure to toxic materials and the disproportionate impact on women's health, also ordering remedies tailored to these specific needs and concerns.[91]

3.2 Broadening the Picture: Recent developments in the ECtHR's case-law on the Application of General Measures in Environmental Matters

Parallel to the significant developments in the Inter-American human rights system, the ECtHR's recent case law on reparations for high-level pollution is worth examining.

Regarding climate-change-related concerns, the *KlimaSeniorinnen* case[92] raised the issue of the adequacy of the ECHR remedial toolbox to address ECEs. In its complaint, the KlimaSeniorinnen association—the only applicant to whom the ECtHR recognized victim status under Article 34 ECHR[93]—did not claim compensation under Article 41 ECHR, but invoked the application of Article 46 ECHR[94]. This request was intended to provide a legal basis for the application, in climate cases, of general measures, which can be ordered by the ECtHR both within and outside[95] the pilot judgment procedure provided by Article 61 of the Rules of the Court.[96] In this regard, the ECtHR stressed that it was impossible to specify the measures that Switzerland should take, since it is primarily up to states to choose suitable measures to implement the judgment. Coherently with that, the ECtHR indicated some general yet very detailed measures to reduce emissions, but missed the opportunity to engage in deeper clarifications on the possible remedies in climate-change-related disputes.[97]

---

91 Enzamaria Tramontana, 'Environmental Chronic Emergencies, Women's Inequality, and International Law', in this Volume.

92 *KlimaSeniorinnen* (n 27).

93 On this issue, Acconciamessa (n 34) 369–82.

94 *KlimaSeniorinnen* (n 27) 647.

95 Andrea Saccucci, *La responsabilità internazionale dello Stato per violazioni strutturali dei diritti umani* (Editoriale Scientifica 2018), 35, with references at note 75. See also Philip Leach et al., *Responding to Systemic Human Rights Violations. An Analysis of the 'Pilot Judgments' of the European Court of Human Rights and their Impact at National Level* (Antwerp-Oxford-Portland 2010), 24–5.

96 Article 61 Rules of the Court.

97 Miriam Cohen et al., 'Reparation for Climate Change at the ECtHR: A Missed Opportunity or the First of Many Decisions to Come?' <https://verfassungsblog.de/reparation-for-climate-change-at-the-ecthr/> accessed 30 March 2025.

However, in a very recent judgment, *Cannavacciuolo and Others v Italy,*[98] the ECtHR took further steps towards renewed attention to the complexities in addressing environmental harm. In this case, Italy was held responsible for breaching Article 2 ECHR by failing to deal with the large-scale pollution arising from the dumping, burying or burning of waste in the area known as *Terra dei fuochi*. According to the ECtHR, Italy had not adequately protected the applicants' lives with the due diligence specifically required to assess serious health risks, prevent their continuation and communicate them to the affected public. Nevertheless, the State was deemed aware of the illegal dumping and burial of hazardous waste since at least the early 1990s, and of illegal incineration since at least 2004.[99] Analogously, Italian authorities have been considered aware that increased rates of cancer and groundwater pollution had been recorded in the area.[100]

The seriousness of such circumstances led the Strasbourg Court to review its previous case law on the 'causation test' in environment-related human rights violations. In earlier cases involving the threat to life in highly polluted areas,[101] the ECtHR had held that a violation of Article 2 ECHR could only be established in light of evidence of a causal link between the pollution and the applicants' illness. Accordingly, it was considered necessary to demonstrate that exposure to an identifiable type of pollution had caused the onset of a *specific*, life-threatening illness or death.[102] The same high threshold was also required in most environmental cases concerning Article 8 ECHR.[103]

By contrast, in *Cannavacciuolo and Others v Italy*, an 'imminent', '*ongoing, omnipresent* and *unavoidable for decades*' risk to the applicants' health was found sufficient to trigger positive obligations under Article 2 ECHR.[104]

98 *Cannavacciuolo and Others v Italy*, Apps Nos. 51567/14 and three others (ECtHR 30 January 2025).

99 *Ibid*., para. 387.

100 *Ibid*., para. 388.

101 See, for example, *Cordella and Others v Italy*, Apps. 54414/13 and 54264/15 (ECtHR 24 January 2019) paras 100–109.

102 *Brincat v Italy*, App. no. 13867/88 (ECtHR 26 November 1992), para. 83.

103 The *KlimaSeniorinnen* judgment makes an exception, as noted by Lorenzo Acconciamessa, 'The Strange Case of Dr Jeckyll and Mr Hyde: Victim Status for Life-Threatening Environmental Harm in the ECtHR's Judgment *Cannavacciuolo and Others v Italy*', (*SIDIBlog* 28 February 2025) <http://www.sidiblog.org/2025/02/28/the-strange-case-of-dr-jeckyll-and-mr-hyde-victim-status-for-life-threatening-environmental-harm-in-the-ecthrs-judgment-cannavacciuolo-and-others-v-italy/> accessed 30 March 2025.

104 *Cannavacciuolo* (n 98) para. 390 (emphasis added). The ECtHR found it unnecessary to deal with Article 8 ECHR, also invoked by the applicants, given its findings on Article 2 ECHR.

Therefore, this standing can be read as an endorsement of a precautionary approach, which had rarely been applied by the ECtHR to date.[105] In fact, the prolonged inaction of the Italian Government in handling the contamination of *Terra dei Fuochi* was considered unacceptable, given that 'the general risk had been known *for a long time* [. . .]' and that 'no scientific certainty about the precise effects the pollution may have had on the health of a particular applicant can negate the existence of a protective duty'.[106]

These findings are reflected in the reparation order. The 'systematic failure to respond adequately, both in terms of time and effort, to the pollution problem under scrutiny'[107] and the 'ongoing' and '*persistent* nature' of the widespread pollution also led the ECtHR to apply the pilot-judgment procedure for the first time in environmental matters.[108] As is known, this procedure—which is conceived as a means to reduce the Court's caseload—applies to cases that reveal the existence of 'a structural or systemic problem or *other similar dysfunction*',[109] and it is often combined with the indication of general remedial measures to be taken at the domestic level within a determined time limit. Despite the ECtHR usually being reluctant to indicate these measures in cases featuring high 'technical complexity',[110] the *Cannavacciuolo* judgment indicated several general measures to be implemented within a 2-year time limit. These include the development of a comprehensive strategy, the setup of an independent monitoring system, consultations with local stakeholders to identify actions to combat illegal waste disposal and investigate health impacts and, lastly, the creation of a public information platform to update the community on interventions and their status.

In light of its recentness, it is still uncertain if these assumptions from the ECtHR will lead to a real jurisprudential development. However, the acknowledgement and subsequent remedial response to an *ongoing* environmental emergency may also have significant implications for future disputes related to ECEs. To this end, it is essential that judges underscore the 'unseen' and persistent nature of *slow violence*, which requires a precautionary approach. Hopefully, future judgments could also engage in critical considerations of the gendered burden of serious and continuous environmental challenges. Indeed,

105 See, for example, *Tătar v Romania*, App. 67021/01 (ECtHR 27 January 2009), para. 107.

106 *Cannavacciuolo*, (n 98) para. 391.

107 *Ibid*., para. 490.

108 Jasmine Sommardal, 'A Landmark Judgment: Three Crucial Aspects of *Cannavacciuolo and Others v Italy*' (*ECHR Blog* 4 February 2025) <https://www.echrblog.com/2025/02/by-dr.html> accessed 30 March 2025.

109 Article 61 ECHR Rules of the Court.

110 Sommardal (n 108), with reference to *Cordella and Others v Italy*.

the *Cannavacciuolo* judgment, in line with the ECtHR's previous case law, is silent on the differentiated impact of environmental challenges on groups with less power and fewer resources in society, such as women. As a result, reparations in the European human rights regional system are far less progressive and articulated than those in the Inter-American regional system.

4. FROM REPARATIONS TO SOCIAL JUSTICE: INCLUSION AND PARTICIPATION AS PATHWAYS OF TRANSFORMATION

The above analysis highlights several critical points regarding reparations for victims of ECEs, whose harm is both difficult to localize and to monetise. However, it may be argued that international law has been adapting to these challenges to provide redress for victims. To this end, several measures have been implemented: remedies beyond monetary compensation, a focus on collective measures and the strengthening of preventive actions. In this context, for reparation to adequately respond to ECEs, the identification of their 'chronic' character—combined with an evolutive interpretation of international legal categories—is indispensable for embracing comprehensive solutions instead of short-term, individualized remedies.

This transformative approach to reparations is reflected in measures that foster social dialogue and participation among previously excluded social groups, in line with the *ratio* of the Convention of Aarhus.[111] Greater inclusion and participation of people with less power and fewer resources in society's decision-making contribute to overturning previous exclusionary dynamics, as partially emerges from the *La Oroya* case, which even differentiates reparations depending on the gender or age of victims, including women and children.

This differentiated approach to reparations, modeled on specific vulnerabilities, may potentially be strengthened in the future in light of the unequal impacts of environmental challenges—including climate change—depending on gender,[112] age or both at the same time.[113] In particular, international

---

[111] Convention on Access to Information, Public Participation in Decision-making and Access to Justice in Environmental Matters, adopted on 25 June 1998 in Aarhus (Denmark). The Aarhus Convention put Principle 10 of the Rio Declaration on Environment and Development into practice. This principle provides that access to information, access to public participation and access to justice are key pillars of environmental governance.

[112] Lupin, Tigre and Gutiérrez (n 88).

[113] Angela Hefti, *Intersectionality and Standing in Climate-Related Human Rights Cases* (2024), <https://hrp.law.harvard.edu/intersectionality-standing-and

practice on reparations remains largely silent on how climate change perpetuates gender inequality.[114] Even the IACtHR's jurisprudence, which reflects a truly progressive and articulated approach to reparations, still overlooks the existing connection between gender and human rights. For example, the landmark judgment in *La Oroya,* despite acknowledging the specific vulnerabilities of some of the case's applicants, did not include specialized reparation measures for women. Similarly, in *Lhaka Honat v Argentina,*[115] the active role that Indigenous women might play in the climate change mitigation process was not considered in the reparation order, although this aspect had been highlighted in the *amicus curiae* brief submitted to the court by the Fundación Ambiente y Recursos Naturales (FARN).[116]

In light of these circumstances, some scholars have already advocated for a change in legal methodology by relying on the contribution of feminist or ecofeminist theories and approaches.[117] According to this growing body of literature, considering gender issues in environmental jurisprudence could potentially reduce existing gender-based inequalities, stereotypes and oppression in society, thereby contributing to reducing women's vulnerability to discrimination and abuses in the future.[118] Moreover, as to reparation, 'the possibilities for a project of reparations that seeks both corrective redress for victims and (transformative) progress in dismantling patriarchy'[119] must not be underestimated.

-climate-change-and-human-rights/> accessed 9 December 2025.

114 OHCHR, 'Analytical study on gender-responsive climate action for the full and effective enjoyment of the rights of women. Report of the Office of the United Nations High Commissioner for Human Rights' (1 May 2021), UN Doc. A/HRC/41/26, 3.

115 *Lhaka Honhat* (n 74).

116 Specifically, the FARN's amicus *curiae brief* stressed how Indigenous women's special traditional ecological knowledge should be considered 'one of the most appropriate solutions to climate change' (see note no. 251 in *Lhaka Honhat,* (n 74)). However, this issue does not have space in the *corpus* of the legal reasoning.

117 Among others, Cathi Albertyn et al., *Feminist Frontiers in Climate Justice* (Edward Elgar Publishing 2023); Ruth Rubio Marin, *The Gender of Reparations: Unsettling Sexual Hierarchies While Redressing Human Rights Violations* (CUP 2009). See also Sara De Vido, 'Violenza di genere e migrazione climatica nel diritto internazionale', ('Violence Against Women and Climate Migration in International Law'), in Angela Di Stasi et al. (eds), *Donne migranti e violenza di genere nel contesto giuridico internazionale ed europeo* (Editoriale Scientifica 2023) 137, in which an innovative reading of the *Tetiota* case is proposed.

118 Odier Contreras-Garduno, *Collective Reparations* (n 7) 9.

119 Rubio Marìn, 'Gender and Collective Reparation in the Aftermath of Conflict and Political Repression' (n 5) 384.

From this perspective, some authors criticized the *KlimaSeniorinnen* judgment, in which the ECtHR did not even consider the specific vulnerability of the individual applicants, elderly women alleging suffering a disproportionate impact of climate change due to their gender and age.[120] In particular, the Court rejected the applicants' argument that they met the conditions set forth under Article 34 of the ECHR.[121] Moreover, someone has noted that even women's marginalization from the climate-related decision-making process, also emerging from the complaint, could have triggered the right to access to justice.[122] Both these stances impacted the remedy part of the judgment, as the *KlimaSeniorinnen* association was the only applicant entitled to reparation in the case at stake. Consequently, this judgment provided only partial redress to the marginalization of women from environmental decision-making. By contrast, in this context, giving voice to women's specific needs and concerns—especially those at the intersection of different grounds of discrimination—is essential to shed light on the disproportionate impact they are suffering from due to climate change and empower them as 'agents of change'.[123] Social dialogue may also contribute to eroding discriminatory patterns and ensuring women's participatory rights in environmental decision-making,[124] as recently advocated by General Recommendation No. 37[125] and General Recommendation No. 40[126] of the CEDAW Committee.

5. CONCLUSION

A broader understanding of remedies, based on enhancing their transformative potential, is consistent with the quest for a paradigm shift in the international legal approach to environmental challenges, which should no longer be

---

[120] Lupin, Tigre and Gutiérrez (n 88).

[121] *KlimaSeniorinnen* (n 27) paras 477–88. For a critical perspective, see also: in this volume, Tramontana (n 70), at 10.

[122] *Ibid.*

[123] In this perspective, see Angela Hefti, 'Intersectional Victims as Agents of Change in International Human Rights-Based Climate Litigation' (2024), in *Transnational Environmental Law*, 1.

[124] Meghan Campbell, 'A Greener CEDAW: Adopting a Women's Substantive Equality Approach to Climate Change', in C. Albertyn et al. (eds) (n 117) 112.

[125] CEDAW Committee (n 89).

[126] CEDAW Committee, 'General recommendation No. 40 (2024) on the equal and inclusive representation of women in decision-making systems' (24 October 2024), UN Doc CEDAW/C/GC/40.

regarded as temporary and exceptional, but rather as inherent to the social dynamics of 'everyday life'.[127]

This chapter has highlighted juridical limits and hurdles for an effective result to be achieved. Most of them lie in the disruptive nature of ECEs, which challenges the longest-standing understanding of international law categories. However, possible solutions could be elaborated to meet the needs and concerns of a constantly evolving society. From this perspective, this paper argues that case law enhancing the principles of prevention and precaution is also reflected in reparations aimed at long-term strategies to settle environment-related disputes. Such an evolutive interpretation of reparations could fruitfully contribute to eroding the unjust, unequal social patterns upon which ECEs are grounded.

---

127 Interpreting the words of Hilary Charlesworth, 'International Law: A Discipline of Crisis' (2002) 65 (3) *The Modern Law Review Limited* 377.

PART IV

Concluding Remarks

14. Conclusion

Meghan Campbell

When conjuring images of climate change disasters, the mind turns to torrential rains pounding the pavement, the ravages of forest fires, the punishing speed of typhoon winds and the crashing force of oceanic waves and flooding waters. These images are traumatic and staggering. The destructive power of climate change is readily visible. The aftermath of a climate change disaster is punctuated with similarly striking and upsetting images of homes, families, lives, communities, animals, plants, trees, nature and environments devastated and destroyed. These images implicitly shape our understanding of what climate change is: a short, dramatic or sensational temporal event that creates seismic shifts and enduring consequences. Legal and policy responses to disasters have echoed this understanding of climate change, with mitigation and resilience efforts directed towards urgent, short-term events.

This edited collection stands out by challenging these commonplace narratives on climate change disasters and exposing how law can dangerously replicate these narratives. The editors brilliantly shift the analytical lens, asking what it would mean to rethink climate change in terms of environmental chronic emergencies (ECEs). Building on Rob Nixon's conceptualization of 'slow violence',[1] the editors put forward the concept of ECEs. Violence cannot only be understood as a short temporal burst but as something that can slowly erode and accumulate over days, months, weeks and years, often in ways that are difficult to detect. De Vido, Russo and Tramontana take this understanding of violence and direct it towards climate change and environmental degradation. Their concept of ECE takes seriously the 'deeper and more complex ongoing' process of the changing climate and considers how this emergency challenges 'traditional categories of time, space, and legal obligations in international law.'[2] Their conception of ECEs calls law to consider not only the slow

[1] Rob Nixon, *Slow Violence and the Environmentalism of the Poor* (Harvard University Press 2011).

[2] Sara De Vido, Deborah Russo and Enzamaria Tramontana, 'Introduction' in this Volume.

manifestations of climate change and the violence it wreaks on humans and the environment, but the micro, meso and macro processes and decisions that underpin these slow disasters. To shift the gaze away from the stark images of climate change disasters and to instead examine the everyday, the ordinary, the seemingly benign, and its role in pushing the planetary boundaries to the brink. The editors demonstrate how this reorientation correspondingly requires a radical rethinking of a panoply of legal concepts and doctrines. At its heart, this edited collection is a push to look beyond the impacts of climate change and to give careful legal attention to the causes. This, however, is not to say that De Vido, Russo and Tramontana are indifferent to impacts. The collection is adamant that the ECEs are gendered and that women and girls are situationally vulnerable and disproportionately experience the impacts of these emergencies. The entire collection is alive to how chronic emergencies are not slow levellers but fracture around and further cement existing inequalities against women. By bringing a new understanding of climate change and environmental degradation, along with a commitment to women's equality, this collection forensically uncovers untenable legal assumptions and probes legal innovations that can more accurately respond to the forces that have precipitated environmental degradation.

De Vido's opening chapter lays the theoretical foundations for the collection, exploring with nuance and precision the dissonances between lived reality and traditional conceptions of violence, emergencies and disasters. Rather than exclusively framing climate change as a tragic or upsetting phenomenon, she argues we should see these events as diagnostic, as 'something that comes to light, that reveals itself if we have eyes open to see it.' Chronic emergencies can reveal normative hierarchies, political neglect and indifference, sociocultural acceptance of inequality and the inadequacy of domestic and international legal regimes. Women's inequality is brought into sharp relief by chronic environmental emergencies. De Vido adopts an ecofeminist lens for the project, arguing that it offers an analytical frame to harmoniously redress the oppression of women and girls and the oppression and commodification of the environment. Russo delves more deeply into the structural dimensions of ECEs. She points out how current legal approaches, the 'disaster-based approach fail to comprehensively account for the harms of climate change and continue to elide confronting the causes of disasters'. By adopting the approach proposed in this collection, the law can be more expansive and can pummel the forces that underpin the emergency. She patiently charts how human rights law has begun to adopt this approach, but points out where further engagement is required. And to round out the introductory chapters, Tramontana focuses the analysis on the gendered aspects of ECEs. She begins by mapping how these emergencies are gendered. Her investigation then proceeds to illuminate how law currently defaults to only examining the role of gender in the context of crisis and points out the need for this examination to extend to chronic emergencies. She saliently warns that the process of responding to slower emergencies can build upon and entrench gender inequalities. International human rights law must, she argues, expand, using an ecofeminist lens to capture how women experience and navigate ECEs and ensure that responses do not trap women in further webs of inequality.

There is no shortage of examples of chronic emergencies, and several chapters in this collection detail the facets of these emergencies with a high degree of granularity. Minamata disease is a paradigmatic example of a chronic emergency. It is caused by the slow build-up of mercury in the food chain, and symptoms manifest over a prolonged period of time. It is a poisoning of the environment and humans that occurs over years and decades. While all humans in the contaminated area are vulnerable to Minamata disease, the impacts on women, particularly on their sexual and reproductive health, are pronounced. Furuya observes that rather than regulating to prevent mercury from infecting the food supply, the state sought to regulate women's fertility to protect them from passing Minamata disease to their children. Directly redressing the ECE would have required regulating powerful economic actors, and Furuya lays out how the state's initial legal response was to blame and control women. This is a stark reminder, as Tramontana's chapter warns, that remedial efforts can exacerbate inequalities. Furuya concludes with a plea that the legal framework must evolve to ensure victims of protracted and cumulative harms are not shut out of accountability structures. Furuya also supports the claims made in Russo's chapter that law seeks to avoid grappling with the root causes of environmental degradation, particularly when this grappling would require destabilizing power hierarchies.

Many of the legal responses to Minamata disease in post-World War II Japan resonate in the dangers posed by mine shafts in Victorian-era Cornwall (UK). When the mining industry collapsed in the southwest of England, the corporations left behind an area of derelict buildings and abandoned mine shafts, which were only rudimentarily 'sollared-over'. These hazards were egalitarian in that all socioeconomic classes were at risk of injury or death from these mines. Cooper, in his vivid chapter on the ECE in Cornwall, uncovers the histories of individuals who fell victim to these mine shafts. He then questions why the legal response to this danger was so slow and why this danger was tolerated for such a long time. In part, this was a function of the key accountability question: who should bear responsibility for redressing this emergency? Since chronic emergencies occur slowly, this is a crucial question, as in the case of Cornwall, the companies that had created the mine shafts were no longer in existence. Who should bear the costs of ensuring the safety of the community? The obvious answer would be the state, but the state, Cooper argues, chose to tolerate the risk rather than expend resources to erase it. Chronic emergencies permit the state to ignore the real and severe risks of dangers because they are not sensationalized, not captured in dramatic images, but quietly exist in the everyday.

This rich collection exposes multiple points of disjuncture between law and ECEs. Perhaps none more so than the law's concept of time. Implicitly, the law adopts a simple, linear understanding of time, placing firm boundaries between the past, present and future. Yet, Scott's thoughtful chapter charts how this vision of time sits ill with ECEs. International law, he argues, is overly preoccupied with the present, seeking to quickly fix the contemporaneous crisis and then move to a brighter, more hopeful future. This results in the law failing to grapple with the past decisions, past choices and past structures that precipitated the crisis. International law needs to shift its understanding of time. Scott observes that the future is no longer an 'open horizon' but rather a looming catastrophe, and the present must seek to prevent that catastrophe by wrestling with the past.

Another clear point of disjuncture is the subject of international law. It assigns rights to human beings because they are human beings. But what about those who are not yet human but will become so in the future? Building on Cooper's insights into the temporal fluidity of ECEs, where past and present collide, Magi explores what chronic emergencies mean in relation to the future. This raises the challenging question of what rights future generations possess in the present moment. Conceptualizing future generations as rights holders could lead to tensions with women's rights to sexual and reproductive health, but completely ignoring future generations ignores intergenerational equity. The rights of those living today and the interests of those in the future can be in conflict. Realizing the right to an adequate standard of living through processes and consumption patterns that increase CO_2 may have a detrimental impact on the right to health of future generations. Different courts are alive to these tensions, struggling to balance the temporality of chronic emergencies and the realization of human rights. Magi's chapter pushes us to think more carefully about how the future rights of future generations and the principle of intergenerational equity could be harnessed in the present to tackle today's ineffectual laws and policies to prevent and combat contemporaneous chronic emergencies.

Transnational corporations repeatedly play a causative role in more typical or traditional disasters and slow environmental degradation, yet they often evade legal accountability. Barabirotto observes that efforts to hold transnational corporations to account have sprung from a crisis management ethos and rightly questions whether these nascent legal frameworks are well-placed to redress ECEs. The due diligence principle to protect and prevent against harm, which in theory could also be utilized to redress these types of emergencies. Recent jurisprudence from the European Court of Human Rights points towards states having obligations to implement adaptive measures to severe and foreseeable effects of climate change. Baade, however, observes that the stringency of the due diligence obligation increases only when the nature of the harm becomes clear, making it ill-suited to emergencies where the harm unfolds slowly across time. Moreover, procedural rules make it difficult to obtain legal accountability for this type of harm, as rules of standing often require that a victim has experienced a rights violation, and with respect to chronic emergencies, by the time the harm has reached this threshold, it may already be too late.

The violence of climate change and environmental degradation, whether slow or fast, creates real impacts that negatively shape the lives of thousands. Many would seek reparations for these impacts. However, legal reparations were not designed in light of ECEs, and seeking reparations in this context raises many challenging questions. Reparations are awarded to recompense for harm that has materialized at a certain moment in time, but for many of these emergencies, the harm is not so time-bound and can continue to manifest after remedies have been put in place. The temporality certainty demanded of reparations may fit ill with ECEs. Moreover, reparations can be myopically backwards focusing, ascertaining the wrongs that have been done in the past and less towards the future and remedies that will prevent future harms. Tammone observes changes in remedial jurisprudence from international and regional human rights bodies and calls on courts to reflect on the unseen nature of ECEs and how they intersect with gendered inequalities.

How can the law better respond to chronic emergencies? All chapters stress the importance of women's equal participation in all environmental and climate change law and policymaking spaces. Many argue for the importance of gender action plans so that women's voices and concerns are not sidelined or marginalized in these legal and policy regimes. There is no doubt that women's right to equality requires women's active and meaningful participation. However, it is important not to overly romanticize participation. First, there are real constraints on women's agency that must be accounted for when demanding their participation, and efforts to increase meaningful participation must redress these constraints. Moreover, the violence of climate change demands real substantive action, and efforts should not be reduced to procedural obligations. More radically, Feria-Tinta pushes us to think beyond the anthropocentric model that has dominated international law. What would it look like to craft law and policy in a way that decenters human beings? She charts how the seeds of this approach have already been planted in international law and begins to reflect on how this could be strengthened, exploring the nascent movement to grant legal personhood to forests, rivers, lagoons and mountains.

Morrow, in her chapter in this collection, argues that disaster-based frameworks to climate change continue to place humans at the centre; correspondingly, legal solutions are too focused on addressing human interests. This approach not only misses accounting for the severe environmental harm and degradation caused by the climate crisis, but it also eschews addressing human (in)actions that have placed all living things on this planet in significant peril. Adopting an ecofeminist approach, she holds that taking a holistic account of 'human flourishing and a sustaining and sustainable environment would give not only a new temporality to thinking about climate change but also new relations between humans and between the environment. Sardo explores the underutilized duty to cooperate in numerous UN treaties, declarations and frameworks. Climate change does not respect national borders or territorial boundaries, yet legal obligations are almost invariably shaped by concepts of state sovereignty. The duty to cooperate, which seeks to transcend borders and boundaries, could be instrumental in responding to ECEs. Sardo's chapter charts how the duty is evolving across a range of legal instruments, observing a common theme that collapses the duty to the exchange of scientific knowledge, technology and data. Much like the concerns regarding participation and climate change, the duty to cooperate should not be conceptualized in such a unidimensional manner. A more radical understanding would push towards the pooling of financial resources, cross-border shifts in consumption and living patterns, which in turn could also simultaneously redress many of the current inequalities.

In sum, the chapters in this collection are intellectually rich and inspiring. They respond to the unseen violence of environmental degradation, exploring its connections to broader human patterns of inequality, and passionately call on the law to change, modify and innovate in light of this degradation. *Gendering international legal responses to environmental chronic emergencies* is a collection to return to again and again, as climate change may defy traditional disaster categories as it is both a fast and slow event, with rapid shifts and slow accumulative events, but our response to this emergency cannot be slow, and this collection marks out the transformations needed to respond with speed and urgency.

Index

2030 Agenda (UN 2015) 193

Aarhus Convention 222, 269
accountability 51, 108–9, 112, 114–15, 177, 184, 188, 190–92, 194, 196, 198, 202–3, 208, 276, 278
ACHR *see* American Convention on Human Rights (ACHR)
acidification 2, 11, 25, 29
Action Plan on Gender Equality (UNCCD) 244
Advisory Opinion on Nuclear Weapons 144
Advisory Opinion on Obligations of States in respect of Climate Change 128–9, 131, 176
Advisory Opinion on the Chagos Islands 146
Advisory Opinion on The Environment and Human Rights (2017) 231
Afghanistan 10
Africa 187, 241
African Charter on Human and Peoples' Rights 217, 260
Agreement Establishing the Caribbean Disaster Emergency Response Agency (!991) 26
agriculture 2, 25, 44, 171–2, 175, 189, 192
Albania 128
Amazon rainforest 182
American Convention on Human Rights (ACHR) 37, 164, 217, 254, 262
Anthropocene 66–7, 70–74, 80, 83–5
anthropocentrism 21–2, 31–2, 35, 56, 72, 79, 168, 178, 182–3, 262–3, 278
Antigua and Barbuda 171
Argentina 263
Assmann, Aleida 141, 143
Atrato envenenao: la huella del mercurio ('Poisoned Atrato: the footprint of mercury') 180
Atrato river litigation case 168, 180–81, 183
Australia 37, 130, 149, 261

Bahamas 171
Basel Convention (1989) 122
Basic Principles and Guidelines on the Right to a Remedy and Reparation for Victims of Gross Violations of International Human Rights Law and Serious Violation of International Humanitarian Law (2005) 256
Bawden, Mary 97
Belize 171
Berryman, Irene 90, 93, 106
Berryman, John 89–91, 94, 106
Beyond Mothering Earth (Sherilyn MacGregor) 16
Bhopal disaster 186
biodiversity 2, 19, 25, 31–2, 42, 44, 50, 57–8, 142, 156–7, 168, 179–80, 182, 240, 244
birth control 113
Blacks 7, 45, 68
Bolivia 199
Budayeva and Others v Russia 208
business *see* companies

Cambodia 198
Canada 181
Cannavacciuolo and Others v Italy 36, 162, 267–9
capitalism 19, 88, 91, 141
Caribbean 168–76
CARICOM 171
Carson, Rachel 3, 5–6

Cartagena Protocol on Biodiversity 31
Cartí Sugdupu 171
CEDAW *see* Convention on the Elimination of All Forms of Discrimination against Women (CEDAW)
Chagos Archipelago 146
Charlesworth, Hilary 7–8, 10, 24, 132–5, 139
Chisso Corporation 108, 111–13, 115–16, 118, 121
Chocó 180–81
climate change 2, 5–6, 9–10, 13, 16, 20, 25, 29, 31, 36–8, 40, 42–3, 50, 54–5, 57, 59, 66, 73, 75, 77, 82, 129–31, 140, 142–4, 146–7, 149, 152, 157, 160–63, 168–70, 172–9, 182, 192, 210–17, 219–28, 230, 232–4, 239, 241–4, 247–8, 254–5, 259, 261, 266, 269–71, 274–5, 278–9
  aim of limiting effects of 31
  anthropocentrism and 168, 182, 279
  companies' responsibilities for 177, 192
  conventions on 30, 57–8, 130, 143, 239, 241–2
  cooperation needed to combat 130, 233, 241–3, 247, 249, 279
  COVID-19 pandemic and 10
  decision-making on issues concerning 66
  defined as crisis 9, 168
  different impacts of 6, 173, 222
  disasters and 40, 274–5
  disproportionate effect on women 55, 59, 66, 174–6, 225–6, 270–71
  effect on children 173
  effects 170
  environmental degradation leading to 31
  example of environmental chronic emergency 2, 50, 147, 227, 242, 275
  form of slow violence 5, 275
  fossil fuels causing 142, 169
  future generations and 37, 147, 149, 160–61
  gender-sensitive solutions needed 59
  human acts causing 73, 147
  human rights and 37–8, 54–5, 75, 77, 152, 169, 179, 210–11, 217, 221, 223, 232–4, 255
  impacts exacerbated by discrimination 13, 20
  increasing awareness of 132, 259
  international law and 131, 223, 225
  law 13, 228, 230, 239, 242, 278
  litigation 176–9, 210, 213–16, 224, 254, 259, 261, 266
  most affected communities 16
  part of triple environmental crisis 82
  policies to combat 36, 244, 248
  reduction of greenhouse gas emissions necessary 211, 213
  reparations for impacts of 270, 278
  result of colonialism 129
  role of NGOs in combating 222
  social inequalities and 11, 13
  some states bearing cost of actions of others 129, 131, 170, 172–3, 242
  States' responsibility to combat 37, 157, 160, 163, 211–14, 217, 219–20, 225, 255, 261, 278
  Sustainable Development Goals addressing 243
  time and 129, 131–2, 140, 144
  UN framework on 29, 31, 58, 130–31, 146, 219, 244
Collin, Timothy 97
Collins, Wilkie 101–2
Colombia 18, 20, 149, 180–81
colonialism 12–13, 23, 88, 91, 129, 141
Commission on the Status of Women 66
Committee on Economic, Social and Cultural Rights (CESCR) 34, 148, 232
Committee on the Protection of the Rights of All Migrant Workers 234
Committee on the Rights of Persons with Disabilities 234
Committee on the Rights of the Child (CRC) 54, 148, 163
communism 141
companies *see* transnational corporations (TNCs)
  accountability 115, 188, 194, 197, 277
  commitment to sustainable development 193, 197–8
  contributing to slow violence 6

damaging environment 164, 277
denying responsibility 108, 111–12, 115
greenhouse gas emissions 177
human rights and 121, 184, 187, 194, 197–8, 204, 207
involvement in environmental chronic emergencies 185
jurisdictions and 191, 195, 200
liability 252
litigation against 115, 177, 187
mining industry 164, 276
power of 109, 112
prioritizing economic growth over public health 122
responsibilities 121, 185, 187, 194, 196, 276
responsible for pollution 108, 111, 115, 118, 121, 187–8
state-owned 164
States protecting 112, 118, 121, 200
women in 40
compound events 73
Comprehensive Environmental Response, Compensation, and Liability Act (CERCLA, 1980) 188
Conferences of the State Parties 32
Congo, Democratic Republic of (DRC) 188, 190
Convention on Biological Diversity (UNCBD, 1992) 31–2, 57, 59, 240, 244
Convention on Climate Change (UNFCCC) 29–30, 58–9, 130, 219, 243
Convention on the Elimination of All Forms of Discrimination against Women (CEDAW) 34, 40, 50, 125, 233, 243, 248, 271
Convention on the Rights of Persons with Disabilities 53
Convention on the Rights of the Child 163
Convention to Combat Desertification (UNCCD, 1994) 31, 57, 59, 241, 244
Cook Islands 129
cooperation 24, 30, 37, 121, 129, 155, 228–43, 247–9, 279
to address gendered effects of environmental chronic emergencies 229
in addressing environmental chronic emergencies 228–30, 232–3, 238–9, 243, 248, 279
in disaster risk reduction 37, 237–9, 243
duty for 230–31, 233–4, 236, 239–43, 248, 279
in international law 229, 234
international organizations 239–40
need for addressing structural inequalities for 249
need for integration of women's rights into 243, 247–9
on climate change 129, 233, 240–41
on disasters 24, 234–6
on environmental law 30, 239, 242
on pollution 121
in science 240
States and private sector 239–40
voluntary 241
COP27 (Egypt 2022) 242
COP28 (Dubai 2023) 242
Cornwall 89, 91–4, 96–102, 105–7, 276
Costa Rica v Nicaragua 258
Covenant on Civil and Political Rights 149
COVID-19 pandemic 5, 10
Crenshaw, Kimberle 81
crises 8–11, 13, 21, 24, 30, 32–3, 35, 40–41, 53, 67, 70, 74, 81–2, 109, 111, 113, 117–20, 122, 126–7, 129–40, 142, 144–5, 167, 169, 174, 179, 182, 185, 189, 199, 207, 222, 228, 247, 249, 276–7, 279
biodiversity 167, 179, 182
climate change 9, 11, 13, 129–32, 140, 167, 169, 174, 179, 182, 222, 279
coinciding 10
defined as emergencies 33, 35
emergency law and 33
environmental 30, 32, 67, 70, 82, 111, 117–18, 120, 126, 133, 167, 249
environmental chronic emergencies as prolonged 109
as historiographical category 132, 137–9
humanitarian 9, 189

idea reclaimed by feminism 21
impact on vulnerable groups 249
international law and 8–9, 24, 30, 41, 132, 134–6, 139–40, 145, 228, 277
management 199, 277
marginalized communities victims of 122
migration 9
modernity and 138, 142, 144
need for challenging monolithic category of 21, 81
need to switch focus to environmental chronic emergencies 185
original meaning 137–8
pollution causing 113
public health 109, 117–20, 126, 207
responsive approach to 40, 74
review of concept of 247
securitization as response to 10, 21
social-ecological 13
victims bearing costs of 129
women and 8, 53, 109, 127, 174, 276
Cusato, Eliana 5

Daniel Billy et al. v Australia 37, 149, 169, 178–9, 261
Daniel, James 98
Dayton Accords 135
De Vido, Sara 24
Deacon, Bernard 91–2
d'Eaubonne, Françoise 13
decarbonization 36, 163, 213, 219
decision-making 40–41, 45, 49, 52, 58–61, 66, 77, 80, 109, 124–7, 160, 175, 212, 216, 221, 243, 247–9, 265, 269, 271, 278
Declaration on Principles of International Law concerning Friendly Relations and Cooperation among States (UN 1970) 229
decolonization 7, 15, 204
deforestation 5, 25, 151, 159, 189–90, 257, 262
desertification 2, 11, 29, 42–3, 45–6, 50, 54, 57, 187, 192
developing countries 8, 23, 200, 227, 232, 234, 237–8, 240–43
disabilities 18, 20, 45, 47, 53, 68, 77, 152, 245
disasters 4, 10, 13, 24–30, 33–5, 37, 39–42, 53, 65–6, 71–2, 74, 76–7, 80, 82, 84–5, 88, 108–11, 115, 117–22, 125–6, 131, 143, 147, 187, 206–8, 228, 230, 232, 234–9, 243, 246, 248, 252, 274–5, 277–9
call for equal participation of women in decision-making on 39, 66, 246
causes 27, 275
climate change causing 65, 274–5
companies causing 108, 121, 186–7, 277
cooperation on 24, 37, 230, 234–9, 243, 248
definitions 27–8
difference to environmental chronic emergencies 41, 131
disproportionate impact on women 66, 125, 246
ecofeminism for more contextualized approach to 76
environmental chronic emergencies resulting in 4, 25, 29, 147, 234
environmental law on 72
examples 42, 108
human actions responsible for 74, 84
human rights and 33, 74, 206–7, 278
inequalities exacerbated by 10, 246
international law on 26–7, 41, 75, 77, 228, 230, 234, 238, 252
invisible 88
laws on 10
looming 143
measures in case of 77
need for different approach by international law 24, 67, 74, 82, 110
need for reframing of understanding of 72
no distinction between natural and human-made 27
pollution leading to 108, 118, 120
public health 108, 117–18, 120
reparations for victims of 115, 119, 122
responsive approach to 40
risk reduction 27, 30, 40, 66, 80, 208, 230, 235–8, 243, 246
sexual violence and 10

solutions aiming at security 13
States allowed to declare emergency law in 33, 35
States' obligation to help victims of 33, 232
States' obligation to reduce risk of 27, 208, 236
stressing of inevitability of 13
sudden-onset and slow-onset 28, 77, 109, 126, 275
traditional conception of 275, 279
underlying structural inequalities and 74
women's inequality in 42, 53
discrimination 4, 11, 13, 17–22, 27, 29, 34–5, 38–9, 41, 44–5, 48, 51–2, 54–5, 64, 77, 151–2, 164, 186, 220, 225–6, 228–9, 238, 243, 247–9, 262, 270–71
against women 13, 18–20, 39, 44, 51, 54, 64, 243
climate change impacts exacerbated by 13, 55, 77, 220, 225
ecofeminism highlighting 4, 17, 48, 229, 270
environmental chronic emergencies impact exacerbated by 19, 51, 54
exacerbating vulnerability in disasters 246
future generations and 152
human rights and 226
international law and 21–2, 41, 247
intersectionality in 4, 18, 22, 45, 52, 54–5, 151, 164, 186, 225, 249, 271
structural 27, 29, 35, 41, 228, 238, 246, 249, 262
systemic 11, 248
Dominica 171, 173
Dominican Republic 171
Draft Articles on Responsibility of States for Internationally Wrongful Acts (ARSIWA) 253, 256–7
Draft Articles on the Protection of Persons in the Event of Disasters (ILC) 24, 26–8, 67, 74–5, 235–6, 238, 246
Draft Conclusions on General Principles of Law (ILC 2023) 155
Draft Declaration on Reparation for Victims of Armed Conflict (2010) 256
Draft Norms on the Responsibilities of Transnational Corporations and Other Business Enterprises with regard to Human Rights (UN 2003) 193, 199
DRC *see* Congo, Democratic Republic of (DRC)
Dupuy, Pierre-Marie 182

Earth systems science 71–2, 83–4
ECD Due Diligence Guidance for Responsible Business Conduct (2018) 194, 197
ECEs *see* environmental chronic emergencies (ECEs)
ECHR *see* European Convention on Human Rights (ECHR)
ecofeminism 4, 14–22, 43, 46–50, 56–7, 61, 63, 66–8, 70–71, 73, 75, 82–5, 185, 204, 228, 248, 270, 276, 279
approach to environmental chronic emergencies 21–2, 43, 63, 276
call for end of structural discrimination against women 48, 56, 228, 248, 276
call for environmental equity 14
call for women's rights and environmental protection 49
criticism of existing environmental law 61, 63
criticism of mainstream science 48
criticism of sanctioning of exploitation of nature 57, 68, 83, 248, 276
discipline of practice 14
essentialism and 15
ethics of care 67, 82–5
holistic view of human-environment nexus 71, 75, 83
intersectional approach to law 20, 46–7, 82
long-term silence on 15
nuances 16
on disasters and structural inequalities 73
origins 13

potential role in international law 14, 16–18, 21–2, 47, 185, 204, 270
revitalization of 4, 17
stressing marginalization of women and nature 19, 46
sustainable development and 70, 279
Ecology of War, The (Eliana Cusato) 5
Economic Commission for Latin America and the Caribbean (ECLAC) 174, 176
ECtHR *see* European Court of Human Rights (ECtHR)
Ecuador 19, 182
education 21, 51, 58, 238, 240, 247, 249
Eicke, Judge Tim 216, 221
employment 19, 25, 44, 46, 51, 93, 124–5, 189
England 67
Enlightenment 141
Environment and Planning C: Politics and Space (Rob Nixon) 6
environmental chronic emergencies (ECEs) 2–4, 7–10, 13–14, 16–17, 19–20, 22, 24–5, 27–9, 31–3, 36, 38, 41–3, 45–6, 48–51, 53–4, 56–7, 61, 63, 67, 69–71, 74, 76, 81–2, 85–6, 88–9, 104, 106, 108, 111, 113–14, 126, 131, 133, 140, 142–4, 146–8, 151–2, 158–9, 162–4, 167, 169, 176, 178, 184–5, 187–92, 195, 198–9, 201–2, 204, 209–10, 220, 224–6, 228–30, 233–4, 236–9, 242–3, 246–9, 252–5, 258–60, 263, 266, 268–9, 272, 275–9
anthropocentrism and 31, 56
causes 32, 53, 210, 254
cooperation necessary to combat 228–30, 232–3, 236, 238–9, 243, 249, 279
crisis escalating into 111, 167
decision-making on 49
definition 25, 185, 210, 234
developing countries 238
disasters and 4, 41, 74, 237
disproportionate impact on women 3, 22, 25, 31, 43, 45–6, 48, 53–4, 56, 61, 184, 187, 201, 229, 243, 246–7, 275
access to healthcare 45
because of stereotypes and biases 45
because of structural disadvantages 22, 48, 61
call for cooperation to combat causes of 229, 243
due to migration 187
ecofeminism calling for new approach to 43, 48
gender-based violence 46
growing recognition of 247
international agreements not dealing with 25, 31
international law on 56, 61, 275
lack of addressing by human rights organizations 53–4
liability of companies for 184, 201
One Health Initiative investigating 3
recent frameworks giving more consideration to 246
women with disabilities 54
due diligence as tool for addressing 209, 225
ecofeminism and 13–14, 16–17, 22, 46, 63, 276
evolving gradually 108
examples 2, 43, 51, 147, 167, 169, 210, 227, 242, 263
fossil fuels and 142–3
future generations and 148, 151–2, 158–9, 162
gender identity and 19
gender-sensitive response needed 22, 247, 249
in history 88–9, 104, 276
human rights and 20, 22, 50, 54, 76, 230
impacts exacerbated by discrimination 19, 27, 43, 51, 276
international law and 10, 22, 25, 42, 50, 57, 61, 63, 132–3, 144, 151, 158–9, 201, 224, 230, 234, 252, 255, 266, 268, 272, 275, 277
concept shaping new developments in 25
cooperation in key fields 230
difficulties in conceptualizing 133, 272

difficulties in digesting complexities 132, 201, 275, 277
ecofeminism and 22
human rights 57, 234, 266
innovative interpretation required 255
intergenerational equity as principle 151, 158–9
law of the everyday 10
profound demands on 144
progress through precedence cases 224, 268
recognition of gendered impacts 61, 63
reparations 252
women's inequality 42, 50
international treaties not addressing 33
intersectionality and 151, 248
lack of conceptualization 28, 176, 178, 199
lack of recognition of 25, 76, 86, 190, 238
mining industry and 189, 202, 210
need for shift in environmental law 67, 69, 85, 199
new concept 2, 22, 67, 74, 82, 147, 204, 253, 275
obligation for States to respond to 3, 9, 36, 54, 114, 163–4
obligations of companies 185, 187, 191, 195
pollution 108, 113
reparations and 126, 253, 258–9, 269, 272, 278
responsibility and accountability for 104, 202, 239, 248, 253, 259, 263
role of NGOs in exposing 198
slow violence and 3, 88, 260, 268
systemic and structural dimensions of 41, 49, 63, 132, 220, 226, 276
time and 106, 133, 140, 143, 277
transboundary effects of 254
transnational corporations and 189–92, 195, 198, 202, 204, 277
triple environmental crisis 67, 70, 82
environmental degradation 3, 8, 14, 18, 20, 23–5, 27–8, 30–31, 35–8, 40–41, 43–9, 53–8, 61, 63, 69, 76–7, 79, 108, 142–3, 147, 149, 164, 168, 178, 189, 227, 232, 254, 263, 265, 275–9
beginnings in Industrial Revolution 169
call for new legal approach to 275
call for women's involvement in decision-making on 61
caused by exploitation of natural resources 23, 25, 189
combating of effects instead of causes of 36
development into crisis 108
differentiated impact on population 38, 76, 265
disasters and 232
driving migration 77
ecofeminism highlighting connection to women's inequality 43, 46, 48
effects 24
environmental chronic emergencies and 8, 25, 147, 228
fossil fuels and 142
future generations and 143, 149, 164
human rights and 30, 35, 37, 54, 56, 79, 263
impact on women 14, 18, 43–6, 48, 50, 53, 55–7
interconnection with discrimination 20
international agreements for combating 57
known phenomenon for a long time 3
lack of measures to prevent 69, 108, 147
leading to climate change 31
reparations and 278
responsibilities for 254, 277
rights of non-human life and 178, 279
slow violence and 275, 279
standards for level of tolerance of 38
underlying structural causes 27–8, 31, 40–41, 46, 49, 58, 276
women's contributions to confront 53
women's inequality and 43–6, 48, 53, 56, 63
environmental law 14, 30, 35, 43, 50, 61, 67, 69–70, 72, 79, 119, 126, 167,

182, 187, 228, 230, 239, 242, 252, 278
concept of strict liability 188
consideration of future generations 79
cooperation on 31, 230, 239, 242
dealing with women's inequality in environmental chronic emergencies 43, 61
developed from soft law principles 182
ecofeminism and 14
history 67, 73
human rights law and 50, 167
importance of women's equal participation in 278
international 35, 61, 119, 188, 252
need for early warning systems 126
need to protect environment in its own right 69
new approach needed 67, 182
pollution prevention 70, 119
reparations in 252
responding to environmental degradation 30
ethics of care 67, 82, 84–5
EU Corporate Sustainability Due Diligence Directive (CSDDD) 194
EU Corporate Sustainability Reporting Directive (CSRD) 194
Eurocentrism 7, 12
European Convention on Human Rights (ECHR) 207–12, 214, 216–18, 220–23, 225–6, 255, 260, 266–7, 271
European Court of Human Rights (ECtHR) 36, 55, 160, 201, 204, 208, 210–25, 256, 259–61, 266–8, 271, 277
European Social Charter 34
European Union (EU) 194, 215
exploitation 13, 19, 21, 23, 25, 27, 30, 46–7, 57, 63, 66, 68, 82, 92, 106, 129, 156, 169, 173, 189–90, 248, 262
by privileged minority 66
of children 173
colonial 23, 92, 129
interlocking systems of 13
of local populations 23
of natural resources 23, 25, 27, 30, 92, 106, 156, 262
of nature 13, 19, 21, 47, 57, 63, 68, 169, 248
systemic 82, 248
of women 19, 21, 46, 189–90
extractive industries *see* mining industry

feminism 4, 6–7, 9, 11, 13–14, 16–17, 21, 81–2, 152, 185, 270
Folkers, Andreas 142–3
food security 9, 31, 38, 44, 46, 50–51, 171, 173, 175, 189
fossil fuels 142–3, 169
Foster, Clement Le Neve 99–100
fracking 53
Framework Principles on Human Rights and the Environment 78
France 130
Frecheville, Robert James 99
Fundación Ambiente y Recursos Naturales (FARN) 270

Gaard, Greta 4
Galilee Basin 158
Gender Action Plan (GAP) 109, 123–7, 243
gender equality 11, 16, 20, 22, 32, 40–41, 58–61, 123–4, 126–7, 152, 243–5, 275
Gender Plan of Action (UNCBD) 244
general principle of international law (GPIL) 151, 153–5, 158–9
GenREM 4, 7
Germany 128, 149, 156, 177, 221
Gill, Frederick Charles 97
Gilligan, Carole 83
Global Climate Risk Index 170
Global Compact (UN 1999) 193, 197
Global North 219
Global South 88, 188, 219, 221
governments *see* States
GPIL 151
greenhouse gas emissions 30, 65, 77, 129, 157, 169, 177, 210–11, 213–14, 217, 220, 255, 277
Gripe, Arthur 98–9
Guiding Principles on Business and Human Rights (UN 2011) 184, 193, 196–7, 200, 202

Gumbrecht, Hans Ulrich 141
Guterres, Antonio 169

Hague Rules on Arbitration Relating to Business and Human Rights (2019) 202
Haiti 170
Handbook for Travellers in Cornwall (John Murray) 102
Harris, Edwin 97
Hartog, Francois 140–41
healthcare 45, 51, 122, 124, 127, 189, 246, 249
Heathcote, Gina 11
Higgins, Judge Rosalyn 145
Hooker Chemical Company 187
Huaraz 177–8
human rights 14, 20, 22, 24, 30, 33, 35–6, 38–40, 43, 48, 50, 53–4, 56–7, 75–7, 79, 81, 108–10, 114, 119–24, 126–7, 130, 133, 135, 148–53, 163, 168, 176, 178–82, 184–6, 189–90, 194–8, 200, 202, 204, 206–7, 209–12, 216–24, 226, 228–30, 232–4, 237, 243, 247–8, 255–7, 260–61, 266–7, 269–70, 276–8
  anthropocentrism and 56, 168, 178, 181
  bodies 24, 33, 39, 50, 76, 78, 226, 234, 247, 261, 266, 269, 278
  children 163
  climate change and 39, 210–12, 217, 232–4, 255
  companies and 121, 184, 186, 189–90, 194–8, 200, 204
  cooperation for 229–30, 233–4, 248
  due diligence 198, 206–7, 209–10
  environmental chronic emergencies and 20, 22, 24, 33, 35, 50, 54, 56, 110, 230
  environmental protection and 36, 76, 79, 168, 178–9, 218, 223
  future generations 148–51
  gender equality 123–4, 126
  healthy environment 50, 121
  law 20, 22, 40, 43, 50, 56–7, 75, 79, 81, 109, 120–21, 130, 152, 168, 178, 182, 206–7, 212, 216, 219, 228, 230, 276
    addressing disasters 206
    anthropocentric perspective 168, 178, 182
    due diligence obligations 206–7
    environmental law and 50, 168
    expansion to rights of nature 178
    lack of obligations for tackling climate change 130, 216
    need to recognize structural dimensions of environmental chronic emergencies 276
    perspective of vulnerable populations neglected 216
    progressive recognition of environmental chronic emergencies 40, 57, 75, 79, 228, 230
    recognition of impact of chronic environmental emergencies on women 43, 56
    reparations for environmental chronic emergencies 20, 22
    resolution of conflicts on combating climate change 219
    right to environmental protection 120, 212
    right to health 120
    right to participation in environmental governance 120
    use of intersectionality 20, 81, 152
  litigation 168
  migrants 50
  NGOs reporting violations 189, 198
  obligations of States 77, 124, 176, 184, 196, 207, 217, 233, 243, 256
  principles 122–3, 127
  redressing of imbalances 76
  reparations for violation of 222, 257, 270
  States failing to protect 108–9, 114, 119, 126
  systemic risk to 209
  transnational arbitration on 202
  treaties 30, 33, 122, 168, 207, 260
  women's disadvantages 48, 53–4, 270
Human Rights Committee (UN) 20, 37, 54, 178–9, 260–61
Human Rights Council (UNHRC) 78, 81, 193, 232

Humboldt, Alexander von 183

IACtHR *see* Inter-American Court of Human Rights (IACtHR)
ICJ *see* International Court of Justice (ICJ)
Indigenous peoples 3, 7, 11–12, 18–19, 45, 59, 68, 77, 125, 149, 152, 183, 244–6, 261–3, 270
Industrial Revolution 67, 169
inequalities 4, 9–10, 13, 21, 32, 38, 42–3, 49–50, 53–4, 56–63, 73, 77, 81, 88, 131, 143, 151, 201, 220, 228, 238, 243, 246–7, 249, 270, 275–6, 278–9
  climate change and 13, 59, 77, 270
  disasters exacerbating 10
  ecofeminism addressing 4, 43, 63, 270
    addressed in context of crises 53
  environmental chronic emergencies and 43, 49–50, 53–4, 61, 131, 275–6, 278
  environmental degradation and 279
  international law and 21, 42, 247
  intersectionality in 61
  projected into future 151
  structural 9, 38, 58, 73, 151, 220, 228, 238, 247
  sustainable development and 62
  women 12–13, 21, 32, 42, 49–50, 53–4, 56–7, 60–61, 81, 243, 247, 270, 275–6, 278
    climate change and 12
    colonialism and 13
    complicity of law in 21
    ecofeminism combating 56, 270
    in environmental chronic emergencies 50, 53–4, 61, 247, 275–6, 278
    international human rights bodies dealing with 53
    need for consideration in environmental law 270
    need for cooperation to eliminate 243
    need to address root causes of 247
    recognized in international environmental agreements 57, 60
    state of international law on 42, 50
    strategies to address 60–61, 81
  structural dimensions 32, 49, 56
Inter-American Court of Human Rights (IACtHR) 37, 55, 163, 169, 176, 178, 183, 201, 204, 231, 254, 257, 262–5, 270
intergenerational equity (IGE) 148, 151–4, 156, 158–60, 162–4, 277
Intergovernmental Panel on Climate Change (IPCC) 147, 211–13, 218, 220
International Court of Justice (ICJ) 128–30, 144, 146, 153, 254, 258
international courts 164, 179, 201, 223, 234, 239, 252–3, 255–6, 259
International Covenant on Civil and Political Rights (ICCPR) 20, 260–61
International Covenant on Economic, Social and Cultural Rights 34
international law 4–5, 7–9, 11, 13, 16–18, 21–5, 27, 29–31, 35, 41–3, 46–7, 49, 57, 61, 63–4, 67, 69, 74, 77, 79, 85, 109, 119–21, 130–36, 139–40, 143–6, 150–51, 154–5, 158, 160, 168, 178–9, 182, 184–5, 187, 191–2, 195–6, 200, 204, 207, 225, 228–30, 234, 236, 238–9, 242, 247, 250–52, 254, 257–8, 269, 271–2, 274, 277–8
  anthropocentrism 178, 278
  bodies 35, 252–3, 256
  call for addressing of structural inequalities 8
  climate change and 130–31
  colonialism 23
  companies and 185, 187, 191–2, 195–6, 201, 204
  cooperation in 228–30, 234, 242
  customary 254
  dealing with gender equality 21
  environmental chronic emergencies and 11, 21, 41, 43, 132–3, 144, 151, 252, 269, 272, 274
  environmental protection 25, 31, 35, 50, 61, 69, 79, 85, 119, 168, 179, 187, 228, 239, 242, 252
  feminist method challenging 4, 7, 11
  General Principles of 151, 154–5, 158
  human rights 50, 56–7, 109, 120–21, 130, 178, 182, 228, 230, 234, 276
  law of crisis 7–9, 25, 132–6, 139, 228

male players dominating 8, 17
monolithic categories of 4
need for reorientation towards everyday life 136, 271
on disasters 25, 27–9, 41–2, 228, 234, 236, 238, 252
potential role of ecofeminism in 13, 16–18, 22, 46–7, 63, 184
private 200
protection of future generations 151, 158, 277
reparations 251–2, 257–8, 269
slow violence challenging concept for 5
soft law 67, 74
stance on women's inequality 42–3, 247
States as empowered actors 77
time and 132–5, 139–40, 144–6, 277
underestimation of 225
International Law Commission (ILC) 24, 26–7, 29, 67, 74–5, 155, 246
international organizations 20, 28, 128, 232, 239
International Relief Union 25
International Tribunal for the Law of the Sea (ITLOS) 179
intersectionality 7, 13, 18, 20, 22, 41, 45, 47, 50, 52, 54–6, 61, 68, 81–2, 151–2, 164, 185, 203, 225, 247, 249, 271
IPCC *see* Intergovernmental Panel on Climate Change (IPCC)
Italy 157, 162, 267–8

Jamaica 173
Japan 108, 112, 114, 116–22, 276
Joint Statement on Human Rights and Climate Change 38

Kapur, Ratna 8
Kenya Green Belt Movement 6
KlimaSeniorinnen et al v Switzerland (2024) 36, 160, 162, 255, 266, 271
KlimaSeniorinnen et al v Switzerland (2024) 202, 210, 216–17, 223–4
Koselleck, Reinhart 132, 136, 138–40
Geschichtliche Grundbegriffe: Historisches Lexikon zur Politisch-sozialen Sprache in Deutschland (*Basic Concepts in History: A Historical Dictionary of Political and Social Language in Germany*) 137
Kosovo 133, 135
Kumamoto 112, 115–17
Kumamoto University 112

La Oroya Population v Peru 38, 168, 178–9, 183
La Oroya Population v Peru 163, 263–4, 269–70
LaDuke, Winona 3
Land Court of Queensland in Australia in the Waratah Coal Pty Ltd v Youth Verdict Ltd and Others 158
land rights 45, 51, 54, 58, 61, 244, 246, 261–2
Latin America 173–4, 180
Le féminisme ou la mort (Françoise d'Eaubonne) 13
leadership 59, 66, 246, 249
Letcher, John 94, 96
Lewes 181
LGBT+ 45
Lhaka Honhat v Argentina 263, 270
Lliuya, Saul Luciano 177
Lliuya v RWE 168–9, 177
Lopez Ostra v Spain 260
Los Cedros case 182
Loss and Damage Fund 242
Love Canal disaster 10, 188
Lozano Barragán case 149

Maastricht Principles on the Human Rights of Future Generations (2023) 148
Maathai, Wangari 6
MacGregor, Sherilyn 16
Magpie river 181
Mar Menor 181
Marxism 17
Mauritius 146
Melanesian Spearhead Group 129
Merchant, Carolyn 14–15
Mies, Maria 14–15
migration 9, 46, 50, 77, 176, 187, 246
Miller, Elizabeth 106
Minamata 9, 108–13, 118–19, 122, 124–5, 127, 187, 201

Minamata Convention on Mercury (2013) 21, 31, 57, 59–60, 109, 119–27, 240, 245
Minamata disease 9, 108–11, 113–18, 120, 122, 124, 126–7, 186, 276
mining industry 21, 53, 60, 89, 91, 93–4, 97, 99, 101–6, 120, 122, 124–5, 151, 164, 178, 182, 188–90, 240, 261
Minors Oposa v Secretary of the Department of Environment and Natural Resources (Philippines 1993) 158
Morgera, Elisa 81
Morrow, Karen 18
Murray, John 102

Nagoya Protocol on Access and Benefit-sharing 31
NATO (North Atlantic Treaty Organization) 135
natural resources 6, 12, 19, 23, 25, 27, 30, 35–6, 42, 44, 46, 51, 54, 58, 61–2, 91, 93, 107, 156, 192, 210, 262–3, 265
Neubauer et al. case 149, 156
Newquay 102
Newton, Richard 96
NGOs *see* non-governmental organizations (NGOs)
Niagara Falls 187
Niigata 113–15
Niigata University 113
Nike 198
Nike Sweatshops controversy 198
Nixon, Rob 3–4, 6–7, 73, 88–9, 109, 274
  Slow Violence and the Environmentalism of the Poor (Rob Nixon) 4, 88
non-anthropocentric model 17, 168, 181
non-governmental organizations (NGOs) 188, 196, 198, 203, 222, 224
Norway 234

OECD Guidelines for Multinational Enterprises on Responsible Business Conduct (1976) 192, 194
One Health Initiative 3
Otto, Diane 9, 20
overpopulation 14

Pact for the Future (UN 2024) 67, 75, 80–81
Pakistan 198
Palcacocha, Lake 177
Paris Agreement (2015) 31, 36, 152, 194, 212, 214, 218, 223, 226, 241, 243
Pease, William 100
Penhale, J.H.D. 93
Penzance 102
Peru 164, 177–8, 190, 263–4
Philippines 158
pollution 9, 25, 36, 38, 42, 44, 50, 54–5, 57, 65, 68–70, 108–9, 111–16, 118–23, 126, 130, 135, 162, 164, 177, 180, 188–90, 210, 227, 242, 253, 255, 263–8
  accountability for 188
  caused by companies 108, 111–15, 177, 188
  causing disasters 65
  causing environmental chronic emergencies 25, 42, 108, 210, 227
  combating of effects instead of causes 36
  control laws 68, 70, 118, 123, 264
  cooperation to combat 242
  displacement 113
  disproportionate impact on women 44, 50, 55, 109, 265
  early approach to 68–9
  greenhouse gas emissions 65
  high-polluting States 130
  impact on children 54, 164
  impact on future generations 54
  impact on local communities 265
  impacting human rights 54
  international law on 135, 267
  mercury 9, 119–22, 126, 180, 242
  mining and 122, 189–90
  neglecting of effects 9
  regulation of 38
  reparations for 266, 268
  responsibility for 253, 255, 263, 267
  rights for nature and 180
  States' failure to combat 108, 114, 116, 162, 263, 265, 267–8
polychlorinated biphenyls (PCBs) 3
Portillo Cáceres v Paraguay 260
Puerto Rico 171

racism 20
Rambles Beyond Railways (Wilkie Collins) 101
rare earth elements 188
RCHSE *see* Resolution on the Right to a Clean, Healthy and Sustainable Environment (2022)
Red Crescent Movement 235
Red Cross 235
Redruth 91, 93, 97
Reisman, Michael 134
reparations 3, 5, 20, 22, 45, 115–17, 119, 122, 126, 188, 250–53, 256–9, 261, 263–6, 268–72, 278
reproductive health 8–9, 12, 21, 39, 41, 45, 186–7, 276–7
reproductive rights 114, 187, 265
Resolution on the Right to a Clean, Healthy and Sustainable Environment (2022) 75–6, 78
responsibilities 5, 13, 30, 44, 46, 51, 62, 70, 74, 82–3, 86, 96, 98–101, 104–5, 111–12, 115–17, 121, 127, 131, 141, 145, 150–51, 157, 163–4, 175, 177, 184–6, 188, 190–91, 193–6, 201, 205, 207–8, 233, 237, 239, 241–2, 248, 250, 253–6, 259, 263–4, 267, 276
  accountability and 51, 188, 190–91, 194
  companies 111–12, 115, 121, 177, 185–6, 188, 190–91, 193–5, 205
  for disasters 13
  for environmental chronic emergencies 248, 253
  ethics of care and 83, 86
  historic 145
  international 253–6, 259
  international organizations 233
  landowners 96, 98–101, 105
  local authorities 98, 100, 116–17
  of men 175
  mining industry 96, 98, 101, 190
  nuanced nature of human 82
  reparations and 250, 253, 256, 259
  shared international 30, 233, 239, 241
  for slow violence 5
  States 74, 116–17, 163–4, 184, 188, 196, 201, 205, 207–8, 233, 237, 241, 248, 255, 259, 263–4, 267, 276
    combating climate change 241
    combating of environmental chronic emergencies 164
    disaster risk reduction 208, 237
    joint with international organizations 233
    monitoring of harmful activities of companies 117, 188, 201, 205, 255, 263
    neglect of 116–17, 259, 267
    protection of human rights 163, 184, 207, 233, 263, 267
    protection of the environment 264, 267
    protection of vulnerable populations 74
    reparations and 188, 259
    resource allocation in emergencies 74, 233
    safety of citizens 276
    women's role in reinforcing 248
  towards future generations 150–51, 157
  unequal distribution of 70, 131, 242
  of women 44, 46, 62, 127, 175, 190
Rio Conventions (1992) 57, 59, 79, 183, 239
Robinson, George 102
Rogers, Nicole 6, 12
Roman Law 250
Rousseau, Jean Jacques 138
Rowse, Peter 97–8
Russia 130
RWE 177

Sacchi and Others v Argentina and Others 163
salinization 2, 43–4
San José Court *see* Inter-American Court of Human Rights (IACtHR)
San Salvador Protocol to the American Convention on Human Rights 34, 260, 262
Sands, Philippe 144
SDGs *see* sustainable development goals (SDGs)
sea level rise 2, 12, 25, 29, 42, 46, 169, 171, 192

Second World War 167
Sendai Framework for Disaster Risk Reduction 26, 28, 237–8, 245–6
Sharpe, Adam 92
Shiva, Vandana 14–15
Showa Denko 115
Silent Spring (Rachel Carson) 3
slow violence 3–4, 6–7, 73, 88, 109–10, 114, 210, 260, 268, 274
social chronic emergencies 25
South Africa 199
Special Rapporteur on human rights and the environment (UN) 38, 75, 79
Special Rapporteur on violence against women and girls (UN) 50
States 3, 5, 9, 20, 22–4, 27, 30, 32, 34–41, 48, 51, 53–4, 67, 74, 76–8, 108, 111–12, 114–29, 131, 144, 150, 155–7, 160, 163–5, 169, 171, 176, 179–81, 184–5, 190–96, 199–205, 207–14, 217–21, 228, 230–41, 243, 245, 248–9, 251, 254–5, 259, 264, 267, 276–9
  Colombia 180–81
  commitment to sustainable development 35, 37, 54, 243
  company host and home 185, 190, 194–6, 199–202
  as company owners 192
  cooperation in environmental law 30, 239
  cooperation in international law 229
  cooperation on climate change 128, 130–31, 144, 233–4, 241
  cooperation on disasters 24, 27, 41, 233–8, 243
  cooperation on environmental chronic emergencies 228, 230–32, 237–8, 249
  co-responsibility for pollution 188, 267
  disaster risk reduction 208, 211, 236–8, 243
  duty to dismantle structural discrimination 35, 37–8, 51
  early environmental laws 67
  emergency measures 34
  empowered actors of international law 77, 191
  feminism demanding reconceptualization of obligations of 9, 20, 22
  freedom to exploit natural resources 30
  Germany 157
  high-polluting 130
  imperialist aims of Western 23
  inadequate track record in environmental protection 212, 220
  international wrongdoing 253–4
  Italy 162, 267
  Japan 108, 111–12, 114–20, 276
  litigation against 36, 157, 163–4, 201, 203, 208, 213–14, 255, 267
  neglecting to act in environmental chronic emergencies 111–12, 118, 120, 164, 277
  not holding companies accountable 112, 114, 118, 164, 204–5
  obligation to combat climate change 55, 77, 157, 160, 163, 211–12, 214, 217, 219, 255, 278
  obligation to combat environmental chronic emergencies 3, 36, 53–4, 118–19
  obligation to ensure women's rights 39–40, 48, 53, 243
  obligation to protect human rights 32, 34, 54, 76, 176, 184, 193, 207, 209–10, 218, 233
  obligation to protect non-human life 179–81
  obligation to reduce greenhouse gas emissions 212–13, 217, 220
  obligation to respond to needs of specific groups 165
  obligation to respond to slow violence 5
  obligations under present framework 20, 22
  Peru 164
  prioritizing economic growth over public health 122
  reparations and 115–16, 251, 259, 264
  responsibilities for environmental chronic emergencies 116–17

responsibilities towards future generations 150, 156, 160, 163–4, 221
some bearing costs of actions of others 129–30, 169, 171
sovereignty 279
Switzerland 213–14, 255
United States 188
work on human rights and environment 78
Stockholm Conference on the Human Environment (1972) 79, 239
Stockholm Convention on Persistent Organic Pollutants (2001) 31, 57, 59–60
Stockholm Declaration (1972) 182
Study Group on Sea Level Rise (ILC) 28
Sultana, Fahrana 13
Summit of the Future (2024) 80
sustainable development *see* sustainable development
sustainable development goals (SDGs) 193, 197, 243
Swiss People's Party (SVP) 223
Switzerland 160, 210, 213–14, 216, 219, 223, 225, 255, 266
Symonds, John 94

Tampere Convention on the Provision of Telecommunication Resources for Disaster Mitigation and Relief Operations (1998) 26
Teitiota v New Zealand 260
Terra dei Fuochi ('Land of Fires') 162, 267–8
Tetiota case 37
Tierra Digna 180
Timor-Leste 129, 234
TNCs *see* transnational corporations (TNCs)
Torpey, John 141
Torres Strait Islanders case *see* Daniel Billy et al. v Australia
transnational corporations (TNCs) 6, 184–7, 189–92, 194–202, 205, 277
Tripartite Declaration of Principles concerning Multinational Enterprises and Social Policy (1977) 193–4
Tronto, Joan 83

UN Declaration for Future Generations (2024) 75, 80, 148, 150
UN Office for the Coordination of Humanitarian Affairs (OCHA) 29, 73
UNCBD *see* Convention on Biological Diversity (UNCBD, 1992)
UNCCD *see* Convention to Combat Desertification (UNCCD, 1994)
UNHRC *see* Human Rights Council (UNHRC)
UNICEF 173
United Kingdom (UK) 130, 146, 183, 276
United Nations (UN) 4, 26, 29–31, 34, 36, 38–9, 50, 53, 57, 73, 75–8, 80, 85, 130–31, 133, 146, 168–9, 193, 218, 224, 227, 229–30, 235, 238, 279
United States (US) 9, 128–30, 144, 146, 187, 224
urbanization 25, 42, 210

Vanuatu 128–30, 143–4
Vienna Convention on the Law of Treaties 212, 218
violence, gender-based 10, 46, 51, 133, 189–90, 207, 209, 247

Wales 67, 159
Waratah Coal Pty Ltd 158
wars 5, 134, 251
water management 9, 19, 38, 44–5, 50–51, 61, 118, 175, 189
Waters, John 99
Watt, James 91
Wheatley, Steven 146
women's rights 49–50, 53, 110, 184, 190, 198, 277–8
World Charter for Nature (1982) 168, 183
WTO (World Trade Organization) 35

Yugoslavia 135

Printed and bound by CPI Group (UK) Ltd, Croydon, CR0 4YY
17/06/2026
14902650-0002